Education, Skills and International Cooperation

Comparative and Historical Perspectives

CERC Studies in Comparative Education

36. Kenneth King (2019): *Education, Skills and International Cooperation: Comparative and Historical Perspectives*. ISBN 978-988-14241-7-4, 381pp. HK$250/US$38

35. Anatoly V. Oleksiyenko, Qiang Zha, Igor Chirikov & Jun Li (eds.) (2018): *International Status Anxiety and Higher Education: The Soviet Legacy in China and Russia*. ISBN 978-988-14241-6-7, 402pp. HK$250/US$38.

34. Magda Nutsa Kobakhidze (2018): *Teachers as Tutors: Shadow Education Market Dynamics in Georgia*. ISBN 978-988-14241-5-0. 262pp. HK$250/US$38.

33. Erwin H. Epstein (ed.) (2016): *Crafting a Global Field: Six Decades of the Comparative and International Education Society*. ISBN 978-988-14241-4-3. 316pp. HK$250/US$38

32. Mark Bray, Ora Kwo & Boris Jokić (eds.) (2015): *Researching Private Supplementary Tutoring: Methodological Lessons from Diverse Cultures*. ISBN 978-988-14241-3-6. 292pp. HK$250/US$38.

31. Bob Adamson, Jon Nixon, Feng Su (eds.) (2012): *The Reorientation of Higher Education: Challenging the East-West Dichotomy*. ISBN 978-988-1785-27-5. 314pp. HK$250/US$38.

30. Ruth Hayhoe, Jun Li, Jing Lin, Qiang Zha (2011): *Portraits of 21st Century Chinese Universities: In the Move to Mass Higher Education*. ISBN 978-988-1785-23-7. 486pp. HK$300/US$45.

29. Maria Manzon (2011): *Comparative Education: The Construction of a Field*. ISBN 978-988-17852- 6-8. 295pp. HK$200/US$32.

28. Kerry J. Kennedy, Wing On Lee & David L. Grossman (eds.) (2010): *Citizenship Pedagogies in Asia and the Pacific*. ISBN 978-988-17852-2-0. 407pp. HK$250/US$38.

27. David Chapman, William K. Cummings & Gerard A. Postiglione (eds.) (2010): *Crossing Borders in East Asian Higher Education*. ISBN 978-962-8093-98-4. 388pp. HK$250/US$38.

26. Ora Kwo (ed.) (2010): *Teachers as Learners: Critical Discourse on Challenges and Opportunities*. ISBN 978-962-8093-55-7. 349pp. HK$250/US$38.

25. Carol K.K. Chan & Nirmala Rao (eds.) (2009): *Revisiting the Chinese Learner: Changing Contexts, Changing Education*. ISBN 978-962-8093-16-8. 360pp. HK$250/US$38.

24. Donald B. Holsinger & W. James Jacob (eds.) (2008): *Inequality in Education: Comparative and International Perspectives*. ISBN 978-962-8093-14-4. 584pp. HK$300/US$45.

23. Nancy Law, Willem J Pelgrum & Tjeerd Plomp (eds.) (2008): *Pedagogy and ICT Use in Schools around the World: Findings from the IEA SITES 2006 Study*. ISBN 978-962-8093-65-6. 296pp. HK$250/ US$38.

22. David L. Grossman, Wing On Lee & Kerry J. Kennedy (eds.) (2008): *Citizenship Curriculum in Asia and the Pacific*. ISBN 978-962-8093-69-4. 268pp. HK$200/US$32.

21. Vandra Masemann, Mark Bray & Maria Manzon (eds.) (2007): *Common Interests, Uncommon Goals: Histories of the World Council of Comparative Education Societies and its Members*. ISBN 978-962- 8093-10-6. 384pp. HK$250/US$38.

20. Peter D. Hershock, Mark Mason & John N. Hawkins (eds.) (2007): *Changing Education: Leadership, Innovation and Development in a Globalizing Asia Pacific*. ISBN 978-962-8093-54-0. 348pp. HK$200/US$32.

19. Mark Bray, Bob Adamson & Mark Mason (eds.) (2014): *Comparative Education Research: Approaches and Methods. Second edition*. ISBN 978-988-17852-8-2. 453pp. HK$250/US$38.

18. Aaron Benavot & Cecilia Braslavsky (eds.) (2006): *School Knowledge in Comparative and Historical Perspective: Changing Curricula in Primary and Secondary Education*. ISBN 978-962-8093- 52-6. 315pp. HK$200/US$3

17. Ruth Hayhoe (2006): *Portraits of Influential Chinese Educators*. ISBN 978-962-8093-40-3. 398pp. HK$250/US$38.

16. Peter Ninnes & Meeri Hellstén (eds.) (2005): *Internationalizing Higher Education: Critical Explorations of Pedagogy and Policy*. ISBN 978-962-8093-37-3. 231pp. HK$200/US$32.

Earlier titles in the series are listed at the back of the book.

CERC Studies in Comparative Education 36

Education, Skills and International Cooperation

Comparative and Historical Perspectives

Kenneth King

Springer Comparative Education Research Centre
The University of Hong Kong

Comparative Education Research Centre
Faculty of Education, The University of Hong Kong,
Pokfulam Road, Hong Kong, China

Copyright © Comparative Education Research Centre
First published 2019
ISBN 978-988-14241-7-4
Paperback

CERC Studies in Comparative Education
ISBN 978-3-030-29789-3   ISBN 978-3-030-29790-9   (eBook)
https://doi.org/10.1007/978-3-030-29790-9

Cover: Gutsage
Layout: Toby Law and Emily Mang
Printed and bound by The Central Printing Press Ltd. in Hong Kong, China

This Springer imprint is published by the registered company Springer Nature Switzerland AG.
The registered company address is: Gewerbestrasse 11, 6330 Cham, Switzerland

Contents

List of Abbreviations   *ix*

List of Tables   *xii*

List of Figures   *xii*

Foreword   1
  Mark Bray

Introduction   11

Chapter 1   33
  The Phelps-Stokes Commissions and the Politics of   43
  Negro Education

Chapter 2   65
  Skill Acquisition in the Informal Sector   69

Chapter 3   93
  Aid, Research and Education   99

Chapter 4   135
  Education and Training for Self-Employment in Kenya   137

Chapter 5   149
  Exploring the Impact of Primary Education   151

Chapter 6   156
  The Vocational School Fallacy Revisited   158

Chapter 7   196
  Africa's Informal Economies: Thirty Years On   198

Chapter 8   209
  Re-targeting Schools, Skills and Jobs in Kenya: Quality,   212
  Quantity and Outcomes

Chapter 9   232
  Skills and Education for All from Jomtien (1990) to the   235
  GMR of 2012: A Policy History

Chapter 10 266
Experience, Experts and Knowledge in Japanese Aid 271
Policy and Practice

Chapter 11 296
African Students in China: Changing Characteristics, 298
Contexts and Challenges

Chapter 12 344
The Geopolitics and Meanings of India's Massive Skills 347
Development Ambitions

Chapter 13 372
Conclusions around Education, Skills, Knowledge and
Work – and the Role of Aid

List of Abbreviations

AIDS	Acquired immune deficiency syndrome
ASU	African Students' Union
ADB	Asian Development Bank
ADEA	Association for the Development of Education in Africa
AfDB	African Development Bank
BIFS	Bilateral Information Feedback System
CIDA	Canadian International Development Agency
CDF	Comprehensive Development Framework
CESO	Centre for the Study of Education in Developing Societies
CICC	China Information and Culture Communications
CMU	Chongqing Medical University
CRIDE	Centre de Recherche Interdisciplinaire pour le Développement de l'Éducation
CSC	China Scholarship Council
CSCUK	Commonwealth Scholarship Commission in the UK
CUSO	Canadian University Service Overseas
DAC	Development Assistance Committee
DFID	Department for International Development
DSE	Deutsche Stiftung für Internationale Entwicklung
EC	European Commission
ECCE	Early Childhood Care and Education
ECNU	East China Normal University
EFA	Education for All
FASID	Foundation for Advanced Studies on International Development
FOCAC	Forum on China-Africa Cooperation
FPE	Free Primary Education
GIZ	Deutsche Gesellschaft für Internationale Zusammenarbeit
GMR	Global Monitoring Report
GTZ	Deutsche Gesellschaft für Technische Zusammenarbeit
GUAST	General Union of African Students in Tianjin
IAMR	Institute of Applied Manpower Research

IBRD	International Bank for Reconstruction and Development
ICEG	International Centre for Economic Growth
IDRC	International Development Research Centre
IDTs	International Development Targets
IERS	International Educational Reporting Service
IIEP	International Institute for Educational Planning
IJED	International Journal of Educational Development
ILO	International Labour Organization
IWGE	International Working Group on Education
JICA	Japan International Cooperation Agency
JOCV	Japanese Overseas Co-operation Volunteers
JSS	junior secondary school
KM	knowledge management
K-REP	Kenyan Rural Enterprise Programme
KS	knowledge sharing
MDG	Millennium Development Goal
MOFA	Ministry of Foreign Affairs
MOHRD	Ministry of Human Resource Development
MOLE	Ministry of Labour and Employment
MSE	Micro- and small enterprise
MTA	Mid-term appraisal
NCCK	National Christian Council in Kenya
NCEUS	National Commission for Enterprises in the Unorganised Sector
NDS	New development strategy
NFE	Non-formal education
NGO	Non-governmental organisation
NORAD	Norwegian Agency for International Development
NORRAG	Network for International Policies and Cooperation in Education and Training
NSDP	National Skill Development Policy
NUGS	National Union of Ghanaian Students
NVQF	National Vocational Qualifications Framework
OAU	Organisation for African Unity
ODA	Overseas Development Administration
OECD	Organisation for Economic Co-operation and Development
PhD	Doctor of Philosophy (doctoral degree)
PTTC	project-type technical co-operation

RRAG	Research Review and Advisory Group
SAREC	Swedish Agency for Research Cooperation
SDC	Skill Development Centres
SDG	Sustainable Development Goal
SIDA	Swedish International Development Authority
SOVP	Senior Overseas Volunteer Programme
SSS	senior secondary school
TICAD	Tokyo International Conference on African Development
TVET	Technical and Vocational Education and Training
UIE	UNESCO Institute of Education
UIL	UNESCO Institute for Lifelong Learning
UIS	UNESCO Institute for Statistics
UKFIET	UK Forum for International Education and Training
UN	United Nations
UNDP	United Nations Development Programme
UNESCO	United Nations Educational, Scientific and Cultural Organization
USA	United States of America
UNGEI	United Nations Girls' Education Initiative
UNICEF	United Nations Children's Fund
UPE	Universal Primary Education
USAID	United States Agency for International Development
VSF	Vocational School Fallacy
VSO	Voluntary Service Overseas
VTET	Vocational and Technical Education and Training
WCEFA	World Conference on Education for All
WEF	World Economic Forum
WGICSD	Working Group for International Cooperation in Skills Development
WHO	World Health Organization
WSSD	World Summit for Social Development
YMCA	Young Men's Christian Association
YAPS	Young African Professionals and Students
ZNU	Zhejiang Normal University

List of Tables

1	Work and self-employment preferences of senior secondary pupils in Ghana (multiple choices: N=522)	174
2	Work and self-employment preferences of senior secondary pupils in Ghana (single choice: N=522)	174
3	Preferred employer by school track – Who would you most like to work for?	181
4	Who do you think you will work for?	182
5	Occupational Rankings by importance, status and income	186
6	The Six Dakar goals	235
7	The Six Dimensions of EFA Targets at Jomtien	238

List of Figures

| 1 | An urban informal sector workplace. Note the temporary structure of wood and cardboard walls. | 73 |
| 2 | Improvisation in hand-tools. Tinsmiths in Nairobi shaping their own soldering irons. | 87 |

Foreword

Mark Bray

It is a great pleasure to write this Foreword in two major capacities. The first is as editor of the series 'CERC Studies in Comparative Education', and the second is as an individual who has known and looked up to Kenneth King for over four decades and who has benefited from significant mentoring.

Beginning with the first, I welcome this selection of Kenneth King's previously-published works, together with his newly-written commentaries prepared through the lens of the contemporary era. CERC has published three previous volumes in a similar genre (Noah & Eckstein, 1998; Gu, 2001; LeVine, 2003). Each has shown not only ways in which the authors' careers and scholarly works developed over the decades, but also how the fields to which they contributed changed. A similar remark applies to the present book. As explained in the Introduction, Kenneth King's career commenced with school teaching in Ethiopia and then doctoral studies at the University of Edinburgh where he focused on the politics of the first education commissions to Africa. Kenneth King then took a post at the University of Nairobi before returning to the University of Edinburgh as a lecturer. From the Edinburgh base he has made enormous professional contributions in all continents, working with and for international agencies, national governments, and other bodies. All the chapters in this book derive from research projects yet benefit from insider perspectives gained through other activities.

The juxtaposition of these chapters within the covers of a single book permits instructive comparisons not only across place but also across time, showing how the wider field has changed in emphases and priorities. For example Chapter 2 focuses on skills in the informal sector of the Kenyan economy in the 1970s, and Chapter 4 revisits the scene in

Kenneth King (2019): *Education, Skills and International Cooperation: Comparative and Historical Perspectives*. Hong Kong: Comparative Education Research Centre (CERC), The University of Hong Kong, and Dordrecht: Springer. © CERC the 1990s. During the 1970s it had been possible to identify at the secondary level a small number of technical secondary schools and a slightly larger number of diversified (industrial arts) schools, but two decades later all primary and secondary schools offered what could be called pre-vocational education as a component of all-round general education, and the 19 technical secondary schools had become post-secondary Technical Training Institutes. This was part of the massive expansion of schooling not only in Kenya but also across Africa and indeed the globe. Interacting with these changes were economic adjustments, Chapter 7 views Africa's informal economies from the vantage point of 2001, and points out that the understandings of the informal sector had changed from something limited to particular artisan groups in major cities to something that cut across entire economies. "The old certainties of being a full-time pastor, primary school teacher, or government clerk," King remarked, "have been replaced by a new world in which many individuals switch back and forth between a main job and other types of work."

These shifts were partly the result of changed economic approaches in the context of globalisation and major developments in the agendas of national governments and international agencies. Kenneth King has analysed these themes with care, particularly as they relate to (i) the global Education for All (EFA) movement launched in Jomtien, Thailand, in 1990, (ii) its successor 2000 World Education Forum in Dakar, Senegal, and (iii) the 2015 World Education Forum in Incheon, Republic of Korea. The 1990 event was convened by UNESCO, UNICEF, the UNDP and the World Bank,[1] and the sequels were convened by these bodies with additional partners. The resolutions of the 2000 event fed into the education component of the United Nations' eight Millennium Development Goals (MDGs), and the resolutions of the 2015 event fed into the counterpart component of the United Nations' 17 Sustainable Development Goals (SDGs). Kenneth King was already sufficiently senior in the field to attend the 1990 event, and made major preparatory contributions to the 2000 one. He thus had a special sense of both continuity and change when participating in the 2015 event. He had a particular interest in Technical and Vocational Education and Training (TVET), but also in wider themes from early childhood

---

[1] UNESCO = United Nations Educational, Scientific and Cultural Organization; UNICEF = United Nations Children's Fund; UNDP = United Nations Development Programme.

to adult education. Chapter 9 reports on insights in the domains of TVET and skills from the perspective of 2012, and other writings (e.g. King, 2017) have included insights from the continued trajectory including the 2015 World Education Forum and the SDGs.

In all of these analyses, Kenneth King had a particular though far from exclusive interest in Africa. Much of his fieldwork, as illustrated in the chapters on skills development in Kenya, was locally grounded; but he also had a broader picture concerned with aid flows across continents. The first chapter in this book is an extract from his early writings about such flows from North America at the beginning of the 20th century, and Chapter 3 illustrates his focus on patterns towards the end of the 20th century. Much of his attention has focused on the bilateral agencies of European and North American countries but since the turn of the present century he has conducted much path-breaking work on the African-oriented roles of Japanese, Chinese and Indian development aid. This work has brought a very different set of insights into the agendas for international cooperation on both sides of such bilateral relationships, and has enhanced broader conceptual understanding about power relations in international contexts.

Turning to the second reason why I have great pleasure in writing this Foreword, I have been personally inspired by Kenneth King and his work since the mid-1970s. At the beginning of that decade I was a volunteer teacher first in Kenya and then in Nigeria, and during school vacations took every opportunity to travel not only within those countries but also in other parts of Africa. In 1975, holding a degree in Economics and with strong interest in Africa, I applied for a Masters programme in African Studies at the University of Edinburgh. I was delighted to be accepted, and in those studies focused mainly on Economics and Education. Because of Kenneth King, Education rapidly became the dominant emphasis, and the seeds were sown for the rest of my career. Following the Masters degree I became Kenneth King's first PhD student. I returned to Nigeria to collect data for a thesis on the Universal Primary Education (UPE) scheme launched in 1976.[2] I felt that the best way to be anchored in the Nigerian education system was again to take a teaching post, which I did in 1976/77. I returned to Edinburgh in September 1977 to continue work on the thesis. Kenneth King had diligently and helpfully communicated with me by airmail to Nigeria,

---

[2] The thesis was in due course published in revised form as a book (Bray, 1981).

3

and I was glad then to be able to receive further direct supervision in person.

As it happened, circumstances soon required further long-distance supervision. In this book Kenneth King mentions that in January 1978 he moved on leave from the University of Edinburgh to the International Development Research Centre (IDRC), which was Canada's path-breaking bilateral research aid organisation headquartered in Ottawa. This could have been disconcerting for me, but fortunately both of us were already familiar with supervision by airmail. Perhaps even more dramatic, and a further great boost to my career, was that the University of Edinburgh advertised a lectureship on a two-year temporary basis to replace Kenneth King. I applied, was shortlisted, and was awarded the post. Two years became two and a half, and eventually three and a half. Kenneth King returned to Edinburgh in mid-1981, at which point I moved to the Papua New Guinea. My three years in that country was followed by a period at the University of London, and from 1986 the University of Hong Kong.

Moving fast-forward a couple of decades, in this book Kenneth King also mentions that in 2006 he became a Distinguished Visiting Professor at the University of Hong Kong. By that time I was Dean of the Faculty of Education, and had had the honour first of inviting him to apply for this very competitive scheme and then of welcoming him following his success in that competition. In what seemed a parallel turn of events, shortly after his arrival I moved on leave to Paris to take up the Directorship of UNESCO's International Institute for Educational Planning (IIEP). Yet the collaboration continued during my absence – not just by airmail this time, because e-mail had been invented; and Kenneth King facilitated continuities by taking over supervision of some of my own PhD students. I returned to Hong Kong in 2010, and it has been a pleasure to welcome him on multiple further visits since that time.

These remarks highlight personal connections and also underscore Kenneth King's observations about the roles of chance and serendipity in the ways that careers and research agendas take shape. They also highlight evolutions within and beyond disciplinary foundations. Kenneth King studied Classics (ancient Greek and Latin) at the University of Cambridge from which, as he explains in the Introduction, he gained a sharpened interest in language and a lifelong concern with the meanings of texts. The classics are of course linked to history, and his doctoral studies were accomplished under the direction of a distinguished professor in the Department of History at the University of Edinburgh. At the University of Nairobi he was again in the Department of History, but contributed to its Institute of Development Studies. Then, on his return to the University of Edinburgh he moved to a joint appointment with the Centre of African Studies and the Department of Educational Studies, both in the Faculty of Social Sciences.

These labels raise themes about fields of studies and about disciplinary boundaries and interactions. When appointed to a chair at the University of Edinburgh, Kenneth King chose International and Comparative Education for the title of his chair. The series in which this book is published only has Comparative Education in its title, but the editorial team responsible for the series certainly recognises the close links between Comparative Education and International Education. Indeed, one much-cited paper by Wilson (1994) described them as Siamese twins. Wilson had in mind the description by Epstein (1994) of Comparative Education as a conceptual field of study and of International Education as a more applied field including professional action especially in less developed countries. Wilson showed how the two domains had productively complemented each other not only in his own career but also in the careers of others, and these remarks certainly apply also to Kenneth King. They can also be viewed within the context of wider discussions on contours within fields of enquiry, both generally (see e.g. Becher & Trowler, 2001) and specifically in the domain(s) of Comparative and International Education (e.g. Olivera 1988, 2009; Bray, 2014, 2015).

Wilson made his remarks in his Presidential Address for a United States body that had been founded in 1956 as the Comparative Education Society (CES) and had in 1968 had been renamed as the Comparative and International Education Society (CIES) (Berends & Trakas, 2016, p.91). Parallel events occurred in the United Kingdom, where in 1966 a British Section was created within the Comparative Education Society in Europe (CESE), which itself had been formed in 1963 (Sutherland et al., 2007, p.156). In 1979 the British Section split from CESE to become the British Comparative Education Society (BCES) and then from 1983 the British Comparative and International Education Society (BCIES) of which Kenneth King was Vice-Chairperson from 1988 to 1990 and Chairperson from 1990 to 1994. In 1997, the BCIES merged with a related body to become the British Association for International and Comparative Education (BAICE), of which Kenneth King was President in 2015/16.

These dimensions are highlighted here to help readers identify strands both in Kenneth King's career and in the wider arena in which he worked. Not included in the title of his chair at the University of Edinburgh, but very evident in the chapters of this book, are other fields of enquiry which overlap and are related. One is geographic in labelling, namely African Studies. As mentioned, Kenneth King was appointed to the Centre of African Studies at the University of Edinburgh in 1972, and he later served for two decades as its Director. During this time he promoted the interdisciplinary status of the Centre and led a vigorous programme of conferences, research and teaching. He also retained a strong interest in Development Studies, evidenced in his career-long membership of and contributions to the Development Studies Association (DSA) and the European Association of Development Research and Training Institutes (EADI). And in 1991 he was a key member of a small group forming the United Kingdom Forum for International Education and Training (UKFIET), which became known for its biennial International Conferences on Education and Development at the University of Oxford. UKFIET is an umbrella body for a number of professional organisations including BAICE. Its website (www.ukfiet. org) explains that UKFIET "provides a proactive forum for universities, non-governmental organisations, consultancy groups and professional associations to share ideas, knowledge and expertise". The website adds that the Forum's diverse membership is "engaged in research, training, teaching, and campaigning and serve as a significant advisory resource to policy makers and practitioners in government, development agencies and non-governmental organizations". Kenneth King has been much involved in UKFIET throughout its history, and was its Chair from 1999 to 2001.

Again linking back to overlap between but differences in the orientations of sub-fields of research and enquiry, UKFIET elaborates on its history with reference to a publishing initiative. In 1979, the website narrates, two businessmen decided to launch the *International Journal of Educational Development*. The website explains that:

> They were concerned about the cynicism that they encountered in the developing countries with regard to the so-called 'experts' who arrived for brief visits and then felt able to write definitive reports. They were also concerned that the importance of education in the development discourse was being squeezed out by economists. They therefore aimed to publish a journal containing articles based

on research into policy and practice in the developing world which might influence policy-makers.

The journal rapidly gained respect in the community concerned not only with direct influence on policy-makers but also with conceptual themes, and in 1989 a conference was organised in Oxford to celebrate its first decade. Discussions during and following the conference led to the formation of UKFIET, as narrated elsewhere by Kenneth King (Watson & King, 1991; Dyer & King, 1993). The *International Journal of Educational Development* maintained an identity different from journals such as *Comparative Education* that had a narrower academic focus. Perhaps in the middle ground was the BCES journal *Compare: A Journal of Comparative Education*, for which the sub-title was retained unchanged during the BCIES era and the first part of the BAICE era but which in 2009 became *A Journal of Comparative and International Education* (Bray, 2010, p.712). Kenneth King's publication list to date includes articles in all three of these journals, but with the majority in the *International Journal of Educational Development*.[3]

These remarks are presented to contextualise the chapters that follow in this book. Kenneth King has made major contributions to the field(s) of Comparative and International Education. Perhaps as significantly, throughout five decades he has uniquely brought his educational research insights to bear in the fields of African History, Development Studies, and African Studies. Few Comparative and International Education specialists have also published in such prestigious journals as the *Journal of African History*, in Development Studies journals such as *World Development*, the *Journal of Development Studies*, and the *European Journal of Development Research*, or in African Studies journals such as *African Affairs*. His doctoral thesis connected the politics of education in the Southern States of the USA with education in colonial Africa, and notably Kenya, and was published by Clarendon Press in revised form in the respected series entitled Oxford Studies in African Affairs (King, 1971).[4] Alongside Kenneth King's membership of BCIES/BAICE and the DSA has been his membership of the African Studies Association of the United Kingdom (ASAUK) which in 2012 honoured him with the Distinguished Africanist Award. Thus his impact

---

[3] For a list of Kenneth King's publications, see   http://www.cas.ed.ac.uk/data/assets/pdf file/0017/ 251027/K.King_List_of_publications_002.pdf
[4] The book was re-issued by Diasporic Africa Press, New York, in 2016.

and influence have been very marked in multiple fields.

With such factors in mind, it has been a challenge to select just 12 items for the present book. Kenneth King has to date (co-)authored nine books and (co-)edited a further 29 books. Alongside these are over 200 chapters and articles, as well as some 60 substantial reports and monographs. The items have been selected for coherence in showing ways in which conceptions of education and skills development have evolved in Africa and elsewhere, accompanied and influenced by the changing roles of international and bilateral agencies. The focus is encapsulated in the title: *Education, Skills and International Cooperation: Comparative and Historical Perspectives*.

Kenneth King has had a huge influence on the field as a whole, and is much respected both in his home country and internationally. I am personally grateful for the modelling provided to me during the last four decades, and I commend this book to readers who may not know him personally but who will find inspiration from both the individual chapters and the collection as a whole.

UNESCO Chair Professor in Comparative Education
Comparative Education Research Centre
The University of Hong Kong

References

Becher, Tony & Trowler, Paul R. 2001. *Academic Tribes and Territories: Intellectual Enquiry and the Cultures of Disciplines*. 2nd edition, The Society for Research into Higher Education and Open University Press, Buckingham.

Berends, Louis & Trakas, Maria 2016. 'Inserting International Education into the Comparative Education Society', in Epstein, Erwin H. (ed.), *Crafting a Global Field: Six Decades of the Comparative and International Education Society*. CERC Studies in Comparative Education 33, Comparative Education Research Centre, The University of Hong Kong, and Springer, Dordrecht, pp.91-109.

Bray, Mark 1981. *Universal Primary Education in Nigeria: A Study of Kano State*. Routledge & Kegan Paul, London.

Bray, Mark 2010. 'Comparative Education and International Education in the History of *Compare*: Boundaries, Overlaps and Ambiguities'.

Compare: A Journal of Comparative and International Education, Vol.40, No.6, pp.711-725.

Bray, Mark 2014. 'Scholarly Enquiry and the Field of Comparative Education', in Bray, Mark; Adamson, Bob & Mason, Mark (eds.), *Comparative Education Research: Approaches and Methods*. CERC Studies in Comparative Education 19, 2nd edition, Comparative Education Research Centre, The University of Hong Kong, and Springer, Dordrecht, pp.19-46.

Bray, Mark 2015. 'International and Comparative Education: Boundaries, Ambiguities and Synergies', in Hayden, Mary; Levy, Jack & Thompson, Jeff (eds.), *Handbook of Research in International Education*. 2nd edition, Sage, London, pp.122-129.

Dyer, Caroline & King, Kenneth 1993. *The British Resource on International Training and Education: An Inventory*, Department of Education, University of Edinburgh.

Epstein, E.H. 1994. 'Comparative and International Education: Overview and Historical Development', in Husén, Torsten & Postlethwaite, T. Neville (eds.), *The International Encyclopedia of Education*. 2nd edition, Pergamon Press, Oxford, pp.918-923.

Gu, Mingyuan 2001. *Education in China and Abroad: Perspectives from a Lifetime in Comparative Education*. CERC Studies in Comparative Education 9, Comparative Education Research Centre, The University of Hong Kong.

King, Kenneth 1971. *Pan-Africanism and Education: A Study of Race, Philanthropy and Education in the Southern States of the USA and East Africa*, Clarendon Press, Oxford. Also 2016, Diasporic Africa Press, New York.

King, Kenneth 2017. 'Lost in Translation: The Challenge of Translating the Global Education Goal and Targets into Global Indicators'. *Compare: A Journal of Comparative and International Education*, Vol.47, No.6, pp.801-817.

LeVine, Robert A. 2003. *Childhood Socialization: Comparative Studies of Parenting, Learning and Educational Change*. CERC Studies in Comparative Education 12, Comparative Education Research Centre, The University of Hong Kong.

Noah, Harold & Eckstein, Max A. 1998. *Doing Comparative Education: Three Decades of Collaboration*. CERC Studies in Comparative Education 5, Comparative Education Research Centre, The University of Hong Kong.

Olivera, Carlos E. (1988): 'Comparative Education: Towards a Basic Theory', *Prospects: Quarterly Review of Education*, Vol.XVIII, No.2, pp.167-185.

Olivera, Carlos E. (2009): *Introducción a la Educación Comparada*. Editorial Universidad Estatal a Distancia, San José, Costa Rica.

Sutherland, Margaret B., Watson, Keith & Crossley, Michael 2007. 'The British Association for International and Comparative Education (BAICE)', in Masemann, Vandra; Bray, Mark & Manzon, Maria (eds.), *Common Interests, Uncommon Goals: Histories of the World Council of Comparative Education Societies and its Members*. CERC Studies in Comparative Education 21, Comparative Education Research Centre, The University of Hong Kong, and Springer, Dordrecht, pp.155-169.

Watson, Keith & King, Kenneth 1991. 'From Comparative to International Studies in Education: Towards the Co-ordination of a British Resource of Expertise'. *International Journal of Educational Development*, Vol.11, No.3, pp.245-253.

Wilson, David N. 1994. 'Comparative and International Education: Fraternal or Siamese Twins? A Preliminary Genealogy of Our Twin Fields'. *Comparative Education Review*, Vol.38, No.4, pp.449-486.

Introduction

This book interweaves education and skills development with international aid. It is concerned with both the history of their interactions and their more recent synergies. Its focus is on the policies and politics of their national and international engagement. In the book, the location of these encounters is frequently Africa, but the scene changes to Japan and to China, and also to India. The analysis draws upon my long-term attachment to the Centre of African Studies and School of Education in the University of Edinburgh (30 years), but also to the University of Nairobi (3 years), Wingate School, Ethiopia (3 years) and the International Development Research Centre (IDRC) in Ottawa (4 years). My insights and changing research focus have been influenced by these locations, but also by building upon a certain amount of serendipity (see further Chapter 1).

The term 'education and skills' covers not only their location in all the formal levels of education and training, but also some of their development in informal settings, including the massive informal economies of so many countries. 'Skills' embraces foundation, transferable and technical and vocational skills, and especially the last. The analysis of aid, on the other hand, is not just concerned with bilateral and multilateral assistance primarily from countries of the Organisation for Economic Co-operation and Development (OECD), but it also covers support from philanthropic foundations, and non-governmental organisations (NGOs). In addition, it looks carefully at the international cooperation associated with countries outside the OECD, and particularly at China and India whose so-called South-South Cooperation in the sphere of education is at least as old as the initiatives of the OECD's aid agencies.

The audience for this book is partly the masters or doctoral student setting out to explore a topic of their choice, whether in Hong Kong,

Kenneth King (2019): *Education, Skills and International Cooperation: Comparative and Historical Perspectives*. Hong Kong: Comparative Education Research Centre (CERC), The University of Hong Kong, and Dordrecht: Springer. © CERC

Johannesburg, Santiago or Edinburgh. However, the book is not about the merits of a particular research method - though the merits of an historical lens are acknowledged throughout. It is also testimony to the key role of chance, coincidence and of serendipity, along with career planning and professorial advice, in identifying key research topics to pursue.

The audience is, in addition, colleagues in the aid policy and international education communities whether in London, Bern, Beijing, New Delhi, Nairobi or Tokyo. Many of these I have learnt from over the years.

General readers who want to understand what lies behind some of the education and skill development narratives of the last 50 years will also find many leads and clues here – whether in exploring why it was once thought that Western education should be 'adapted' for Africa; or what were the implications for education and skill when the 'informal sector' was found to be such an enormous dimension of so many economies. Then there was the sudden consensus that 'Education for All' and 'Meeting basic learning needs' should be central to both national and international agendas. Often, a single phrase, such as the 'vocational school fallacy' has set off ripples right round the international education community. The same would be true of 'appropriate learning and life-skills'.

Development cooperation agencies and philanthropic foundations have played a key role in both agenda-setting and target-setting, but their agendas and targets have shifted markedly over the last century, with significant impacts on their recipients as well as on the wider narratives about education and skills. The World Bank, regional banks and the United Nations agencies have been central players in these narratives about education and skills, and have directly influenced the policy and academic communities with their changing priorities. The terms such as 'international development targets', 'Millennium Development Goals', 'Education for All' and 'Sustainable Development Goals' have all been crucially identified by and supported by development agencies.

Development assistance or aid have not promoted only Western or Northern education and research priorities; countries such as China and India have also been directly involved in education and skills agenda-setting since the early 1960s. However, the language of China's or India's narratives about aid has been sharply different from that of the West. They have talked about 'South-South Cooperation', as already mentioned, and about 'mutual benefit' or 'common development'. And they have not focused very much on basic education or on Education for All, but much more on higher education.

These are the concerns of this book: the shifting agendas for education and skills, and the role of many different development agencies in shaping these.

If this volume is to be of value to students or researchers of international and comparative education, African Studies or development studies, it may be useful to outline the history of the author's professional years so that these different pieces can be better understood in particular historical contexts.

Connecting with African history, development studies, and education in Kenya and UK

Reading ancient Greek and Latin at the University of Cambridge sharpened my interest in language and gave me a lifelong concern with the meanings of texts. Being in Cambridge from 1958 to 1961 also introduced me to Africa for the first time, as there were students in my college from Uganda, Nigeria, Southern Rhodesia (as was) and Tanganyika (as was), and others from Japan and India. Others were British but had families working in countries such as Rwanda.

In the early 1960s, when a large number of African countries achieved independence, the desperate shortages of secondary schools and universities for the majority black African populations became sharply evident. Aid operations, particularly from Europe and North America but also Japan, were mounted to construct new universities and to provide large numbers of secondary and university teachers for Africa. Along with many thousands of others who responded to volunteer schemes such as VSO, which had started in 1958, the Peace Corps initiated by US President Kennedy in 1961, the related US initiative Teachers for East Africa in 1961, Japan's JOCV in 1961, and Canadian CUSO also in 1961, to mention just a few,[1] I responded to a new British Council scheme for teaching English as a foreign language abroad, and found myself teaching English in the premier school in Ethiopia from 1962 to 1965. Ethiopia's Emperor Haile Selassie had seized the opportunity to establish the new Organisation for African Unity (OAU)

---

[1] On this vast multi-stakeholder technical assistance operation, see further King and McGrath (2012). VSO – Voluntary Service Overseas; JOCV – Japanese Overseas Cooperation Volunteers; CUSO – Canadian University Service Overseas.

in the capital in 1963, and offered a large number of foreign African students the opportunity to study in what had been for most of its long history Africa's only independent country. There was therefore something of a Pan-African flavour in the student body of Haile Selassie First University where I also taught English literature in the evenings, drawing on the newly available African Writers Series published by Heinemann (Currey, 2008). I also taught in an extraordinary self-help school started in 1961 by Asfaw Yemiru whilst a student at our school, dedicated to offer good quality free education to poor children. Asfaw and his Asra Hawariat school still thrive on the same principle of providing free education to families without the ability to pay (Asra Hawariat, 2017).

This was also the period, with the end of colonial empires, when area studies centres were being established in order to engage in both policy and academic terms with a very large number of independent countries. The movement was not just a European or North American project, for African studies centres, for example, were also set up in New Delhi, Beijing, Moscow and Tokyo. One of these was established in the University of Edinburgh following the UK Foreign and Commonwealth Office's Hayter Report (FCO, 1961). Illustrating the role of chance in careers, one of my fellow-teachers in Wingate happened to go there in 1964; and I decided to follow suit a year later. Like Addis Ababa, the University of Edinburgh had something of a Pan-African presence with students from all over Anglophone Africa, as well as others from Britain and the USA.

Students interested in African history in the University of Edinburgh were fortunate to have the presence of George (Sam) Shepperson, one of the founders of the academic study of Pan-Africanism (Shepperson & Price, 1959), and Christopher Fyfe, the renowned historian of Sierra Leone (Fyfe, 1962). But setting out on a doctorate in the mid-1960s was very different from contemporary procedures. There were no prescribed methods courses; indeed there were no prescribed courses at all. Several of us elected to attend Christopher Fyfe's undergraduate African history lectures at 9.00 am in Old College. Graduate students learnt a great deal from each other. But you were on your own. It used to be said that if you survived until the second term, you had a chance of staying till the end.

My own doctoral thesis area I came upon completely by chance in the University of Edinburgh library, underlining the need to be flexible however careful your academic career planning. I found copies of the first ever educational aid missions to Sub-Saharan Africa (see further on these Phelps-Stokes Commissions in the introduction to Chapter 1 below). The exploration of the politics and Pan-Africanism of this international initiative in the early 1920s convinced me of the value of historical approaches to complex educational processes. Shortly, thanks to my father having found a small grant from the Aberdeenshire Educational Trust, I found myself in the archives of black institutes and colleges in the Southern States of the USA, including Tuskegee and Hampton Institutes, as well as missionary and government collections in the UK. It was also a time to learn the key contribution of oral interviews in both historical and contemporary research (King, 1971a). This set of issues is taken further in Chapter 1.

I had stumbled across the Phelps-Stokes reports by accident, but this occurrence was also the very beginning, again by chance, of my life-long interest in technical and vocational education and training. The promotion of what was then called 'industrial education' was one of the central messages of the Phelps-Stokes missions to Africa.

Three years later, in 1968, the venture into the political history of education in Africa, and particularly in Kenya, was deepened by the opportunity to be one of several non-Kenyan staff in the History Department of what would shortly become the University of Nairobi. There were larger numbers of so-called international staff in many other departments, particularly in the sciences, engineering and architecture. The History Department was unusual in having a strong local staff drawn from all the major provinces of Kenya. It had a powerful research culture, a regular conference of the Kenya Historical Association, and a valuable synergy with Tanzania and Uganda through the annual East African social sciences conference (Court, 1979).

Oral history was a special, pioneering strength of the Department of History. My own contribution to this was recording and introducing a book with Kenya's first nationalist leader, Harry Thuku, who had been very active in the 1920s before being sent into exile in Kismayu (Somalia) by the British (Thuku, 1971). A second oral history was with T. Ras Makonnen, a noted Pan-Africanist from British Guyana who had migrated to USA and taken an Ethiopian name to register support for that country on its invasion by Italy in 1936. Although he had gone to Ghana shortly after its independence in solidarity with the Pan-African ideals of Kwame Nkrumah, he had to leave Ghana with the fall of

Nkrumah in 1966. As an intriguing example of the crucial element of serendipity in research enterprise, I was told about Ras Makonnen by a black academic, St. Clair Drake, from Roosevelt and later Stanford University, USA. When we met round a camp-fire in 1967, St. Clair Drake was preparing Peace Corps volunteers to go abroad – and was doing so in the Tuskegee Institute where I was working in the archives. He mentioned that Ras Makonnen had been sent to Kenya a year earlier by the Ghanaian authorities, at the request of Kenyan President Jomo Kenyatta who had known him well in the UK. Makonnen had no personal papers; so it was necessary in preparing a book to rely almost entirely on oral interviews, supplemented and sharpened by review of the relevant literature (Makonnen and King, 1972).

Though I was located in the University's History Department, I continued my doctoral interest in education, and began to explore the history and politics of education in the pastoral economy of the Maasai. This also brought me to contemporary educational issues, as other non-pastoral communities such as the Kikuyu and the Kisii were migrating into traditional Maasai areas in order to access schools in which the Maasai were less interested than the agricultural peoples. Thanks to the presence in the University of Nairobi of the pioneering Institute for Development Studies, it was possible to present a first contemporary paper to an audience of economists, sociologists and political scientists. It was the beginning of a lifelong interest in connecting Education with Development Studies (King, 1971b; 1972a). Just before leaving Kenya, I had an opportunity to study the emergence of *Harambee* (self-help) Institutes of Technology in different parts of the country providing a fascinating connection back to the world of Hampton and Tuskegee but in a fundamentally different African context (King, 1972b).

At the end of three years in Kenya with these growing interdisciplinary connections, I had an opportunity to return to the University of Edinburgh having secured an advertised position in African Education at its Centre of African Studies. This provided a chance to work alongside colleagues in the Centre who were concerned with African geography, history, economics, politics, and anthropology. As this was a joint appointment with the Department of Educational Studies of the University, it offered a valuable first connection with comparative and international education through the comparativist Nigel Grant, as well as with adult and community education through John Lowe and, very briefly, Lalage Bown. By this time in 1972, I was becoming a participant in three disciplinary communities with their conferences, journals, networks and meetings: African Studies, Development Studies and Comparative and International Education; and in all of these there were strong engagements with History.

Stumbling across Kenya's informal sector

During the University's long vacation of 1972, I returned with research funding to examine in more detail the *Harambee* Institutes of Technology which I had been reviewing shortly before leaving the University of Nairobi. I do not want to overstate the role of chance or of serendipity in my research career, but nevertheless stress that readiness to seize and build on such openings is critical even though the roles of chance opportunities do not play any part in most research methodology courses. In the first few days of my time in Kenya, I was looking around Kariakor and Burma Markets in Nairobi – named for the Kenyan troops of the Carrier Corps in the First World War, and for those who served in Burma in the Second World War. I spotted on open waste-land a small number of men who had mounted metal-cutting machines on wooden poles. They were cutting and riveting metal to form bicycle carriers and other items appropriate to strengthening bicycles for Kenya's roads.

Talking to them, I learned they had gained their metal-working skills from a family member in a village not far from Nairobi. Within a day, they had taken me there, to find a compound filled with every kind of metal-cutting machine, all made locally. I had accidentally come across what was, unknown to me, being pursued that very same year by the International Labour Organization (ILO) Employment Mission to Kenya, and being termed the informal sector. I switched the focus of my research to follow these first machine-makers in Kenya and the role of their education and skills acquisition.

Unlike the economists, political scientists and manpower planners who were excited about the discovery of the informal sector for its links to employment, unemployment, productivity and income generation, my concern was primarily with the education and skills dimensions. Accordingly, I examined what training systems were associated with the informal economy and how those differed from training in the formal, so-called modern sector. Equally, I noted the emerging powerful political rhetoric around the slogan 'education for self-employment', as well some considerable international agency interest in non-formal education which had become manifest at almost the same time as the informal sector.

17

Chapter 2 on 'skills acquisition in the informal sector' teases out some of these connections as well as exploring the culture and context of skills development in Kenya's informal sector.

The role of aid in international education and skills development

Although my doctorate had been concerned with the analysis of philanthropy both in the Southern States of the USA and in Africa, I had not had much direct contact with philanthropy or with international development cooperation since then. Admittedly, my research on skills development in Kenya for several years after 1972 was supported by British aid through the Overseas Development Administration. In addition, my very presence in Kenya, as earlier in Ethiopia, had been part of a vast series of technical assistance projects from USA, UK, France, Denmark, Germany, Canada and Sweden –amongst many others – which were providing the many new universities and colleges across Sub-Saharan Africa with temporary staff while local staff were trained to replace them.

My direct contacts with aid agencies during my Kenyan research were restricted to those bodies such as Swedish SIDA and Canadian CIDA[2] that were supporting Kenya's technical and vocational schools, along with the ILO that was more concerned with industrial training. Then in 1975, when I had finished a first draft of *The African Artisan* and was attending a conference in Sèvres (outside Paris) of the Comparative Education Society in Europe, I was approached by Robert Myers of the Ford Foundation. He was a consummate networker, and had noted some of my articles on skill acquisition and the informal sector. He asked if I knew the renowned economists of education, C. Arnold Anderson and Mary Jean Bowman from the University of Chicago, as they were also in this conference. They had read my work, he said, and would like to meet. Though I had not previously met them, I knew of their influential edited book, *Education and Economic Development* (1965), not least because it contained the controversial chapter by Philip Foster on 'The vocational school fallacy in development planning' (Foster, 1965a). Also, Foster's *Education and social change in Ghana* (1965b) was one of the first things I had read once I had discovered the Phelps-Stokes Commissions, as he had a short section critical of their approach to education in Africa.

Anderson and Bowman in turn asked me if I knew Hans Weiler who

---

[2] SIDA Swedish International Development Cooperation Agency. SIDA later became Sida; CIDA Canadian International Development Agency

was the director of UNESCO's International Institute for Educational Planning (IIEP) in Paris. Despite knowing neither Weiler nor the IIEP, an appointment was arranged for me, and within a day I was meeting Weiler and then Neville Postlethwaite, a staff member of the Institute. By the time I left the Institute an hour or two later, I had been given a contract to work in Kenya on 'Curriculum development for basic education in rural areas'. It was my first piece of contract research for an international agency (King with Postlethwaite, 1975). Like my discovery of Phelps-Stokesism and the informal sector, it had come about almost entirely by chance and Myers' networking.

When I had completed the assignment later that year, I was invited to present its findings to the IIEP's annual conference of donor agencies. During that same conference, I was asked by Don Simpson, a Canadian working for a new organisation called the International Development Research Centre (IDRC), if I would be interested in directing its education research funding programme worldwide. By January 1978, I had taken leave of absence from Edinburgh University to pursue this new opportunity for what was initially two years and was then extended to three and a half years. I had also agreed to a request from Robert Myers to join a new 12-person group, which he would lead, termed the Research Review and Advisory Group (RRAG), set up with the agreement of the Bellagio group of donor agencies to review and synthesise educational research in the developing world.

These two developments opened my eyes to the new world of donor or development agencies, or development partners, as they have been termed more recently. IDRC was unique at the time it was set up since it took seriously the research priorities of partner institutions in the global South, and did not make it mandatory to have a Canadian collaborator. From being concerned with my own research in a single country, Kenya, I was suddenly visiting research centres in Latin America, the Caribbean, South and South East Asia, and Western and North Africa. Chapter 3, drawn from *Aid and education in the developing world* (King, 1991), covers the extraordinary range and reach of the research-related activities of the donor agencies.

Education and training for self-employment: Kenya's informal sector revisited

One theme that runs through this book is the vital importance of historical depth. This is why I have looked at aid to skills development in

19

the Southern States of the USA and in Kenya 40 years before the first development agencies were established in the early 1960s. This is also why, after stumbling across the informal sector in Kenya in 1972, I wanted to explore the 'pre-history' of the informal sector in the insights of the *East African Royal Commission of 1953-1955*. The Commission had noted that the informal settlements just outside the formal town and city boundaries were 'important as centres of African trade', and warned against destroying them as they were 'the only development of African commercial enterprise' (EARC, 1955: 208). They were among other predecessors in Kenya to the 'discovery' of the informal sector by the ILO Employment Mission when visiting that country in 1972 (King, 1996: 5).

Another example of historical sequence is that I was lucky enough to publish a second book on Kenya's informal artisans in 1996 almost 20 years after the first one in 1977. I say lucky advisedly since chance has also been a theme to which I have referred on several occasions already in this introduction. In the case of this second book, was it by chance that President Arap Moi (1979-2002) stopped at Kamukunji, near the Burma and Kariakor markets in Nairobi, where there was a huge concentration of informal sector activities one afternoon in November 1985? Or was there some reason that he visited these informal sector workers four more times in the next four months, promising them protective sheds and title deeds? Within a few months, the government produced a *Sessional Paper No. 1 of 1986 on economic management for renewed growth*. This promised a crucial role for technical and vocational education 'in developing artisans, managers and entrepreneurs for the informal sector' (Kenya, 1986: 57). The next year I was invited to a seminar on this *Sessional Paper* in Kenya. It rekindled my interest in the informal sector on which I had last worked in 1974. I found time after the seminar to visit the areas in which I had previously worked, and noticed profound changes. By the summer of 1987, I had secured funding to return to Kenya. In addition, I was fortunate enough to trace the artisans with whom I had worked closely in the early 1970s, including the one who was on the front cover of my book *The African artisan.*

Over the next seven to eight years, I reviewed the changes in technology, policy and financing in the informal sector – which was now widely termed *jua kali* in Kenya, meaning hot sun workers, or rather all those working in self-employment. In addition I thought it would be vital to see how the schools and the training system had reacted to the new, official support for *jua kali*. This thread led to a chapter on 'Education and training for self-employment'. A great deal had been achieved since the research for *The African artisan*. Curricula with an orientation to self-employment had been introduced at many different levels, including at primary. Some of these key issues are taken forward in Chapter 4.

Research about the impact of primary education
Having just looked at how a single country, Kenya, had tried to create an educational environment supportive of self-employment, it may be worth looking at the international research findings that commented so powerfully on the alleged impact of primary education. In this sphere, one of the best-known research claims has been that four years of education make a difference to agricultural productivity. This finding by Lockheed, Jamison and Lau (1980) emerged at the time when the increased research capacity in the World Bank had allowed it to make a series of claims, including the impact of education on the reduction of female fertility, and on education's impact on the informal sector.

I have selected in Chapter 5 the famous 'four years of education' finding because it illustrates the importance of looking critically at the basis of these iconic pieces of research evidence. In the case of this well-known claim, I illustrate the vital need to examine what precisely was claimed, and the danger of simply using a short form of the findings for policy convenience.

Researching text
With the benefit of hindsight, I can see that one red thread running through much of my work has been the critical analysis of text. This may have been encouraged by reading classics (i.e. ancient Greek and Latin) as a student, as already mentioned. But whatever the source, my long-standing academic concern has been to interrogate what lies behind a particular report or policy – whether the Phelps-Stokes Commissions (Jones, 1922: 1925) or the *Declaration* and *Framework for Action* from the Jomtien World Conference on Education for All (UNESCO, 1990a; b), or the very first Global Monitoring Report (UNESCO, 2001) before the well-known series started in 2002. Equally, the hugely influential 'vocational school fallacy' caught my attention from early on, not least because it had some controversial things to say about the limits of school curricula to influence attitudes to vocation and work (Foster, 1965).

Sometimes this fascination with peeling off the layers of a particular report has been helped by being present or being involved in some capacity with the report, as in Jomtien, or in the World Bank's controversial *Education in Sub-Saharan Africa* (World Bank, 1988). On other occasions such as the Dakar World Education Forum of 2000, I wanted to understand why a particular piece of text had been agreed, and by which particular parties. This was the case with 'access to appropriate learning and life-skills programmes' which appeared as part of the six EFA goals (UNESCO, 2000: 7). This single word, life-skills, had a hugely deleterious impact on the positioning of technical and vocational education and training (TVET) internationally. The word 'skills' has been equally challenging because in English it can cover such a wide range of abilities or capacities. It was revealing how it had been used over the course of a decade of Education for All Global Monitoring Reports (King, 2011), as indicated in Chapter 9. In the same way, it was fascinating to follow how the idea of skilling 500 million people in India had come about in Manmohan Singh's government (2004-2014), as explained in Chapter 12 (King, 2012), and to explore whether it had been modified by Narendra Modi's term in office (Sharma and King, 2019).

A further example would come from the term 'informal sector', first used half a century ago, though of course it had antecedents historically in both industrialised and developing economies. It also widened its use over time; so what had started as a term to describe a wide range of mechanics, carpenters and other artisans operating where they could find a space, under the hot sun, over the next 30 years it could be applied to a whole range of informal, second or third jobs, frequently untaxed and unrecognised in national accounts. Many of these could be found right inside the formal sector, as noted in Chapter 7. I shall note many other examples of this interrogation of text, but turn now to the revisit of the 'vocational school fallacy'.

Revisiting the 'vocational school fallacy'
Foster's hugely influential article came out in the year, 1965, that I was starting on my doctoral work in Edinburgh, and was clearly concerned with the vocational arena – which was also the case with the Phelps-Stokes Commissions which I was investigating. The 1960s were an intriguing moment to be looking at vocational education in Africa. The World Bank had just made its first loan in support of diversified secondary education in Tunisia in 1963, a policy it would continue for 15-20 years across the world. Several other bilateral agencies such as Swedish SIDA and Canadian CIDA were also supporting technical and

vocational education. Yet a number of countries including Kenya were dropping vocational education from their basic cycles with the attainment of Independence and as a reaction to colonial policies which had encouraged vocational rather than academic education.

Forty years after Foster had collected his first data, I had an opportunity to work in Ghana under the umbrella of the UK-funded Research Consortium on Educational Outcomes and Poverty (RECOUP) which was led by Christopher Colclough. This provided a chance to try out the vocational school fallacy's approaches and assumptions within a very different Ghanaian educational context, including the very school, Achimota, where James Aggrey had been the assistant principal (See further Chapter 1 for Aggrey).

The article in Chapter 6 drew on the vital importance of Ghanaian educational history, including from colonial times, but like many other pieces in this book it provided a chance to examine very carefully what Foster had actually tried to carry out, and what he had not. For example, the vocational school fallacy, paradoxically, does not draw at all on any vocational school! Most fortunately, however, it was possible to discuss our article and his own one with Philip Foster himself, providing a unique commentary all these years later (Chapter 6). The article followed Foster's in having both an historical and a quantitative approach. My colleague, Chris Martin, then in Edinburgh's Centre for Educational Sociology, was vital in critically analysing the questionnaires and the subsequent data I had gathered in Ghana as part of revisiting Foster's thesis with more recent data.

Africa's informal economies: Thirty years on

The importance of historical depth in research is something on which I have already commented several times. It is a luxury to be able to work on a small number of topics over time. Unfortunately, this has become much more difficult in a number of universities in Sub-Saharan Africa. The salary situation in some of these institutions is such that staff have turned to consultancy, making capitalisation of research much more of a challenge.

In my own case, it has been possible to return to the research on the informal sector on a continuous basis, but basically in the early 1970s and late 1980s and early 1990s. These lengthy periods of research led to two books, already mentioned. It was a welcome opportunity, three decades on from the first use of the term 'informal sector' to be asked to reflect briefly on 'Africa's informal economies: thirty years on'. This is explored in Chapter 7.

Re-targeting schools, skills and jobs

The red threads that run through these different chapters cover schools, skills and jobs, and their multiple interactions. I have also followed the informal sector from its origins, and noted its connections with education and training. The political concern with a 'relevant' curriculum has been teased out from the days of the Phelps-Stokes Commissions, right through to the vocational school fallacy and beyond. USA, Kenya and Ghana have been the sites for many of these synergies, but we shall note they also occur in India in Chapter 12.

Another red thread that goes back far into the 20th century is the setting of goals and targets for education and skills (King, 2016). At the international level, goals and targets were associated with UNESCO's regional conferences in the 1960s, and then taken up by the World Conference in Jomtien in 1990, and again in the six Dakar Education for All (EFA) Goals in 2000, as well as the Millennium Development Goals that same year. The national ambitions for the targeting of new jobs is also widespread, but will be looked at in Chapter 8 in Kenya against the implications for quantity and quality (King 2005). Later a parallel exploration will look at the massive ambitions and targets of India for 500 million skilled workers (Chapter 12).

The global monitoring of skills – 1990-2012

I have already mentioned, in assessing the crucial importance of text, how sometimes a single phrase or even a word can hugely affect education or training policy at the national or international levels. The term, 'informal', would be one such word, and another, already mentioned, would be 'life-skills'. The framers of the influential text of the *World Declaration on Education for All* and the *Framework for Action* (1990) had deliberately sought to promote the terms, 'Education or All', and Basic Education, rather than the traditional 'primary' or 'secondary' school or 'vocational' education.[3] The *Declaration* and *Framework* do actually use the term 'skills' in many different ways, but in the critical six suggested dimensions for national targets, they employ the phrase 'expansion of provisions of basic education and training in other

---

[3] The terms 'primary education' and 'primary school' are scarcely used in the *World Declaration* or the *Framework for Action*. 'Basic education', by contrast, is used 162 times in some 30 pages.

essential skills for youth and adults' (UNESCO, 1990b: 3).

Though I was present in Jomtien, and had prepared much of one whole issue of *NORRAG⁴ News (7)* on how the final text of Jomtien was reached, through its several drafts, I was not representing any particular skills constituency; so I contented myself by commenting that the *Framework*'s 'expanded provision of skills is by far the most vague; it seems to address many different conceptions of skills-for-motherhood, for life and for formal employment' (King, 1990: 30). The Dakar World Education Forum in 2000 had not helped; it had taken Jomtien's 'education and training in other essential skills for youth and adults' and had turned it into 'ensuring that the learning needs of all young people and adults are met through equitable access to appropriate learning and life-skills programmes'.

Nevertheless, once the Global Monitoring Report series began in 2002, as noted above I sought to follow through each volume what had actually happened to this commitment about appropriate learning and life-skills as one of the six EFA Dakar goals.

The paper in which I analysed the first 10 EFA Global Monitoring Reports from this particular angle is another example of the kind of policy history to which I have referred. This is taken further in Chapter 9. I wrote a whole series of other papers on TVET in this period leading up to the 2012 Global Monitoring Report. This raises the very old question of the extent to which research can influence policy, on which there are, of course, no easy answers.

Research and knowledge in development aid

I wrote earlier about how my participation in RRAG from 1977 and my move in 1978 to the International Development Research Centre (IDRC) in Ottawa to take responsibility for their educational research funding worldwide had opened my eyes to the world of development agencies, both bilateral and multilateral. I had come across a whole language that I had not met before. What was unique to IDRC when it was established in the early 1970s was that it sought to fund directly research institutions in the South. It did not go via Canadian partners. Thus, at a time when research priorities were almost entirely set in the North, IDRC was clear that the ownership of research should be secured in the South. This involved discussions with independent research centres all over the

---

⁴ Network for International Policies and Cooperation in Education and Training

world, but also the encouragement of research networking.

My membership of RRAG, along with 11 other academics and policy people, supported this approach as it was based on the belief that there was a great deal of research in the South that it would make sense to synthesise and summarise. One of the first examples of this was a review of teacher effectiveness research in six regions and countries in the South by Beatrice Avalos and Wadi Haddad (1981). Another early RRAG product examined the *Educational research environments in the developing world* (1983), edited by Sheldon Shaeffer, who joined me in IDRC, and John Nkinyangi. This focused on the different cultures and contexts in which research was conducted, whether in Colombia, Kenya or the Caribbean.

There was little time to carry out any of my own research during my four years in IDRC. The focus was on organising research meetings and encouraging research networking, mostly in the South, but also liaising with agencies that carried out research – much of it for their own work in the education sector. The few papers there was time to write were on subjects such as 'Dilemmas of research aid to education in developing countries' (King, 1981).

The great privilege of the time in IDRC and in RRAG was that it allowed me to build friendships and research networks with colleagues in and from the South, such as Ernesto Schiefelbein, Patricio Cariola and Beatrice Avalos from Chile, Wadi Haddad, originally from Lebanon, J. P. Naik from India, Tunde Yoloye from Nigeria, Katherine Namuddu from Uganda and Pablo Latapi from Mexico. There were a host of others, including Aklilu Habte, originally from the Ethiopia, who had moved to the World Bank. My colleagues in IDRC, Sheldon Shaeffer and Nelly Stromquist, contributed crucially to our team.

The academic and research legacy from this IDRC and RRAG focus on working with the South, and not for the South, was an awareness of how agendas for educational development as well as for research continued to be set in the North for many decades after my time in IDRC, and my return to African Studies in Edinburgh. This focus on work with colleagues in the South, and looking critically at the role of agenda setting and knowledge production in the North was to be one of the key motives in setting up a child of RRAG in the North, called NORRAG, in 1986. This became possible through the support of Swedish SIDA, and its education staff, Lennart Wohlgemuth, Ingemar Gustafsson and Christine McNab. The first issue of *NORRAG News* appeared in 1986, and was co-edited by Christine McNab and myself till Jomtien in 1990, and for two further years with Wim Biervliet from the Hague. NORRAG's critical stance on major education and skills developments meant close ties with analysts and policy people in agencies, such as Peter Williams in the Commonwealth Secretariat, Birger Fredriksen, Jamil Salmi and Arvil Van Adams in the World Bank, as well as Wolfgang Kuper in GIZ and Wolfgang Gmelin in DSE.[5]

Chance stepped in once more shortly after Jomtien. Because I had dedicated almost all of *NORRAG News 7* (1990), and the whole of *NORRAG News 8* (1990) to a critical analysis of how the text of the *Declaration* and *Framework for Action* were constructed for the World Conference, and to what happened in Jomtien, the OECD's Development Assistance Committee (DAC) had asked me to assess what had been the impact of this World Conference on the aid community worldwide. I had constructed a detailed questionnaire, along with Roy Carr-Hill (of York University and the London Institute of Education), whom I had invited to join me on this task. In approaching the Japanese delegation to the OECD, I was told that merely sending a questionnaire would not work well in the aid culture of Tokyo; would it be alright if we both went there personally? It was the beginning of a long engagement with Japan, its international education community and its aid programme. Thus, ten years later, when Simon Mcgrath and I were looking for a non-Western example of a knowledge agency, it was natural to consider the Japan International Cooperation Agency (JICA). This is explored further in chapter 10

Discovering China's aid to Africa
Shortly after I had 'retired' from the University of Edinburgh in September 2005, Mark Bray, who was the Dean of the Faculty of Education in the University of Hong Kong (HKU), asked if I would like to apply for the position of Distinguished Visiting Professor. Mark had been my first doctoral student in the Department of Educational Studies and in the Centre of African Studies. Naturally I was delighted when this worked out.

A few days after arriving in Hong Kong in March 2006, I was asked by Mark Bray and his colleague, Mark Mason, to do a first seminar. What

---

[5] Germany's GIZ – German Agency for International Cooperation – previously GTZ. DSE –German Foundation for International Development.

would it be on? The informal sector? Knowledge for development? TVET? Once more, fortune stepped in; the government of the People's Republic of China had published its *China's Africa policy* in January that same year. Thus my first paper to the Comparative Education Research Centre in HKU in March was on 'China and Africa: New approaches to aid, trade and international cooperation'. It was the beginning of a ten-year engagement with China's expanding cooperation with Africa, not in the realm of building roads, railways, stadia, and parliament buildings, but in the sphere of its support to education, training and capacity building.

One of the most dramatic changes in this area was in the rapidly expanding numbers of African students in China. Therefore, one theme of our research was the history of African students in China, some 40 years after pursuing 'African students in the States' in my published thesis (King, 1971a: 212-251). I say 'our' advisedly since my wife, Pravina, carried out hundreds of interviews with me on the broader theme of *China's aid and soft power in Africa: The case of education and training* (2013). The focus on history and change over time remained important: how had things changed since China first brought over a hundred students to study at the beginning of the 1960s, when it too, like the West, was beginning its more formal aid, and setting up institutes to study Asia and Africa? I explore this theme in Chapter 11.

India's massive skills development ambitions
I didn't visit India until August 1968 when Pravina and I were married in New Delhi *en route* to going to teach in the University of Nairobi. With my interest in the informal sector kindled in Kenya, I would become interested in the way that there had been a good deal of informal technological learning from Indian artisans in Kenya by their African workers. But I found the sheer scale of the informal – or the 'unorganised' sector as it is termed in India – staggering in the many times I visited it in Old Delhi, Ahmedabad and Kolkata during the 1970s.

My next research interest in India resulted from my time in IDRC (1978-1981) where there had been a very active science and technology policy programme driven by my colleague, Tony Tillet. It was thought valuable to explore some of the synergies with those of the education programme. One result was a conference and a volume by IDRC on *Science, education and society: Perspectives from India and South East Asia* (IDRC, 1985).

A continuing concern remained with skills development, not least because of the lengthy process whereby the EFA Global Monitoring Report decided to pay serious attention to skills in 2010 and 2012 (see Chapter 9). Further, when the government of Manmohan Singh laid out plans for a skills mission that would move India from having only 2% to 50% of its workforce trained, with a total of no less than 500 million skilled people by 2022, it looked like an area worth critical attention. Chapter 12 analyses India's ambitious plan to reap a 'demographic dividend' from providing both its own labour market and international markets with millions of Indian skilled workers (King, 2012).

Preliminary conclusions

There are no full conclusions to this safari from Addis Ababa, Tuskegee and Nairobi to Tokyo, Hong Kong and New Delhi - principally because it is not finished. Since the last article in this selection, there have been lots more stops along the way. One of these has been reflecting on the century of target-setting in education and skills through the lens of the BAICE Presidential Address (King, 2016).[6] Another has been the beginning in 2016 of an exploration of India's aid to Africa over the period since Independence, or the completion in that same year, 2016, of 30 years of editing *NORRAG News.*

One of the differences between the beginnings of the journey and later stages is that it was possible at the beginning to spend a full three years each in Ethiopia, Kenya and Canada. This makes such a difference to understandings of culture and context, not to mention developing friendships and networks. Further down the track, the stops along the way have been shorter, but the year and a half in the University of Hong Kong and in what is now the Hong Kong University of Education allowed the time to engage much more fully with China and its international connections, including with Africa. In the same way, the three months in Hiroshima University in 2000 and four months in Nagoya University in 2014-2015 offered the privileges of extended academic involvement and new friendships. This was also the advantage of spending three months in New Delhi in early 2018.

Interweaving the long histories of the red threads of aid, skills, education and work in their different patterns in Kenya, Ghana, Canada, USA, Switzerland, Japan, China and India has been fascinating, and

---

[6] BAICE – British Association for International and Comparative Education. As BAICE President, I delivered a paper at the UKFIET Oxford Conference in 2015, a shortened version of which appeared in *Compare* (King, 2016).

made more so by serendipity and good fortune along the way. I hope that they will offer some insights to other younger scholars and policy people as they explore the advantages of looking over time through the lenses of area studies, and development studies, but especially comparative and international education.

References

Avalos, B. and Haddad, W. 1981. *A review of teacher effectiveness research in Africa, India, Latin America, Middle East, Malaysia, Philippines and Thailand: Synthesis of results.* International Development Research Centre, Ottawa.

Asra Hawariat School Fund, 2017. *Annual Report.* www.asrahawariatschool. org

Court, D. 1979. 'The idea of social science in East Africa: An aspect of the development of higher education', *Minerva*, 17, 2, pp.244-282.

Currey, J. 2008. *Africa writes back: The African Writers Series and the launch of African literature*, James Currey, Oxford.

East Africa Royal Commission, 1953-1955 (EARC), 1955, Cmd. 9475, Her Majesty's Stationery Office, London.

Foreign and Commonwealth Office 1961, *Hayter Committee Report*, Foreign and Commonwealth Office, London.

Foster, P. 1965a.'The vocational school fallacy in development planning' in Anderson, C.A. and Bowman, M.J. (Eds.) *Education and economic development*, Aldine, Chicago.

Foster, P. 1965b. *Education and social change in Ghana*, Routledge and Kegan Paul, London.

Fyfe, C. 1962. *A history of Sierra Leone*, Oxford University Press, Oxford.

IDRC, 1985. *Science, education and society: Perspectives from India and South East Asia.* IDRC Manuscript Series, IDRC, Ottawa.

Jones, T. J. 1922. *Education in Africa: A study of West, South and Equatorial Africa by the African Education Commission, under the auspices of the Phelps-Stokes Fund and the Foreign Mission Societies of North America and Europe*, Phelps-Stokes Fund, New York.

Jones, T. J. 1925. *Education in East Africa: A study of East, Central and South Africa by the second African Education Commission, under the auspices of the Phelps-Stokes Fund, in cooperation with the International Education Board*, Phelps-Stokes Fund, New York.

King, K. 1971a. *Pan-Africanism and education: A study of race, philanthropy* and education in the Southern States of the USA and East Africa, Clarendon Press, Oxford. A new edition of *Pan-Africanism and education* is available from Diasporic Africa Press, since 2016 www. dafricapress.com

King, K. 1971b. 'Primary schools in Kenya: Some critical constraints on their effectiveness', Institute for Development Studies, Discussion Paper 130, University of Nairobi, Nairobi; reprinted in Court, D. and Ghai, D. (Eds.) 1974, *Education, society and development: New perspectives from Kenya*, Oxford University Press, Nairobi, 123-148.

King, K. 1972a. Education and development in the Narok District of Kenya', *African Affairs*, LXXX1, 3, 1972, 389-407.

King, K. 1972b. 'Technological self-help in Kenya: The *Harambee* institutes', in: Centre of African Studies (ed.), *Developmental trends in Kenya*, Centre of African Studies, University of Edinburgh, 175-203.

King, K. 1977. *The African artisan: Education and the informal sector.* Heinemann, London.

King, K. 1981. 'Dilemmas of research aid to education in developing countries' *Comparative Education Review* 17, 2, 247-254; also in *Prospects*, XI, 3, 343-351.

King, K. 1990. 'World Conference on Education for All' in *NORRAG News 7, Special issue on World Conference on Education for All and International Literacy Year,* University of Edinburgh and University of Stockholm, accessed at www.norrag.org

King, K. 1991. *Aid and education in the developing world.* Longman, Harlow, UK.

King, K. 1996. *Jua kali Kenya: Change and development in an informal economy.* James Currey, London.

King, K. 2011. 'Skills and education for all from Jomtien (1990) to the GMR of 2012: A policy history', *International Journal of Training Research*, 9: 16-34.

King, K. 2012. 'The geopolitics and meanings of India's massive skills development ambitions'. *International Journal of Educational Development*, 32, 665-673.

King, K. 2013. *China's aid and soft power in Africa: The case of education and training,* James Currey, Woodbridge, UK

King, K. 2016. 'The global targeting of education and skill: Policy history and comparative perspectives' *Compare: A Journal of Comparative and International Education*, 46, 6, 952-975.

King, K. with Postlethwaite, T. N. 1975. 'Curriculum development for basic education in rural areas' in *Planning Problems in Rural Education,* International Institute for Educational Planning, UNESCO, Paris.

King, K. and McGrath, S. 2012. 'Education and development in Africa: Lessons of the past 50 years for Beyond 2015', paper to Conference on Centre of African Studies @ 50, Centre of African Studies, University of Edinburgh. Accessible at: http://eprints.nottingham. ac.uk/1640/1/Kenneth.King%26Simon.McGrath.CAS@50.pdf

Lockheed, M., Jamison, D. and Lau, L. 1980. 'Farmer education and farm efficiency: A survey', *Economic Development and Cultural Change,* 29, 1, 37-76.

Makonnen, T. R. and King, K. 1972. *Pan-Africanism from within,* Oxford University Press, Nairobi.

NORRAG News 7, 1990. *Special Issue on the World Conference on Education for All and International Literacy Year,* University of Edinburgh and University of Stockholm, accessed at www.norrag.org

NORRAG News 8, 1990. University of Edinburgh, Edinburgh, accessed at www.norrag.org

Sharma, A. and King, K. 2019. "Skill India": The "modification" of skill development in India' in McGrath, S., Papier, J., Mulder, M. and Suart, R. (Eds.) *International Handbook of Vocational Education and Training for the Changing World of Work,* Springer, New York.

Shaeffer, S. and Nkinyangi, J. 1983. *Educational research environments in the developing world,* International Development Research Centre, Ottawa.

Shepperson, G. and Price, T., 1959. *The Independent African: John Chilembwe and the origins, setting and significance of the Nyasaland native rising of 1915,* Edinburgh University Press, Edinburgh.

Thuku, H. 1971. *Harry Thuku: An autobiography,* Oxford University Press, Nairobi.

UNESCO, 1990a. *World Declaration on Education for All.* UNESCO, Paris.

UNESCO. 1990b. *Framework for action to meet basic learning needs.* UNESCO, Paris.

UNESCO, 2000. *The Dakar framework for action: Education for all: Meeting our collective commitments.* World Education Forum, 26-28 April 2000, Dakar,

UNESCO, 2001. *Monitoring report on education for all, 2001.* UNESCO, Paris.

World Bank, 1988. *Education in Sub-Saharan Africa: Policies for adjustment, revitalisation and expansion,* World Bank, Washington DC.

Chapter 1

Debates about education have always been a central concern of
development aid and international cooperation. Right back to when
Christian missionary endeavours spread outwards from Europe and
North America to the rest of the world, there have been discussions about
the most appropriate education for the peoples reached by missions.
Colonisation added a layer of complexity to this debate about education.
Even after the end of empire, education remained a key dimension of the
programming of the bilateral aid agencies that came into being during the
1960s, just as it had been for the UN specialised agencies, such as
UNESCO and UNICEF, from the 1940s. Provision of educational aid was
not confined to the European and North American nations, however; it
was also associated with China, India and Japan from at least as early as
Western nations established their development agencies.

Sub-Saharan Africa has been at the centre of many of these debates
by external bodies about the role of education and skills in the continent's
development. With the end of slavery in the American South after the
Civil War in 1866, the discussion about African education began to be
linked to options for the newly liberated populations of the Southern
USA. No topic was hotter than whether African Americans should
directly aspire to the kinds of education available to the white population
or whether they should adapt their aspirations to the realities of
continuing white power and show themselves worthy through espousing
agricultural and industrial education. Eminent black proponents of both
options emerged in the last two decades of the 19th century. Booker T.
Washington, a former slave, developed Tuskegee Institute in Alabama,
USA, from 1881 as a beacon of black gradualism through industrial
education, while W.E.B. DuBois, the first African American to receive a

Kenneth King (2019): *Education, Skills and International Cooperation: Comparative and Historical
Perspectives*. Hong Kong: Comparative Education Research Centre (CERC), The University of Hong
Kong, and Dordrecht: Springer. © CERC

© Springer Nature Switzerland AG 2019
K. King, *Education, Skills and International Cooperation*, CERC Studies
in Comparative Education 36, https://doi.org/10.1007/978-3-030-29790-9_1

doctorate at Harvard, presented himself as a spokesman for college education for emancipated blacks (King, 1971: ch. 1).

Significantly, both men perceived that there were significant implications for African education and skills development in the increasingly polarised positions which they had adopted. Thus, DuBois, in the first Pan-African Conference in London in 1900, and in the Universal Races Congress, also in London in 1911, was able sharply to separate his educational ambitions for black people from those 'of Booker T. Washington and others' who were said to be compromising their future through the gospel of industrial education (King, 1971: 11). Meanwhile, the International Conference on the Negro,[1] held in Tuskegee in 1912, provided an opportunity to internationalise the merits of industrial education to many interested participants, including from Africa.

Tuskegee was more than an American symbol of black industrial ambition; its graduates had actually appeared in African projects from as early as 1900. Major figures concerned with the analysis of what would now be called international and comparative education, such as Michael Sadler, had visited Tuskegee, which may have been in part the inspiration for his 'Education of the Coloured Race' in 1902.[2] Sadler became a proponent for the ideals of Tuskegee and its mother school, Hampton Institute, over a period of many years:

> The work which is going forward in the industrial and agricultural training schools for the coloured race in the United States, is one of great significance. Lessons can be learned from it which are of value for those engaged in education in parts of the British Empire; for example, in West Africa and the West Indies, where there are large black populations. (Sadler, 1902, quoted in King, 1971: 48)

Sadler had picked out some of the features of Tuskegee which would later appeal to many hundreds of visitors to the Institute – from mission, government and civil society – an educational formula that would counter urbanisation, an experience that would compensate for a backward home, and 'the kind of *practical* instruction which the coloured people would specially need' (Sadler, 1902 quoted in King, 1971: 48). Sadler paid little attention to the political and economic value of

---

[1] The terms 'Negro' and 'American Negro' continued to be acceptable in both academic and popular discourse until the very early 1970s, after which they were replaced by 'black' and 'African-American'.
[2] Sadler had a government position in the UK as Director of the Office of Special Reports and Inquiries.

Hampton and Tuskegee to a white-dominated society, or to their implicit rejection of competition with whites in higher skills and the professions. This omission was remedied by Sir Harry Johnston, the great British traveller, botanist and Africanist, who visited the two institutes in 1908, and devoted no less than 46 pages to their virtues in his *The Negro in the New World*, while the black colleges got half a page of ridicule. These struggling colleges did not 'solve the tremendous need of the United States for field-hands – INTELLIGENT field-hands; they don't turn out cooks – and cooks, as Booker Washington points out … are more necessary than preachers' (Johnston, 1908, quoted in King, 1971: 49, emphasis in the original).

This tension between technical and vocational education and training (TVET) on the one hand and academic, college education on the other was much more than a curricular issue. It was not just another version of the widespread preference for academic streams or schools over vocational schools on the grounds of greater mobility, later choice of options, and negative stereotyping of the vocational. Rather, it was the promotion of the vocational as particularly suitable for the black populations of USA and elsewhere that jarred with critics such as Dubois. Five decades later the politics of vocational education would be rerun in South Africa in the promotion by its government of the *Bantu Education Act* of 1953 as part of apartheid and its proposal for blacks to prepare to be mere hewers of wood and drawers of water (Union of South Africa, 1953).

The critics of what could be termed the 'racialisation' of the vocational argued that for black populations to accept the differentiation of the curriculum before the achievement of political and economic equality would be hugely problematic. The politics of this choice were made sharper in the United States by the role of aid moneys. The majority of the Northern US foundations operating in the education sphere in the Southern states were solid supporters of the Hampton-Tuskegee approach to industrial education. One of these, the Phelps-Stokes Fund, established in 1911, actually had written into its charter that one of its aims should be 'the education of negroes, both in Africa and the United States' (Jones, 1923, quoted in King 1971: 3). Accordingly, the secretary to its trustees, Anson Phelps Stokes, in his first official move, wrote to Booker Washington to ask him what would be a valuable contribution to the cause. It was rapidly agreed that a survey of all the black schools and colleges in the American South would be invaluable in sorting out the wheat from the chaff, especially in the area of quality industrial education (King, 1971: 31).

The survey was duly carried out over a period of three years, published in 1916, and widely publicised. It should perhaps not be surprising that the researcher chosen to direct this highly controversial study should be someone who was already persuaded of the value of the Tuskegee-Hampton approach to education, Thomas Jesse Jones. At the time of leading this inquiry, Jones was working in the research department of Hampton Institute.

Jones seized the opportunity to apply Tuskegee criteria of rural relevance through agricultural and industrial education across the whole of the segregated school and college system for blacks in the USA. He used the study to underline the advantages of rural education, and to dismiss the movement of Southern blacks to greater safety and opportunity in towns, both North and South, as a delusion. The two-volume report, *Negro education: A study of the private and higher schools for coloured people in the United States* (1916) was arguably an exercise in special pleading, and a restatement of the founder of Hampton Institute's conviction that 'the temporal salvation of the coloured race for some time to come is to be won out of the ground' (Armstrong, 1901, quoted in King, 1971: 33). Armstrong had managed to devise a programme for educating blacks that met with the approbation of Northern philanthropists and white Southerners. The few concessions in the report to the needs of higher education for blacks were all but swamped by Jones's enthusiasm for industrial and agricultural education. He had managed to give Booker Washington's educational formula a national currency. He would soon have the opportunity to apply 'Tuskegeeism' to the whole of Sub-Saharan Africa.

Washington's international influence on educational policy had been very evident for years even before his visit to London in 1899, and the publication of his autobiography, *Up from slavery*, two years later (Washington, 1901). In the first World Missionary Conference of 1910 in Edinburgh, Scotland, Commission III focused on the appropriate education to accompany 'the evangelisation of the world in this generation'. From many different sources and authorities, the methods of Hampton and Tuskegee received the strongest possible approbation, and especially, but not exclusively, for Africa (World Missionary Conference, 1910, quoted in King, 1971: 50). Two of the most influential visitors for promoting Tuskegee and Hampton through English-speaking missionary circles were A.G. Fraser, known for his work in Ceylon and later as co-principal of Achimota College in the Gold Coast, and his brother in law, J.H. Oldham, editor of the new journal, *International Review of Missions* and secretary to the continuation committee of the World Missionary Conference. Both visited Hampton in 1912, and felt they had learned more than ever before in the same amount of time. They were determined to make the Hampton-Tuskegee message bear fruit in other countries.

Two other visits to Tuskegee and Hampton were critical in the chemistry that led to the Phelps-Stokes education commissions to Africa in the early 1920s. One was C.T. Loram whose book on *The education of the South African native* appeared in 1917, just a year after Jones's *Negro education*. He was looking for ammunition in the Southern states that would convince his fellow whites in South Africa that 'with proper training and education the negro can be made a valuable asset to any country' (Loram, 1914, quoted in King, 1971: 52). The second was a man from the Gold Coast, J.E.K. Aggrey, who had finished his education at Livingstone College in North Carolina (USA) but had met with Jones in 1904. Jones had immediately recognised that Aggrey was working on the same educational lines as himself, and had ensured that he visited Hampton in 1904 to lecture, preach and learn more. Jones maintained contact with Aggrey over the next decade and a half, and when the North American Missionary Conference proposed to the Phelps-Stokes Fund that there be a survey of West African education, and that Jones should be asked to carry it out, he immediately thought that Aggrey should be a member of the Commission. Doubtless, he recalled DuBois's criticism of his *Negro Education* report: 'that the Phelps-Stokes Fund find it so much easier to work for the Negro than *with* him' (DuBois, 1918, quoted in King, 1971: 56-7). At the time it was a courageous and almost unprecedented move to include an African in such an international commission. But it was one where only the Tuskegee spirit could overcome the discrimination that could be encountered, and especially in Southern Africa. Accordingly, Aggrey was sent by Jones to Tuskegee shortly before the Commission sailed for West, Central and Southern Africa – with its mandate now extended from just West Africa.

All the pieces were falling into place for what would be the first educational commission to report on the whole of West, Central and Southern Africa: the American foundations, both American and European missionary bodies, representatives of the British colonial office and C.T. Loram, who was directly appointed by the South African prime-minister, Jan Smuts, to be on the Commission. Its report would be available in 1922, and it would be followed two years later by a second Commission to East Africa – from Ethiopia to South Africa (Jones, 1922; 1925). Both commissions were led by Jones, by now the Educational Director of the Phelps-Stokes Fund. Both would have Aggrey participate as a full member.

Before illustrating how these two commissions presented very powerfully the case for a kind of education 'adapted' to the needs of the Africans, and particularly the great majority who were in rural areas, it should be acknowledged that these two 'aid' missions to Africa were carried out against a background of alternative approaches for African development – not just by critics of colonial education from within Africa, but also by critics, both black and white, of industrial education for Africa within the USA and Europe. I have already mentioned W.E.B. DuBois as a powerful voice for the necessity of good college education for black populations, as well as the case for Pan-African solidarity; but there was also the widespread appeal of the Jamaican, Marcus Garvey, with his Universal Negro Improvement Association, founded in 1914, and his publication, *Negro World*. Both encouraged black Americans and Africans to aspire for greater independence, educationally, economically and politically.

Chapter 1, which follows, illustrates the complexity of how an aid mission on education was constructed and how many different constituencies influenced its messages, impact and influence. The same remains true of more recent aid reports, as can be seen in the missions of the International Labour Organization (ILO), the World Bank, and bilateral aid agencies many decades after the Education Commissions of the Phelps-Stokes Fund.

Context, culture and chance

The Introduction to this book pointed out that the history of an individual's research journey contains many side roads, even cul de sacs, but that serendipity also plays a role. In my own case, in 1965 I had returned to Edinburgh from teaching in Ethiopia with the funding to do a PhD, and a possible field of inquiry – Ethiopian education. However, the head of the Department of Educational Studies in the University fell ill, no education staff had any experience of Africa, and the library contained very little material on Ethiopian education. In touring alternative departments, I was offered options in applied linguistics, psychology, and even theology. But then in browsing the old university library, I stumbled by chance across the two books by Jesse Jones: *Education in Africa*, and *Education in East Africa* which were mentioned in the Introduction. Both were fully illustrated from mission and government schools, local communities, arts, crafts and farming. They contained detailed accounts of good practice in individual mission and government schools. But what was particularly intriguing was the commentary right up front, in the introduction, that the members of the Commission:

> had been profoundly impressed by the ideals of education developed by General Armstrong at the Hampton Institute in Virginia, immediately after the Civil War. He saw that book learning of the old type was entirely inadequate: that the plow, the anvil, the hammer, the broom, the frying pan and the needle must all be used to supplement the customary instruction.... He saw that the training in agriculture, in industry, and in home economics could not only be made to subserve a useful end, but that the processes used in acquiring skill as a farmer, as a mechanic, or as a cook ... have large educational value, both mental and moral. Armstrong's theories of education have been developed at Hampton, Tuskegee and scores of other institutions in America, and are beginning to take firm root in Africa. (Anson Phelps Stokes in Jones, 1925: xvii)

Here, in the very core of the first two education commissions to Sub-Saharan Africa was an explicit proposal for policy transfer: that African education should learn from the example of particular institutions in the Southern States of USA, notably Hampton and Tuskegee, and also from the Jeanes system of visiting teachers in rural areas.[3]

A little more research revealed that the roles of Hampton and Tuskegee Institutes were part of a contested history of black education in the Southern USA. There were many different strands of African involvement with black American education, and also black American engagements and initiatives with education in Africa. It was moreover clear that many missionaries and philanthropic societies saw the education of Africans and of American blacks as a single interdependent problem. I coined the term 'educational Pan-Africanism' to cover this

---

[3] On policy borrowing in the history of comparative education, see Crossley, 2008. On the Jeanes Schools and their transfer to East Africa, see King, 1971, ch. vi. 'The Jeanes School: An experiment in Phelps-Stokesism'

complexity. Fortunately, the University of Edinburgh's history department was a pioneering centre for the study of Pan-Africanism more
generally (Shepperson and Price, 1959). Within three years, my doctorate
on *Pan-Africanism and Education* had been completed, with a particular
focus on the Phelps-Stokes Commission in Kenya. Then a first university
job in the University College of Nairobi made it possible to do further
field research before its publication within the series, Oxford Studies in
African Affairs (King, 1971).[4]

Several chapters of this thesis could have illustrated the Phelps-
Stokes Commissions' proposals for the 'adaptation' of African education
to a model that was influenced by best practice in Hampton and Tuskegee
Institutes. There were the particular politics of the East African
Phelps-Stokes Commission's experience in Kenya; the establishment of a
Jeanes School in Kenya, directly influenced and funded by American
foundations; the 20-year experience of missionaries and administrators
from Africa visiting the model schools and institutes of the American
South, and notably Hampton and Tuskegee; or the experiences of African
students in the USA, and Jones's ambitions for them to remain 'good
Africans' like Aggrey and not be radicalised. The selected chapter with its
original title has been preferred for the first chapter in this book because it
exemplifies the complexity of this first educational aid mission to
Sub-Saharan Africa. The Commission's selection of one particular strand
of heavily-aided black education in the Southern States to recommend to
the whole of Sub-Saharan Africa was an extraordinary initiative in policy
transfer. This had to be done in the face of highly articulate critical
commentary from black constituencies other than those associated with
the Hampton-Tuskegee consensus, notably DuBois and Garvey, as well as
white critics of Phelps-Stokesism, such as Norman Leys.[5]

For students of policy transfer today, seeking to understand the exact
origins of powerful themes such as 'Education for All' in Jomtien (1990) or
the Millennium Development Goal (MDG) of universal primary
education (2000), tracing the origins may be very difficult as they may not
have access to the culture of letter-writing that was so commonplace in
the 1920s. Tying down crucial influences which have been based on email
traffic, from the late 1990s, may be hugely daunting as the systems for

---

[4] A new edition of *Pan-Africanism and education* is available from the Diasporic Africa Press, New
York (2016).
[5] Leys's highly critical account of Kenya in a book of that name appeared the year before the
Phelps-Stokes report on *Education in East Africa* (Leys, 1924).

accessing and recording emails for posterity are seldom in place. It may be true that the process around the construction of sustainable development goal 4 on education 'resulted from what is **arguably the most inclusive process of consultation in the history of the United Nations'** (Naidoo, 2017: 6, emphasis in original), but identification of who was actually responsible for the wording or editing of the finally agreed text remains challenging.

'The politics of Negro education' has been chosen for highlighting here because it provides a lens on the richness of the policy and political context in which two international commissions reported on Africa. Like several subsequent reports, such as the World Bank's *Education in Sub-Saharan Africa* (1988), these Phelps-Stokes Commissions were enormously influential; but they courted controversy by their views on the very purpose of education in colonised Africa, on skills development versus higher education, and on interracial cooperation. A large part of Tuskegee's appeal to blacks and whites alike was that it was developed and led by a black American. This paralleled the widespread attraction of Nyerere's *Education for Self-Reliance* in 1967. In the case of the Phelps-Stokes Commissions to Africa, there was a central role for Aggrey, from the Gold Coast, who had profited from education at home and also in the Southern States, and yet had not been radicalised by the process. For Jones and the rest of the team, he was the 'good African', but he had an influence far beyond the hundreds of speeches he made on these two commissions to Africa. Paradoxically, he was a powerful illustration of the vital importance of higher education for Africa even as he spoke up for a very different curriculum in the continent (King, 1969).

References

Crossley, M. 2008. 'Bridging cultures and traditions for educational and international development: Comparative research, dialogue and difference', *International Review of Education*, 54: 319-336.

Johnston, H. 1911. *The Negro in the New World*, Methuen, London.

Jones, T.J. 1916. *Negro Education: A study of the private and higher schools for coloured people in the United States*, US Bureau of Education Bulletin No. 38. Vol.1, Government Printing Office, Washington.

Jones, T.J. 1922. *Education in Africa: A study of West, South and Equatorial Africa by the African Education Commission, under the auspices of the*

Phelps-Stokes Fund and the Foreign Mission Societies of North America and Europe, Phelps-Stokes Fund, New York.

Jones, T.J. 1925. *Education in East Africa: A study of East, Central and South Africa by the second African Education Commission, under the auspices of the Phelps-Stokes Fund, in cooperation with the International Education Board*, Phelps-Stokes Fund, New York.

King, K. 1969. 'James E.K. Aggrey: Collaborator, nationalist, Pan-African', *Canadian Journal of African Studies*, 3, 3, 511-530.

King, K. 1971. *Pan-Africanism and education: A study of race, philanthropy and education in the Southern States of the USA and East Africa*, Clarendon Press, Oxford. A new edition of *Pan-Africanism and education* is available from Diasporic Africa Press, since 2016 www.dafricapress.com

Leys, N. 1924. *Kenya*, Hogarth Press, London.

Nyerere, J.K. 1967. *Education for self-reliance*, in Nyerere, J.K. *Freedom and socialism*, Oxford University Press, Dar es Salaam.

Sadler, M. 1902. 'The education of the coloured race' in *Special reports on educational subjects*, Vol. 11, XXIX, Cmd. 1156, His Majesty's Stationery Office, London.

Shepperson, G. and Price, T., 1959. *The Independent African: John Chilembwe and the origins, setting and significance of the Nyasaland native rising of 1915*, Edinburgh University Press, Edinburgh.

Washington, B.T. 1901. *Up from slavery: An autobiography*, Doubleday and Co., New York.

World Missionary Conference, 1910. *Report of Commission III, Education in relation to the Christianisation of national life*, Edinburgh, Fleming H. Revell, New York.

The Phelps-Stokes Commissions and the Politics of Negro Education (1971)[6]

The Phelps-Stokes Commissions to Africa and their published findings were very far from being isolated attempts at recommending the educational values of Tuskegee to Africa. They had grown out of the bitter conflicts to work out an education relevant to Negro political status in America, and were only one episode in the extension of those disputes to Africa. At times it was not so much that they were recommending Tuskegee as that they were promoting it deliberately to counterbalance the Africa programmes of two other American Negro creeds—DuBois's pan-Africanism and Garveyism. This fact made it increasingly difficult to regard 'adaptation' as a purely educational formula, since Garvey and DuBois (the latter with more valuable white support than he had had over Jones's *Negro Education*) showed the concept to be closely allied to African docility and continuing dependence on white leadership.

All three approaches to Africa were launched within the space of little more than a year, at the end of the First World War. Dr. Moton of Tuskegee had been directed into African affairs in December 1918 with his appointment to represent Africa at the Peace Conference,[7] and had by January decided that an educational survey of Africa might be the best contribution he could make:

> I am hoping the Phelps-Stokes Fund as soon as possible will study the African situation as Dr. Jones proposes, with a view as far as possible to helping those of the Peace Conference who will settle forever, I hope, the situation as regards Africa on a basis of human brotherhood, that is the development of the natives as the only safe method of colonization from a selfish as well as from a humanitarian viewpoint.[8]

---

[6] This chapter derives from my doctoral dissertation (1968), revised by field research in Kenya, and published in King (1971), *Pan-Africanism and education Pan-Africanism and education: A study of race, philanthropy and education in the Southern States of the USA and East Africa,* Clarendon Press, Oxford.

[7] Moton's role on the Presidential Peace Commission was to be on hand at t he Peace Conference for consultation on African colonies. He did not in fact attend, but had some informal discussions with English and American authorities.

[8] Moton to Phelps Stokes, 19 Jan. 1919, Box 71, Peabody Papers, L.C.

Dubois inaugurated the first of his pan-African congresses the next month in Paris, a project which had only become a reality after Blaise Diagne, the Senegalese deputy, and Moton had intervened diplomatically with the French and American authorities.[9] There, to a relatively small Negro elite from the West Indies, Africa, and America, DuBois proposed a more radical readjustment of the African colonies than Moton was contemplating. Then on 1 August 1920, at a great international Negro convention in Harlem, Marcus Garvey blazoned forth his own declaration of the rights of the Negro peoples of the world.[10] Three weeks later the first Phelps-Stokes Commission sailed for Africa, with Aggrey groomed 'to introduce many features of Tuskegee and Hampton' wherever they went.[11]

The British missionary leaders most concerned with sending the Commission had believed from the beginning that there were serious political issues potentially involved, and were prepared to make these quite clear to Jones in the months before he left. A.G. Fraser, for instance (at this point leading his Village Education Commission to India via a tour of Negro education in the United States), found it possible to combine the greatest admiration for Tuskegee and its president with the conviction that the Phelps-Stokes Commission should be used to investigate the evils of exploitation in South and East Africa.[12] J.H. Oldham thought it conceivable that some useful alliance could be forged between Jones's ideals and those of Norman Leys, a retired medical officer. The latter's outspokenness over the Coast administration and Masai land policy in the East Africa Protectorate had earned him his dismissal,[13] but in 1919 he was, with Oldham's close co-operation, continuing his attack on settler power in East Africa by exposing the recent Labour Ordinance of the East Africa Protectorate.[14] In an attempt to initiate some form of collaboration between the two men, *Negro Education*

---

[9] Moton to DuBois, 5 July 1919, R.R.M./G.C. (1919), T.U.A.; also Moton, *Finding a Way Out* (New York, 1921), p.253. For Moton and the Second Pan-African Congress, see p.222.

[10] See Declaration in R. Buell, *The Native Problem in Africa* (New York, 1928), Vol. ii, Appendix XLIX, pp.965-71. For an account of Garvey, see E.D. Cronon, *Black Moses* (Madison, 1955). Much recent material is contained in J.A. Langley, 'West African Aspects of the Pan-African Movements: 1900-1945' (Univ. of Edinburgh Ph.D. thesis, 1968).

[11] Aggrey to Moton, 16 Apr. 1923, R.R.M./G.C. (1923), T.U.A.; Jones to Moton, 17 Jan. 1920, R.R.M./G.C. (1919), T.U.A.

[12] Fraser to Peabody, 12 July 1919, R.R.M./G.C. (1919), T.U.A.

[13] Denham to the Colonial Secretary, 27 Mar. 1925, C.O. 533/327, P.R.O. For Leys on the Masai, see Leys, *Kenya*, pp.86-125.

[14] For co-operation between Oldham and Leys on the labour situation in East Africa, see File on Leys (hereafter File Q-B), E.H.

was recommended to Leys as 'exceedingly valuable',[15] while Jones was sent a detailed analysis of the causes and solutions of African unrest which summarized Leys's sixteen years' experience in British East Africa, Nyasaland, and Portuguese East Africa.[16]

Leys's document could have been exceedingly relevant to Jones's purposes, since he was chiefly concerned like Jones to propose a colonial policy that would make for African stability through education; moreover, he too had had first-hand experience of the results of American Negro education which had helped to confirm his African proposals. But here the similarity ended. For the Negro education Leys had in mind was that of John Chilembwe, leader of the abortive 1915 Nyasaland rising.[17] Leys deliberately stressed in this memorandum of 1918 the fact that Chilembwe's 'knowledge of English was perfect, he had read widely and had sent his sons to America for education'.[18] The point was introduced, however, not as an obvious reason for curtailing such literary education, but as a plea for even wider education, and for giving responsibility and respect to those who secured it:

> The touchstone of educational policy, and through education of all policy in Africa, is the relation of governments with the class of educated natives ... The importance of these men lies, not in their being a necessity, as clerks and so forth, to the machinery of Government, but in their being taken as models by an increasing number of their countrymen...
>
> Nevertheless, to guide the thought and ambition of these men, and to gain their sympathy and cooperation, should be part of Government's deliberate policy. A place must be given them in the state comparable with their influence on society. Otherwise they inevitably pass into opposition.[19]

Although both men attached supreme importance to the role of the school,[20] it is difficult to understand how Oldham could have con-

---

[15] Oldham to Leys, 3 Sept. 1919, File Q-B, E.H.

[16] Leys to the Colonial Secretary, 7 Feb. 1918, copy in File Q-B, E.H.

[17] Ibid., pp.30-4; for the full significance of this rising, which Leys believed to be 'the first attack of a new malady', see Shepperson and Price, *Independent African.*

[18] Leys to the Colonial Secretary, 7 Feb. 1918, p.31. For the exact nature of Chilembwe's English see Shepperson and Price, op. cit., pp.537-8.

[19] Leys to the Colonial Secretary, 7 Feb. 1918, pp.45-6.

[20] For Leys's views on missions and education, see Fulani bin Fulani (pseudonym for Leys), 'A Problem in East African Missions', viii (1919), 155-72; 'Native Races and their Rulers', *I.R.M.* viii (1919), 263-6; 'Christianity and Labour Conditions in Africa', *I.R.M.* ix (1920), 544-51.'

templated any form of alliance between them, for basically Leys would make Africa safe by more independence and Jones by less. For industrial education, too, Leys had already stated the consequences of his own political philosophy: industrial training should aim neither at providing artisans for the European commercial community, nor at reviving village anachronisms, but primarily it should develop 'real, large-scale industries, having insatiable demand from wide markets, like cotton or oil seed growing'.[21] Scarcely surprising in the light of all this, was that sector of American Negro opinion which Leys was beginning to heed: after the 1919 Pan-African Congress in Paris, he had begun to be impressed by a 'M. Burghardt du Bois, a man of character, ability and power to lead in quite exceptional degree', and had shown some considerable sympathy for 'his new liberation campaign, to be preached to Africans'.[22]

There is, however, little evidence from the West Africa Report that Jones thought Leys's document anything more than an indirect confirmation of his own outlook. His own report was studded with references to the education of American Negroes, but they were all to that type which had received the greatest publicity in his earlier *Negro Education*. Attention was continually focused on Washington and Moton, Tuskegee and Hampton, and the little Penn School on St. Helena Island was declared to be the best model for African education.[23] The casual reader would scarcely have gained any idea that Negroes had ever aspired any higher, apart from one short passage in Anson Phelps Stokes's introduction to the volume:

> The time has passed when the old thesis can be successfully maintained that a curriculum well suited to the needs of a group on a given scale of civilization in one country is necessarily the best for other groups on a different level of advancement in another country or section.

> This was the natural mistake generally made by New England in dealing with the Negro in the southern states of America immediately after emancipation. For the many as distinct from the few, the results were small in comparison with those that came later based on General Armstrong's vital work at Hampton, where

---

[21] Leys to the Colonial Secretary, 7 Feb. 1918, p.45.
[22] Leys to B. Turner, 3 May 1921, File Q-B, E.H.
[23] Jones, *Education in Africa*, see index for references to Hampton Institute, Jeanes Fund, Rosenwald Schools, Washington, Moton, Tuskegee, Armstrong; for Penn School, see pp.34-5.

education was adapted directly to a people's needs. Here there was real education.[24]

Furthermore, the two colleges for higher education that there were in Africa received a comment somewhat similar to that made on Lincoln and other universities in the *Negro Education* report.[25]

There were further parallels with Jones's earlier work. The general effect of the first Phelps-Stokes Report upon independent Negro initiatives was not so readily ascertainable as in America. The Yergan affair, however, had already shown Jones over-anxious to scrutinize the safety of individual Negroes for African work.[26] Nor was that an isolated episode, but part of a definite policy to play down those types of independent American Negro and African enterprise in Africa that commended themselves to DuBois and Garvey, even to the extent of not mentioning when mission stations were headed by American Negroes. An extreme example of Jones's caution in this matter was shown in his description of the work of the American Congregational Mission in Angola. In the published report, there was no mention that the oldest station of this mission was under the direction of Mr. Hastings, a native Jamaican, and another station under Mr. Hector McDowell, an American Negro graduate of Talladega College.[27] That this reticence was no accident was shown in Jones's more private account of the commission's tour:

> The home board [of the Congregational Church] plan to have Negro churches send more workers supported by themselves. It is to be hoped that the board will exercise great care in pursuing this policy. The relationship of missionaries on the field to the government and to the natives is exceedingly delicate. Our observations in Africa indicate that only the most thoughtful, cooperative type of American or English Negro can be helpful with the mission fields.[28]

More than this, there was even a parallel to the way that, in the States, Jones's word had become almost necessary to ensure philanthropic support. Mrs. Adelaide Casely Hayford, the wife of the famous Gold

---

[24] Ibid., p.xxiii.
[25] Ibid., pp.109, 205, for Fourah Bay College and the South African Native College. For Lincoln University, Pennsylvania, see p.41.
[26] See pp.81-2.
[27] T.J. Jones, 'Journal of the West Africa Phelps-Stokes Commission' (copy in E.H.), entry for 4 Feb. 1921; p.186; see also Jones, *Education in Africa*, pp.239-43.
[28] Jones, 'Journal', p.186.

Coast barrister, had been in the States raising funds for a new girls' school for Sierra Leone, run in fact on model Phelps-Stokes lines.[29] Yet Jones had been instrumental in at least one donor's withdrawing her contribution, by pointing out 'the relative usefulness of money placed in a school that had no assurance of going on, or the number of schools like Tuskegee and others in this country which are assured of continuance'.[30] This incident, with several others like it, were no doubt of little enough significance in themselves. They do, however, illustrate a point which has been touched on before — Jones's fear not only of the radical Negro, but also of the uncommitted or marginal man.[31] They also put into somewhat more accurate perspective the claims for Tuskegee methods that the commission was expounding.

Once the commission had returned to England in August 1921, the confrontation between Tuskegee and pan-African propaganda for Africa was accentuated by both Jones and DuBois again being in England at the same time, and seeking to put their own points of view before various groups of people.[32] One of the people with whom they both conferred at some length during the same week was Dr. Norman Leys,[33] who was thus ideally placed to judge the issues that had divided the two men for more than ten years. He had read widely both Washington's writings and some of DuBois's work, but had not felt it necessary to judge between the two schools.[34] The outcome was not now difficult to predict. Leys began to see a good deal of DuBois, subscribed to the *Crisis*, and attended the second Pan-African Congress at the end of August.[35] For Jones it was a very important reverse; Leys had become convinced that the Phelps-Stokes Africa policy, as expressed by its chief architect, presupposed for Negroes a permanent status significantly different from that of whites. He

---

[29] Adelaide Casely Hayford, A Girls' School in West Africa', *Southern Workman,* lv (Oct. 1926), 449-56. For Jones's attitude to African independent schools see further p.239. See also Mrs. Casely Hayford's reminiscences, serialized in the *West African Review,* from vol. xxiv, No. 313 (Oct. 1953) to vol. xxv, No. 323 (Aug. 1954).

[30] Peabody to Mrs. Casely Hayford, 7 Jan. 1924, Box 20, Peabody Papers, L.C. Tuskegee itself contributed money through its Y.M.C.A. to her school; R.R.M./L.C. (1920), T.U.A.

[31] See p.85, n. 1. For Jones's 'fear of radical negroes', see Peabody to Dillard, 7 Dec. 1921, Box 15, Peabody Papers, L.C. Cf. also DuBois, 'Thomas Jesse Jones', p.256.

[32] Jones and DuBois had coincided once before in England, see p.56.

[33] Leys to Oldham, 22 Aug. 1921, File Q-A, E.H.

[34] Leys to Moton, 11 Jan. 1922, R.R.M. Misc. Papers, (1922), T.U.A.

[35] DuBois met Leys at a meeting of the Advisory Committee on International Questions of the Labour Party, 26 Aug. 1921, along with Sidney Webb, John Harris, and Leonard Woolf. For Leys's views of the importance of the *Crisis,* see Leys to Miss G. Gollock, 18 Dec. 1921, 'Race' Folder, E.H., now IMCA, Geneva. The Pan-African Congress (London session) took place on 28 and 29 Aug. 1921. For this second Pan-African Congress, see DuBois, 'A Second Journey to Pan-Africa', pp.39-42.

confided this view at a very crucial time to Oldham, who was working on a book about Christianity and the race problem:[36]

> There is no sense whatever in trying to treat the least of human creatures as a Jesus if in his soul there are innate deficiencies. Let me give you an illustration of how intensely practical a question the alternative raises. I pressed Jesse Jones to tell me whether he thought American negroes as a whole different in nature and capacity from the Europeans they live among and whether he expected from them a different kind of future. He admitted that he did. I told him that explained everything, to me, of his differences with Du Bois and others... Jones in effect says it isn't wise, it isn't sensible to teach a negro child what European children are taught because as men they have a different status.[37]

It is interesting that Leys considered the issue sufficiently important for him to write direct to Moton at Tuskegee, and ask him to confirm or deny the impression he had just gained of Jones and DuBois.[38]

What Moton replied is not known, but it is clear on other evidence that Moton was not prepared to be pressed by his white supporters into a personal vendetta with DuBois. Despite this, he was increasingly being elevated by white missionary leaders into a position of Negro spokesman on Africa, which had the effect, albeit involuntarily, of throwing him into apparent competition with DuBois.

Oldham, on his second visit to Tuskegee, had co-opted Moton to be one of the representatives for Africa on the I.M.C., and Moton had therefore an influence at the highest level on missionary policy in Africa at the 1921 session.[39] Jones and Aggrey were also prominent at the same conference, and this monopoly of Phelps-Stokes and Tuskegee opinion over education in Africa understandably gave DuBois the feeling that policy-making was quite out of his hands. He commented bitterly: 'A secret conference on missionary and educational work among Negroes in Africa and elsewhere has been held at Lake Mohonk. The Negro race was represented by Thomas Jesse Jones and R.R. Moton.'[40] Whatever DuBois's reaction, Jones's and Aggrey's personal pre-eminence in missionary

---

[36] J.H. Oldham, *Christianity and the Race Problem* (London, 1924).
[37] Leys to Oldham, 14 Nov. 1921, Folder on Race, E.H., now I.M.C.A., Geneva.
[38] Leys to Moton, 11 Jan. 1922.
[25] Oldham to Moton, 5 Mar. 1921, R.R.M./G.C. (1921), T.U.A.; see also F. Lenwood, 'The International Missionary Council', *I.R.M.* xi (1922), 41.
[40] DuBois, *Crisis,* xxiii, No. 2 (Dec. 1921), 81.

conventions on Africa was assured, for they had now a quite unrivalled knowledge of mission work throughout the western, central and southern areas of Africa. It was therefore very natural that they should dominate the Foreign Mission Convention of North America when they discussed education in its 1922 session.[41] It is some indication of the success that both they and J.H. Oldham had had in pointing to Tuskegee as the source of missionary inspiration for Africa that Dr. Robert Moton should be called across to the great Scottish Churches Missionary Conference in Glasgow later that year.[42] There he linked the 'conspicuous' progress of the Negro population of America to the education of Tuskegee and Hampton, and both of these to the development of Africa. In this light, he explained, even the slave trade now appeared as the working of Providence.[43]

Marcus Garvey, however, would not be spoken for on Africa in this manner any more than DuBois. Himself an ardent admirer of Tuskegee,[44] he nevertheless felt that Moton should guard himself against manipulation; for whether Moton realized it or not, he was being used to recommend to Africans continued dependence on the white man:

> Now that the Negro has started to think for himself the white Christian leaders and philanthropists realise that it will be very hard for them to convince us to accept their 'friendly protection'. Hence they feel that the best that can be done would be to get a representative Negro to say for them what they would very much like to have said. Our friend Dr. Moton is the fittest man for such a job, because he and his institution as well as Hampton Institute... are the two Negro institutions that have received millions of dollars from white philanthropists to teach Negroes in the way that they should go...

> We hope that no member of our race will pay any attention to what Dr. Moton says in the matter of Africa's needs, because it is strange

---

[41] T.J. Jones, 'The Educational Needs of the People of Equatorial Africa', *The Foreign Mission Conference of North America: Twenty-Ninth Annual Session, 1922* (New York, 1922), pp.168-76. See also address by Aggrey therein, pp.176-80.

[42] D. Fraser, 'The Scottish Churches' Missionary Campaign', *I.R.M.* xi (1922), 286-94.

[43] R.R. Moton, 'Problems a nd Development of the Negro Race', (address at Scottish Churches' Missionary Conference, Glasgow, 17 Oct. 1922), printed in the *Tuskegee Student*, xxxii, No. 17 (1 Nov. 1922); see also 'Missionary Methods', *Tuskegee Student*, xxxii, No.18, (15 Nov. 1922).

[44] Garvey to Moton, 1 June 1917, R.R.M./G.C. (1917), T.U.A. See further p.18, n.3.

that he had nothing to say about Africa until he was called by these white missionaries and philanthropists to speak.[45]

It was a charge that was echoed by several leading American Negroes at this time, however bitterly opposed to each other they might be on other matters.[46] What seems strange in retrospect, however, is not that the charge was made, but that it never more openly attached to Aggrey's role in the Phelps-Stokes Commissions. This may perhaps be partly explained by Aggrey's capacity for understanding of and friendship with those very Negroes most critical of Jones and the Fund, in particular Max Yergan, Carter G. Woodson, and such Coloured Y.M.C.A. leaders as Jesse E. Moorland.[47] Indeed, with the exception of his attacks on Garvey, Aggrey seems to have been determined to avoid that internecine strife that had so weakened the Negro leadership during the early twentieth century. It was a conviction he only spoke of to all-black audiences, using the following parable:

> The cardinal sin of whites is arrogance—the trouble with us Africans is jealousy. If we have a leader, even a first-class one, we want to pull him down.
>
> I once went to a lumber camp in Canada, and I saw an enormous fir being felled with ropes right up to the top—scores of men pulling. Finally down it came. 'Have you ever seen such a wonderful sight?', the foreman asked. 'It's not wonderful so much as amazing. You have missed the whole point. Look who was pulling on the ropes—Canadian Negroes! Have you ever seen one hundred Negroes pulling together?'[48]

At any rate, even if Aggrey was himself too occupied in gaining everybody's co-operation for Africa to notice the peculiar vulnerability of

---

[45] *The Negro World*, xiii, No. 10(21 Oct. 1922), 1. Garvey underestimated Moton's personal interest in Africa, expressed most obviously in the encouragement of African staff and students at Tuskegee, see Ch. VIII.

[46] Cf. p.84.

[47] Aggrey to Peabody, 17 Nov. 1923, Box 18, Peabody Papers/L.C.; Aggrey to Woodson, 13 July 1927, Box 6, acc. 3579, add. 1, Woodson Papers, L.C.

[48] I am indebted for this anecdote to Mr. A.G. Fraser (son of Principal Fraser, leader of the Village Education Commission, and later of Achimota College). For a more detailed discussion of Aggrey, see K.J. King, 'James E.K. Aggrey: Collaborator, Nationalist, Pan -African', *Canadian Journal of African Studies*, iii, No. 3 (1970).

his role, there can be little doubt that Jones did increasingly see Aggrey and others as fulfilling precisely the function Garvey had mentioned.[49]

As Jones had been under severe attack from all sectors of radical Negro opinion both during and after the West African Phelps-Stokes Commission,[50] it is not perhaps surprising that the second (East African) Education Commission and its report had an even greater propaganda content than the first. Indeed, many of its actions and much of the subsequent report can only be fully understood as part of a continuing crusade by Jones against DuBois, Garvey, and Woodson.

Much more time both in Africa and in the writing of the report was consequently spent on explaining away the recent demands for racial equality and the various forms of independence claimed by Africans. Nor was Jones concerned only to counteract radical American Negro propaganda; he was possibly also reacting to his encounter with Leys on the question of race equalities. For it was strongly denied that any rating of equalities or inequalities was valuable; instead, it was 'sound and helpful' to appreciate the reality of racial differences.[51]

On the issue of greater independence for Africans, there was a further reference to programmes for Africa politically different from his own:

> The conflicting ideals of those who would serve are in some instances as divisive and unfortunate as selfishness and prejudice. The more recent of these ideals are represented by such words as 'Self-Determination', 'Self-government', 'Self-expression'... Liberty, independence and self-determination, with their comparatively unknown or untried experiments, are far more attractive to idealistic temperaments than trusteeship, protectorate and colony, whose failures have often been allowed to over-shadow their successes. The thought of freedom seems to have far more charm than that of direction and discipline and order.[52]

As has been seen in Kenya itself, Aggrey had been of great value in preaching against Garveyism, an activity which he had later continued in

---

[49] On Jones's scheme to finance a Negro journalist, Lester Walton, to conduct constructive propaganda among Negroes and whites, see Jones to W.W. Alexander, 22 Dec. 1922, R.R.M./G.C. (1923), T.U.A.
[50] DuBois, 'Thomas Jesse Jones', pp.253-6.
[51] Jones, *Education in East Africa*, p.77.
[52] Ibid.

southern Africa.[53] It was generally the commission's policy to leave the winning of Africans themselves to Aggrey, but on more than one occasion Jones seems to have taken the initiative himself with a local ruler, and used Tuskegee's good offices to anticipate propaganda from other Negro sources. He sought Moton's co-operation in one of these plans: 'Today I conferred with His Highness, the Sultan of Zanzibar. He is an able and delightful man. I wish you could send him *Finding a Way Out* with a brief letter of appreciation for his kindness to us. You would thus begin to bind him to you and so help avoid a relationship to the radical forces of our country.'[54]

In discussing the reports from this propagandist angle, it has been implied throughout that they could be taken as expressing Jones's views rather than those of any other members of the commission. Both reports were indeed almost entirely of his authorship, but it is significant that his monopoly over the contents had not been ceded willingly in the East Africa report. While they were still on tour, Garfield Williams and others had been so alarmed at Jones's dictating the mind of the commission that a form of joint authorship had been agreed on.[55] This had, however, been reversed on the return to London, and the Report was written by Jones alone, under a serious threat of non-cooperation from the two English authorities, Vischer and Williams.[56] Their differences with Jones can only be conjectured, but some light is thrown on possible areas of disagreement from one of Jones's co-workers at Edinburgh House.

Miss Georgina Gollock, co-editor with Oldham of the I.R.M. had noted in the draft of the report the almost complete absence of any criticism of white settlers and government, and thought this was a potential danger to the report's intended objectivity. She had made therefore an attempt to have the balance redressed by Anson Phelps Stokes:

> I believe that his [Jones's] attitude may be the means of inaugurating a new kind of fellowship, a new and fuller understanding just where it is needed most; but the reality and the extent of this sympathy has

---

[53] Smith, *Aggrey of Africa,* pp 122, 124, 176; see also p.118 and p.223.

[54] Jones to Moton, 14 Apr. 1922, R.R.M./G.C. (1925), T.U.A. Jones was also anxious that Moton should use his influence with President Coolidge to arrange for the Prince Regent of Ethiopia, Ras Tafari (Haile Selassie) to come to the States; Jones to Moton, 6 Feb. 1924, R.R.M./G.C. (1925), T.U.A. The book mentioned was R.R. Moton's, *Finding a Way Out: an autobiography* (London, 1920).

[55] Vischer to Oldham, 8 Apr. 1924, File Q-E, E.H.

[56] Miss Gollock to Oldham, undated memo of 1924/5, File Q-R, E.H.

a side of danger, and it is for this I think a very careful reading should be given to the Report as it nears completion. Individual sentences or paragraphs in a certain chapter may be in true proportion. When they recur in chapter after chapter, they may make a total impression of something that is more than the truth ... I am anxious lest there should be anything in the Report which should seem in the least degree to condone actions which are not quite worthy, or to fail to hold an even balance where the interests of the Africans are at stake.[57]

Miss Gollock was anxious that Anson Phelps Stokes should insert somewhere an explanation for this absence of criticism of the white settlers and government. He could, she suggested, stress that the commission had deliberately steered clear of political issues as beyond their brief. What Miss Gollock failed to see in the report, however, was that, far from playing down white injustice and avoiding controversy, it rather invited controversy by enthusiastically supporting a large increase in white settlement. The report gave the strongest possible backing to the idea of a great white belt extending from East to South Africa, in which South Africans would play the dominant part, and where "possession' would be 'nine points of the law'.[58] It is not improbable, therefore, that it was with something in these assumptions that Vischer, Williams, and Shantz quarrelled.[59]

It might equally well have been the question of cultural education for Africans or the place of African leadership in East Africa that caused disagreement, for on both these matters Miss Gollock also felt that there was a danger of the report's appearing reactionary and attracting adverse criticism. [60] Indeed, it seems not impossible that the criticism she anticipated was from DuBois.[61] Her suggestions on the report, however, appear to have had no more effect on Jones than Leys had had earlier, and if she foresaw DuBois's hostility, it was probably no more than Jones did himself.

---

[57] Miss Gollock to Phelps Stokes, 15 Jan. 1925, File L-l, P.S.F.A.
[58] Jones, *Education in East Africa*, pp.82-3.
[59] H.L. Shantz to Oldham 2 June 1925, Box 314, E.H., now I.M.C.A., Geneva. For Jones's own confidential analysis of his tactics in the report, see Jones to Owen, 18 Dec. 1924, Acc. 83, Owen Papers, C.M.S.A., London; and Jones to Arthur, 18 Dec. 1924, Education Bundle, P.C.E.A.
[60] Miss Gollock to Phelps Stokes, 15 Jan. 1925, File L-l, P.S.F.A.
[61] DuBois was quick to note the praise for Jones's Report coming from *East Africa*, a magazine exclusively interested in white settlement and business throughout Eastern Africa. *Crisis*, xxx (May 1925), 40. *East Africa*, i, No. 32 (Apr. 1925), 676-8; No. 33 (May 7, 1925), 694-5.

Fresh fuel was to be added to the flames of this antagonism to DuBois and his supporters soon after the commission had returned to England for the second time. It consisted of the publication in October 1924 of Norman Leys's book, *Kenya,* one of the most ruthlessly outspoken exposés of white exploitation to appear in the inter-war years. The timing was crucial; it antedated Jones's East Africa report by several months, and took good care to condemn in advance what Leys believed to be its educational heresies and its accommodation to white settlement. In three pages of passionate analysis of Jones's ideology, it demonstrated the central political importance of African education, and concluded:

> The reader may consider that too much attention has been paid to these false educational ideals. He may be assured that in Africa the obscurantist is an even greater danger than the exploiter. What the African in Kenya needs is knowledge, enlightenment, the acquisition of the appetite which makes men seek the truth. He needs these exactly as the whole human race needs them.[62]

The publicity which attended *Kenya*[63] and its attempt to discredit Jones's policies was only the beginning of a series of reverses that threatened completely to undermine Jones's position as expert on the Negro in America and Africa. DuBois had himself travelled to West Africa in the winter of 1923, and on his return had had published in a nationally respected journal his famous 'Worlds of Color'. [64] It was a sort of miniature second instalment of Leys's work, investigating the 'dark colonial shadow' that walked behind every great European power, and reserving for Britain's African governments the heaviest strictures of all; on any rating of colonial racism, DuBois argued, Britain had no competitor.[65] This was, of course, in direct contradiction to everything that the Phelps-Stokes report would claim the month afterwards, and it made both Jones and Oldham feel that something must be done to set the record straight on British colonial policy.[66]

The contemporary situation in the Negro colleges was equally crucial for Jones, and was an inevitable counterpart to the conflicts over African education and white rule. Since June 1924 DuBois had been waging a campaign to free Fisk University, his own Alma Mater, from what he

---

[62] Leys, *Kenya*, p.392.
[63] It had run through two editions before Jones's *Education in East Africa* was published.
[64] W.E.B. DuBois, 'Worlds of Color', *Foreign Affairs* (Washington), iii, No. 3 (Apr. 1925), 423-44.
[65] Ibid., p.423.
[66] Oldham to Jones, 5 May 1925, Jones File (hereafter Q-J), E.H.

considered to be the oppressive white leadership of President McKenzie. Indeed, at the Alumni commemoration address at Fisk in 1924, DuBois had suggested to McKenzie's face that he should resign and that his place should be taken by a Negro.[67] Even here there was an element of the old vendetta; Jones was the secretary of the Fisk board of trustees, and believed that McKenzie was one of the only men who had really tried to adapt Negro college education to his own ideals.[68] He assured the board that a blow would be struck for 'Fisk, Negro education and for race relationships in America and Africa' if McKenzie could weather the storm.[69] But DuBois was more than ready, for once, to come down into the arena and distribute his own printed statements among the student body, to encourage them in their protest. Student rioting broke out at least twice at DuBois's incitement, and on the most serious breakdown of order, in February 1925, the president's account left no doubt about where some of the inspiration came from:

> This Wednesday night two of these leaders told Miss Boynton that it would be of no use for the President or any other representative of the faculty to come, and that they were going to keep up this sort of thing until the President's hair was white. The disorderly students overturned chapel seats, broke windows and fired shots terrifying the neighborhood for blocks around all the while keeping up a steady shouting of 'DuBois' and 'Before I'd be a slave'.[70]

In the event, President McKenzie was forced into resignation two months later, and Jones, in complete confusion, had to admit the apparent defeat of the Hampton principle of white leadership in Negro colleges.[71] While the *Crisis* was blazing its victory to other colleges,[72] however, Jones suggested a new policy to his board: a completely coloured faculty from the president down, with W.T.B. Williams, a member of the staff at

---

[67] W.E.B. DuBois, 'Diutumi Silenti', *Fisk Herald,* xxxiii, No. 1 (1924), see also L.A. Roy to Jones, 19 June 1924, File A-22, P.S.F.A.
[68] Jones to P. Cravath, 20 Aug. 1924, R.R.M./G.C. (1925), T.U.A.
[69] Ibid.
[70] F.A. McKenzie, 14 Feb. 1925, 'Letter written to an Alumnus who asked for information', File III, b.6, Acc. No. 329, McKenzie Papers, Tennessee State Archives, Nashville. Also Broderick, *W.E.B. DuBois,* pp.163-4.
[71] Jones to McKenzie, 6 May 1925, File III, b. 6, Acc. No. 329, McKenzie Papers, Tennessee State Archives: 'I am all mixed up. I have been saying things that do not belong in Sunday School...Well, what next? After us, the Deluge.'
[72] DuBois thought the time appropriate for a general attack on restrictive philanthropy; see especially his 'Gifts and Education',*Crisis,* xxix, No. 4, (Feb. 1925). See further, p.246, n.3, and Broderick, op. cit., pp.163-4.

Tuskegee, and field agent of the Jeanes and Slater Boards, as the new President. The rationale of this proposal was exactly what Garvey had three years earlier analysed as the new philanthropic and missionary method of controlling Negroes in the post-war era. A safe Negro could more plausibly suggest unpopular methods than a white man.[73]

Jones indeed realized that the same principle might be applied equally well in the international sphere, and, if the right candidate could be found, would effectively nullify some of the recent radical statements about Africa. Here there could be no doubt whom Jones would select:

> I have been giving serious consideration to some plans for Aggrey.... They are as follows. 1. That influences unfriendly to British Colonial policy, such as the articles in *Foreign Affairs* and the *New York Times Current History* by Dubois; Leys' book; the propaganda of Indians and others in this country, make it very desirable that the carefully presented statement of an educated African like Aggrey should be produced.[74]

Jones proceeded to outline how Aggrey's still uncompleted Ph.D., along with other articles, could be used for this larger end, and proposed that the Colonial Office could grant him study leave from Achimota College, where Aggrey was by this time assistant vice-principal.[75] As Achimota had not yet even opened, however, it was impossible at this stage that Aggrey should be spared; his role in recommending to his fellow-Africans a new kind of college that started from the bottom with a kindergarten and not a degree was much too vital.[76] Nevertheless, it was a pointer towards this more deliberate use of Aggrey in redressing slurs on British African policies that he was given the opportunity to justify the new African education on the B.B.C. in November 1925.[77]

These provisional plans for Aggrey were becoming in Jones's mind only a part of a wider scheme whereby the peculiar appropriateness of Tuskegee-Hampton education could make itself felt throughout Africa. He now projected that white men with the right experience of Southern education should go out to each African country, paired with American

---

[73] Jones to McKenzie, 6 May 1923; Fisk did not in the event have a black president then since many Negro leaders, including Moton, thought it highly inadvisable; Moton to Jones, 14 May 1925, RRM./G.C. (1925), TUA.

[74] Jones to Oldham, 14 July 1925, File Q-J, E.H.

[75] Smith, *Aggrey of Africa*, p.230.

[76] Ibid., pp.225-45.

[77] J.E.K. Aggrey, 'The Prince of Wales College' broadcast talk, reproduced in *Southern Workman*, lv (Jan. 1926), pp.39-42.

Negroes who had been trained in the Hampton and Tuskegee ideals.[78] By the end of 1925 the first white educator had been selected for this programme, and had been sent to Liberia as supervisor of missionary education;[79] but, as has been seen already, the real difficulty was finding suitable American Negro partners—a task that had become doubly difficult after Woodson's and DuBois's critique of 'hand-picked' Negroes.[80]

Associated with this new conception of the value of the American Negro propagandist in Africa was the notion, now suddenly popular among mission leaders in Britain and Africa, that Dr. Moton himself should make an African tour. It had originated with Donald Fraser, who had called Moton to the Scottish Conference earlier, and was taken up by Loram.[81] Oldham too thought that 'a visit to Africa by Moton, rightly prepared for, might have a most valuable and far reaching influence'. He had evidence from Uganda that Moton could most usefully reinforce the impetus towards co-operation given by Aggrey's earlier visit, and thought it possible that he would also be welcome in Kenya.[82]

Both these projects were made even more relevant by the fact that a major conference at Le Zoute on Christian mission and education in Africa was being prepared for 1926. Organized primarily by Oldham, its educational objective was to ratify the new outlook of both the Phelps-Stokes Commissions and the Colonial Office Advisory Committee,[83] and link once and for all the development of African education with the philanthropic traditions of the Southern States.[84] Oldham, in recognition of this connection, had made it quite clear to Jones that everything would 'depend on getting over the right representatives of the coloured people in America, and of those among the whites who have been leaders in the work for the Negroes'.[85] Jones, for his part, had by now quite recovered from the upsets of the previous year, and, with a World Conference in the offing, it was a temptation to feel that Africa really might soon be won for

---

[78] Jones to E. C. Sage, 18 Dec. 1925, File C-3, P.S.F.A.

[79] W.E.B. DuBois, 'The New African Program', *Crisis,* xxxi, No. 3 (Jan. 1926), 113-14.

[80] See p.79 ff.

[81] Jones to Moton, 2 Aug. 1923, R.R.M./G.C. (1923), T.U.A., and Oldham to Jones, 3 Dec. 1925, File Q-J, E.H.

[82] Moton did not eventually go to Kenya or Uganda on his African tour.

[83] Smith, *Christian Mission in Africa, passim.* The first Command Paper of the Advisory Committee for Native Education in Africa (*Educational Policy in British Tropical Africa,* Cmd. 2374 Mar. 1925) had been timed to coincide with the publication of Jones's *Education in East Africa.*

[84] Sage (asst, secretary of the General Education Board) to Jones, 10 Dec. 1925, File C-3, P.S.F.A.

[85] Oldham to Jones, 5 Nov. 1925, File Q-J, E.H.

his four 'Simples' of education.[86] The policy was there; all that was required was for Loram, Oldham, and himself to work as a triumvirate for its acceptance. He explained this, their continent wide potential, to Loram:

> The three of us have real possibilities for the future of Africa.... It is thus important that we shall work out the bases of cooperation....
>
> That Oldham shall win Mission Societies and European Governments to our education programs; that you shall help formulate the administrative problems of both schools and Governments, and of course win Governments and others to these programs; that I shall help formulate the adaptations of education and exert any influence I may have in winning the support of America.[87]

If this master plan to be ratified at the September World Conference took no account of African or American Negro reaction, that very soon occurred. Two months before the conference, DuBois delivered his most stinging indictment yet of the two Phelps-Stokes African education reports.[88] He took up the same points that he had made earlier in his critique of Jones's *Negro Education:* Jones's animus against African higher education, his fear of all forms of Negro independence, and his accommodation to the commercial requirements of the white minorities in Africa. To DuBois both Africa reports were simply further proof of the essentially political nature of Negro education: 'This is the program of Thomas Jesse Jones and the Phelps-Stokes Fund in Africa. They are defending situations like that in Kenya, warning against agitation, seeking to substitute white leadership, white teachers and white missionaries for coloured missionaries, and decrying and discrediting the educated black man the world over.'[89]

This tirade, which concluded that 'the Phelps-Stokes Fund was making Africa safe for white folks',[90] did not fail to be heard. Indeed, the reverberations were soon felt in the Gold Coast, and Aggrey was thrown

---

[86] See the full statement of his educational philosophy in *The Four Essentials of Education* (New York, 1926); and A.V. Murray's critique of this in *The School in the Bush*, pp.300-4.
[87] Jones to Loram, 7 June 1926, File Q-J, E.H.
[88] W.E.B. DuBois, 'Education in Africa: A Review of the Recommendations of the African Education Committee', *Crisis*, xxxii, No. 2 (June 1926), 86-9. DuBois had shown further evidence of his continuing association with Norman Leys by devoting some considerable space in the *Crisis* to a review of Leys's *Kenya*, viz. 'Kenya–A Study of East African conditions as revealed by Norman Leys', *Crisis*, xxxi (Feb. 1926), 188-91.
[89] DuBois, 'Education in Africa', p.88.
[90] Ibid., p.89.

into the role, which Jones had cast for him, of counteracting DuBois's propaganda and justifying the Phelps-Stokes Fund. [91] Furthermore, Aggrey's task was not made any easier by propaganda from the *Negro World* at this time. Just a month before the Le Zoute conference, it brought out a full-page editorial, demonstrating that Africans 'need the same sort of education that Europeans need.'[92]

None of this could, of course, prevent the conference from reaching a very satisfactory consensus; its effect would come later, in making it just a little more difficult to convince Africans that they needed a specially adapted type of education. The conference itself, however, was a success on its own terms, for its membership did indeed symbolize just such a union of the Southern States and Africa as Jones and Oldham had worked for. Every major fund that worked in the American South was represented at the highest level: Dr. Dillard of the Jeanes and Slater Funds, E.C. Sage and Jackson Davis of the General Education Board, Leonard Outhwaite of the Spelman Rockefeller Board, Canon Anson Phelps Stokes and Jesse Jones of the Phelps-Stokes Fund.[93] More than this, the educational methods of the South of which Jones most approved were represented by Miss Thorn, Principal of Calhoun Coloured School, and Miss House of the Penn School. [94] The extent to which the conference was an endorsement of Jones's overall vision for education was no more expressively summed up than by E.W. Smith: 'Scarcely a speech at Le Zoute was complete without the words "adaptation", "cooperation". They were reiterated so frequently that at last speakers felt inclined to apologise for pronouncing them.'[95]

As far as the attitudes of Leys and DuBois were concerned, such conspicuous missionary and philanthropic unanimity over the form of African education could only give further grounds for indignation and dispute. Another clash over the politics of African education was inevitable. The only difference this time was that the protagonists were not DuBois and Jones, but Leys and Oldham, by now in open hostility. The complete break between these two men, who had cooperated to such effect in their resistance to Kenya's labour ordinances, had been coming for some time, but was very largely due to just those issues of race and education that the Phelps-Stokes Commission had raised but not

[91] Smith, *Aggrey of Africa*, pp.255-7.
[92] 'The Sort of Education Africans Need', *Negro World*, xxi, No.1 (14 Aug.1926)
[93] Smith, *The Christian Mission in Africa*, pp.187-8.
[94] Ibid.; for the Penn School, see further, p.41, and pp.184-5.
[95] *Smith, Christian Mission in Africa*, p.92.

resolved. In Leys's view, Oldham's book, *Christianity and the Race Problem,* had failed to take account of the racial undercurrents in Jones's educational theories, and had, instead of dismissing the notion of race itself as illusory, returned with 'conspicuous fairness' a verdict of not proven.[96]

It was on these grounds that Leys now castigated him for his part in spreading Phelps-Stokesism; for Oldham had not only been instrumental in getting the missionary societies to ratify Jones's adapted education, but he had also been largely responsible for its becoming the official doctrine of the Colonial Office Advisory Committee on African Education.[97] In the bitter correspondence which they carried on in the national press over Jones's reports and African education,[98] the key term was 'adaptation', with all its widely different interpretations. For Oldham this was an educational term, for Leys a thinly disguised formula for political inferiority. The truth was that it could assuredly be both, and, as has been noticed in Kenya, it was very largely its ambiguity that temporarily secured the co-operation of all the various white groups in the cause of African education.

Although co-operation between Jones and Oldham was going to become progressively strained in the later twenties and early thirties, as Oldham's doubts about white settlers' good intentions in Eastern Africa revived,[99] there were substantial grounds during the years 1923-7 for Jones to believe Oldham committed to the same approach as himself on the best way to resolve Kenya's political crises. Oldham does seem to have adopted Jones's conviction that constant criticism from London could only impede any settlement of Kenya's race-torn politics, and that the better element among the whites on the spot should be trusted to work out for themselves problems of native welfare. In addition, he came near to letting himself be appointed the Governor of Kenya's research

---

[96] Leys to Oldham, 14 Nov. 1921, Folder on Race, E.H., now I.M.C.A., Geneva; also Leys to Oldham, 2 July 1924, File Q-B, E.H.

[97] N.M. Leys, *The Scots Observer,* 27 Nov. 1926, p.13.

[98] N.M. Leys, letter to *Manchester Guardian,* 26 Oct. 1926; J.H. Oldham, letter to *Manchester Guardian,* 29 Oct. 1926; N. M. Leys, 'Christianity and Race: A New Policy for Missions'*The Scots Observer,* i, 13 Nov. 1926, p.4. N.M. Leys, 'Missions and Governments: Objects of C hristian Education', *The Scots Observer,* i, 27 Nov. 1926, p.13; J.H. Oldham, 'African Education: Missions and Governments', *The Scots Observer,* i, 11 Dec. 1926, p.13; N.M. Leys, letter to *The Scots Observer,* i, 18 Dec. 1926, p.11.

[99] Cf. Oldham's membership of the Hilton Young Commission (Cmd. 3378, 1929), and commentary by Bennett, *Kenya,* pp.67-9. See also J.H. Oldham, *White and Black in Africa: A Critical Examination of the Rhodes Lectures of General Smuts* (London, 1930); and Jones to Oldham, 17 Jan. 1930, File L-l, P.S.F.A.

director, a position that would have allowed him to bring to bear on racial tensions the sort of objective analysis that Jones was in the habit of advocating.[100] Moreover, Oldham had recently written articles in *The Times,* asking for more public recognition of Kenya's progress, which Jones thought surpassed even his own 'appreciation of the terrible Nordics in that part of the world !'[101] For his own part, Jones continued in America to take every available opportunity of protecting white Kenya's image against corrosion.[102] As for West Africa, he had just successfully persuaded A.G. Fraser to release Aggrey for the important propaganda work against the detractors of British colonial policy.[103] It had begun to look as if the propaganda conflict was entering a new phase.

Aggrey's research work on the subject of Jones's choice was to be undertaken between May and November 1927. 'It is now going to be about British rule in West Africa,' he wrote to Jones. 'Those who hate Great Britain and are Anglophobists will have their eyes opened.'[104] It must remain a very open question, however, whether Aggrey's work would really have served the purpose Jones intended, even if it had been completed.[105] As it was, J.E.K. Aggrey died quite unexpectedly in New York only two months after starting on his project, with his thesis still in note form.[106]

Aggrey's death was a much greater blow to Jones than anything else could have been. It was not simply a question of losing after twenty-five years the only African he had ever really known well. His single most perfect exemplar of Negro behaviour had been removed. For Aggrey had embodied the very spirit of the adaptation and co-operation that Jones had preached in Africa. Yet it must be seriously doubted whether the uniqueness of Aggrey had not in the long run had an unfortunate effect on Jones's view of African and American Negro progress. For Aggrey had been a continual reminder to Jones that protest was not essential to

[100] Oldham to Sir Edward Grigg (Governor), 28 July 1926, General Correspondence 1927, Grigg Papers, (John Grigg, London; microfilm at Queens University, Kingston, Ontario, Canada); Oldham to Ormsby-Gore, 'Research into Native Welfare in East Africa', Grigg Papers; Oldham to R.T. Davidson (Archbishop of Canterbury), 2 Mar. 1927, ibid. See also G. Bennett, 'Paramountcy to Partnership: J.H. Oldham and Africa', *Africa*, xxx, No. 4, (Oct. 1960), 358.
[101] J.H. Oldham, leading articles on Kenya, *The Times,* 9 June 1926, and 10 June 1926. Jones to Gibson, 28 June 1926, File Q-J, E.H.
[102] Jones to Orr, 1 Feb. 1926, File Q-G, E.H.
[103] Smith, *Aggrey of Africa,* p.271.
[104] Ibid.
[105] Aggrey was soliciting C.G. Woodson's aid for his thesis just two weeks before he died; Aggrey to Woodson, 13 July 1927, Box 6, acc. 3579, add. i, Woodson Papers, L.C.
[106] Smith, *Aggrey of Africa,* pp.276-7.

leadership, and that a Negro could reach the highest point of development without rejecting his white counsellors. Aggrey had further taken the greatest pride in the differences between races, and frequently talked of the Negro's distinctive contribution. He had even pleaded fervently for an African curriculum differentiated from that of the whites, and had worked to make that a reality at Achimota. Most important of all for its influence on Jones, Aggrey had believed the race problem soluble by the initiative of enlightened individuals, and not by political alliances. As an individual he felt complete racial equality with all his white friends, but he did not realize that the Africanization he emphasized so strongly could only enhance his already high personal status, while it might still be dangerous for Africans in general. He then proclaimed differentiation for his people's education before it was politically safe and in the process underestimated the value for others of the twenty years of undifferentiated higher education that had largely given him his own equality.

After Aggrey's death the propaganda conflict over African education continued unabated, with Jones proceeding on an opposite set of assumptions from DuBois and Leys. It was, however, becoming increasingly clear that the debate was less about education than the political futures that were open to Africans. Because of his conviction that white rule in Africa was as unchangeable as white supremacy in the Southern States, Jones believed that the most that was open to Africans was, like Aggrey, to imbibe on an individual level the Tuskegee spirit; they could then make a successful adaptation to the white *status quo*. DuBois and Leys, on the contrary, sought out those Africans who had formed or belonged to African political associations, and encouraged them to aspire to independence. It was entirely consonant, therefore, with their vision of Africans for Leys to adopt and co-operate with the secretary of the Kikuyu Central Association, Jomo Kenyatta,[107] and for DuBois to be enlisted by the A.S.U. as 'the most logical candidate' to help them 'to do the things that will benefit Africa in its march toward race consciousness and self-determination'. [108] For Jones it was no less appropriate that he should have continued to work to create such leaders as Aggrey. At this time, very few Africans could, of course, go and hear

---

[107] For evidence of co-operation between Leys and Kenyatta, see Hooper to Miss Soles, 26 Sept. 1929, Letterbooks of the Africa Secretary, C.M.S.A., London. Cf. also correspondence in Winifred Holtby Papers, File 8, Hull Public Library.

[108] T. Dosuma-Johnson to DuBois, 27 Jan. 1933, DuBois papers, Park Johnson Archives, Fisk University, Nashville, Tenn.

Aggrey's message in the Southern States; however, for the vast majority who did not, it was Jones's largest ambition that the Tuskegee spirit of the Southern States should come—as it did now to Kenya, in the form of the Jeanes School.

Chapter 2

I have already mentioned the serendipity with which I stumbled across Kenya's informal sector in 1972, the very year that the term was first widely used by the ILO's *Employment Mission* who were also visiting Kenya (ILO, 1972). The recollection underlines the importance for researchers to keep open minds – and eyes – as they seek to follow their research plans in the field.

For the policy community, the discovery of the informal sector[1] was a relief at a time of growing concern about the possible political impact of unemployment of primary school leavers emerging from the dramatically expanded school systems after independence. This paralleled the discovery of non-formal education (NFE) at almost the same time. Arguably, the latter term[2] emerged from the thinking associated with Coombs' book on *The world educational crisis* (1968) and was promoted by Coombs and others in the early 1970s (Coombs, 1968; King, 1969; Sheffield and Diejomaoh, 1972; Coombs and Ahmed, 1974). In the face of the expense of formal education and its tendency to favour educational access for better-off, urban populations, by contrast, NFE was thought to be particularly relevant for the great majority of poorer rural communities; it was seen to be more appropriate than formal schooling because of its strong connections to agricultural, technical and vocational opportunities, most provided through other ministries and agencies than the Ministry of Education.

As a historian, with an interest in education and development in Kenya, I was able to combine research insights into both the informal sector and non-formal education (King, 1977: chapter 1). It was noticeable

---

Kenneth King (2019): *Education, Skills and International Cooperation: Comparative and Historical Perspectives*. Hong Kong: Comparative Education Research Centre (CERC), The University of Hong Kong, and Dordrecht: Springer. © CERC

[1] Keith Hart used the term 'informal economic opportunities' of migrants in Accra, Ghana in 1971, but it was not published until 1973 (Hart, 1973).

[2] NFE was defined as 'any organised educational activity outside the formal system' (Coombs et al., 1973: 11).

© Springer Nature Switzerland AG 2019
K. King, *Education, Skills and International Cooperation*, CERC Studies
in Comparative Education 36, https://doi.org/10.1007/978-3-030-29790-9_2

that international organisations, and notably the World Bank (1974), the ILO (1972) and the International Council for Educational Development (Coombs et al., 1973), took up different dimensions of these two developments as perceived solutions to the problems of both formal education and of the formal or 'modern' sector of the economy. There were parallels to the way that philanthropic agencies and missionary societies had zeroed in on Tuskegeeism as being particularly relevant to the great bulk of black rural communities in USA and then later in Sub-Saharan Africa.

One great attraction of the recognition of the informal sector was that it demonstrated that hundreds of thousands of young people were not turning to despair or political bitterness when they failed to enter secondary school or college, but were actually *working* (King, 1974). Another huge policy attraction was that these people were creating their own jobs. In countries without unemployment insurance, the evidence that self-employment was a major element in the informal economy was highly significant. It was only a short step to argue that 'education for self-employment' seemed to hold out 'answers to many of the problems associated with the saturated labour market, the aspirations of school-leavers, and the budgetary restrictions on higher formal education' (King, 1980: 219). School systems were widely encouraged to develop a culture of enterprise and self-help. This was evident at the highest level in Tanzania where its president, Julius Nyerere, was responsible for promoting, through his *Education for self-reliance*, an approach to primary education that was 'a complete education in itself' and had a strong practical and community orientation (Nyerere, 1967).

Researchers were able to demonstrate that there were already systems for skill acquisition that could be linked to what would be termed the informal sector after 1972. This was not only true of countries such as Nigeria, Ghana and Côte d'Ivoire which had long-established traditional or indigenous apprenticeships (Callaway, 1964; McLaughlin, 1979), but also in countries like Kenya where no such traditions had been present amongst Africans in most of the country (King, 1975a).

It was possible to show that compared with the systems of apprenticeship for the formal sector which had been imported by the colonial powers and were then adopted by the independent states, the indigenous systems for skill acquisition in the informal sector were dramatically larger (King, 1977). The very few technical and vocational schools in the countries were not always popular and were poorly linked to employers' demands; by contrast, large numbers of young people were prepared actually to pay their masters to secure skills through the informal sector.

In the particular chapter ('Skill acquisition in the informal sector') which is taken from *The African artisan: Education and the informal sector in Kenya* (King, 1977), the importance of an historical lens is again underlined. During the years between the First and Second World Wars, large numbers of Indian skilled workers had migrated to Kenya. Many of these had practised their skills of tin-smithing, welding, carpentry, construction, automotive repairs, forging and a great deal else. They were in a sense an early example of the informal sector, transferred from India to Africa. But gradually, Africans had been taken on as employees, and in turn they had left to become self-employed. Arguably, Indo-African skill transfer was a crucial source of some of the skills which I came upon in Nairobi's Burma and Kariokoo markets in 1972 on my first research trip to Kenya from the University of Edinburgh (King, 1975b).

What had first caught my attention, as mentioned in the Introduction to this book, was a group of young men with metal-cutting machines mounted on poles, working in the open, under the hot sun (*jua kali* in Swahili). But after more investigation, I realised that there were many ways to acquire skills in the informal sector, including the young paying the older artisans to be taught auto-mechanics, tin-smithing, carpentry, metal work, etc.. Other pathways encompassed getting skills gradually on-the-job through casual labour. It was a complex picture, and was constantly changing. Clearly there was considerable interaction between the so-called formal or modern sector and the informal sector. Indeed, informal skill acquisition could be found right inside the formal sector.

References

Callaway, A. 1964. 'Nigeria's indigenous education: The apprenticeship system', *ODU: University of Ife Journal of African Studies,* I, 1, 62-79.

Coombs, P. 1968. *The world educational crisis: A systems analysis,* Oxford University Press, Oxford.

Coombs, P., Prosser, R. and Ahmed, M. 1973. *New paths to learning for rural children and youth,* International Council for Educational Development, New York.

Coombs, P. with Ahmed, M. 1974. *Attacking rural poverty: How non-formal education can help,* Johns Hopkins University Press, Baltimore.

Hart, K. 1973. 'Informal income opportunities and urban employment in Ghana', *Journal of Modern African Studies*, 11, 1, 61-89.

ILO, 1972. *Employment, incomes and inequality: A strategy for increasing productive employment in Kenya.* World Employment Programme, ILO, Geneva.

King, J. 1969. 'Planning non-formal education in Tanzania', *Educational development in Africa: Vol. III. Integration and administration,* UNESCO International Institute for Educational Planning (IIEP), Paris.

King, K. 1974. 'Kenya's informal machine-makers: A study of small-scale industry in Kenya's emergent artisan society'. *World Development,* 2, 4-5, 9-28.

King, K. 1975a. 'Skill acquisition in the informal sector of an African economy: The Kenya case', *The Journal of Development Studies. Special issue on employment and income distribution,* 11, 2, 108-122.

King, K. 1975b. 'Indo-African skill transfer in an East African economy', *African Affairs,* 74, 29, 65-71.

King, K. 1977. *The African artisan: Education and the informal sector in Kenya,* Heinemann, London.

King, K. 1980. 'Education and self-employment', in IIEP, *Education, work and employment II,* UNESCO International Institute for Educational Planning (IIEP), Paris, 217-283.

McLauchlin, S. 1979, *The wayside mechanic: An analysis of skill acquisition in Ghana,* Centre for International Education, University of Massachusetts, Amherst.

Nyerere, J. K. 1967. *Education for self-reliance.* Government Printer, Dar es Salaam.

Sheffield, J. and Diejomaoh, V. 1972. *Non-formal education in African development,* African American Institute, New York.

World Bank, The, 1974. *Education sector working paper,* The World Bank, Washington DC.

Skill Acquisition in the Informal Sector[3]

The informal sector has caught the attention of many international concerns, and is the object of research by the ILO and other bodies in a number of countries. Shortly, therefore, a good deal more data will be available on the personnel and operations within it. At the moment, however, the words 'informal sector' do not presumably convey very much to the general reader, with no direct experience of the Third World, and it may perhaps be useful initially to sketch in some of the dimensions this sector has in Kenya.

From one angle it may be represented perhaps by the image of a man pushing the entire shell of a used car on his little handcart to one of the areas where the metal will be recycled into some household goods. Geographically, it may be taken to refer to whole concentrated sections of Nairobi, for instance, where without demarcation of plot from plot, petty producers are packed tightly on to the slopes of the Nairobi River, or cluster on a piece of open ground at Eastleigh, Kariobangi or Shauri Moyo. On the Gikomba site, along the Nairobi River, the debris from the reworked and gouged-out cars and lorries rises higher and higher, and threatens to overwhelm the diminishing open ground left to the petty mechanics, tinsmiths and woodworkers. In the smaller towns, by contrast, there are no really large unregulated areas where workers may carry on their trade; here and there activity seems to have spilled out into the open, but generally artisans operate out of some kind of premise or fenced off area. And in the villages, again, petty artisan activity tends to be closely associated with a homestead or semi-permanent work area.

The impression of such activity, particularly in the Nairobi concentrations, is one of exceedingly hard work for long hours under the sun or a makeshift shelter. In parts of the Burma market, near the Nairobi Stadium, the din of metal being beaten and reworked is maintained from dawn till nightfall. There is no hush at the lunch hour, as there is in Nairobi's formal Industrial Area next door. It is an interesting historical twist that one of the areas of most intensive day-long production along the Nairobi River is still called Grogan, after the notorious early white settler who caricatured and occasionally whipped his labour for their 'inherent' laziness.

---

[3] This chapter is taken from King (1977), *The African artisan* – see bibliography in introduction above.

The image, then, is of hard work in adverse conditions, on sites that may be required for redevelopment in a few months' time. It is not surprising therefore that the ILO mission that visited Kenya in 1972 were impressed by the dynamism of the informal sector, particularly in Nairobi.[4] Unlike the rather gloomy predictions about employment in large scale business, evidence of employment potential in petty activity declared itself loudly from all these jostling sites. Perhaps the most important impact of the sector was that it now clearly had a *productive* side, or a manufacturing side; it was not restricted to the older petty service image of match-girls, maize-roasters, shoe-shiners and hawkers.

The Span of Informal Sector Activity

Before coming to examine the implications for education and training of such strenuous activity, it is worth trying to put the productive or craft side of the informal sector into some kind of perspective. This needs to be done particularly in relation to the *'service'* side of the sector. Clearly a very great deal of what shelters under the informal sector umbrella appears to be service activity. Again, naturally this is at its most conspicuous in Nairobi where hundreds of rickety roadside 'Hiltons' provide tea and hot food to the lower paid people of the large scale firms as well as to the informal sector. Many young boys and girls assist these canteen owners. The same is true of food preparation in the small town and rural areas although there the bars and hotels are licensed registered premises in permanent or semi-permanent buildings. This question of premises in urban and rural areas immediately raises a point that I shall need to recur to: *in what does the informality consist?* It seems difficult to consider premises alone as crucial; otherwise the boy who cooks, serves and cleans in a rural hotel for two or three shillings a day is somehow outside the informal sector, while the boy who works in a Nairobi canteen of sticks, stones, cardboard and polythene, teetering on the banks of the Nairobi River, is firmly informal. Nor is it a question of wages or of being enumerated in official labour statistics, since neither boy will have been officially counted, and neither will be receiving anything approaching the rural or urban minimum wage.

I shall come back to the complexity of defining informal again a little later. Still on the service side of the sector, several points need to be made

---

[4] International Labour Office, *Employment, iincomes and equality: A strategy for increasing productive employment in Kenya* (Geneva, 1972), Ch. 13 passim.

on other issues. First, the service occupations within the informal sector (whether fetching and carrying, acting as a domestic servant in the village or town, washing and guarding cars in the city) should not be seen as rigorously separate from the productive craft activities. In many cases, indeed, service jobs are determined by the youthfulness of the boy who knows that he could not be accepted on a building site or at a factory gate. They are used consequently as a place to mark time in the village or town while waiting to enter other kinds of jobs. Often a boy will wait for a year or two after primary school, moving from small hotel, to small store, to domestic servant, to milk-boy, to turn-boy, before he even tries to begin some productive course.

The second point to be made concerns girls. Much that will be said later in this chapter about informal education and indigenous apprenticeship does not apply to girls. In both the formal and informal sectors, there are very few productive or craft activities that girls can enter as yet. They are much more likely therefore to get stuck in the service occupations of the informal sector, such as bar girl, servant, village or city prostitute, or in the casual work of tea- and coffee-picking than the boys are in their service sector. There have been a few innovations recently as for instance with the knitting machine which has allowed women to set up on their own in many towns, but this kind of independent craft activity still only affects a handful.

In general, therefore, in examining some of the service occupations of the informal sector, it is important to try for an analysis over time. The rate at which at least the young move through service jobs can then be documented. It seems likely for instance even on present limited evidence that mobility in this sector is more marked than in the craft occupations, which could mean that the most significant thing to be said about, say, Nairobi's shoe-shiners is that they are likely to stop shoe-shining.

This is not to suggest that the actual occupations in the service side are likely to diminish in importance. Indeed, there is every· indication that they will expand and diversify to offer a wider range of cheap services to both rich and poor than they do at the moment. In this event, the present mobility in and out of the service sector might well be reduced. For the moment, however, I may consider some aspects of skilled productive work in the informal sector, as these raise some questions about training.

Productive Crafts in the Informal Sector

I have suggested that this aspect of the urban informal sector is the easiest to admire. Clearly in a city like Nairobi there are several thousands of skilled men (and some women) engaged in such craft practice, and who carry on their trade or business against what seem considerable odds. The discovery of these thousands of petty producers appeared particularly heartening in Kenya since the primary and secondary leaver problems had been presenting great difficulties to national planners. It was all the more admirable since this productive low-cost world seemed to have thrown itself up without any official encouragement; if anything, indeed, it had been discouraged and harassed by being shunted summarily from site to site. Yet it had survived, and showed every sign of expanding dramatically. How had this come about?

In examining the training component of this productive wing, it is important to distinguish the *informal* sector from *nonformal* education. It was stressed that nonformal education, as referred to in the literature, tends to mean *sponsored* training opportunities, usually offered outside the Ministry of Education. These turn out to be programmes, more or less institutionalised, on which data are readily available, and whose clients can be enumerated. The better known of these in Kenya are the village polytechnics, the National Youth Service, and skills courses offered by official agencies and voluntary bodies. By contrast, training in the informal sector is not sponsored, and numbers and methods not widely known at all. As there is, however, rather a significant training function attached to much of the productive and skilled areas of the informal sector, it may be useful to gauge something of its dimensions, its internal structure, diffusion potential, attitudes and aspirations of its participants, and its links with the more formal Indian and Western production enterprises. It is perhaps easier to make this analysis concrete if it is linked to the different *products* of the sector.

1. *Exclusively informal sector products and skills*[5]

Many of the basic commodities necessary to a low income household are *only* produced in the informal sector. These items include the cheapest form of lighting – the tin lamp; the brazier or cooking stove; some kitchen utensils, for cooking and frying; and some containers and measures.

---

[5] For a typology of informal sector activity more concerned with roles, see K. Hart, 'Informal income opportunities and urban employment in Ghana', *Journal of Modern African Studies*, 11, 1 (1973).

Figure 1. An urban informal sector workplace. Note the temporary structure of wood and cardboard walls.

Again, in Nairobi, where the cheapest productive activity has outrun available accommodation, these commodities are made almost exclusively out of doors, on open ground or under temporary shelters. The makers are not randomly scattered on the city fringes, but following the existing Nairobi pattern of specialised streets (for cloth, vegetables, auto spare parts, etc.), these informal operators tend to cluster into concentrations of tin, wood and metal workers. The pattern is different in the small town and rural areas where such products are almost invariably associated with some kind of permanent or semi-permanent premise. This accommodation variable is not itself critical in determining differences in production and technology at this low level. In fact, elsewhere I have examined for one particular item – the oil lamp – the nature of its manufacture right across Kenya, from the urban wastelands, to the market towns, to the village centres. It will appear that questions of market, distribution, technology and incomes are of rather more importance than the nature of the premises.

As far as training for production is concerned, these particular items are much easier to separate off from the formal education system than many others I shall shortly come to. There is simply no provision for teaching their manufacture in the formal training system, or in the nonformal setting. The skill has to be acquired on the job, at the hands of a local artisan (or *fundi*, in Swahili).

2. *Industries and skills common to formal and informal sectors*

I enter a much more complex area with these skills since the craft practice can be acquired in a variety of modes, and the skill carried on equally easily in large-scale, small-scale or petty enterprises. The most common of such skills would be: building and contracting skills; auto-mechanic, spray painting, panel beating; metal, blacksmith and welding; making household furniture; shoemaking, tailoring; and driving. The skills required for such activity can be learnt in at least three main modes.

Formally

It is possible to acquire competence in most of the above skills through attending government technical secondary schools, though learning by no means assumes subsequent entry to the trade. A little less formally, there are ways to master many of these crafts by entering the National Youth Service, a local village polytechnic, youth centres, and private technical colleges.

Through casual labour to skilled man

The majority of skilled people in Nairobi's industrial area (as in the other large towns) were originally taken on at the gate as casual labourers (*kibarua* men); their skills were learnt exclusively *on the job)* by a process of the more productive casual labourers being attached over the years to the Asian (now African) *mistri* (master). This method of reproducing skills is central to the Indian firms in Kenya, but common also in the less technologically sophisticated European and all the emerging African firms. Employers tend not to be interested in grades, trade tests or salary linked to formal qualifications. And this tends to raise a number of difficulties for any attempt by the government to encourage formal technical training, as opposed to acquiring very specific skills of value to particular firms. For the moment, the point is that all the skills listed above can be acquired more or less rapidly on the job.

It is necessary to stress that this is not at present a rather uncommon event, but it is widely and explicitly acknowledged by workers to be a way of becoming skilled. It is not therefore particularly useful to transfer to the Kenya context the standardised western job classifications of unskilled, semi-skilled, skilled and professional, because this static picture distorts the widespread manipulation of the unskilled casual category to attain skilled status.

Indigenous skill acquisition
In addition to the formal and *kibarua* modes of skill attainment, there has emerged over the last thirty to forty years a process whereby an individual can attach himself to a skilled man (or woman) in a type of informal apprenticeship. It is particularly apparent in these skills and industries which are common to both the formal and informal sectors, but it also embraces those exclusively informal sector skills that were mentioned earlier. As there is a good deal of interest in the varieties of African apprenticeship, and the potential or obstacles they present to rapid employment generation, it is worth examining rather carefully the particular characteristics of Kenya's present style.

In contrast to the formal mode of apprenticeship in Kenya, the indigenous system operates on almost completely different assumptions. The former is increasingly formalised, being tied to years and qualifications in a very limited number of schools. In addition it is part of rather an elaborate Industrial Training Act, and the apprentices are given considerable attention by the Ministry of Labour, its training officers and training institutions. Wages and conditions are rigorously laid down, and can be enforced.[6]

The indigenous system works on a set of quite different principles.

1. Fees.
Like the apprenticeship principle in Britain until the early years of the 20th century, trainees pay their masters to accept them, and expect some form of maintenance or subsistence in return. There is, however, a very great variety in what needs to be paid; the premiums may fall anywhere in the range from 100/- Kenya shillings to 600/-, depending on the skill desired. For instance, it is fairly standard in the central area of Kenya to expect to

---

[6] Republic of Kenya, Ministry of Labour, *The National Industrial Training Scheme for the Training of Craft Apprentices* (Nairobi, Government Printer, 1973).

pay 450/- to learn auto repair. But the fee can be reduced or waived altogether if there is some relationship of kin or friendship.

There is no doubt of the readiness of many parents to pay fees of this order for a 'course'; 450/- is, after all, the same as one year's fees in a government boarding school, and only half what it costs to attend some of the *harambee* (self-help) boarding schools. Furthermore, it is now relatively well known that one year in secondary school, without the other three, is not worth the expense; whereas most courses in the informal sector are completed in a year.

This system of payment in exchange for skill is not unique to Kenya, but appears elsewhere in the East African territories as well as in Cameroon, Ghana and Nigeria. There are, however, some fundamental differences in the East and West African modes as will appear shortly. Within the Kenya context, the widespread interest in acquiring a skill for money means that there is sometimes the possibility of the training function displacing the productive element in importance. If it is possible to get nine or ten young boys to pay 300/- to 400/- at the same time to learn car repair, then the income from fees can become as important to the master as the cheap labour. It is easy then to visualise the growth of garage-cum-schools which have begun to spring up here and there in Kenya's central belt.

Obviously when an artisan decides to try combining his garage or workshop with a boarding wing, and begins to advertise for students, he has in a sense crossed into the formal sector. His technical 'college' or 'academy' can be registered with the Ministry of Education, and he may proceed to charge fees of up to 1500/- a year if the student is boarding. In terms of value for money, what students receive from some of these institutions is clearly inferior to straight one-to-one apprenticeship in the informal sector. These colleges do, however, point to a demand even in the remoter areas of Kenya to get access somehow to a marketable skill. Indeed, the majority of the trainees in such institutions are migrants from up-country Kenya or neighbouring Tanzania. Lacking government technical facilities in their home areas, or relatives with whom they may board in Nairobi, they respond to the advertising of the private technical academies:

We are among the First Kenya Schools to introduce this system of Education which presently provides technical training opportunities to students in Secondary Schools. What is one's hope nowadays in the Continent of Africa without a technical qualification?[7]

2. *Length of training.*

As soon as there is this transition into the formal sector, the fees become much higher, and are related to specific terms and years of study. The courses, too, make much of being geared towards government trade tests, to be taken at the end of the period. With the smaller fabricator and his one or two trainees, by contrast, the fee is for the length of time it takes the individual student to master the skill – the bright student being expected to serve his time in under a year perhaps, and the slower student up to a year or more. Apprenticeship can be a few months in some of the tinsmith operations, and not much above a year in many of the automotive related trades. This is what principally differentiates the East African system of apprenticeship from the traditional British, or the West African variety. In Dakar, in Senegal, and Togo, for example, the apprentice is given over to a master (or *patron),* and will be attached to him without wages for five years and more.[8] Apparently in such a situation, many apprentices still aspire to become masters, and the masters for their part insist that youths *can* become masters as rapidly as their intelligence allows. The reality is, however, different. Apprenticeship in these circumstances is much closer to its original European characteristics of restricting access to journeyman status, and reducing any chance of over-competition amongst those practising the same trade.

In Kenya, on the other hand, whatever else may be alleged of the indigenous apprentice system, it seems hard to picture it as an arena of extended exploitation of cheap labour. Admittedly, apprentices pay premiums, but over the period of a year, a good deal of the 450/- will have been returned to them through daily subsistence and the provision of somewhere to sleep. So far in Kenya there is none of the codification and formality of the West African system, with its written contract, and the elaborate ritual of freeing the apprentice at the end of his indenture. At the moment there seem to be no sanctions that the master can use to hold on to his trainees beyond the time they wish to stay.

Indeed, the most obvious feature of the system is the determination of those under training to move as rapidly as possible to establishing their

---

[7] Brochure of Universal Central Academy, Thika, 1972.
[8] I am indebted to Alphonse Tay and Olivier Le Brun for discussions of apprenticeship in Togo and Dakar respectively.

own little workshop or industry. Very often the brightest trainees are absorbed within a short time into a co-operative arrangement with their former masters. They may begin to do a little work on a contract business, but as soon as they see how much their master gets from a single job in, say, panel beating, they will either ask to become one of the qualified helpers in the company and share its profits, or will, after accumulating sufficient capital from piece work or contracts, set up on their own. Within a year or two, therefore, it is quite possible for the former trainee to have his own apprentices. Also, many of the older masters seem very aware of the number of people who have gone through their hands, between 1950 and 1970, and are able to identify with some pride precisely where their former pupils are now operating their own-businesses. The system in fact seems so open that it scarcely merits the narrow traditional use of the term apprenticeship.

3. *The paradox of the open apprenticeship.*

The openness of Kenya's apprenticeship system is perhaps better understood in some historical framework. First, with the exception of blacksmithing, there had in most of the East African hinterland been no long pre-colonial tradition of local craft communities. Second, the major eruption of specialised craft communities to Kenya was associated with the waves of Indian immigration. These Indian craft workers in building, tin, wood, steel, car repair and many other skills, found themselves operating in a much more monopolistic situation in Kenya than they had left at home. And there is little doubt that they did restrict their craft expertise as far as possible to their own community. In doing so, they were acting in a similar fashion to the white settlers who, in their own struggle for survival against Indian and African competition, arrogated to themselves monopolies in land, marketing and the most profitable cash crops (coffee, tea and pyrethrum). Moreover, the skill monopoly of Indian craft groups was further protected even amongst themselves by the rather rigid internal differentiation of the various communities. The result was that it was possible for certain Indian manual workers to accumulate a significant surplus even by the mid-1930s; this could then be ploughed into simple machinery, and by the second or third generation, the family had, in many cases, differentiated into ownership of a small factory, a small precision engineering workshop or a contracting business.

In this process, but particularly after the Second World War, the Indians became much less possessive of some of the skills that they had once deliberately guarded from their African employees or fellow workers, who now began to take over the production of a whole range of goods that had originally been made entirely by Indian skilled labour. And it should be noted that these include all the items that I have described above as 'exclusively informal sector' products. I shall look in more detail at the Africanisation of some of these craft processes in some of the other original chapters. Here I am concerned with the effects of the colonial restrictions on land, crops, schools, skill, urban trade, etc. Fundamentally, in all these areas it became politically difficult at Independence to stand for a policy of restriction, monopoly and limited access. It proved impossible to legislate against the expansion of self-help schooling, despite the initial concern expressed in 1964 and 1965 by the Kenya Education Commission. Certainly, the groups who had managed to get primary or secondary schooling were not able to prevent thousands of others from getting access almost immediately, with the result that any slight educational head-start tended to be rapidly eroded. It was the same story with coffee and tea, and, in a different sphere, with licences to carry people in motor vehicles. In the matter of inheriting certain skills from the Indians, it was no different. Particularly as the first learners had no ancient prerogative over such and such a skill, but were often the first in their family, clan or tribe to become a welder or panel beater, it was inconceivable that they should act like medieval masters and restrict access.

In the late colonial period, payment in exchange for skill was a method that a number of Africans had arranged with members of the Indian skilled class. But because of the hostility of the colonial government, it was not uncommon during the late 1950s and early 1960s for Africans who agreed to such an arrangement to sign a lawyer's letter to the effect that they were receiving wages of so many pounds (even though they were getting nothing). This proved, however, not to be a very effective protection against some of the labour inspectors, and once a few Indian firms had been prosecuted and forced to pay several thousand shillings of back pay to their one-time apprentices, there was a general reluctance among Indians to become involved further in fee-paying training. In fact, in a brief survey of the small Indian workshops in one area of Nairobi in 1972, only two or three were found who were prepared to risk becoming skill models in the way that the Africans had meanwhile developed into an accepted pattern on the waste lots nearby. The very hostility of the colonial government, however, meant that the system has not yet really come into the open as in West Africa, even though it expanded very rapidly in the post-colonial period.

A final aspect of this openness concerns the relations of these petty producers with the large scale formal sector of the economy. It could be suggested that the seemingly progressive spread of local skill into areas forbidden or restricted during the colonial period actually benefits the large-scale firms, and the elite who work in them and in the public sector. Clearly, the large concentrations of informal spray painters, panel beaters and mechanics across the Nairobi River allow many car and lorry owners to get a relatively good job done at half the price of the large-scale car agencies. Africans who patronise these workers do obviously benefit from the intense competition which along with stolen or second-hand parts keeps the prices low. It is similarly the case that the African and remaining Indian retailers in the formal sector of Nairobi do benefit from the numbers of informal metal workers who compete to sell them their braziers, water cans, rat traps and much else. In fact, elsewhere I have a particular case study of the manufacture of bicycle carriers in the informal sector which highlights some of these aspects of dependency (see King 1974 in the Introduction).

It is one thing to note this phenomenon, and it is of course rather the fashion to analyse the ways in which the apparent expansion of the informal sector makes for greater dependency, ultimately making the differential between rich and poor even greater. On the other hand, in analysing the current attack on formal schools, I noted that the espousal of the working poor, and the disillusion with the elite has come about so rapidly in the international literature that it runs the risk of neglecting local African opinion. Fifteen years ago probably no Kenyan African possessed an electric welding machine, or a motorised spray paint machine; just as few possessed a form four certificate. Yet, as soon as small numbers did manage to obtain such equipment, they are seen by some analysts as confirmation of the widening income differentials. It might of course be preferable for the Nairobi mechanics and spray painters to combine in some sort of closed shop, to keep their prices nearer the going rate in the formal large-scale sector. It seems equally important, however, that this sort of monopoly should not precede the spread of many of Nairobi's cheap services into the rural areas. I shall mention shortly the attraction of doing informal sector apprenticeship in Nairobi; many apprentices are, nevertheless, aware that the competitiveness of Nairobi and its critical housing shortage will drive them to try out their new craft in some smaller up-country town. If rural and agricultural development can create conditions that will provide work in crafts that have never been practised there before, this is surely more important than worrying about the possible overproduction of certain skills in Nairobi.

In brief, the present openness of Kenya's indigenous apprenticeship system seems likely to spread rather widely in the rural areas a range cheap products and a group of versatile artisans.

4. *Character of the trainees.*

I suggested elsewhere, in a discussion of the ordinariness of Kenya's primary schools, that school leavers have no great difficulty in adjusting their sights to whatever job is available. In this sense they measure up to the conventional picture of the cooling-out of the standard-seven leavers, as they compete to grasp in the 1970s the sort of openings that their protected predecessors despised in the late 1950s: shoe-shiner, shamba-boy, spanner-boy, day-labourer on building sites, tea- and coffee picker. I have said that some of these are seen as temporary jobs, to allow them to grow a little older. In other cases what is taken as a temporary job may gradually become permanent. However, this image of cooling-out does not adequately cover the self-employed petty producers, and those who train to become like them. Many of these see themselves training for a situation where they will be rather better off than those in the lower echelons of, say, government service. Indeed, in a number of cases, contrary perhaps to expectations, trainees or their masters had come to the informal sector of the economy not because they could not obtain a position in the enumerated sector, but because the jobs they had in the modern sector had insufficient pay and prospects. Often such a distinction is drawn in the literature between the wage-and-salary sector and the unenumerated, informal sector that it is assumed that *any* job in the former is worth retaining for its security and steady income. The reality in Kenya is that there is a great deal of restless movement in the bottom reaches of the modern sector as people search out an income outside the range of 80/- to 200/- per month. Once they have set up on their own, several claim that they found they make more in a week than they previously made in the month, while avoiding most of the former expenses and overheads. Whatever the reality of their earnings may be, most artisans or their trainees have a fierce determination not to be employed again. As is seen elsewhere (see King, 1974, in this introducetion), there are sufficient examples of successful operators in the informal productive world, for it to appear as an alternative route of upward mobility to many who enter.

In most cases, still, would-be trainees are the first generation of their families to take up a particular trade, although in a few skills like woodcarving and blacksmithing there is already some continuity from father to son. Consequently, the commonest pattern is for the young man to approach a friend or an acquaintance of the family who has been following a trade for some time; he is usually a man of the same tribe, but by no means always so in Nairobi. Taken as a group the trainees are largely drawn from the poorer strata of society (though not the poorest). Their parents have not been able to afford secondary school, even though their children might have won a place there. In many cases the result is that younger and more schooled boys are going, in order to gain their skill, to craftsmen who are frequently illiterate or have had minimal schooling. So rapid, however, is the reproduction of skill in the informal sector that most of the workers are young men.

It is difficult to estimate to what extent this expanding group sees itself as set apart from the industrial mainstream. There is admittedly a tendency for operators within it to stress that only those prepared to work hard and long in dirty conditions need think of entering apprenticeship. A number of the owners actually share with their European and Indian counterparts in the modern sector the disdain for the secondary school boy, seeing him as someone who will be unable to accommodate himself to the work. It is assumed by all three that his education will have unfitted him for hard labour in exacting conditions, even though, increasingly, poor secondary school leavers are turning to this type of training. Amongst the majority of secondary school boys, however, it is still regarded as something of a joke to find one of their classmates translated into a self-employed carpenter ('doing what he shouldn't be doing' in popular parlance). However despite the disadvantages of working in Nairobi without access to piped water, electricity or shelter from rain or mud, it seems difficult to conceive of the informal artisans as a race a part. For one thing, while it remains true that the informal sector aims its products principally at the low income African market, some of its wares cannot be distinguished from modern sector artefacts. Cars that have been spray-painted or been panel-beaten in a vacant lot only substantially differ from Indian garage workmanship in price, – the informal operators nearly always having initially learnt their skill from the Indians. Similarly, the wardrobes and kitchen furniture that are made under makeshift shelters of polythene duplicate the products of some formal operators. In fact, there are only a handful of items, as mentioned earlier, that can be considered informal-sector products exclusively, since scrap materials are widely used by artisans who have moved into permanent premises. Furthermore, the majority of roadside operators aspire to get formal workshop premises, presently in very short supply in Nairobi, and probably do not see themselves as different in kind from those earlier and more successful ones who have managed to rent or buy accommodation already. If the informal areas of Nairobi are inspected carefully, it will be seen that there are constant attempts by the more successful artisans to stake out, and demarcate with bamboo, an area where their equipment and materials can be secure. Many such little tentative plots turn out to be rented from people who work in the modern sector. For these kinds of reasons, whether looked at from the angle of materials, product, premises or personnel, the attempt very rigorously to dichotomise formal from informal appears rather an academic exercise.

As was hinted at the beginning of this chapter, it becomes more and more difficult to put a finger on what essentially constitutes the informality of the informal sector. Not premises. Not wages. Not product. At first sight it looks as if there might be something in the attitude to training that would differentiate formal from informal. This might be summed up in the Kikuyu axiom which is readily produced in the informal sector in any discussion of government trade tests, or formal certification: 'Ti ngirindi irutaga wira, ni mundu' – 'It's not the grade that works, it's the man'. It expresses an antipathy to the government trade certification system as something that is not relevant to the small man and his workforce. Petty producers will admit that trade tests are valuable if someone has got connections to enter the large-scale European firms or the Ministry of Works; they can then be used to secure automatic increases in wages depending on the grade of trade test. It can be seen, incidentally, that this axiom is in line with what many educational reformers would like to see being adopted in the Third World. Such reformers despair of the way they think industry automatically raises its recruitment criteria to the certificate level of school leavers, regardless of whether a higher school grade is necessary for the job in hand. Strictly speaking, this is not an accurate generalisation across industry in Kenya, for a considerable part of local industry has needed rather strong government sanctions to make it accept even a handful of formally trained and certified school products.

It has to be admitted in fact that this Kikuyu axiom which seems to express so accurately the spirit of the informal sector is equally applicable to the bulk of Indian enterprise, and a section of western firms also. So it looks as if the informal sector eludes definition on this score as well.

5. *Product technology and urban-rural diffusion.*

As far as a separate product technology is concerned, it is not easy to generalise when there is such a range of cheap and expensive goods and services offered in the informal sector. It is interesting to observe that some of those for which there is an insatiable export demand to the smaller towns and rural areas are the originally Indian artefacts, principally charcoal-burning braziers, tin lamps, and metal kitchen bowls and pans. It is common to see the top of country buses leaving Nairobi festooned with braziers and other informal sector products. But this should not be taken to mean that Nairobi exerts a monopoly over such goods. Indeed, even during the last three years, there has been a very marked decentralisation from Nairobi, and the dynamism of new local operators has reduced the need to depend on the capital. There is, however, a difficulty about the promotion of certain goods in the rural areas, for even though many of the informal sector products are now admired by economists for their labour intensity, it should be realised that a good deal of the informal sphere is very much a satellite of the large-scale firms or of some of the products they import at first hand. That is to say, the appropriate technology of the informal sector may be derived from the allegedly inappropriate technology and import patterns of the modern large-scale sector.

To take an example, Kenya's policy on the importation of cars has been frequently criticised for being too *laissez faire*, it being considered inappropriate that so much foreign exchange should go on the purchase of these for the still rather small local and foreign elite. On the other hand, the informal metal-working industry is directly dependent on the detritus from the modern car industry for much of its own dynamism. The vast numbers of motor oil cans collected daily by the service side of the informal sector from Nairobi petrol stations provide the producers with the most satisfactory supply of cans for the making of the tin lamps. Bought at approximately 5/- or less per hundred from the petrol stations, these cans are converted the same day into lamps that retail at 60-70 cents each depending on the area and style. Additionally, oil and petrol drums and much of the car body is central to the fabrication of the charcoal braziers which retail at 4/- to 6/- for the cheaper versions. Oil drums are also sliced into very effective containers for cattle feed or water. Even the bed-making industry – which is one of the fastest growing on the carpentry side – is dependent for all its springing on the availability of second-hand tyres from which the long crisscross strips can be cut. The car, therefore, inappropriate and expensive as it may be, makes a rather important contribution to informal sector products, quite apart from the numbers of mechanics and panel beaters who keep cars, buses and lorries on the road long after they would have been scrapped in the West. Any decision, such as that of Tanzania recently, to restrict radically the import of new cars could well alter patterns of production amongst the various informal ancillary industries. This is not intended as a defence of high cost consumer goods any ·more than one would try to defend an inappropriate school system on the grounds that it did at least *employ* thousands of teachers. It is, however, worth establishing some of the link between formal and informal before considering any policy questions.

There is a set of problems when it comes to the diffusion of the actual craftsmen into the rural areas. Some of these will only be touched on here, as they are dealt with in a later chapter of the original book, but they do highlight the difficulty of surmounting urban-rural imbalance even in the informal sector. Initially, of course, it has to be admitted that the market for informal sector goods, though vast and still largely untapped, is determined to a considerable extent by the state of agricultural incomes, and can therefore be sluggish in taking up even cheap innovations quite close to Nairobi. The craftsmen who do however decide to practise in their home area (after acquiring the skill perhaps in Nairobi) are naturally attracted by the idea of being one of the few or often the only such in the village or small town. In conversation, however, with some who had taken this step, or who had taken it and then returned to practising in Nairobi, it became clear that there could still be quite substantial difficulties in operating outside the metropolis.

First, there is the task of obtaining scrap materials from Nairobi in sufficient quantity to maintain production. This is particularly critical with the tin- and metal-based industries, but is naturally much less true of carpentry. The road system is now very adequate to the majority of small trade centres in the middle belt of Kenya at least, but even this is a mixed blessing to the young rural entrepreneur; the very multiplicity of country buses, and the tendency for most rural families to have some member of their family in the town, mean that it is very often easier to buy beds, chests and cooking equipment from amongst the much greater variety of Nairobi and send them up on the bus. The quality is also still very much better in Nairobi than in the smaller market centres.

Secondly, the would-be rural entrepreneur cannot take advantage of the apprentice system to the same extent as his urban counterpart, Especially at the village level, he often does not have sufficient work to justify keeping an apprentice, and as it is not customary to sack or send off apprentices for lack of work, they would have to be maintained during periods of slack. By contrast, daily paid labour can be taken on and dropped as the occasion arises. In fact, at the very lowest level of the village carpenter or tinsmith, apprenticeship is often not a feasible proposition. Many of the craftsmen combine their craft with agriculture and only make one-off goods to order. Things are admittedly better in the larger district towns like Nakuru, Murang'a, Thika, Machakos and Kisumu, where apprenticing is much more common. Even so, the result is that many intending apprentices who have Nairobi contacts will prefer to acquire their training there. For one thing, they will learn a much wider range of skills through urban apprenticeship than by attending a master who is restricted by limited rural demand and lack of materials. In the automotive trade, for example, they find it very difficult to get experience of lorry repair, unless they learn in Nairobi, Mombasa and the few other large towns.

Thirdly, a number of artisans give the definite impression that they are much more troubled over licensing in the rural areas than if they were set up on one of the large vacant lots in Nairobi. There, at the moment, the City Council do not attempt to enforce licensing upon whole sections of the carpenters, mechanics and scrap metal workers. But it is almost impossible to avoid it in many rural areas; which is why rural petty producers almost always operate out of permanent or semi-permanent premises.

Nevertheless, despite the attractions of Nairobi for migrant apprentices, the informal fabrication sector is very much on the increase in the smaller towns right across Kenya. Unlike the picture of the decay of rural crafts so often drawn for other parts of the Third World, Kenya is witnessing a rather dramatic rise in the level of craft activity in the post-colonial period. It should be added that as long as rents remain as high as they presently are in Nairobi, youths who have learnt informally will continue to try their luck in their own village or town.

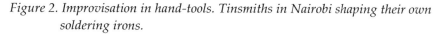

Figure 2. Improvisation in hand-tools. Tinsmiths in Nairobi shaping their own soldering irons.

Note: heat from the locally made brazier and the imported blowlamp.

It should finally be noted in this section on technology that there is a very marked innovative strain in much of the production in the informal sector, contrary to the usual picture of its doing second-hand things in a second-rate way. As seen elsewhere with oil lamps and machine-making in the informal sector, a considerable range of variations and improvements have been made in the rather short span that Africans have been involved in their manufacture. In general, there has been product development and design improvement in a whole range of items in the last ten to twenty years, as would be expected. Because of economic necessity, the key characteristic of informal sector technology is its emphasis on repair and improvisation in the use of scrap and of available tools. This places it in direct contrast with the technology in the capital intensive large-scale sector of the economy, where it is increasingly the case that workers in Kenya as in Britain are taught to replace rather to than repair the products of the industrialised nations.

Laudable though this technology of improvisation is for urban and rural artisans, it is still not possible to regard it as unique to what has been loosely called the informal sector. I noted earlier that improvisation and adaptability were the mark of the· small-scale Indian *fundi* in the colonial period, and it has remained today characteristic of Indian car repair, and the Indian precision workshops. They continue in the 1970s as earlier to improvise and make on the spot complicated parts and components that would otherwise need to come from abroad. This technology of adaptation, therefore, is much more widespread than the small-scale African work places.

Policy Conclusions and Definitions

From a policy point of view, there has already been a recognition of the value of the product, the technology and the employment potential of the informal sector. Indeed, in September-October of 1974, the government embarked on a policy of giving limited credit to some of Nairobi's petty producers who did not have permanent workshops.[9] It would seem to be in line with this move if policy were also able to allocate site and service areas where craft communities could gain some security of tenure and provide premises for themselves in time. This would only be to adopt a trend that is already under way amongst the artisans themselves, as they combine to demarcate provisional boundaries.

As far as the present fee-paying element of apprenticeship is concerned, there seems little ground for indignant attempts at eradication, such as marked the late colonial period. It does, of course, mean that apprentices may not be drawn from the most indigent households, just as the earlier British system of apprentice premiums discriminated against the lowest income levels. Similarly, some young people who possibly lack parents or favourable extended family connections cannot afford not to be paid a wage. At the moment this appears to be much more true of the rural areas where money is tighter than of the cities. But even so, the Kenya informal learning system does not mean foregoing real wages for the five to seven year period that was

---

[9] *Daily Nation*, November 17, 1971

the norm in Britain until the early 20th century and which, from some accounts, still is the norm in cities like Dakar and Lomé in West Africa. It may transgress the letter of the Industrial Training Act, but then, as can be shown relatively easily, the Industrial Training Act is not even concerned at the moment with the thousands who acquire skill outside the sponsored official routes.

Over the last 20 to 30 years a system has grown up, almost entirely unnoticed by educationists, which has quietly been producing hundreds of artisans yearly with basic craft skills. Most important, the bulk of the group in their anxiety to be *self-employed* have paid little attention to the system of government trade tests which are decisive in assessing salary in the public sector and the larger firms. They share with the Indian artisans a healthy disregard for paper qualifications and schooling credentials; they are aware that grade tests on certain occasions can actually be 'purchased', but know for all this that grades are irrelevant in a situation where the hardest worker makes the most money. Like the Indians, they say of a skilled colleague: he's illiterate, unqualified, but equivalent to Government trade test, Grade 1. Over against this ungraded sector with its very low training costs (a fraction of the National Youth Service's per capita costs or the village polytechnic's), there is a counter ideology spreading throughout the country that there is still a vast reservoir of intermediate and higher level wage-and-salary technical positions waiting to be Africanised. For example, never until the last few years have there been so many applications for entry into some of the eight secondary technical schools. And to provide institutions for the higher reaches of technical training (sub-university), communities have been competing to tax themselves on a scale unprecedented in the history of African self-help. Both these thrusts are directed to the hope of technical employment (rather than self-employment) whatever their prospectuses may claim to the contrary; and unfortunately not very much attention has been paid to the difficulties already encountered by many technical school graduates in finding a job today. Technical preparation for formal sector employment is in fact rapidly becoming a high cost activity, and the tendency for its products will be, in Kenya as in Zambia and in Nigeria, to have technical qualifications without real industrial or workshop experience.

A case could, however, be made out that there is really a very limited demand in the short term for candidates with these higher technical aspirations. The problem rather is how first to provide all of Kenya with the variety of informal sector skills available to Nairobi. And this, it is suggested, is proceeding apace. And, second, how to produce for both urban and rural areas people of a skill level immediately above that of the present informal sector operator. The latter could conceivably be provided by those whose aspirations for high technical positions become gradually adjusted downwards through unemployment. It is much more likely that as with the Indians in the 1920s and 1930s it will come from hand-tool operators moving upwards into hand-operated machinery. Neither the conditions nor the available machinery are as conducive to this move in the 1970s as they were when the industrialised countries still produced a wide range of extremely cheap hand-operated machines. Nevertheless, a small Indian skill reservoir does exist still in Nairobi and Mombasa, and it may prove possible for the precision workshop sector to be Africanised in a way that retains and promotes its methods in Kenya. The people most likely to adopt and spread this next level of machine technology are the more successful informal sector operators, who have in a sense been made in the Indian image. They are not, however, in political and economic terms, the group most able to get the credit necessary to do this. Still, the need for simple and power-driven machines is already felt very strongly by artisans in the informal sector, and it should perhaps be possible to design a sufficiently sensitive credit or hire-purchase system to take account of their needs.

Again, it has to be stressed that the motivation and aspirations of many in this sector for upward mobility and technological advance continue to make it difficult to separate off the informal sector from the rest of the economy. In fact, the more the informal mode has been examined in this chapter, the more difficult it has been to isolate it from the rest. The difficulty arises in part from the term being first used for the most conspicuous unregulated urban sector of a particular city, Nairobi; whereas there is very little to distinguish the urban mode of either the service or productive side from that operating elsewhere in the country. The second, and perhaps major difficulty has arisen from a perhaps unconscious use of the term 'informal sector' to mean *African* (at least in the Kenya context) so that attempts at definition are implicitly only concerned with descriptions of the African artisan and service communities. This is really rather unhelpful. It would be more useful to talk of a series of informal modes, and demonstrate how widespread they are throughout the economy. When this is done, it will be noticed that a good deal of the entire economy is informal on some criteria.

Informal education and training
By this criterion, perhaps most of the economy can be judged informal. Preference for on-the-job and other informal skill acquisition is common to petty rural and urban African concerns, to the majority of larger African and Indian business, and to the European large farm and plantation sector, as well as to the less sophisticated urban European firms.

Technology of improvisation with labour intensity
On this variable also, the informal mode penetrates a very large part of the country's large- and small-scale industry. It is particularly characteristic of the Indian sector of the economy, but is conspicuous also in the use of machinery in the large farm and plantation sector. It is of course already well-established in the petty and larger African enterprises.

Informal wage structures, determined by productivity not certification
High wage rates associated with level of school certification or trade test are really only common in a part of the public sector and the more sophisticated subsidiaries of multinational companies. In much of the rest of the economy, wages are arrived at without regard to schooling or formal trade competence. The indigenous apprentice system has a wage system irregular by official standards, but then wages much lower than official minimum rates are common to many other enterprises. The large European (and now also African) farm sector although often regarded as a formal, enumerated sphere, can pay rates to its casual workers which are often less than the daily casual rate of 5/- amongst petty producers in the town. Similarly, large-scale urban firms can pay low rates by keeping a substantial number of their workforce on casual terms. Obviously also, the Indian method of taking on casual labour and gradually paying more to the more productive keeps wage rates low.

Informal products and services
I have shown that with the exception of a handful of items, very few products are exclusive to the lowest stratum of African artisan. And even these were made in the Indian sector of the economy only a short time ago. Nor can it be made out that various sorts of illegitimate activity or reliance on stolen goods are somehow a special feature of this most petty

stratum. *Magendo* (stolen) business, to use the local term, is by no means restricted to this smallest scale of operators.

From this kind of perspective, it appears that informal criteria permeate a major part of Kenya's economy. There may be good reasons for examining obstacles such as licensing, harassment and lack of premises that presently seem to afflict the bottom end of the informal sector, but it is probably not helpful in analysis to regard that bottom section as somehow a separate entity. Although indigenous apprenticeship is common in this lowest sphere, it is also found among the more established African businessmen. Similarly, on-the-job training is common both at the bottom of the economy and in many of the higher reaches of Nairobi's industrial area. Indeed, if the informal modes were not so deeply entrenched throughout a good part of modern industry, it would not have proved so difficult to suggest that it accept highly schooled and certificated apprentices. A good deal more of the relation between the formal and informal modes of production becomes clearer in the next chapter of the original book, where I examine the resistance to the *formally* trained apprentice in what has perhaps too glibly been called the formal sector of the economy.

Chapter 3

I have noted that development cooperation agencies have played major roles in the transition from colonies to independent countries. In the education sector, these agencies supported tens of thousands of teachers at school and university levels in the newly independent countries, and also administrators in Ministries of Education. They also provided expatriate staff in other sectoral ministries, especially the treasury and economic planning.

The influence of one small philanthropic agency in setting the agenda for education in Sub-Saharan Africa during the 1920s and 1930s was noted in Chapter 1. In the last 60 years what had not been widely appreciated was how central both knowledge and research were to all stages of agency projects and programmes. Initially, such knowledge was principally for satisfying the internal processes of project development, analysis and evaluation. Increasingly from the early 1960s, the capacity became more evident of multilateral bodies such as UNESCO to convene international conferences on education relating to different regions[1] and of bodies like the World Bank from the 1970s to publicise their education policies. What the Bank termed *Education sector papers* were particularly influential. As early as 1974, the Bank's positive views about non-formal education and vocational education were clear along with their criticism of the 'dysfunctional' nature of general academic education (World Bank, 1974: 21; King, 2003).

By the 1970s, as I noted in 1991 (King, 1991: 1), an 'enormous trade in appraisals, review missions, sector assessments, manpower reviews, evaluations and completion reports' had grown. This was not only the case for education but for all sectors in which developing countries were

---

Kenneth King (2019): *Education, Skills and International Cooperation: Comparative and Historical Perspectives*. Hong Kong: Comparative Education Research Centre (CERC), The University of Hong Kong, and Dordrecht: Springer. © CERC

[1] For example, UNESCO and United Nations Economic Commission for Africa (UNECA) (1961) *Conference of African States on the Development of Education in Africa.*

© Springer Nature Switzerland AG 2019
K. King, *Education, Skills and International Cooperation*, CERC Studies in Comparative Education 36, https://doi.org/10.1007/978-3-030-29790-9_3

seeking loans or credits for development. It was not uncommon for individual countries to have between 20 and 50 bilateral and multilateral agreements with donors in the education sector alone.

Increasingly the World Bank in particular, as it built up its research capacity in the late 1970s, began to publicise its views about female education, science education, technical and vocational education, higher education and a great deal else, including its views about the rates of return to different levels of education. Lending and credits in support of education were directly influenced by these policies. What is more, these policies did not remain the same. For instance, longstanding Bank policies in support of secondary schools 'diversified' towards agriculture and vocational skills could be changed by a new policy paper on vocational and technical education and training (World Bank, 1991). Indeed, in all the main fields of education and training – from early childhood and literacy to higher education and skills development – there have been substantial changes in agency policy between the beginnings of formal educational aid in the 1960s and the present.

International conferences convened by multilateral agencies provided forums for discussing and shaping education policy priorities. They included UNESCO's pioneering regional education conferences in the 1960s (Fredriksen, 1981), the World Conference on Education for All in Jomtien, Thailand, in 1990, the World Education Forum in Dakar, Senegal, in 2000, and the World Education Forum in Incheon, Republic of Korea, in 2015.

Another modality has been the agency sector policy paper – whether for all developing countries or for specific regions, and whether for the whole of education or for particular levels of education. Thus, for the education sector as a whole, the Bank's 1980 *Education sector policy paper* looked across all the Bank's regions. By contrast, its *Education in Sub-Saharan Africa* in 1988 focused on this single region, but made judgments across all levels of education, attracting particular controversy for its comments on higher education (World Bank, 1988).

Though the Bank remained the most influential source of commentary in the aid sector on broad policies for education through the late 1970s, 1980s and 1990s, other UN agencies also made significant contributions, notably UNESCO, UNICEF, UNDP and the ILO. Bilateral agencies contained substantially less analytic capacity than the Bank. Nevertheless, Swedish SIDA's *Education Division Documents* (both old and new series) provided unique and detailed insights into their support to most of their programme countries. UK's DFID likewise covered a very diverse set of topics in their 70 volumes of *Researching the issues*. Both drew on external researchers for many topics.

Inter-agency analytic capacity

While individual agencies remained responsible for massive amounts of appraisal, assessment and evaluation, much of it outsourced to consultancy firms, powerful forces also supported inter-agency collaboration. Indeed, some of the most influential initiatives in educational policy development emerged from coordination amongst key groups of multilateral and bilateral donors. Thus, the Bank's *Education in Sub-Saharan Africa* (1988) was followed up by the inter-agency Donors to African Education, which subsequently morphed into the Association for the Development of Education in Africa (ADEA) in which agencies continued to play an active role. Similarly, the initiative for the movement that led to the World Conference on Education for All in 1990 originally came from the World Bank and UNICEF, but UNESCO and UNDP joined these sponsors and 18 other agencies and national governments were rapidly drawn in. The resulting Declaration and Framework for Action had an international appeal (UNESCO, 1990a), but the crucial *Background document* was drawn together by the World Bank and UNICEF, synthesising a great deal of the available agency research (UNESCO, 1990b).

The same was true of the sponsorship of the World Education Forum in Dakar in 2000. Its influence through the six Education for All (EFA) Goals was massively greater because of the convening power of its sponsoring agencies. Equally, the *Education for All Global Monitoring Report* which annually reviewed these EFA Goals between 2002 and 2015 had a huge impact especially because of the diverse donor support. Once the 10 targets of the Sustainable Development Goal (SDG) 4 for Education had been agreed in 2015, the *Global Education Monitoring Report* continued to draw on the support of the following national donors in reviewing SDG4's targets: Australia, Canada, France, Germany, Ireland, Finland, Norway, the Netherlands, Sweden, Switzerland, and the United Kingdom, as well as on UNESCO, UNGEI, the Open Society Foundations, Master Card Foundation and Hewlett Foundation (UNESCO, 2016). However, this is not to say that all influential education reports were inter-agency products. For instance, the first *World Development Report* (WDR 2018) to focus primarily on education was the responsibility of the

Development Economics vice-presidency in the World Bank (World Bank, 2017).

Development of research capacity in the South

From 1978, my new position in an organisation, the International Development Research Centre (IDRC) which was charged with funding and building research capacity in the South, permitted and required work with like-minded donors such as the Swedish Agency for Research Cooperation (SAREC), Rockefeller and Ford Foundations, along with the education divisions of many bilateral and multilateral agencies. It focused on sponsoring rather than doing research, and adopted a whole new language such as 'capacity building' which I had never used before as an education researcher. The IDRC approach encouraged a critical perspective on agencies setting out their own priorities for education research and policy in the South. It contributed to understanding and funding institutional research priorities in many different world regions.

This shift in employment location and focus did not mean that I myself abandoned research or analysis. In 1977 (i.e. the year before I moved to IDRC) I had become a member of the newly formed and IDRC-sponsored Research Review and Advisory Group (RRAG) whose remit was to review and analyse the large amount of existing research in the developing world. It became particularly interested in understanding the differing research environments and cultures in the South. This duly led to the publication of *Education research environments in the developing world* (Shaeffer and Nkinyangi, 1983). RRAG eventually developed into a series of regional RRAGs, one of which – NORRAG – I helped to found in 1986 with strong support from Swedish SIDA. Over the last 30 years, *NORRAG News (1-54)* has continued the RRAG tradition of critically analysing education research priorities set in the North, and has actively involved hundreds of Southern researchers as contributors.

The chapter selected to provide a lens on the range of educational data and analysis connected to development agencies is taken from a book, *Aid and education in the developing world* (King, 1991). This research had been commissioned by the UK's Overseas Development Administration (ODA), and I delayed the publication in order to capture the significance of the 1990 World Conference on Education for All. Its chapters review the elaborate coverage of agency research and analysis. This insight into the role of the agencies in reviewing and prioritising certain approaches to education research illustrated the continuing dramatic asymmetry between the North and the South in terms of development knowledge. It is a theme to which I shall return in chapter 10 of this book, and whose wider context Weiler (1983: 21) had acknowledged:

> The transnational system of knowledge production is inextricably linked to a transnational system of power, in which publishing interests, research funding, consulting firms, testing services, professional associations and development assistance agencies all form part of a powerful – if less than perfectly coordinated – centre.

References

Fredriksen, B. 1981. Progress towards regional targets for universal primary education: A statistical review. *International Journal of Educational Development* 1 (1), pp. 1-16.

King, K. 2003. 'The international steering of education systems: The case of the World Bank in the fields of work, education and occupation', in J. Oelkers (Ed.) *Futures of education I*, Peter Lang, Bern.

NORRAG News (King, K. Ed.) 1986-2017. See complete listing: http://resources.norrag.org/

Shaeffer, S. and Nkinyangi, J. (Eds.), 1983. *Education research environments in the developing world*, IDRC, Ottawa.

UNESCO, 1990a. *World declaration on Education for All* and *Framework for action to meet basic learning needs*, UNESCO, Paris.

UNESCO, 1990b. *Meeting basic learning needs: A vision for the 1990s. Background document.* World Conference on Education for All, 5-9 March 1990, Jomtien, Thailand, UNESCO, Paris.

UNESCO, 2016. *Education for people and planet: Creating sustainable futures for all. Global Education Monitoring Report, 2016*, UNESCO, Paris.

UNESCO and UNECA, 1961. *Final report. Conference of African states on the development of education in Africa, 15-25 May 1961.* (UNESCO/ED/181) UNESCO, Paris.

Weiler, H. 1983. 'Knowledge and legitimation: The national and international politics of educational research' paper presented at annual conference of the Comparative and International Education Society, Atlanta, March, p. 21.

World Bank, 1974. *Education sector working paper*, World Bank, Washington, DC.

World Bank, 1980. *Education sector policy paper*, World Bank, Washington, DC.

World Bank, 1988. *Education in Sub-Saharan Africa: policies for adjustment, revitalisation and adjustment*, World Bank, Washington DC.

World Bank, 1991. *Vocational and technical education and training: A World Bank policy paper*, World Bank, Washington DC.

World Bank, 2017. *Learning to realise education's promise: World development report 2018.* World Bank, Washington DC.

Aid, Research and Education[2]

> Rather than to do the thinking for a country ... the panel felt that we
> should help create an awareness of objectives, in order that they can
> be appraised by the country itself and used as an index for the
> success or failure of the programme.[3]

So ran one of the final recommendations of *Education in the Far East*, a
report of a major conference organised in 1956 by the International
Cooperation Administration, forerunner to USAID (United States Agency
for International Development). This was not a conference report full of
discussions about educational research and evaluation, but in these early
years it was interesting to note delegates asking each other questions like
'Has any country started a long-term programme by getting the Ministry
of Education to set up a committee for self-study and then use the results
for building into different parts of the programme?' It was also refreshing
in this era before the invention of professional educational planning to
hear delegates remark that 'We need to be pretty sympathetic toward
every country, for their plans are no worse for the short time they have
had educational programmes than the U.S. for as long as we have had
them.'[4]

These comments are an appropriate introduction to the scope of
educational research on developing countries over the last decade and
more. They are peculiarly relevant since what follows is not a description
of what might be called national education research, pursued, for
instance, in Thailand through Thai government or Thai university funds.
It describes instead a type of investigation which few industrialised
nations experience as 'recipients' in their own countries except when the
Organisation for Economic Co-operation and Development (OECD)
occasionally sends one of its expert groups to carry out a country review.
It is, in a word, externally-funded analysis, designed and executed by an
external aid agency, and frequently carried out by agency or other foreign
personnel.

---

[2] This chapter is taken from the first chapter of King (1991), *Aid and education in the developing world*.

[3] International Cooperation Administration, *Education in the Far East: A summary report of the ICA regional Conference on education*, ICA, Manila, 1956, p.71.

[4] Ibid.

What is exceedingly rare in the industrialised countries is absolutely commonplace in virtually all the poorer countries of the world. One of the characteristics of being a heavily-aided economy is that for each of the aided sectors – from health, to roads, to education, to small-scale enterprise – there is a requirement to allow the external aid agencies to satisfy themselves that there is a need for the particular items requested. Given the fact that in many poorer countries every single major development project in education – from university, to technical college, to vocational training centre – appears to be initially dependent on external loans or credits, *there is a simply enormous trade in appraisals, review missions, sector assessments, manpower reviews, evaluations and completion reports.* Most of these review and analysis activities are carried out by the agents of those providing the funds, and at the beginning of the 1990s a very considerable proportion of these agents came from outside the country receiving the funds.

During the colonial era the traffic in aid to education in developing countries was very restricted, and what few commissions of inquiry there were naturally tended to be carried out by the metropolitan authorities of the particular colonies. But beginning from the early 1960s when the bulk of the colonies received their political independence, aid negotiations started up with many of the new bilateral assistance agencies that came into being during the 1960s as well as with the multilateral agencies, and in particular the World Bank which started its educational lending in 1963. Aid negotiations also intensified with the private agencies, such as the Ford and Rockefeller Foundations, and with non-governmental organisations (NGOs). By the 1970s it was not uncommon for countries to have between 20 and 40 separate bi- and multi-lateral agreements in the education sector. Though not all of these would require extensive justification and documentation, the larger ones certainly would. To appreciate the scale and complexity of these 'external education relations', it may be of interest to record that one Central African country in 1986 had separate project agreements with the following donors in the education sector: UNICEF (3); UNESCO (2); Australia (3); Belgium; Canada (6); Cuba; Denmark (2); Egypt (2); Finland (2); West Germany (2); India; Greece; France (2); Italy; Netherlands; Romania; Switzerland; USA (3); Commonwealth Fund for Technical Cooperation (2); EC (2); UK (3).[5] This range would not be untypical of other countries.

---

[5] UNDP, 'Report on development cooperation, 1985', Harare, November 1986.

The above group of some 40 education agreements only includes those negotiated with the central government, and within that, only those falling within the formal education sector. Beyond these would be significant numbers of training projects negotiated with other ministries, such as Labour, Manpower, Social Services etc., and there would be several times more than these negotiated between non-governmental organisations in the OECD countries and their counterparts in the developing country. Often these latter would be in the area of non-formal and adult education, including skill development and income-generating projects for groups in both urban and rural areas. In many cases, funds corning from NGOs in the industrialised world would be derived in part from the bilateral agencies through various types of co-financing arrangement.

The totality of these aided links, ties, education and training projects is large and complex for many developing countries. But surprisingly, despite this, there exists virtually no account of these education-systems-as-aided. Nor does there exist except at the very general level any detailed account of the impact of educational aid upon the recipient systems of the developing world.

This present account does not intend to provide a map of educational aid. Indeed to do it thoroughly for even one country would be a considerable undertaking, and to calculate its influence would be even more demanding. The purpose, rather, is to examine just one major strand in this whole complex of international educational relations, and that is the crucial role played by external assistance in educational research and evaluation. Agency analysis has become an increasingly dominant element in the thinking about educational development needs. Accordingly, this chapter starts with the growth of the capacity of agencies to carry out research and evaluation in the education sector. It pays attention particularly to the coordination of the various strands of agency analysis. This is contrasted with the continuing weakness in many developing countries of local education research capacity.

The range for the analysis is broadly from 1960 to 1990, and the sub-sectors selected in the original book are those that have been important to the donor community. It would have been equally possible to have examined other sub-sectors, such as early childhood education, or other cross-cutting themes like curriculum development, teacher training, or educational financing or planning. Indeed, to an extent some of these themes are captured. But it is doubtful if the message would have been very different with a different set of educational themes: that over the three development decades, from 1960-1980, the agency vision of the educational requirements for poor countries has grown in sharpness of focus, confidence and authority. A huge range of analytical work has increasingly underpinned this vision.

The Scope of Aid-related Educational Research and Evaluation

It might be thought that formal education research would not constitute a significant part of most donors' aid portfolios. And this would certainly be true if by research is meant activities derived from ear-marked research budgets for which individual scholars and institutions compete and succeed following on peer reviews of the sort associated with research councils. Very few donor agencies, except those dedicated to the pursuit of research, like Canada's International Development Research Centre (IDRC) and Sweden's SAREC (Swedish Agency for Research Cooperation with Developing Countries), have major budgets allocated to support of social science research in developing countries, and of these, IDRC has traditionally had funds specifically allocated to educational research. Other agencies may have a department or a section concerned with research, as for example does the World Bank. Others such as Britain's Overseas Development Administration (ODA) or SIDA (Swedish International Development Authority) may have a fund for educational research which is under the control of their Education Divisions. But these 'dedicated' research funds are not particularly large. In the case of the Bank's Research Committee, Bank staff members in the field of education can submit proposals which compete with proposals from all the other departments of the Bank. In the case of ODA and SIDA the funds are relatively closely linked to the work of their Education Divisions, and with ODA it is made clear that the principal beneficiary of the research is the agency itself:

> Funds are used to commission from institutions...projects that benefit the bilateral aid programme by providing fresh information that can be fed back into ODA's work.[6]

But the role of agency research is much more significant than might be suggested by the 30 or so education projects funded by the Bank's Research Committee since the early 1970s, or the smaller number of very

---

[6] ODA, *British aid to education in developing countries*, London, 1986, p.15.

much smaller research projects funded by ODA or SIDA. Such formally defined research activities are too few to justify extended investigation, though much important work has been funded through such mechanisms. But by far the largest amount of research and evaluation supported by the development assistance community is embedded in their regular activity of making educational loans and credits to large numbers of developing countries. And it is this 'embeddedness' of research and evaluation within the very large number of individual aid projects we have referred to that makes it worthy of some serious analysis.

Sector Assessments as Educational Research

Applied educational research is widely deployed at every stage of the project cycle of aid in most bilateral and multilateral agencies. It is very seldom called research, but collection, analysis and interpretation of educational data are commonplace from project development to project completion. The terminology differs from agency to agency, but the initial elaboration of a project is frequently based on consultant missions, project identification activities, or 'sector work' as it is called in some agencies. This part of the aid process is more formalised in some agencies than in others, but generally there has been a trend towards greater analytical underpinning of what may emerge as a project lasting a decade and costing millions of pounds in loans or credits. This stage of the aid cycle can typically require manpower reviews, state-of-the-art reviews on what other donors have funded in the proposed area of new activity, analysis of policy options, or sub-sector surveys of costs and financing. The products of this stage, depending on the size of the team that is involved, are often very extensive. But they are effectively invisible outside the agency that commissioned them.

This provides one of the first paradoxes of this form of educational investigation – that it often involves a good deal of high-level manpower both in the recipient country and from the donor, and it results in the collection and interpretation of significant amounts of educational data and yet the results are usually not available in the public domain. What makes this conclusion more pointed is that many of the countries involved in negotiating for aid do not have abundant research materials on education for use in university departments or in teacher training colleges. But this abundant source of analytical material on the education sector is seldom tapped or 'translated' for use by the local education research community. This is not of course to urge the publication and dissemination of all such agency feasibility reports and sector assessments – many of them contain much frank assessment of the education sector as well as financial data that might be considered sensitive. This point contrasts the scarcity of serious analytical work on education in the public domain in many developing countries with the sheer abundance of educational analysis associated with aid agency negotiations.

Educational Data in the Agencies and its Availability

It may be worth remarking, however, that a partial insight into the quality and relevance of this type of normally inaccessible data can be gained from looking at some of SIDA's Education Division Documents. This series was at one point almost unique in the agency world since many of the almost 50 documents published between 1980 and 1989 were in fact sector or sub-sector assessments of education and training for countries such as Botswana, India, Ethiopia, Sri Lanka, and Zambia with which SIDA has ongoing programmes of education support.[7] Since 1984, however, the United States Agency for International Development (USAID) has also made public the series of sector assessments on Botswana, Yemen Arab Republic, Somalia, Indonesia, Haiti and Liberia which were an integral part of its large project on Improving the Efficiency of Educational Systems. These were a little different since they were part of a large research and development project rather than the feasibility component of a regular aid package.

There would certainly seem to be a trend towards greater openness with these assessments and reviews of the education sector. Thus the Norwegian Ministry of Development Cooperation has also begun a series of Educational Reports, its first one being a lengthy report of a team from the Norwegian Agency for International Development (NORAD) which summarised 'past achievements and trends of educational policies in Zambia' and investigated 'possible fields of Norwegian assistance to primary and adult education'. The result was a published volume by Trevor Coombe and Per Lauvas: *Facilitating self-renewal in Zambian education: Report by a NORAD consultant team*.[8]

One factor which has certainly made for greater openness in these feasibility reports as well as the major interim and final evaluation missions has been a tendency for them increasingly to be carried out by

---

[7] See the Education Division Documents, SIDA, Stockholm.
[8] Trevor Coombe and Per Lauvas, *Facilitating self-renewal in Zambian education: Report by a NORAD consultant team*, Educational Reports No.1, 1984, Oslo.

teams composed of both external and internal members. The incorporation of local education officials and other experts in such teams not only involves them directly in the analysis that leads to the project proposals, but the production of a published document, even with a very small circulation, acts as a public confirmation of the educational agreements within.

This trend is also evident within agencies that currently do not make widely available the results of major review missions. The form and content of several recent ODA reviews, such as *Kenya: Second joint review of education projects* (1987) are not dissimilar to the kind of data that are routinely included in SIDA's Education Division Documents series.[9] And the same would be true of reports funded by the French Ministry of Cooperation such as *Succès de l'école au Sénégal: un pari difficile ... qui peut être gagné.*[10] It would in fact be useful for the education research and policy community to know the status of such reports in the various bilateral and multilateral agencies. But the sheer quantity and diversity of such materials are in no doubt.

For instance, SIDA's *Annual Report 1987: Education, culture and public administration* lists no fewer than 57 separate evaluation reports and studies conducted that year alone in the Education Division.[11] West Germany's Agency for Technical Cooperation (GTZ) has produced a highly comprehensive volume (of over 600 pages) detailing all the education projects of the division responsible for Education, Science and Sport: *Bildung und Wissenschaft in der Technischen Zusammenarbeit mit Entwicklungslandern* (1982). And in a section of over 50 pages are laid out all the titles of reports, reviews, occasional papers, internal documents, broken down by topic, country and sub-sector.[12] A similar document is available on all the projects from the division responsible for Vocational Training, though this does not contain a listing of evaluation reports and studies.[13]

---

[9] British Development Division in Eastern Africa, 'Kenya: second joint review of education projects, 12-23 October 1987', Nairobi, November 1987.

[10] Pierre Mondon and Claude Thelot, *Succès de l'école au Sénégal: un pari difficile ... qui peut être gagné*, Paris, 1988, draft.

[11] SIDA, *Annual report 1987: Education, culture and public administration*, Education Division, Stockholm, 1987.

[12] GTZ, *Bildung und Wissenschaft in der technischen Zusammenarbeit mit Entwicklungslandern*, Eschborn, West Germany, December 1982.

[13] GTZ, *Gewerbliche Berufsausbildung: Schwerpunkte und laufende Projekte*, Eschborn, West Germany 1986.

As agencies are mandated to assist development rather than publishing, it should not be expected that they should pay a great deal of attention actually to publishing and disseminating these materials. Even SIDA has published only a handful of the range of consultant reports and missions they have executed in the sphere of education. But an important starting point is the detailing of the extraordinary range of what is available. Beyond this, SIDA, with its long tradition of open government, has just completed the entry of all this grey material on a publicly-accessible data base. The first beneficiaries of this are clearly the staff of the agency itself, who can call up, for example, all previous reports on literacy in a particular region. But this type of information system on the agency is obviously also of value for the academic research community, for consultants, and especially for the development education lobby within the home country.

Other agencies have also been moving fast during the 1980s in entering project data into various kinds of management information systems. The assumptions lying behind these moves are the increasing need for accountability in agencies, but also a strong interest in the development of 'institutional memory' or 'corporate memory'. With the expansion and growing complexity of aid processes, and the retirement of many of the aid managers who had worked with agencies in the first two development decades, it became even more necessary to have access to the lessons of the past. The Canadian International Development Agency (CIDA) has, for instance, developed a Bilateral Information Feedback System (BIFS) which was specifically designed to offer agency staff immediate access to 'lessons learned' from bilateral projects. The scale of the exercise (which is agency-wide and not restricted to education) is worth underlining:

> BIFS is now operational, having accumulated tombstone data on 4,900 completed and operational projects approved since 1968. A documents inventory contains information on 12,000 documents, including 1,100 evaluative documents on 830 projects... As well, approximately 12,000 'lessons learned' statements from evaluation reports, or other evaluative documents, are available on about 980 projects approved since 1975.[14]

---

[14] CIDA, 'BIFS corporate memory: bilateral project evaluations', Programme Evaluation Division, Hull, Canada, July 1986, p.1.

Though few agencies have sought to rival this ambitious attempt to extract lessons from the past 20 years of development assistance, it is now commonplace to have project summary information on computerised data bases such as the MINISIS system developed by the IDRC. It is also common for the evaluation divisions or units within the agencies to be seeking ways of organising and even exchanging their formal evaluation reports with each other. Indeed agreements have been reached amongst donors which begin a process of institutional exchange of certain categories of formal project evaluations. But it must be noted that, just like the formal research projects, the formal evaluations of education carried out by the evaluation units of agencies also constitute a tiny proportion of the universe of education reports, consultancies and evaluations held by agencies. Thus in USAID for the period 1980 to 1985, there were only some eight reports published on the education sector by the agency's Programme and Policy Evaluation Division.[15] And for ODA, there appear to be 22 evaluation reports on the area of education out of the evaluation reports produced between 1971 and 1986.[16] The exchange of this type of official evaluation report will only cover a very thin layer of the existing data on education systems held in the bilateral agencies.

The richest and most comprehensive data on education and training in developing countries is held by multilateral agencies, and pre-eminently by the World Bank. Like other agencies, the bulk of the Bank's analytical work in the field of education is not concerned with the small number of projects funded by the Research Committee which we have already referred to. Rather it resides in the major tasks leading up to and including the fully-developed appraisal reports that go to the Board along with the President's report and the loan documents. Until the late 1980s, such preliminary analytical work could include mission reports on particular sectors or sub-sectors undertaken by the UNESCO/World Bank Cooperative Programme. It could also include sector or sub-sector analyses organised by the Bank, as well as very specific research tasks ordered up by the staff responsible for the project development. In addition it could encompass research studies funded in the previous Bank projects and designed to assist in the development of the subsequent projects.

---

[15] See listing in USAID, ' Aid and education: a sector report on lessons learned', A.I.D. programme evaluation report no.12, Washington, DC. January 1984.
[16] ODA, 'Reference list of available reports of evaluation and other studies and other publications about evaluation', Evaluation Department, August 1986.

To give some indication of the scope of this data base, there are well over 150 major reports on the education sectors of developing countries which have been carried out over the last 20 Years under UNESCO's Educational Financing Division for the Cooperative Programme.[17] This programme was terminated in the late 1980s, but although the quality of these reports has been inevitably uneven, there have been some excellent studies carried out through this mechanism. The bulk of all such material is not in the public domain however. The same is true of a great deal of the sector work carried out by the Bank itself. Again, many of the products that emerge from sector work are major studies of basic education, higher education or of the education sector as a whole. They have been produced by teams of experts both inside and outside of the Bank, but their status is usually restricted. Examples of titles of such documents are:

- 'Education sector policy review – Mauritius' (1985)
- 'Education sector memorandum – Rwanda' (1985)
- 'Education and training study – Morocco' (1983)
- 'Sector survey of science education – Korea' (1982)
- 'The costs of higher education sub-sector study – Sudan' (1977)
- 'Pakistan: education sector strategy review' (May 1988).[18]

Given the amount of relatively rigorous, if sometimes controversial, analysis in such sector reports, as well as in the introductory sections of appraisal reports themselves, it is not being argued that there should be a policy of unrestricted access to this documentation. Rather, there are whole sections of sector surveys that could be extracted into a working paper format at very little cost, in time, to the Bank. Some indication of the usefulness of material drawn from such sector work may be seen in the two large volumes of Occasional Papers produced by the Educational Financing Division of UNESCO some ten years back. These useful sets of materials had 'their origin in practical problems or theoretical issues arising during the course of missions carried out by the staff of the Division of Educational Financing to assist governments in the identification and preparation of projects for external financing by IBRD/IDA', *Educational development: some practical issues* (1975 and 1976).[19]

---

[17] UNESCO, Educational Financing Division, 'List of reports on national systems of education prepared under the UNESCO/World Bank Cooperative Programme', Paris, September 1986.
[18] World Bank, project data base.
[19] UNESCO, Educational Financing Division, *Educational development: some practical issues* , Occasional Papers no.1 and 2, Paris, 1975, 1976.

Educational Policy Development as Research

It may appear somewhat churlish to suggest that an agency like the Bank consider giving greater attention to the dissemination of its crucial analytical work at the field level. It could be argued that the Bank has revolutionised its public relations over the past two decades, and now gives serious thought to publicising its formal research findings as well as its syntheses of policy. Indeed the Bank's commitment to educational research and policy studies has grown from a few items that could be counted on the fingers of one hand in the early 1970s to a bibliography of over 150 pages in 1987. Its policy papers on education, such as the *Education sector policy paper* of 1980, and *Education in Sub-Saharan Africa* of 1988, were very vigorously disseminated amongst senior policy-makers and leaders of educational thought. And the same is certain to be true of their policy papers on *Primary education* (1990), and on *Vocational and technical education and training* in 1991.

It is not suggested that such products are necessarily marketed against the wishes of their potential recipients. All the evidence would indicate the opposite: that the data available in these reports and the clarity and confidence with which they are interpreted contrasts with the tremendous scarcity of good national analyses of educational problems and issues in many of the poorer countries of the world. Scholars and teachers of higher degree students in developing countries, as well as their counterparts in centres of expertise on the Third World in OECD countries, are anxious to acquire copies of such Bank policy papers, and it is not uncommon for this material to be treated almost as a set text for courses on international development education.

It is precisely because Bank policy papers have so successfully managed to determine the nature of the debates about education in the developing world that they need to be considered also in this present account. Such policy papers are increasingly infused with the research results from the Bank's policy research, as well as from the field experiences and sector work that we have been discussing. Hence this research base for Bank policy is a legitimate and significant field of study. And this is more so today when many of the poorer countries of the world are in some ways more dependent on external assistance than they were at the time of Independence 20 and more years ago. Strapped by external debt and the conditionalities of structural adjustment agreements, countries are finding that donors are increasingly concerned with the shape, direction, and financing of their educational systems. Donor policies of the late 1980s and early 1990s seem very far removed from Eric Ashby's determination, in outlining the scheme for investing in Nigeria's universities in 1960, that 'our proposals remain massive, expensive and unconventional'.[20] The late 1980s' round of discussions between the World Bank and the universities of Africa was organised around a very different agenda – of constraint, cost-cutting, and accountability.[21]

The Bank increasingly has the capacity to draw into its policy papers an enormous range of experience, including that of other multilaterals such as ILO (International Labour Organization), and UNESCO, as well as policy work done by the bilaterals. Perhaps the pre-eminent example of this is the policy paper on *Vocational and technical education and training* which became available in 1991. Following the example of the Bank, several of the other agencies in the late 1980s developed major education policy documents to guide their negotiations over aid. For instance, both the African Development Bank (AfDB) and the Asian Development Bank (ADB) produced policy papers in this period, the one appearing in 1986 as *Education sector policy paper* and the other in 1988 under the title: *Education and development in Asia and the Pacific*. [22]

The bilateral donors also have been gearing up to produce more professional accounts of their activity in support of education and training. They have always had small booklets describing the scope of their aid, but the indications are that several of them are now moving to develop more analytical accounts of their funding rationales. And in the process, they will inevitably have to draw on their improved 'institutional memories' as well as on field lessons gathered from project implementation and evaluation. USAID produced an *A.I.D. policy paper: basic education and technical training* in 1982. [23] Britain's ODA produced an updated version of its guidelines on *British aid to education in developing countries* in 1986, and then issued its first-ever glossy, illustrated education policy in 1990, under the title *Into the nineties: An education policy*

---

[20] Nigeria, Federal Ministry of Education, *The report of the commission on post-school certificate and higher education in Nigeria*, Lagos, 1960, p.3.

[21] World Bank, ' Nigeria – cost and financing of universities', Washington, November 1987. See Kenneth King, 'The challenge of education for all to higher education in Eastern Africa', Royal African Society one day conference on 'African universities in the 1990s', 9 Nov. 1990.

[22] Asian Development Bank, *Education and development in Asia and the Pacific*, Manila, 1988. For a comment on this, see Mark Bray in *'NORRAG News 5'*, University of Stockholm, November 1988, Also, African Development Bank, *Education sector policy paper*, January 1986, no place of publication; presumably Abidjan.

[23] USAID, *A.I.D. policy paper: basic education and technical training*, USAID, Washington, DC. December 1982.

for British aid. Canadian CIDA had an 'education and training sector issues paper' in draft in 1990 also. Meanwhile in Holland, the Centre for the Study of Education in Developing Societies (CESO) was deeply involved in coordinating an 'Education programming study' which was to lay out new parameters for educational cooperation in the 1990s. By 1989, the first volume, which focused on the Dutch resources of personnel and institutions available for international cooperation in education, had appeared as 'Inventory of Dutch capacity'.[24]

But among the bilaterals, CIDA has probably gone the furthest in what might be termed the professionalisation of support to human resource development. Beyond the sector issues paper in the sphere of education, it has been engaged for four years in articulating a human resource development rationale that would be agency-wide, recognising with most other donors that an enormous amount of project-related education and training goes on outside the field of education narrowly defined. Over this period CIDA has produced a series of major analyses of 'human resource development programming' in the agency, with the ultimate intention of having a policy guideline to inform all its work in 'formal, non-formal and informal education' as well as all the following developmental activities:

- training: task-oriented skills directly related to employment
- research: generation of new ideas and techniques, and their evaluation
- institutional development: structures and processes for the organisation and management of development
- social communications: changing attitudes and mobilising community efforts towards development.

This human resource development analysis has been solidly located within Canada's published policy on international development assistance, *Sharing our future* (1987).[25]

---

[24] ODA, *British aid to education*, op. cit. See also ODA, *Into the nineties: An education policy for British aid*, London, 1990. CIDA, Professional Services Branch, 'Education and training sector issues paper', Dec. 1989 (draft); CESO, 'Programming study. Report 1. Inventory of Dutch capacity', CESO, The Hague, November 1989; to be published 1990.

[25] CIDA, 'CIDA's programming in human resource development', brief for presentation to the standing committee on external affairs and international trade, Hull, 2 Dec. 1986. CIDA, Evaluation Division, 'Evaluation assessment of human resource development in CIDA: part 1, profiles', Hull, March 1984. These should be seen within context of CIDA, 'Canadian International Development Assistance: to benefit a better world' (Min. of Supply and Services, 1987); and CIDA, *Sharing our future: Canadian international development assistance*, Hull, 1987.

Agency Seminars and Expert Meetings as Educational Research

Thus far we have pointed to several elements in the project cycle as producing serious analytical work, and we have also suggested that the policy development process in agencies increasingly seeks to draw on a knowledge base informed by the systematisation of past experience. Apart from these, one of the most common vehicles for the production and synthesis of research information on developing country education issues is the agency-funded expert meeting. These are in one sense highly academic meetings, although their focus is more on 'applied', policy research than on more 'basic' research. They differ fundamentally from regular academic meetings by being paid for entirely by the sponsor, in most cases, and by their being invitational. There is nothing particularly sinister about either of these characteristics. What should be noted, however, is that they play a very crucial role in the policy development process. But it is a role that is not particularly well known or particularly visible to interested members of the academic or policy community in those countries for which the policies are intended.

The argument is not about making all such meetings open, any more than it was suggested that all agency sector work should be in the public domain. Rather, such meetings need to be analysed for their capacity to determine the agenda for research, and for educational debate on the problems of education in developing countries. Agencies have the capacity, through their power to commission position papers, state of the art reviews and other documentation, to draw on some of the best talent both in the industrialised world and in the developing countries. Indeed an agency contract to prepare a paper for an expert meeting is an offer that is difficult to refuse, especially for scholars on university salaries in developing countries. The foreign exchange implications of such an invitation are overwhelming in countries where this commodity is normally unobtainable. And the same argument can be made for many academics in the industrialised world, for whom university salaries have not kept pace with inflation.

The number and variety of these agency-funded expert meetings is prodigious. Some indication of this may be gained by looking at the 40 to 50 meetings referred to in the late 1980s' editions of the journal, *NORRAG News* every six months, but these listings constitute just the tip of the iceberg.[26] There is an immense agency activity in expert meetings, and UNESCO alone would be responsible for a very great number in any one year. However, not all meetings are equally influential in directing educational policy or research down new avenues. In the original chapters we have pointed to key meetings that have developed new interests in literacy, basic education, the informal sector and many other themes. The ingredients of such events differ a good deal from one sponsoring agency to another, but the mechanisms often include the presentation of a small number of papers directed to particular policy issues and options. There may also, depending on the nature of the agency, be country papers that have been targeted on the particular agenda of the meeting. And then there is a synthesis paper at the conclusion of the meeting, which may seek to lay out the areas of agreement. An example at a relatively high level may be suggestive, and it is taken from 1988.

The rekindling of the agency priority towards basic education and literacy for all can be traced to events earlier than 1987, but an important staging post to consensus-building was the 'Educational consultation meeting' organised by UNICEF on 15-17 February 1988 in New York. Out of the total participation of 31, some 26 were from agencies, and three from developing countries. A next stage was the UNICEF-UNESCO-World Bank joint task force meeting of 8-9 September 1988 on 'Moving towards basic education for all', by which time it had already been concluded at the highest level in these three agencies (and shortly also by UNDP) that the time was ripe for a world conference on Basic Education for All. This eventually took place in March 1990.[27]

Obviously to achieve an inter-agency agreement for a world conference to which ministers of education would be invited from all developing countries requires more than a few task force consultations. It demands the agreement of the heads of agencies, and their active support of such an initiative. This happens to have been the case with this particular momentum towards basic education for all. But the issue of inter-agency actions is a sufficiently important element in the whole

---

[26] See listing of meetings in *NORRAG News*, 1986-1990, Education Department, University of Edinburgh. Also at www.norrag.org.

[27] UNICEF, 'Moving towards basic education for all', report of an educational consultation meeting, 15-17 February 1988, UNICEF-UNESCO-World Bank joint task force meeting, Paris, 8-9 September 1988. See also *NORRAG News* Nos. 7 and 8' which analyse in detail the build-up to this world conference. See also www.norrag.org.

complex of international educational relations that it deserves to be specially underlined.

The Inter-agency Dimension of Aid to Education:
The Search for Consensus

So far we have focused largely on the individual agency and the growth of its institutional capacity to analyse education in the Third World. But the inter-agency dimension of educational aid is also a thread that needs to be picked out. It has a potential importance for our topic of research and evaluation that could be considered either an advantage or a disadvantage. If, for instance, as a result of inter-agency consensus, most agencies determine that more aid for the poorest, and for basic and non-formal education, is the top priority, then this may well be a good thing from the point of view of emphasising the quantity and quality of the basic cycle of education. On the other hand, such a consensus may imply that recipient countries may suddenly find it hard to secure agency attention in support for higher education. In the original chapters we point to occasions where the agencies almost appear to have united around a particular option, such as non-formal education.

One of the mechanisms for seeking to direct the attention of many agencies to particular tasks has been the Bellagio education meetings, named after the location of the Rockefeller conference centre in Italy where the heads of many of the development assistance agencies convened several times in the early 1970s.

The search for consensus and for investment priorities in education for the developing world goes back to the hope that concentrated attention might pay off for this field as it had for population and agriculture, with their international consultative committees. It was because of this parallel with the pioneer work on agriculture and population the Rockefeller and Ford Foundations took the initiative in convening these agency meetings on education policies and priorities. This is not to say that there was a deliberate search for an educational technology that might do the equivalent of growing two ears of corn where one grew before, but there was a strong fascination with low-cost innovations, the exchange of educational information, and with the possibility that donor coordination could significantly assist with the state of education in the Third World.

It was widely felt that as countries entered the second development decade, the question of the relationship between education and development was no longer as straightforward as agencies and national governments had thought it in the 1960s. It should be no surprise that the first of the major reports of these inter-agency meetings should be entitled: *Education and development reconsidered: the Bellagio conference papers* (1974). [28] These papers constitute a very useful state of the art of educational assistance in the early 1970s, and they provide an important starting point for any serious student of agency cooperation. At this point there were 15 agencies involved in these activities, with the only bilaterals being Canada, France, Japan, Sweden, United Kingdom and the United States. Our principal interest in their deliberations, however, concerns their conceptualisation of the role of research.

These early Bellagio papers did not emerge with a series of strong recommendations about what areas of research should receive coordinated agency attention. Nevertheless, one of the themes that did stand out as an obvious candidate for agency attention was the need for greater information exchange about educational innovations and reforms that were already in existence. One of the first direct outcomes of inter-agency cooperation was the view that information was simply not reaching educational decision-makers. Accordingly, an International Educational Reporting Service (IERS) was set up within the International Bureau of Education in Geneva in 1975, supported by seven of the Bellagio donors: CIDA, SIDA, ODA, USAID, IDRC, Ford, and UNICEF. It built on an existing series of experiments and innovations in education, but gave them a much more Third World perspective.

Over the following four years, the series produced some 40 separate titles, describing innovative projects, most of them in the developing world. The impression gained from the series, which was wide-ranging, was that somehow the knowledge about these fascinating projects would have a direct impact on the hard-pressed policy-maker. With the benefit of hindsight, this appears rather an optimistic undertaking:

> The principal aim of this service is to provide information about innovations which have a high relevance to developing countries. It will be designed to serve educational leaders in such countries, particularly those who decide policies and plan and administer education systems, *so that they may be aware of the various possibilities*

---

[28] F. Champion Ward (ed.), *Education and development reconsidered: The Bellagio conference papers*, Praeger, New York, 1974.

open to them. Thus the IERS is seen as one instrument for helping in the renovation of national systems of education.[29]

The published examples darted from radio study groups in Tanzania, to the Caribbean mathematics project, to vocational training in Venezuela, to educational innovations in Switzerland. It was all a far cry from the very targeted reforms which policy-makers would be presented with in the late 1980s, and it is doubtful if this early coordinated initiative had much influence at all upon the policy community.

This was not the only area that the donors pursued as a consequence of the Bellagio meetings. They also supported research on the economics of education amongst a network of centres in Latin America, and they encouraged IDRC (one of the newest agencies at that time, and one that was entirely dedicated to developmental research) to pursue a mechanism for synthesising existing research. In its origins this latter donor initiative was a good deal more directive than the IERS. The backdrop to the IDRC task was not providing interesting examples to policy-makers, but it was sharply defined as the 'problem of providing more relevant education more efficiently to larger numbers of people despite resource constraints'.[30] It was hoped that focused research reviews and policy advice could present to both the donors and national governments cost-effective ways of solving these constraints. IDRC's assumption was that the solutions might very well already be present in developing countries. What was needed was a very thorough presentation through state of the art reviews of what was already known, but needed disseminating:

> Before recommending additional investment either for further research or action programmes, it would seem important to learn what we can from available information. For this to be done systematically, we would recommend some form of research coordination.[31]

As a way of implementing this search strategy for what might already be worth acting upon, IDRC set up, on the model of other international advisory committees (e.g. for population), a Research Review and Advisory Group (RRAG). The rationale for the work of the group, and the

---

[29] International Bureau of Education, Geneva; series on 'Experiments and innovations in education', note on International Educational Reporting Service, appended to each volume.
[30] IDRC, *Education research priorities: a collective view*, Ottawa, 1976, p.4.
[31] Ibid. p.12.

six areas where it might focus its initial attention, were set out in *Education research priorities: A collective view* (1976). [32] In the spirit of donor cooperation, Ford provided a coordinator for the group in Robert Myers, and there was further donor involvement from the World Bank, and IIEP. Most of the remaining group members came from developing countries. The expectation was that they would move rapidly to commission state of the art reviews which would effectively sort out the enormous amount of research material already available. A possible model was one of the first World Bank reviews that had just appeared: 'The determinants of school achievement in developing countries'.[33]

This is not the place to trace the history of RRAG from its origins in the Bellagio forum to its regional continuation in the 1990s, but it is worth remarking that though it outlasted IERS, it did not fulfil the ambition of its founders in 'prioritising' research, and sorting out in a series of perhaps 20 key state of the art reviews what was the state of policy-related research. Instead, it did just one really major cross-regional review of teacher effectiveness research before concluding that it should focus instead on the state of the research environment for education in developing countries. In other words, it became more interested in the process of education research rather than a set of policy-oriented products, a priority captured importantly in *Educational research environments in the developing world.*[34]

The Bellagio forum has continued as a research-related meeting of those responsible for education in the bilateral and multilateral donors, but from the mid 1970s it no longer sought jointly to fund research initiatives. Instead it increasingly went down the road of different agencies funding reviews on coordinated themes, and bringing them for discussion and information to the others. In other words the forum (which changed its name to the International Working Group on Education [IWGE]) concentrated on a process of informing itself on major trends in the donor analysis of education. This was the spirit of its 1978 meeting on 'Literacy research in developing countries' as well as its

---

[32] Ibid.

[33] Ibid. p.16.

[34] Sheldon Shaeffer and John Nkinyangi (eds.), *Educational research environments in the developing world*, IDRC, Ottawa, 1983. See Beatrice Avalos and Wadi Haddad, *A review of teacher effectiveness research in Africa, India, Latin America, Middle East, Malaysia, Philippines, and Thailand: Synthesis of results*, Ottawa, 1981. On RRAG in 1990, see report of RRAG Roundtable at World Conference on Education for All, in *'NORRAG News 8'*, June 1990. See norrag.org.

conference on *Financing educational development* in 1981, both of whose proceedings were published.[35]

During the 1980s IWGE met twice, in 1984 and 1988, both meetings in the International Institute for Educational Planning (IIEP). The exclusiveness of the earlier forums has disappeared and they now are open to all the bilateral and multilateral agencies who wish to attend. No less than 37 such agencies were invited to the 1988 meeting, and the agenda on both these meetings has been basic education. Their function of allowing the donor community to communicate with itself about major new agency initiatives also continues, and in the 1988 meeting a primary purpose of the seminar was to give the rest of the donor community an early warning of the momentum towards Basic Education for All, to which we have already referred. The documentation for the 1988 meeting demonstrated the continuing tradition of agencies sharing their research reviews on a central theme. Indeed two of these reviews were actually commissioned as part of the IWGE process:

- Basic education for all (UNICEF)
- Effectiveness and efficiency of primary education (World Bank)
- Indicators of educational effectiveness and efficiency (USAID)
- Adult literacy in the Third World countries: a review of objectives and strategies (SIDA).[36]

Summarising the significance of the Bellagio-IWGE meetings and reviews from our particular perspective of donor-aided research, it is clear that though they have sought to focus agency attention on particular themes, and have always had an important concern with the reporting of research on education, they cannot be characterised as a multinational consortium that actually prioritises donor activities in the Third World. The November 1988 meeting did seek to do some consensus-building amongst the agencies for coordinated action on basic education for all. But this did not constitute a fixing of education priorities for the poorer countries. Although the whole mechanism sounds rather like a donors' club, these agency meetings have always had a small number of Third

[35] IDRC, *Financing educational development*, Ottawa, 1982. DSE, 'The dissemination of educational research results: report of the sixth follow-up meeting to the Bellagio conference on Education and Development, 9-12 February 1981, Berlin', Bonn, 1981. DSE, 'Literacy research in developing countries: report of the Bellagio IV workshop on educational research with special reference to research on literacy', Bonn, 1978.
[36] Gabriel Carron, note in *NORRAG News 5*, Stockholm, November 1988.

World representatives present 'in order to make sure that the recipients' point of view is being duly expressed'.

Before leaving this brief discussion of donor coordination in exchange of information, and especially of relevant research, the existence of a European Aid Donors' conference should also be noted. This development, initiated by the ODA in 1986, has already led to a first meeting in London, a second in Dublin in 1987, a third in the Hague in 1989, and a fourth in Berlin in 1990. One of the more interesting developments from the viewpoint of this present account is that the donors agreed to build up joint inventories of their aid in education to different countries. This 'Survey of aid to education' across the European donor community would appear to have been overtaken by a much larger initiative of the World Bank.

As a direct result of the Bank's policy paper on *Education in Sub-Saharan Africa* (1988), an elaborate process of donor collaboration was initiated through a Task Force of Donors to African Education. This had various subject panels on topics like higher education, vocational education, teacher training, and textbooks, but in terms of the systematisation of donor activity in education, one of the more interesting developments has been the emergence of the 'Donors to African Education Information System'. Already by mid 1990, this had accumulated some 700 entries of donor projects, and was expected to grow rapidly. The results of this donor project data base were not going to be restricted to the aid community, but it was planned that on a country by country basis, they would be made available to African ministers of education. From the viewpoint of research it would be possible also to access those projects which had significant 'research and studies' components.[37]

Summary on the Growth of Institutional Capacity within the Donor Community

In the first part of this chapter we have looked at just a few of the indications of the range and variety of analytical work on education for which the agencies are responsible. The trends we have remarked upon include the development of institutional memory within agencies, the

---

[37] ODA, 'Report on the European aid donors' conference, 12-13 May 1986, organised by the Overseas Development Administration, London'. HEDCO, 'Report on the conference of European donors to education, 10-11th September 1987'. On the Donors to African Education, see the 'Donors to African Education Information System (DIS): Users Guide', World Bank, 1990.

exchange of education-related project and evaluation data, and the sharing of review tasks in particular fields, such as literacy, basic education, or financing of education. We have noted a trend towards greater openness and accountability within agencies, and an increasing readiness to disseminate particular products that synthesise current policy.

One of the reasons for this attention to improving the research base for educational aid, as well as for the commissioning of state of the art reviews by several agencies, is that many of the education donors have been, and in some cases continue to be, active in research administration as well as, occasionally, in its execution. This notion of the donor-as-researcher is one that is perhaps most obvious in certain sections of the World Bank, where the pursuit of policy research is part of the job. This is also the case with the IIEP. But even in many agencies where research is not directly expected of the position, it is plain that the much older Ford and Rockefeller Foundation tradition of appointing officers with significant research experience has spread gradually through the agency world. Not a small part of the literature concerning education research strategies, capacity-building, state of the art reviews of key themes as well as major analytical work is written by education advisors and programme directors in the agencies themselves. The list is extensive but it would include, apart from the many World Bank and IIEP staff, names such as the following who at some point worked in the related agencies: Robert Myers (Ford), David Court (Rockefeller), Gary Theisen and Frank Method (USAID), Richard Jolly (UNICEF), Ingemar Gustafsson (SIDA), Sheldon Shaeffer (IDRC), Wolfgang Kuper and Herbert Bergmann (GTZ), Udo Bude and Wolfgang Gmelin (DSE), Peter Williams (Commonwealth Secretariat), and Fred Fluitman (ILO), to mention only a few of those who have been associated with some substantial piece of analytical work during the 1980s. Many of the others have been active in research prior to joining the agency and they continue an active concern with research direction in their new positions.

In concluding this section, however, we return to our earlier concern with the immense increase of educational data on the Third World that is now available to the donor community. One consequence of the growth in analytical capacity is a greater certainty about educational options for different kinds of developing countries. The ability to synthesise not only the agency's own learning experience in particular fields but also what has been learnt elsewhere across the agency world is now qualitatively different to what was possible when the Bellagio donors first began meeting in the early 1970s. There are occasions in the original chapters to point to particular policy issues in such fields as technical and vocational education and training, or quality in primary education, where the global synthesis of all 'relevant' information is decidedly impressive, but is in glaring contrast with the still very fragile base of policy information in the recipient countries. The situation in which more and more knowledge is acquired in the North about the education sectors of so many developing countries does mean that a fundamental imbalance is being built up between the information-rich North and the information-poor South, which has very long-term implications for research and training of academics and policy-makers from developing countries. This point was made at an ODA-funded meeting on 'Education priorities and aid responses in Sub-Saharan Africa' in 1984, itself a very good example of the invitational agency meetings we have been discussing:

> Sub-sector support to literacy by one donor or to the university by another, if extended over a ten-year period, produces a situation in which the institutional memory on literacy or university develop-ment in Africa may be more detailed in one of the OECD countries than in Africa itself. Hence the colonial tradition of having to study African education in London, Paris or Lisbon is to a limited extent continued through dependence on the data bases of the foundations, the multilaterals and the bilaterals, and of the very large numbers of Northern consultants who have assisted at various stages of the feasibility study, appraisal or evaluation of agency projects.[38]

The Development of Institutional Research Capacity in the South

A lot of what we have been discussing thus far relates to what might be termed the 'professionalisation of educational development', or the improvement of the capacity in the donor community to develop sound projects, better justified, more competently assessed and evaluated, and better disseminated. The obvious question must be 'To what extent has there been a parallel development of capacity to analyse education and training in the developing world?' Or to use the terminology of the quotation from the International Cooperation Administration with which

---

[38] Kenneth King, 'Problems and prospects of aid to education in sub-Saharan Africa', in Hugh Hawes and Trevor Coombe (eds.), *Education priorities and aid responses in Sub-Saharan Africa*, ODA, HMSO, London, 1986, p.117.

this chapter started: 'To what extent are agencies still doing the thinking for a country, rather than encouraging the analysis and appraisal of education objectives in the country itself?'

This is a vast topic and it will only be possible in a few pages to give some suggestions about tendencies, and to point to some examples of relevant work on this area. I start, however, with one or two assertions about the research environment in many developing countries at the very end of the 1980s.

1. In many of the poorer countries of the world, the local capacity confidently to analyse their own educational priorities, and to pursue coherent programmes of research is not stronger than it was in the early 1970s.

2. This local analytical capacity is inseparable from the existence of strong research centres based in universities (or in private institutions) and from strong education planning cells in central and local government. There is unfortunately little evidence for many of the poorer countries of the world that the essential skills for the evaluation and management of increasingly complex education systems are in place. Indeed, for many countries it could be maintained that with instability at the national level, and low morale and flight of talent in many centres of higher education, this critical capacity is actually less apparent now than before. Very few developing countries have the critical mass of expertise available to pursue the range of research tasks necessary in education.

3. The infrastructure of educational research in developing countries in the form of research associations, annual locally funded conferences, healthy journals, and research funds, as well as commissioned work to local researchers from governments, does not seem to be widely in place.

4. In not a few countries, what little educational research is actually conducted is today more dependent on external funding than it was in the 1970s, when universities still had significant research budgets. This agency research is naturally oriented to the information and evaluation needs of the development assistance communities. There are today as few sources of non-project-related research funding in developing countries as there were in the 1970s. Indeed, these sources may actually be fewer.

5. It is now extremely rare for scholars and investigators in many developing countries to be able to continue with a major research topic for an extended period of time. Core funding to allow dedication to policy research on particular themes for several years has been drying up.

6. Where university salaries (traditionally intended to support both research and teaching) only effectively cover the living costs of a few months in the year, there is little alternative to research being regarded as a luxury, when it cannot be seen as a source of income.

The situation is possibly exaggerated for some countries, and in other countries it may actually be more severe. But it does seem likely that Frank Method (then of the Ford Foundation) described an environment in the very early 1970s – at Bellagio – which has not changed much over the following two decades in the direction he had hoped:

> There is much more that can be done to strengthen local research and local educational leadership, particularly in strengthening local research institutions and local or regional professional organisations, but there seems to be a clear and growing pattern of support for such efforts. Perhaps the main criticisms are that despite the growing support for local efforts, there are too few examples as yet of effective partnership or collaborative effort. Cooperation often means the assistance of expert teams ('expert' being nearly always synonymous with 'expatriate'), and assistance agencies themselves have been slow in making use of local expertise and research done in local institutions.[39]

Today it seems far from clear that there is a growing support for the development of local educational research capacity, either from government or from the international community. At the time that Method wrote, the Ford Foundation was in the midst of a massive, long-term project to strengthen education research centres in Latin America, and parts of Asia, and a little later also in Africa. Ford's international (education) division, when at full strength, was substantial, and the international meetings of these education staff could well give the

---

[39] Frank Method, 'National research and development capabilities in education', in F.C. Ward (ed.), *Education and development reconsidered*, p.143. For an analysis of the expatriate expert, see Gerry Fry and Clarence Thurber, *The international education of the development consultant*, Pergamon, Oxford, 1989.

impression that the strengthening of both national and private research centres in education would be on Ford's agenda for a long time to come. As it was, however, the 1979 international division education conference of Ford was really the last, and the staff dispersed to other organisations. Unfortunately, the long-expected historical account of the Ford Foundation by Frank Sutton did not materialise; hence we lack the detailed scholarly attention to the development and legacy of what was probably the largest single long-term programme of support to education research in the developing world. But any such history would probably judge that there was left a lasting impression upon local research capacity in countries like Brazil, Thailand, Indonesia, Chile, Argentina, Mexico and a few others, where the Foundation had a significant presence for several years, but that in Africa Ford in effect withdrew from this form of institution building just a short time after it had started.[40]

In one sense the obvious successor to Ford was the IDRC, whose educational research funding diversified rapidly from the late 1970s and early 1980s. And it was often directed to centres which Ford had assisted with major funding in the earlier years. The funds dedicated to the support of education research within the Third World grew to over two million dollars (Canadian) in the early 1980s. Though much smaller in real terms than Ford's commitment to education overall, IDRC funds played a crucial role in maintaining educational research activity in several situations. This was true of education research in the southern cone of Latin America where IDRC supported education and other social science research throughout periods of great political oppression for national scholars. But the greatest challenge lay in Africa where strong institutions had not really got underway before the larger macro-economic situation became really severe.

IDRC strategy in Africa consisted largely of seeking to hold younger researchers in universities, through small grant schemes of various sorts. And latterly, it has sought directly to address the research infrastructure

---

[40] For a conspectus of Ford's education research activities, see the papers of the International Division Education Conference, 2-4 October 1979, Ford, New York, 1979, mimeo. On Ford's earlier activity in Latin America, see Raj Rao and Kalman Silvert, 'Ford Foundation assistance to Latin American education in the seventies', Ford, New York, 1972. Ford and IDRC, 'Anglophone West African educational research conference, Freetown, Sierra Leone, 7-11 June 1976', University of Sierra Leone, 1976, mimeo. See also, Robert Myers, *Connecting worlds: a survey of developments in educational research*, IDRC, Ottawa, 1981. Also, Melvin Fox, 'Language and development: a retrospective survey of Ford Foundation language projects, 1952-1974 ', Ford, New York, 1975. On the institutional history of the Ford Foundation and Frank Sutton, I am indebted to David Court for information.

through grants to encourage the development of educational research associations, research reviews, and research networking. It has also supported a small number of active researchers within their institutions over a longer period of time. But IDRC's own studies, along with RRAG, on the *Educational research environments in the developing world* (1983) would suggest that without a healthy university infrastructure on which the research superstructure can depend, some of the external support will really be a holding operation.[41] It may hold a small number of key individuals and centres in the business of research until a time when the larger system of national incentives for teaching and research may improve.

But the notion that was so prevalent amongst development agencies in the 1960s and early 1970s – that institutions could be rapidly created, set on the 'right' road, and the donors could withdraw – has been confounded in the 1980s. Foreign debt, lack of foreign exchange, and the impact of structural adjustment measures have all sapped the strength of institutes founded in the post-independence period. Some donors now feel that it is unlikely that they will be able in the foreseeable future to withdraw from their support to certain countries in Africa – and elsewhere. And there is certainly a research counterpart to that feeling. A number of institutions such as the African Curriculum Organisation and the Science Education Programme for Africa remained as dependent (perhaps more dependent) on external funding at the end of the 1970s and in the early 1980s as they had been when they were founded. And the same might be said of institutions such as Centre de Recherche Interdisciplinaire pour le Développement de l'Éducation (CRIDE) founded with Rockefeller aid in Kisangani, on the bend of the Congo River, in the late 1970s.

At the beginning of the 1990s some regional and continental organisations in Africa in the sphere of education were as fragile financially as they had ever been, but it is encouraging to note that the Ford and Rockefeller Foundations have begun in 1990 a process of rethinking and intensifying their support to higher education, and the World Bank also has decided that it will need to give a great deal more attention to the building of **local** education research capacity if the policy work it has invested in so thoroughly is to bear fruit.[42]

---

[41] IDRC, *Educational research environments*, op.cit.
[42] Ford and Rockefeller Foundations funded a ' Consultation on higher education in Africa' in late 1990, conducted by Trevor Coombe. This was intended precisely to indicate strategies for

The Relative Invisibility of Third World Education Research

We have already discussed the invisibility and inaccessibility of much of the analytical work undertaken by the agencies, even though the few general policy documents (e.g. of the Bank) are very widely disseminated, especially in the North. It should not be surprising to hear that the same is true for a good deal of the research that continues to be done all over the Third World. This is not to say that good work is locally invisible, provided there are funds to get the support to publish it at all. But a good piece of analysis produced in a limited edition on a Gestetner machine in a university in one country of Africa is not necessarily known about in the next-door country, let alone in the world of agency reviews of the 'available' research literature. It is precisely because of this low profile of much education research production that it made such very good sense for IDRC's *Teacher effectiveness review* to set out deliberately to discover what was really available internationally. Like Method's comment on 'expert', it must be admitted that the term 'international' is too frequently used to mean what is available in the North. Instead, it should be acknowledged that there is a good deal currently termed 'international' that is effectively parochial, and a good deal that is currently only locally visible in a particular country or region that may deserve a much wider audience.

None of this discussion about relative visibility and internationality would matter very much in a situation of symmetrical academic relations. Doubtless much Dutch research is invisible to Norwegian academics and vice versa. The invisibility of local educational analysis and local research priorities becomes, however, much more critical in a fundamentally asymmetrical relationship, such as many poorer developing countries experience in comparing local research with research on their countries conducted by external agencies. In these environments, local researchers, whose own work is effectively invisible, may have little or no impact upon the debates about education priorities conducted by the various agencies assisting education in these countries.

To such researchers, many of the documents that have been referred to in this chapter are quite unknown. Policy papers by the Bank on Sub-Saharan Africa, or new work by the ILO on training in the informal sector, or research on the Social Dimensions of Adjustment, which are

---

strengthening of African universities once more. See also Birger Fredriksen, 'Increased foreign aid for primary education: the challenge for donors', paper to International Working Group on Education (IWGE), June 1990.

widely known about in the North, may be virtually invisible in the very countries they refer to, and when not invisible, unobtainable. Often it is only through participation in one of the agency meetings that we have referred to that this agency-funded policy research becomes visible to local researchers.

But the issue is not just visibility and access. It is also a question of the extent to which the local research and policy community can effectively participate in and affect the development of educational policies in their own regions. So much of the development of key policies for education appears to take place outside these regions that there can be little immediate expectation of changing the situation. Even the opportunity to discuss such policy papers as the Bank's *Education in Sub-Saharan Africa* is sometimes dependent on donors paying for researchers to attend meetings.

There are some indications in the original chapters that donors such as the World Bank and the USAID have acknowledged that policy change, to be effective, has to grow out of the participation of local people in the formulation of policy options. However evident a particular strategy such as double-shift or multi-grade teaching may be (based on research in other parts of the world), it has to be re-invented locally and adapted if it is to stick. But what is not so clear is whether the packages of options to be experimented with in the South have already been patented in the North. Or to change the metaphor, has the menu for educational reform already been chosen by the Northern agencies? And is the role of the South restricted to choosing amongst a number of tried favourites?

Making the Agency World more Visible

The primary purpose of this chapter is to afford an insight into the literature generated by the agencies. The historical approach to the various themes is intended to demonstrate how a particular idea, such as the diploma disease, non-formal education, or the search for low-cost quality, gets developed and disseminated within the agency world. The topics that have been chosen very much reflect the priorities of many donors, though it would have been possible to add to the discussion by analysing further areas such as early childhood education, or educational management. This would not have altered substantially the central themes. One of these would surely be that locally produced research (in the South) has thus far not had much impact on the development of agency policy, with the possible exception of research on adult education and literacy. 'Learning from the South' remains more of a slogan or an aspiration than a reality.

It is expected that the literature referred to will prove useful to scholars as well as to policy-makers in the South. Many of the materials quoted will not turn up in regular booksellers' catalogues, but they can be ordered from the agencies themselves or from their local representatives in developing country capitals. The discussion is also designed to be of use to agency personnel, who, despite being research-oriented, may not have the time to track down some of the fugitive literature in these chapters. The coverage of the agencies is uneven, inevitably, and it has been affected by the timing of this research. Had this been done in 1978 instead of 1988-90, the Ford Foundation and the Rockefeller Foundation would have taken up a great deal more space, and the World Bank, which was just starting, at Ford's suggestion, to pay much more attention to research, would have been much more in the shadows.

There are some major gaps in agency coverage, and here they should just be listed. They would include the growing importance of Italy in development cooperation; the expanding role of the regional banks (Inter-American Development Bank, African Development Bank and the Asian Development Bank); French Cooperation; the growth of Japanese Development Cooperation; the role of Ireland; and of course the dramatic changes in education cooperation that are likely in the former Eastern bloc countries. There are also a number of significant foundations such as the Aga Khan, and the Bernard van Leer, to mention only two whose contribution is well known.

Lastly, it is hoped that many of these sources of literature may prove valuable to the large number of developing country students who come to pursue research in the major resource centres of the North. They bring with them to their studies in the industrialised world detailed information about their own education systems, but for reasons we have mentioned, they have frequently not been exposed to the 'international' debates about education and training in which they may well discover that their own country features as a source of data. In this sense, this volume can be seen as a companion to the ODA-funded 'Bibliography of policy-related education documents in 28 selected countries in Africa, Asia and the Pacific' (1985).[43] What the title of that volume does not make

---

[43] Diana Clayton and Maggie Smales, 'Bibliography of policy-related education documents in 28 selected countries in Africa, Asia and the Pacific', University of London Institute of Education, 1985; second edition reprinted in Faculty of Education, University of Leeds.

clear is that this bibliography lists the education materials published in developing countries which are to be found in different libraries all over the UK. It is therefore in some sense a guide to a portion of Southern policy literature already in the North.

Some Pointers to the Improvement of Symmetry
There are several very obvious points that need to be restated about the improvement of symmetry between locally-conducted research and much of the research production which features in the following chapters. These are itemised here, but can only be briefly discussed.

1. As IDRC stressed in its pamphlet that led to the setting up of RRAG, more attention should be given to **existing** literature sources in the South. At the time that was written, in 1976, CIDE in Santiago had not yet started its *Resúmenes analíticos en educación,* which developed into an interactive network of centres producing abstracts on educational research across Latin America.[44] This database (Red de Información y Documentación en Educación para América Latina [REDUC]) now contains a very significant part of the research production in education in the region. In this regard it provides a model that other regions are interested to follow, as well as providing a mechanism that makes research data available across many different countries.
2. Even without a data base like REDUC, there are several major sources of educational research data in developing countries. One of the most striking is the nine-volume *Review of the state of the art of educational research: the Philippine experience* which covers the years 1973-83.[45] It is mentioned here, not because it is typical – it clearly is not – but because it gives an insight into the sheer scale of the local knowledge base. There is little doubt that other countries could greatly increase the visibility and the potential value of local research by state of the art reviews of this type. The South East Asian Research Review and Advisory Group

---

[44] For illustration of this Latin American documentation network on education, see REDUC, *Indice de resumenes analyticos sobre educación en America Latina y el Caribe*, CIDE, P.O. Box 13608, Santiago, Chile. Also REDUC newsletter from this address.
[45] PRODED/MECS/PAGE, *A review of the state of the art of educational research: the Philippine experience, vols.1-9*, PRODED, Ministry of Education, Culture and Sports, Manila, 1986. Also, S. Gopinathan and H. Dean Nielsen (eds.), *Educational research environments in Southeast Asia*, Chopmen Publishers, Singapore, 1988. See also the development of SEABAS, the South East Asian Bibliographic and Abstracting Service, linked to SEARRAG, which is based on the REDUC model.

(SEARRAG) has developed this approach in six countries of the region, through mapping the research environment and through state of the art and state of practice reviews. SIDA has also demonstrated through its support to a review of research on primary education in Tanzania just how much data is available at the local level. [46] And the IDRC-funded Education Research Network in Eastern and Southern Africa (ERNESA) has encouraged nine countries in the region to do some serious mapping of local research knowledge on particular themes. In the short term, agencies could play an important role in making such materials more visible in the North.

3. There is also scope for an updating of the kind of agency-generated data with which this chapter is concerned. One thing that should become clear in this and the original chapters is how very rapidly funding priorities change in the North, partly because of political changes in the North, and partly in reaction to the perceptions of the 'educational crisis' in the South. Keeping up with the nature and direction of these developments is notoriously difficult to do from the South, which is one reason why between 1986 and 1990 SIDA supported a network journal linking scholars and agency representatives across the North, in an attempt to access and rapidly make available agency developments that are of importance to research and policy in education in the South. The title of this journal, *NORRAG News*, underlines the connection backwards to the IDRC-sponsored Research Review and Advisory Group (RRAG) which was also mandated to improve this South-North and North-South flow of educational information.

Summary Comments on Research Capacity in the South

In conclusion, we need to underline the fact that the few items just mentioned may help to make existing research in the South better known in the region as well as in the North. But such assistance cannot improve the marginalisation of research in some countries, or its status as a luxury item in others. If the assertions we made at the beginning of this section hold some truth, then the issues are not just visibility and dissemination

---

[46] Roy Carr-Hill, 'Primary education in Tanzania; a review', Education Division Documents no.16, SIDA, Stockholm.

of existing neglected research. The very structures to support that research activity require massive attention, particularly the universities.

When the history of external support to higher education, especially in Africa, gets a much needed update upon the classic work by Ashby, *Universities: British, Indian and African* (1966), it may well be thought that the initially significant external aid to social science research, including to education, was terminated precipitously.[47] There is some evidence of a reawakening of an aid vision that sees long-term collaborative relations between industrialised and developing country universities as necessary to *Sharing our future*, as the new aid literature from CIDA terms it.[48] But many universities of industrialised countries can no longer entertain such aspirations, as the cult of cost-recovery and enterprise threatens to sweep away the obligations of an earlier age. Without the support to long-term symmetrical academic relationships from aid moneys on a very large scale, expertise in Northern universities finds itself increasingly turning to the short-term consultancy mode that has already weakened the research base in many Southern universities.

In moving now to the original chapters mapping the work that the external agencies have funded on educational research and evaluation, we should constantly bear in mind that this is only part of the picture of what is known about science education, vocational training, adult literacy, primary schooling, or higher education. The paradox is that both the local and the agency literature on the education systems of the South take little account of each other, partly because each is relatively invisible or unobtainable by the other. There is accordingly an urgent need for much more work to be funded in the South that is independent of the aid frameworks and policy-related concerns of the agencies. In the short term, and in many of the poorer countries, there will not be national bodies with financial resources available on any significant scale to fund research; hence there will be continued reliance on research and evaluation that are spin-offs from agency projects. Hopefully, however, such donor-aided projects will be able increasingly to encourage research and studies that are locally relevant and appropriate to particular contexts.

---

[47] Eric Ashby, *Universities: British, Indian, African*, Harvard University Press, Cambridge, Mass., 1966.
[48] CIDA, *Sharing our future*, op. cit.

The Limits to Symmetry in Aid Relationships

This may be a forlorn hope. After all, most of the agencies with which we are concerned in this chapter are not independent foundations dedicated to the furtherance of research. They are development agencies, using their funds in many different ways to promote their versions of Third World improvement. Almost inevitably the sheer power of the North in respect of many of the fundamental issues in the South – negotiations about debt, primary commodity prices, technology, access to Northern markets – means that the North-South dialogue is not between equals, whether it is about macro-economic policy or about schooling or health provision. It may not appear to be between such dramatically unequal partners as it did during the era of formal colonisation of the South by the North, when 'native education' was decided on by Northern missionary societies and colonial departments of education. But it is worrying to see that some of the contemporary powerlessness of the South has reawakened images of Northern sovereignty, colonisation, and Southern dependency.

Recent commentary has highlighted the 'new scrambles for Africa' by Northern non-governmental organisations (NGOs) and donor agencies. In some respect even the Northern NGOs – which are not really the subject of this chapter – can be characterised as donor agencies. In many cases their budgets, which partly come from official aid agencies, have risen dramatically during the 1980s, and the largest, such as Oxfam, have added research and evaluation departments. This new economic power, combined with the budgetary crisis in many developing countries, has given NGOs an independence of the state. But in the process, it is doubtful if relations between Southern (partner) and Northern NGOs have become more symmetrical.[49]

This fundamental imbalance between the South and the power of the North, and especially of Northern financial institutions, must be the backcloth to this and all the original chapters. Ultimately, the intellectual agenda of the North – whether of agencies or Northern research centres – is inseparable from these global power relations. The agency priorities for education need to be conceptualised within a highly uneven framework of knowledge distribution between North and South. Hans Weiler has put

---

[49] See for example Alan Fowler, 'New Scrambles for Africa: Non-governmental organisations and their donors in Kenya', March 1989, processed. See also on the imbalance between Northern and Southern NGOs, Centre of African Studies, *New challenges for NGOs: African development in the 1990s*, University of Edinburgh, December, 1990.

this larger setting succinctly, as was mentioned already in the Introduction to this chapter:

> The transnational system of knowledge production is inextricably linked to a transnational system of power, in which publishing interests, research funding, consulting firms, testing services, professional associations and development assistance agencies all form part of a powerful – if less than perfectly coordinated – centre.[50]

This macro-economic context must be borne in mind even when there is evidence of new thinking by agencies about the need to strengthen education research capacities in the South. Thus, some elements within the World Bank have concluded at the beginning of the 1990s that there needs to be much greater intellectual ownership by the South of Bank project assumptions and objectives. For this to happen, the South must be afforded a greater role in the analysis of education projects, and this in turn will imply a general strengthening of education research capacity in developing country governments. In other words, as Birger Fredriksen of the Bank has argued, local analysts and planners should be assisted to reach conclusions about what needs to be changed. Support to local research may achieve this:

> We have already stressed the need for a minimum level of consensus among the main stake-holders in the education sector as a condition of being able to implement process-oriented education reforms. Solid information, derived from analytical work that is 'owned' by the country, constitutes a cornerstone in any consensus-building effort.[51]

It is much too soon to follow up the possible implications of the Bank (and other agencies) more directly entering the field of strengthening research capacity in the South. The focus of this chapter, rather, has been the strengthening of agency capacity over the last two decades. While it may seem logical, at the end of a period of enormous growth in Northern agency capacity, for concern to switch to the South, it must be recognised that research capacity building to facilitate ownership of agency projects is likely to be viewed as a much more questionable activity than agency

---

[50] Hans Weiler, 'Knowledge and legitimation: the national and international politics of educational research', paper to Comparative and International Education Society Meeting, Atlanta, March 1983, p.21. There are several critiques of Northern agency power, notably Graham Hancock' s *Lords of poverty*, Macmillan, London, 1989.

[51] Birger Fredriksen, op.cit., p.14.

support to the general academic infrastructure of universities and research centres in developing countries.

It is time, however, to look in much more detail at the contents of the black box – agency institutional capacity – and to lay out for closer inspection some of the objects which have most attracted agency attention in these past 20 years.

Chapter 4

At the very time that the World Bank was deciding in 1986 that its more than 20 years of support to 'diversified' secondary education – orienting schools to agriculture, construction, automobile repair and domestic science – was no longer justified by the data (King, 1991: 78), Kenya's Ministry of Education was beginning a love affair with vocationalisation of both primary and secondary schools. Kenya's shift was significantly affected by its sudden recognition and national ownership of what it called *jua kali* (informal sector) development,[1] 14 years after the ILO had 'discovered' the informal sector in its Employment Mission to Kenya. This excerpt is about the multi-faceted attempt by the Kenyan government to orient schools more towards self-employment and enterprise – in other words to connect education and the informal sector.

Kenyan policy makers had decided to adopt a modern version of the practical curricular ideas which the Phelps-Stokes Commission had proposed in the early 1920s. This orientation directly affected the curricula of the now eight-year primary cycle, as well as four years of secondary school, and many different kinds of vocational training institutions. These encouragements of enterprise and self-employment were supported by policy papers on the economy as well as on education and training.

The increasingly national ownership of *jua kali* development, including at the highest level by the President, was a crucial factor in supporting curricular changes in the schools and other training institutions. The national trend towards vocationalisation of schools was encouraged by the awareness of the *jua kali* sector of self-employment. Suddenly, from the mid-1980s Kenya's upper primary school years were

Kenneth King (2019): *Education, Skills and International Cooperation: Comparative and Historical Perspectives*. Hong Kong: Comparative Education Research Centre (CERC), The University of Hong Kong, and Dordrecht: Springer. © CERC

[1] *Jua Kali* literally means 'hot sun' in Swahili, and came to mean both the informal sector workers many of whom worked without formal premises or shelter from the sun, as well as the informal sector itself.

© Springer Nature Switzerland AG 2019
K. King, *Education, Skills and International Cooperation*, CERC Studies in Comparative Education 36, https://doi.org/10.1007/978-3-030-29790-9_4

full of texts that spoke of the attractions of skills for self-employment. But what impact did these have in urban or rural schools? There were so many uncertainties in these politically-driven educational innovations. It was not enough just to review the relevant texts, but also to talk to teachers in poorly resourced rural schools.

The excerpt that follows captures some of these dimensions. The original book of which this is a very small part reviews many dimensions of a major change in government policy: in the education policy papers as well as in the economic policies, in the schools, in the rural as well as the urban areas, and in particular in the lives of those who had actually been in self-employment after their schooling.

Reference

King, K. 1991. *Aid and education in the developing world*, Longman, Harlow.

Education and Training for Self-Employment in Kenya[2]

In the decades between the ILO Employment Mission to Kenya in 1971 and the publication of the *Sessional Paper No. 2 of 1992 on Small Enterprise and Jua Kali Development in Kenya* (Kenya, 1992a), an enormous amount has been written about education and training in Kenya. The purpose in this chapter is not to review this general output, but to analyse the extent to which the education and training systems have changed in ways that may have some direct impact on options for self-employment and micro-enterprise. Kenya has often led the rest of Africa in educational innovation, in educational self-reliance, and in access to higher and higher levels of education. But arguably in respect of seeking to orient its system to new kinds of self-employment and vocationalisation, it has also done more than most others. Even within this narrower perspective on education and training there has been a considerable outpouring of literature on Kenya. For instance, in *Jua Kali literature: An annotated bibliography* (K-REP, 1993), no fewer than 81 items fall under the heading 'Education, training and entrepreneurship'.

Vocationalisation of basic education for self-employment in Kenya

There are several ways in which governments in the last decade and more have tried to alter schooling and training so as to affect employment. Some of these could be captured by the term vocationalisation, and in these initiatives the curriculum whether in primary, secondary or tertiary education has been altered in order to give it a greater orientation to work. The varieties of vocationalisation are large, but they have tended, as the term itself might imply, to be most obvious in situations such as Commonwealth Africa where there was not a distinct vocational school system of any magnitude. In such countries, where there might only have been a handful of trade or technical schools, there has been considerable interest in developing a more vocational orientation. In this respect, these Commonwealth countries have not had very different experiences from the UK. Here too there had been no strong tradition of separate vocational and technical schools such as are common in parts of

---

[2] This chapter is taken from King (1996), *Jua kali Kenya: Education and training in an informal economy, 1977-1995.*

Western and Eastern Europe, and yet in the 1980s there was a large-scale attempt to give a more technical orientation to the regular schools through the Technical and Vocational Education Initiative (TVEI).

There was a parallel in Kenya. Influenced originally by the UK, it also had no separate tradition of vocational and technical education but just a very small number of trade and technical schools. Only a handful of the *jua kali* we interviewed had gone to these schools in Machakos and Kabete respectively. To these schools there were added in the 1960s and 1970s, with World Bank and Swedish funding, some schools that were termed 'Industrial Arts' or 'diversified' in the sense that they had workshops for wood, metal and electricity, as well as facilities for home economics and agriculture. Because these schools were high cost and dependent on donor-financing, they never reached large numbers of children (Lauglo, 1985). Nevertheless, these two types continued until the large-scale curricular and structural reform of the mid-1980s.

Running alongside this relatively small, donor-financed version of technical and diversified education has long been a local strain of policy in Kenya which has felt that in both the basic cycle and the secondary school system as a whole there should be a substantial practical emphasis. This goes back to the recommendations of the National Committee on Educational Objectives and Policies in 1976, and the Sessional Paper on the same topic in 1978, which had suggested that a whole range of new subjects should be found in the basic cycle, including business education, home economics, Swahili and traditional arts and crafts. Nor were these to be electives, but rather they should be part of the nationally examined core subjects. Similar recommendations were made for the secondary cycle (Kenya, 1978).

What was unusual about these recommendations was that they were linked very explicitly to new employment and technology policies that went back to the recommendations of the ILO Mission at the beginning of the 1970s, and argued for legislative and administrative measures that would abolish harassment and encourage growth in the informal sector (King, 1990b). Exactly eight years later in December 1984 the government moved decisively to put into place a new structure and content of education in what was called the 8-4-4 System of Education. This with its eight years of basic, four of secondary school and four of university finally put into place in 1985 a curriculum that it was hoped would 'impart the kind of attitude more in tune with the development of the rural areas where 80 per cent of our people live' (Kenya, 1984a: 39).

The new *Syllabuses for Kenya Primary Schools* (1984) made it quite clear that the curriculum was concerned with skills, knowledge, expertise and personal qualities for a growing modern economy. But it added this important emphasis: 'The country requires trained manpower, both self-employed and in paid employment' (Kenya, 1984b: ix).

The notion that schools should prepare young people both for employment and for self-employment, and that both sectors offered opportunities for modern incomes and wealth creation was one of the distinguishing features of the Kenyan education reform (King 1990a). By contrast in Tanzania with its 'Education for Self-reliance', it had been difficult not to conclude that there were modern sector jobs protected by the selective entrance to secondary school, and then for the great majority there was terminal primary education followed by work in the rural areas (King, 1984; Buchert, 1994). The 8-4-4 Reform produced a whole series of basic education syllabuses including Home Science, Art and Craft, Science, Agriculture, and Business Education where there was a strong emphasis on the awareness of income opportunities and of the notion that self-employment could mean making as much money as being in a salaried job. These syllabuses were in due course translated into textbooks and suddenly a whole range of new information about young people and micro-enterprises was offered through the regular school system.

Some of the flavour of this may be worth offering. For example, in one of the new subjects, Business Education, here is some typical exhortation being offered through a textbook to Standard VI (i.e. 12-year-olds):

> All that one needs is to be organized either as an individual or as a group and start a business. You do not need to stay idle in your father's home simply because you have no job in which you are paid regularly. You should actively keep yourself busy by engaging yourself in one of these activities. In other words, when you finish school, the question should not be: WHO WILL EMPLOY ME? BUT HOW WILL I EMPLOY MYSELF? In many cases, you will find that self-employment is more paying than being employed by another person. There are many self-employed people in the rural areas who are very successful. (Gatama, 1986: 66; emphasis in the original)

This particular text goes on to argue that there are many more job openings in the rural areas than in town. And, as if the syllabus committees

139

had known that it had often been said that small businessmen did not seem to know about or to keep accounts, the Standard VI texts give full information about keeping records and different types of personal records and personal budgets (Gatama, 1986; Waithaka, 1987).

But it is not only Business Education that is concerned with the business of being self-employed. Similar encouragement runs through the Home Science texts, Agriculture, Art Education and Craft Education, as well as Primary Science. Here, for example, is an excerpt from one of the best written and most innovative of the Primary Science texts (Standard VIII):

Soon you will be leaving primary school. You will have to decide what to do. There are many possibilities:

1. Self-employment
    This means you work for yourself. For example, you could start a small business – such as making tools, rearing chickens, trading or growing vegetables...

2. Finding out about Self-employment
    To be self-employed, you need to have courage and skill. You need to work hard. However, many people enjoy working for themselves, being their own boss. Many of the following people are self-employed: mechanics, builders, watch-menders, taxi-drivers, tailors, fish-sellers, plumbers, traders, craftsmen, electricians, shoe repairers, potters. Find out what small businesses are needed in your area... (Berluti, 1985)

One of the problems about inserting a great deal of what might be termed 'developmental knowledge' into the primary school curriculum is that, even with the advantages of a progressive examination system (for which Kenya has been justifiably proud), it is difficult to know what, happens to all this potentially valuable information (King, 1989; Eisemon, 1989). There was already within a year or two of its being implemented a good deal of critical comment on the impact of all these new subjects with their demands for practical experimentation and space in the crowded timetable. Indeed, the Presidential Working Party on Education and Manpower Training for the Next Decade and Beyond (which led to the *Sessional Paper No. 6 of 1988 on Education and Manpower Training* [Kenya, 1988c]) had looked carefully at the evidence of how the new system was bedding down. But it certainly did not retreat from the decision to ensure a measure of vocational education for all, both in primary and secondary education. In fact, as a result of the reforms, the proportion of time allocated to broadly vocational subjects in the upper primary schools was no less than 34 per cent.

The original intent of the reform had been that the practical subjects be examined for both their academic and their practical content. This suggested that pupils would actually be assessed for their ability to make such things as simple tinsmith items, a blouse or a shirt, and much else. Because of the disparity in tools, equipment and workshop space, it has always proved problematic to carry out national examination of the practical side of these subjects. An interesting illustration of the problems of the practical examinations is that tinsmiths reported that there was always an increased seasonal demand for their simple tin-lamps from pupils wishing to provide evidence of their practical skills!

In Githiga Primary School in particular, four years after the reform had been implemented, it is perhaps typical of the difficulty of doing in school, for all children, what is commonplace in the self-employment setting for some, that teachers should be appreciative of the reforms but critical about their practical challenges:

> Many practical things are not practised because of the cost or the lack of the materials. Thus in Standard VII, they are meant to make pyjamas, but many children cannot afford the material, and they are kept off school for that reason. Accordingly we only teach them the stitches. The smaller items are easier; and so with the tea-cloth which is only 1/4 metre of cloth, they can do that in school.

> There is the same problem with the woodwork. No timber. They are supposed to make some basic items. But because we have few tools, and no timber, we just show them the joints.

> In Standard VIII for Home Science, we are at the moment trying to collect enough flour to make cakes, but it is difficult.

> In Agriculture in fact quite a lot of the families do not have land – even in Githiga. So they cannot try things out practically; and the school has no room for practical activities.

> Business Education – they do enjoy it in the classroom. And now they do have some ideas about business that they did not have before. But unless they can put it into practice, they won't be able to understand the things that are suggested.

Finally, though primary school is now eight years and not seven, the children nowadays, as compared with the 1960s and 1970s, are not big enough to do *jua kali* practically. (Discussion with teachers, 2 August 1989, Githiga)

It is worth underlining the fact that a decade is a very short period for effective educational reform. For example, children who started in Standard I in 1985 would still not have finished their secondary education in 1995. And there would so far only be three cohorts who would have left primary school (eight years) after experiencing the whole of the new curriculum. Researchers, therefore, have only just begun to investigate the impact on these new generations of primary school leavers of one third of their time being allocated (in upper primary school) to more vocational subjects. Equally, attention has been paid to the impact of the science curriculum. Understandably, assessment has been difficult. For instance one Kenyan researcher discovered that the new primary school curriculum accounted, at least on paper, for 21 out of the 22 skills that were judged essential for welding artisans in *jua kali* workshops. But it was very difficult to be sure how many of these skills had actually been communicated in the very resource-poor settings of the basic cycle of education (Digolo, 1990: 41-2).

Another researcher (Obura, 1993) has investigated whether the new form of 8-4-4 education has been a 'help or a hindrance' to small and intermediate sized enterprises in Kenya. Her preliminary conclusions are that despite the lack of facilities, properly trained teachers and insufficient time allocations, there have certainly been some beneficial outcomes for the school leavers and the community from the reform. These would include:

A more positive attitude on the part of learners towards practical skills.

Increased recognition by many primary learners of the relationship between primary technical subject learning and employment in the informal sector.

Involvement of the wider community in technology learning at school, for example, in the agricultural activities.

The lessening of gender differentiated curriculum through compulsory core, non-traditional curriculum for everyone (including technical and Home Science subjects). (Obura, 1993a: 21-22)

The debate about the cognitive and attitudinal consequences for later work of the particular curriculum in primary and secondary schooling will continue for a long time. But it is at any rate worth noting that the Kenya Government has not been apparently influenced by the World Bank's very forceful argumentation against the vocationalisation or 'diversification' of primary or secondary education. The Bank has commented that 'These 'diversified' programmes are no more effective than academic secondary education in enabling graduates to enter wage or self-employment' (World Bank, 1991: 9), and it has made a similar case for primary education. Indeed the Bank's general position, reinforced by its *Priorities and strategies for education* (World Bank, 1995), continues to be that because the social returns to specialised vocational education are much lower than those to general secondary education, vocational and technical education is best delayed as long as possible, ideally to the workplace, and is best preceded by general education (World Bank, 1995). Admittedly, on this particular occasion it is talking about specialised vocational education, but it has in so many other places talked against the vocationalisation of primary and secondary education that it is worth making the point that Kenya provides one of the most dramatic illustrations of following a reform process directly opposite to the tenor of Bank recommendations.

The fact is, as the Bank has itself admitted, that there hardly exist rigorous evaluations of such programmes (for the vocationalisation of primary education); and yet the Bank argues very strongly against them. What research the Bank itself has supported in this arena is not strictly relevant to what the Kenya Government has done in the 8-4-4 system. Thus in Tanzania and Colombia, the Bank analysed the diversified versus the general secondary schools, and reached a judgement that the former were not cost effective (Psacharopoulos and Loxley, 1985). This research has been challenged for its relevance to Tanzania let alone to Kenya (King, 1987). In addition, the Kenya government could legitimately argue that what they themselves have tried to put into place through the 8-4-4 system is not a high-cost, specialized vocational education system such as has been commonplace in Eastern Europe, but rather a form of low-cost vocational orientation for all. It could be emphasised, therefore, that Kenya's version of the vocational really treats it as an element of general education which every pupil should be exposed to. Furthermore, in Kenya, because of the shortage of materials, tools, equipment and workshops, a good deal of the vocationalised curriculum – whether in primary or secondary school – is actually academic and theoretical, just as science education is frequently theoretical in developing countries.

While it may be legitimate to challenge the Kenya experiment on grounds of overcrowding the curriculum and for expecting too much of children and their families in the practical areas, it certainly cannot be dismissed as yet another version of the diversified school which the Bank believes it has judged and found wanting. Nor can much credence be given to attempts to correlate different kinds of primary school subjects with 'economic development' as has been tried by Benavot (1992). For although the latter research has suggested that science education has a positive and prevocational a negative correlation with economic growth, the same research has also had to admit that maths and language do not turn up positively in these correlations while aesthetic education does!

What probably has to be said is that a good deal of the research that links primary schooling to all kinds of positive developmental outcomes remains mystifying to many members of the policy community and indeed to many researchers. The most heralded of these research results (many of them are associated with the World Bank) would claim that there are direct impacts of even four years of primary schooling on agricultural productivity and there are equally renowned impacts on the reduction of female fertility (World Bank, 1988). And as far as the link between the informal sector and basic education is concerned the Bank feels that basic education is probably one of the best ways to improve the productivity of the sector. Not of course basic education with a bias towards pre-vocational studies, but just plain basic education with a traditional emphasis on numeracy and literacy. Indeed in a Bank-financed study of apprenticeship in West Africa, one of the most important factors for improving productivity in the informal sector is said to be basic education:

> *Increased access to basic education.* This is critical in assisting wider entry to the microenterprise economy, particularly to the 'more attractive' activities and therefore to a more equitable widening of access to microenterprise opportunities. Completion of primary education has become a necessary, though not a sufficient, condition of apprenticeship. (Birks, S. et al., 1992: 99)

Current research by the Bank which connects primary education to the *jua kali* development process ends up arguing that general primary education is highly beneficial to the informal sector, but not, paradoxically, those forms of primary education that seek explicitly to make the content of the primary school curriculum more relevant to self-employment (Riedmiller, 1994).

The Kenyan form of vocational secondary and post-secondary education

Unlike the Kenya of the 1970s where it was possible to identify at the secondary level a small number of technical secondary schools and also a slightly larger number of the diversified (industrial arts) schools, the 8-4-4 system heralded the end of both these as secondary level institutions. In their place, it was recommended that in the first two years all secondary schools offer Agriculture and one subject from Home Science, Industrial Education, or Business Education. And in their last two years, they should still offer Agriculture as well as one other subject from Business Education, Home Science, Industrial Education or Religion or the Arts. In other words, two of the 13 subjects taken in junior secondary were explicitly vocational, and up to two of the nine subjects taken in the second two years of secondary schooling could be vocational (Kenya, 1984a). The 8-4-4 reform could therefore be seen as unifying the secondary education system, so that there were no longer just a small number of schools thought of as technical or industrial. Instead, all secondary schools now offer a modicum of what should probably be termed pre-vocational education, in the sense that these subjects are seen to be an important component of an all-round general education.

By contrast the more specialized institutions – the 19 technical secondary schools – have now become post-secondary, and have been renamed technical training institutes (TTIs). In this post-secondary role, they are now much closer to the 20 Institutes of Technology (ITs) which continue in the 1990s to have special connections with particular districts, reflecting their original self-help (*harambee*) beginnings.

The distinction between the element of some vocational orientation for all (and especially to Agriculture) in the general secondary school and the removal of the more specialized and intensive vocational preparation to institutions outside the formal school system is probably appropriate. The aims and objectives of the secondary school system are now more coherent, and it is likely that the clientele now entering the TTIs or the ITs are doing so much more because of their explicitly vocational or technical mission. In earlier days, as was shown in *The African artisan*

(King, 1977), it had always been unclear to potential employers whether entrants to the national technical secondary schools were more attracted by their being secondary schools than by their technical content.

Jua kali attitudes to school reforms far self-employment
It would be interesting to know more about *jua kali* artisans' attitudes to all these changes in schools, and especially when a great deal of the purpose of the reforms has been to make pupils more aware of opportunities in self-employment. What is intriguing about those artisans for whom we do have data is that their attitudes towards schools are more concerned with school type (government versus harambee versus private) than they are with the content of the curriculum. This should perhaps not be surprising. School reforms in all countries take a very long time to reach small-scale employers' attention, and Kenya is likely to be no exception.

What we can, however, note in some *jua kali* attitudes to schooling is a very shrewd investment approach. Schools, and especially secondary schools in Kenya, cost a good deal of money, and the good quality government schools are normally much less costly than the lower quality *harambee* schools, or *harambee* streams. *Jua kali* were prepared to support their children if they managed in the competitive examinations to reach a government school, but they were not going to throw a great deal of hard-won money after a low-quality education, and then find that the children were no better off in employment terms; they would be better to learn a trade with their father right away, they had thought. In other words, *jua kali* are not even aware of what is meant to be the self-employment orientation of all schools, but are still operating on the basic contrast between government and *harambee*. The same was true of several of our other *jua kali*, including both the candlemakers, with their relatively modest incomes, and metalworkers. They were seeking to ensure that they covered the government school fees of their children, even if this was putting them under very severe pressure. And again the issue seemed to be good government school, and preferably boarding, as opposed to cheaper *harambee* day schools.

Effectively this means that *jua kali* with children of their own of school age seem little different from many other Kenyans in classifying schools according to their traditional capacity to provide better opportunities for a modern sector job. There is some evidence, however, from the next generation of *jua kali* who have just emerged from the exposure to 8-4-4 that they certainly appreciate some of what has been learnt, for example, about the pros and cons of starting a business.

References

Benavot, A., 1992, 'Curriculum content, educational expansion and economic growth', *Comparative Education Review*, Vol.36, No.2: 150-174.

Berluti, A., 1985, *Primary science for standard eight*, Macmillan, Nairobi.

Birks, S. et al., 1992. 'Skill acquisition and work in micro-enterprises: Recent evidence from West Africa', Joint study of World Bank, ILO and the Development Centre, OECD, draft, The World Bank, Washington DC.

Buchert, L., 1994, *Education in the development of Tanzania, 1919-1990*, James Currey, London.

Digolo, O.O., 1990, 'A study of the nature, process and problems of training primary school leavers in jua kali workshops in Kenya', Kenya Education Research Awards/IDRC study, University of Nairobi, Nairobi.

Eisemon, T.O., 1989, 'The impact of primary schooling on agricultural thinking and practices in Kenya and Burundi', *Studies in Science Education*, 17: 5-28.

Gatama, W.M., 1986. *Business education for primary schools: Standard six. Pupils' book*, TransAfrica, Nairobi.

ILO, 1972, *Employment, incomes and equality: A strategy for increasing productive employment in Kenya*, ILO, Geneva.

Kenya Government, 1978, *Sessional paper on educational objectives and policies*, Government Printer, Nairobi.

Kenya Government, Ministry of Education, Science and Technology, 1984a, *8-4-4 System of Education*, Government Printer, Nairobi.

Kenya Government, Ministry of Education, Science and Technology, 1984b, *Syllabuses for Kenya primary schools: Standards VII and VIII*, Jomo Kenyatta Foundation, Nairobi.

Kenya Government, 1988c, *Sessional paper No. 6 of 1988 on education and manpower training for the next decade and beyond*, Government Printer, Nairobi.

Kenya Government, 1992a, *Sessional paper No. 2 of 1992 on small enterprise and jua kali development in Kenya*, Government Printer, Nairobi.

Kenya Rural Enterprise Programme (K-REP), 1993, *Jua kali literature: An annotated bibliography*, K-REP, Nairobi.

King, K., 1977, *The African artisan: Education and the informal sector*, Heinemann Educational Books, London.

King, K., 1984, 'The end of education for self-reliance in Tanzania?' Occasional Paper No. 1, Centre of African Studies, University of Edinburgh, Edinburgh.

King, K., 1987, 'Evaluating the context of diversified secondary education in Tanzania', in J. Lauglo and K. Lillis (eds.) *Vocationalising education*, Pergamon, Oxford.

King, K., 1989, 'Primary schooling and developmental knowledge in Africa', in *African futures*, Centre of African Studies, University of Edinburgh.

King, K., 1990a, 'Education for employment and self-employment interventions in developing countries: Past experience and present prognosis', in International Foundation for Education with Production, *Defusing the time-bomb? Education and employment in Southern Africa*, IFEP, Gaborone.

King, K., 1990b, 'An evaluation of research and policies on informal sector employment in Kenya', in D. Turnham et al. (eds.) *The informal sector revisited*, OECD, Paris.

Lauglo, J., 1985. *Practical subjects in Kenyan academic secondary schools: General report*, Education Division Documents, No.20, SIDA, Stockholm.

Obura, A., 1993, 'Education as support or hindrance of small and intermediate size enterprise in Africa', African Centre for Technology Studies, Nairobi.

Psacharapoulos, G. and Loxley, W., 1985, *Diversified education: Evidence from Colombia and Tanzania*, Johns Hopkins University Press, Baltimore.

Riedmiller, S., 1994, 'Primary school agriculture in Africa', *International Encyclopaedia of Education*. 2nd Edition, Pergamon, Oxford.

Waithaka, J.M., 1987, *Business education for standard six: Pupils' book*, Kenya Literature Bureau, Nairobi.

World Bank, 1988, *Education in Sub-Saharan Africa*, World Bank, Washington DC.

World Bank, 1991, *Vocational and technical education and training*, World Bank, Washington DC.

World Bank, 1995, *Priorities and strategies for education: A World Bank review*, World Bank, Washington DC.

Chapter 5

More than a decade before basic education became one of the key elements of an expanded vision of Education for All in Jomtien, Thailand, in 1990, the World Bank had begun supporting some influential research papers on the value and impact of primary education in other development sectors. One of the first of these underlined the powerful link claimed between education and fertility (Cochrane, 1979). Others linked primary education to several other outcomes, including productivity in the informal sector (Colclough, 1980). The one my colleague, Robert Palmer, and I analysed suggested that there was a very strong connection between just four years of education and farmer productivity (Lockheed, Jamison and Lau, 1980). Within two years there was a book published by two of the authors on *Farmer education and farm efficiency* (Jamison and Lau, 1982).

One of the problems with the finding was that it was very frequently misquoted. The research actually claimed that four years of education made a difference to farmer productivity of about 10% 'in a modernising environment'; but it made almost no difference in a non-modernising environment, where agriculture was traditional and no new methods or crops were being tried out. So merely repeating the short version about four years of education making a difference to farmer productivity was hugely misleading. The key determinant was whether there was an enabling environment in which a more educated farmer could operate.

But we went on to argue that at least two other enabling environments needed to be considered if such a claim was to be secure. One was that there was a post-basic educational environment which was crucial to the performance of schools and agriculture through the presence of teachers and agricultural extension personnel. The other was that the educational environment of the primary school was surely crucial

Kenneth King (2019): *Education, Skills and International Cooperation: Comparative and Historical Perspectives*. Hong Kong: Comparative Education Research Centre (CERC), The University of Hong Kong, and Dordrecht: Springer. © CERC

© Springer Nature Switzerland AG 2019
K. King, *Education, Skills and International Cooperation*, CERC Studies
in Comparative Education 36, https://doi.org/10.1007/978-3-030-29790-9_5

to its impact: if the quality of the four years of education was abysmal, and the school was affected by massive teacher absenteeism, it might have little effect on later developmental outcomes. In other words, just four years of any schooling cannot be assumed to be effective.

The complete paper is 67 pages long and was one outcome of a DFID-funded research project on the role of post-basic education in 'Educating out of poverty'. In this book, we shall just present the executive summary which captures the main argument sufficiently, but the full paper is still accessible (King and Palmer, 2006). Robert Palmer had been a masters and doctoral student in the Centre of African Studies at the University of Edinburgh, and had particularly focused on education and skill acquisition in Ghana's informal economy (Palmer, 2006). He has been with the Queen Rania Foundation in Jordan since it began in 2013.

References

Cochrane, S. 1979. *Fertility and education: What do we really know?* World Bank, Washington DC.

Colclough, C. 1980. 'Primary schooling and economic development: A Review of the evidence', World Bank Staff Working Paper No.399, World Bank, Washington DC.

Lockheed, M., Jamison, D. and Lau, L. 1980. 'Farmer education and farm efficiency: A survey', in *Economic Development and Cultural Change, 29*, 1: 37-76, reprinted as World Bank Report Series No.166, The World Bank, Washington DC.

Jamison, D. and Lau, l. 1982. *Farmer education and farm efficiency*, Johns Hopkins University Press, Baltimore.

King, K. and Palmer, R. 2006. 'Education, training and their enabling environments: A review of research and policy', Post-basic education and training working paper series No.8, Centre of African Studies, University of Edinburgh. Accessed on 22nd October 2017, at https://www.gov.uk/dfid-research-outputs/education-training-and-their-enabling-environments-a-review-of-research-and-policy-post-basic-education-and-training-working-paper-series-n-8.

Palmer, R. 2006. Skills development, the enabling environment and informal micro-enterprise in Ghana, PhD thesis, University of Edinburgh.

Exploring the Impact of Primary Education[1]

This paper focuses on the need for education to be embedded in a wider environment of a particular kind – for its expected social and economic impacts to be most evident. It explores, as a case study of this relationship, the extraordinarily long life of one of the best-known policy claims in the whole sphere of international education and training – that four years of education increase agricultural productivity (cf. Lockheed, Jamison and Lau, 1980). But it also looks more generally at the role of the enabling environment for education and skills development to reach their full potential.

The original policy attractiveness of this case study research was doubtless because it claimed a connection between education and increased farmer productivity. This was particularly attractive in the World Bank at the time, as the Bank wanted to make the case that investment in education was not simply a consumption good or a human right, but that it also translated into economic growth. The same research is now used, far beyond the Bank, to demonstrate the impact basic education has potentially on poverty reduction.

The paper re-examines these particular connections, noting the way that this particular research finding has been translated into policy documents over the last 25 years, but its authors are also interested in a second, and much more general parallel of this early research which has been little analysed – the crucial link between basic education and its surrounding or enabling environment. This concept of the environment includes both, within the education sector, the whole post-basic education and training system, but also the wider non-education environment (for example, macro-economic growth, job creation, good governance, and the availability of credit and agricultural inputs).

The paper first explores what we term the 'farmer education fallacy in development planning', by looking at the origin of the famous farmer education claims just mentioned and seeing how these claims have been used since then in agency and academic policy. It then explores this issue of the need for education to be embedded within a wider environment more generally. This discussion examines the need for a sector-wide 'post-basic education and training environment' – beyond primary

---

[1] This chapter is the executive summary of King and Palmer's working paper (2006), 'Education, training and their enabling environments: A review of research and policy'.

schooling, on the one hand, and the importance of the wider 'non-educational environment' on the other. It also discusses some of the links between the existence of a post-basic education system and this wider enabling environment.

The 'farmer education fallacy in development planning'

We are not examining this renowned World Bank finding because we necessarily doubt the evidence on which it is based, but rather, because the research results have so frequently been oversimplified or misrepresented by those who have used them. Versions of this finding – that four years of education increase agricultural productivity – are quoted, for example, in the Education for All (EFA) Global Monitoring Reports [GMR] of 2002 and 2003, and also in the ILO volume from the 91st session of the International Labour Conference. But these are really misquotations; the original research said education makes a difference to farm productivity of about 10% in 'a modernising environment'. [2] Education makes virtually no difference, the research argued, if the environment is non-modern [where agriculture is traditional and where there are no new methods and new crops being tried out]. If the above finding – that four years of education increase agricultural productivity – is used without a reference to the crucial importance of the economic context or environment, there is a danger of misleading the reader. In other words, if the education is to make a difference to agricultural productivity, this particular research asserted, certain other things needed to be in place in the surrounding environment.

Moreover, the research on farmer education and efficiency provides a dramatic case of how the original research evidence can be stripped of caveats and context, hence resulting in the misrepresentation of the research findings in later policy documents.

The Policy Impact of the Farmer Education Research

The Lockheed et al. research, which explicitly stated that education is more effective in modernizing conditions, points to the fact that education (or literacy), *on its own,* may not be sufficient to result in positive developmental outcomes. This is a very simple message, but it is exactly

---

[2] Referring to a context where there were 'new crop varieties, innovative planting methods, erosion control, and the availability of capital inputs such as insecticides, fertilizers, and tractors or machines. Some other indicators of [a modern] environment were market-orientated production and exposure to extension services'.

the opposite of what many agencies derived from this World Bank research. They chose to represent the research in an 'edu-centric' way – to suggest that education itself has this kind of impact. Although, as we have shown, this core message of the research has often been misrepresented or oversimplified, as it was taken up and translated into policy by the World Bank, development agencies, and NGOs, and as it became accepted in the academic literature, it nevertheless sought to make an important contribution to understanding the role of education in relation to its surrounding contexts.

Education and its Two Enabling Environments

Our paper takes the suggestive concept of the surrounding or enabling environment – from the Lockheed et al. research – and develops it both in relation to the wider educational environment and then to the environment beyond the school and the vocational training system. We argue that the concept of the enabling environment is much more complex than the simple dichotomy between modernizing or stagnant, in economic terms, with which we engage in the first part of this paper. Many other dimensions of the surrounding environment determine whether the investment in basic education will be productive.

We argue that there are, in fact, two main types of surrounding environment that that could catalyse the linkage between basic education and positive developmental outcomes. One might be termed a 'post-basic education and training environment', while the other would be an environment that is outside the education system itself, such as the character of the macro-economic context, or in other words, 'the wider non-educational environment'. Thus, secondary and tertiary education, and (formal and informal) skills development all form part of a post-basic education and training context or environment which may well be required to be substantial and accessible in order to make primary or basic education fully effective. This means that post-basic education and training may themselves be a part of the essential enabling environment for basic education. Alongside this, and equally crucial, there is the need for a 'non-education related environment' if education, in all its sub-sectors, is to deliver its full developmental impact.

The interplay between these two kinds of enabling environment is highly complex, especially since, as we argue in the paper, the post-basic education and training system has itself a direct impact on these non-educational environments. We discuss educational and non-educational environments in turn. We argue, along with Lockheed et al., that there are crucially important differences in the environments which surround basic schooling. In doing so, we are not synthesizing a series of quantitative studies, as Lockheed et al. did. Rather we examine and tease out the shifts in education and development policy, which seem as much to be based on experience and on commonsense as on the review of state of the art economic research. For instance, we note that the terms which Lockheed and others used – stagnant and modernizing – could be applied to the school system itself. In other words, does investment in basic schooling provide all the well-known development benefits if the school system is of abysmal quality, and if teachers are uncommitted and frequently absent. To explore these and other issues we examine the synergy between basic education and the wider educational environment beyond the primary school.

Conclusion on a two-way relationship of education and training with their enabling environments

In research terms, what is intriguing about the argument for seeing education against a background of change in other sectors in the wider environment is that, like the case for the necessary interaction of primary with post-primary education, the policy is not research-based.

It is not just a question of there being more or less influence of education depending on modernising/stagnant or egalitarian/non-egalitarian environments or of education aspirations being determined by external factors – all of which are one-way relationships. More likely, basic education – and particularly post-basic education and training – may itself play a part in whether an environment is actually ready to absorb change or is open to new technology, or is critical of poor governance.

Our paper argues that the process of assisting a country to reach the Education Millennium Development Goals [universal primary education and gender equity] may well require an understanding of two other enabling environments – that of the education and training system itself, and especially the dynamic interaction of primary with post-primary provision – and also the interaction of education as a whole with change in the larger economy. The policy of single-mindedly targeting just one sub-sector, such as primary education or girls' education, in order to reach these education goals may well be inadvisable.

We argue that the politically attractive claims that schooling directly 'makes a difference' to agricultural productivity need to be qualified in two ways. First, these allegedly developmental effects of schooling are almost certainly dependent on other facilitating conditions being present – in the social, cultural, economic and political environments. And, second, these powerful impacts claimed of education are unlikely to be present – even in environmentally promising conditions – if the quality of the schooling or of the skills training is of a very low quality. Common sense would suggest that a school affected by massive teacher absenteeism and low morale can have little impact on other developmental outcomes.

If, in conclusion, there is to be new research on the issues that we have explored in this paper, then it will need to begin to explore new ways of capturing the crucial role of the enabling or disabling environments in affecting how education and training are actually utilized. This will not be a question of reproducing more research like that of Lockheed, Jamison and Lau, valuable and influential though this was in its day. Rather, it will need to move from the 'edu-centricity' of such research towards work that will capture something of the complexity of the social, economic, cultural, legal and political environments in which education and training investments are constantly being affected.

This will not be research, therefore, that measures how education and skills can help break the cycle of poverty or how a certain threshold of secondary education can assist a transition to the brave new world of the knowledge society. But it will be research that will need to develop new tools and artefacts that capture the complexity of the wider environment, while bearing in mind, also, that school and skill are much more than years of education.

Further Reading

Lockheed, M., Jamison, D. and Lau, L. (1980) Farmer Education and Farm Efficiency: A Survey, in *Economic Development and Cultural Change* 29, 1: 37-76, reprinted as World Bank Report Series No. 166, The World Bank: Washington DC.

The full paper – *'Education, Training and their Enabling Environments: A Review of Research and Policy'* is available on the following web link: https://assets.publishing.service.gov.uk/media/57a08c1bed915d3cfd001186/ King_Palmer_Educ_Env_PBET_WP8.pdf. It is part of the DFID-supported project on post-basic education and training for poverty reduction.

Chapter 6

Philip Foster was a critical sociologist of education, spending time first in the University of London and later in the University of Chicago. One of his key contributions was to question the capacity of school systems to change the employment aspirations of children and youth by means of changing the curriculum. He argued persuasively from his research in Ghana shortly after that country's independence in 1957 that student ambitions for work were determined by their perceptions of the opportunities in the 'modern', formal sector of the economy, and not by the specific curricular orientations of schools. He had tried a novel way of checking student ambitions by asking them first to indicate what jobs they would ideally desire, and then asking them to assess realistically what jobs they would end up with. Foster was able to show that farming, for example, did not come at the bottom of the students' prestige rankings, as might have been anticipated in a newly independent country in Sub-Saharan Africa.

Before following up many of Foster's questions 40 years after his 1959 research in Ghana, it was important to recognise that although Foster's work had major implications for the instrumental use of school curricula, he paid very little attention to the curricula in his target schools. Also in one of his chapters which was seen to be crucially concerned with vocational education, he paid almost no attention to the (few) technical schools in the country (Foster, 1965b). Thus the vocational school fallacy did not actually look at the provision of vocational education in Ghana at the time.

In revisiting Foster's classic paper during 1998 and 1999, it proved possible not only to explore reactions to some of the identical themes on which he had worked, but also to introduce new issues of interest to scholars and policymakers such as education and self-employment. In

Kenneth King (2019): *Education, Skills and International Cooperation: Comparative and Historical Perspectives*. Hong Kong: Comparative Education Research Centre (CERC), The University of Hong Kong, and Dordrecht: Springer. © CERC

© Springer Nature Switzerland AG 2019
K. King, *Education, Skills and International Cooperation*, CERC Studies in Comparative Education 36, https://doi.org/10.1007/978-3-030-29790-9_6

addition to the value of an historical perspective over 40 years, it was invaluable to receive comments on our paper from Philip Foster himself. His views of diversified curricula were perhaps surprisingly positive, but so was his amazement that his paper on 'The vocational school fallacy' written in just a few days in 1964, became one of his best-known articles. It is valuable to have his own reactions (Chapter 6b) to the article presented here.

The Vocational School Fallacy Revisited[1]

Kenneth King and Chris Martin[2]

In Accra, Ghana, in December 1959, Philip Foster drew his first sample of 210 middle school boys in their fourth and — for most — last year of formal post-primary education. He asked them about the kind of employment they would like to obtain — if they were "completely free to choose". He then followed this with a query about what kind of employment they "actually expected to be able to obtain". This was one dimension of work that would contribute to Foster's "Vocational School Fallacy in Development Planning" in 1963[3] (1965a), and an important element in his classic case study, *Education and social change in Ghana* (1965b).

Few articles in the field of international and comparative education have been so influential in academic circles, and also amongst some development cooperation personnel, as "The vocational school fallacy". One reason for this justifiably long-standing reputation is that Foster was prepared to stand out, in a period when it was all too easy to suggest that schools could deliver all kinds of attitude change (towards nation building, good citizenship and rural development), and state that "schools are remarkably clumsy instruments for inducing prompt large-scale changes in underdeveloped areas" (1965a: 144). The 1960s was a decade which in Africa witnessed the ambitious targets for all sub-sectors of education in the Addis Ababa conference of 1961 (UNECA & UNESCO, 1961), the excitement about self-help educational expansion (*harambee*) in Kenya, and then a whole series of innovations designed to deal with the sudden arrival of primary school leaver unemployment — from the Brigades in Botswana, to the Workers Brigades in Ghana, to the Village Polytechnics in Kenya, and, most famously, in *Education for self-reliance* in Tanzania.[4]

---

[1] This chapter is taken from King and Martin (2002), ' The vocational school fallacy revisited: Education, aspiration and work in Ghana, 1959-2000'. Martin was responsible for the quantitative analysis and King for the qualitative and historical dimensions.

[2] Chris Martin was a member of the Centre for Educational Sociology, University of Edinburgh.

[3] "The vocational school fallacy in development planning" was first presented at a conference on Education and Economic Development in Chicago in 1963, and first published in the conference proceedings edited by Anderson and Bowman (1965). The article has been reprinted in several forms, but not all of these contain the full original.

[4] For the range of these initiatives, see King (1991). Foster was one of the earliest critics of Nyerere's *Education for self-reliance* (1967); see Foster (1969).

Foster's message about the limitations of schooling to change society arrived early in the decade which saw the application of the new approaches of manpower planning and educational planning to targets for the creation of, usually, high level manpower, through all kinds of exceptional and emergency measures.

What was particularly unusual about Foster's approach was that it was deeply embedded in a knowledge of the educational history of the Gold Coast right back to the 1600s, and his concerns with achievement, selection and recruitment in the early 1960s were founded upon an understanding of recruitment to office, mobility, status and differentiation in the traditional societies that eventually made up the Gold Coast, and later Ghana.[5]

Put perhaps over-simply, Foster was able to argue that for well over 100 years western education had been responsible for a massive amount of social change in this area, but that the schools had very seldom functioned in the manner expected by the educators and the policy makers. In the new era of educational planning, Foster's book was a vivid testimony to what he called the "unplanned consequences of educational growth" (1965b, 303).

What makes Foster's work especially worth revisiting after more than 40 years of Ghanaian independence, and after the decades of 'development', 'basic needs', 'adjustment' and — now — 'globalisation' is that, again, Ghana is a potentially prime candidate for examination. At independence, it was one of the best endowed nations in Africa, in terms of high levels of per capita income and of human resources; in the late 1990s it was felt to have managed the era of structural adjustment in a relatively successful manner. As part of this adjustment era, there have been substantial reductions in public service employment, the privatisation of parastatal companies, and rationalisation and reform of primary, junior and senior secondary education, as well as university (King, 1989). More generally, there have been attempts to encourage an enterprise culture, under the broader Vision 2020 of its National Development Planning Commission (Government of Ghana, 1995).

In this very different economic context from Foster's Ghana of the late 1950s and early 1960s, we administered, in 1998 and 1999, very similar instruments to those used to such effect by Foster. The results

---

[5] In fact, more than half of the volume on *Education and social change in Ghana* is about education and social change in pre-colonial and colonial Gold Coast. Paradoxically, the book, which is a major scholarly work, is now much less known than the article.

powerfully confirm in some measure but also raise important questions about Foster's longstanding findings.[6] Most specifically, they suggest that there could, very possibly, be an identifiable school influence or school effect on attitudes towards employment and self-employment.

1. The central challenge in the vocational school fallacy (VSF)

The two publications by Foster about Ghana mentioned above cover considerable ground. In their own right, they make a major contribution to our understanding of Ghanaian education history against a background of social and political development. But, for many, Foster is best known as the champion of the realism and rationality of Ghanaian middle and secondary school pupils. Over against the multitude of plans, projects and commissions arguing for more practical, adapted and relevant education for Ghanaian youth — from the early Basel mission years, to the Phelps-Stokes recommendations of the 1920s, to the pre- and immediate post-Independence periods — Foster's analysis has consistently backed the good sense of young people (and their parents) to work out what was in their best career interests.[7]

At the heart of the debate lay the issue of vocationalism and its relationship to economic growth. Should not schools, and especially those in predominantly agricultural societies where the formal sector of the economy could only absorb a very small proportion of the economically active population, keenly prepare young people with a substantial measure of the practical, agricultural and technical skills needed for the transformation of their societies?[8] The nub of the argument, therefore, concerns the relationship of the school to its society, and particularly the role that the school can be expected to play in support of economic development. At a time when there were many ambitious schemes involving a central role for the school in national development, Foster

---

[6] This research was carried out in association with the larger study of "Education, Training and Enterprise", supported by the Department for International Development, in Ghana, Kenya and South Africa. Further support was made available from the Moray Endowment at the University of Edinburgh. We were assisted considerably by Dela Afenyadu in pursuing this research, and have profited from his comments and reactions.

[7] For a sustained critique of the Phelps-Stokes Commissions, the most influential of these plans for an 'adapted' education for Africa, see King (1971). I am grateful to Paul Nugent for pointing out that this interest in promoting vocational schooling was especially the case in Northern Ghana where there was a conscious attempt to avoid the 'mistakes' of the South (see further Bening, 1990).

[8] A useful analysis of the range of the literature in the 1960s (much of it written by expatriates) which was preoccupied with the attitudes of young, unemployed school leavers can be found in Hanson (1980).

remained frankly sceptical about the extent to which the school could, alone, become an active instrument in a massive economic and social transformation.[9] Could curricular change at the national level — towards more practical, vocational subjects in the schools — not only have a direct effect on the young people themselves and their choice of careers, but also indirectly on the emerging problems of the time, such as the unemployment of educated school leavers and the slow pace of agricultural and rural development? Foster's answer, after examining the record of 100 years of reforms, was that mission societies, colonial governments, and now the new independent government of Ghana, had frequently been attracted by the apparent logic of this position, and had sought to use schools in this instrumental way. But the plain truth was that "the educational history of the Gold Coast is strewn with the wreckage of schemes" based on these assumptions (1965a: 145).

The reason lay principally in the new occupational opportunities generated by colonialism, and in the role of schools as one of the primary mechanisms for moving young people from subsistence activities to a position in what was then called "the exchange sector" or modern sector of the economy. For clerical and commercial employment in this emerging wage and salary sector, African students had determined quite rationally that academic qualifications were a better preparation than vocational.[10] Such positions as existed for technically trained individuals were both fewer in number and less well paid. In addition, it could be said that for much of the colonial period the emerging West African professionals were very clear that they should pursue for their people the same form of academic education as characterised the education of the European elite in the Gold Coast. Accepting an education 'adapted to Africans', they argued, would compromise aspirations to social and political equality (King, 1971).

2. School data on the vocational school fallacy

---

[9] Foster was not alone in this view of school leavers; he was conscious of the parallels with Callaway's work in Nigeria: "The fact is that school leavers' views of their vocation in life are determined largely by what happens outside the school, in the society and economy" (Callaway, 1963).

[10] Foster made the point that there was a real sense in which 'academic' education was more 'vocational' than so -called vocational education, since it prepared young people for the jobs with the best pay and prospects in the economy of the time. A.G. Fraser, first joint-principal of Achimota College, had made this same point in the 1920s (King, 1977). This is not to say that technical schools could not also become popular with pupils, as for example they were for a short time in Kenya in the 1970s and early 1980s because of their close links with some of the best known employers in the country (King, 1971; Lauglo and Narman, 1987).

In order to explore the rationality of the Ghanaian school pupil, Foster decided to analyse the pattern of career aspirations of pupils at the end of their middle and secondary school years, and to use pupils' own perceptions of good jobs, in terms of status and income, to see what light could be thrown on their commonly-alleged obsession with white collar jobs, and their reluctance to consider manual work, whether in agriculture or in technical or vocational settings. We shall first summarise and comment on his results, and then look at them afresh in the light of new data acquired from secondary school pupils in today's very different Ghana.

Foster collected his pupil data from two rather distinct types of school.[11] First, as we mentioned at the start of the paper, he administered questionnaires to 210 boys in the 4th year of what were called middle schools. To make sense of the answers it should be stressed that these schools (somewhat parallel to the secondary modern schools of the UK in the post-war period) were designed to be terminal, unlike the 5 year, highly selective secondary schools. Fourth year middle school students could realistically have little hope of joining the higher status secondary school stream.[12] Would their responses to a questionnaire show that their aspirations were hopelessly ambitious for white collar employment?

Foster was able to show that even when they were encouraged first to fantasise about their ideal job, and then say what they expected in fact to achieve, their answers were relatively level-headed. In their 'ideal' responses, just over 50% hoped to get artisan and skilled work, while only 30% aspired to get white collar, professional and clerical, jobs. By contrast, in their 'realistic' responses, the white collar proportion fell to 21% and even the aspiration for artisan and skilled work fell sharply to 22%. Instead of their aspirations for skilled work, the largest number now (35%) only expected to get semi-skilled and unskilled work.

It was a small sample of boys from non-selective, low-status middle schools, which were scrapped in the late 1980s, but Foster felt that the results on job aspirations had certainly indicated that the "pupils displayed a remarkable level of realism" (1965a: 149). It may seem strange to readers now to hear that pupils in the fourth year of post-primary (middle school) education in a newly independent country should aspire

---

[11] In 1960, there were some 200,000 pupils in the four-year terminal middle schools, and just 14,000 in the selective public secondary schools.

[12] In the year that Foster carried out this middle school study, nearly all the pupils from middle school who did manage to make the transition to secondary came from Middle I and Middle II, and just a handful from Middle III. So Middle IV was effectively terminal (Philip Foster to King, 3 September 1999).

in such numbers for artisanal and skilled work. But it should be remembered, in the extraordinary state of secondary school arrangements prevailing at that time in Ghana, that if a pupil in the fourth year of middle school did succeed in passing the common entrance to selective secondary education, he or she had to start all over again, in the first of five years of secondary.[13]

The second point that should be noted about this 1959 data from middle schools was that the pupils were asked by Foster about jobs and not about work or about self-employment (1965a: 149). We are told that the category of "Artisans and Skilled Workers" — which was initially so popular with these students — was made up of careers such as electrician, motor mechanic, plumber, carpenter, mason, printer, painter, shoemaker, locomotive engineer, tailor etc. But at this distance from the data, there is no way of knowing whether those who indicated particular artisan trades were (with the exception of locomotive engineer!) thinking of work in the informal apprenticeship system which was very widespread in Ghana or in the formal or modern sector of the economy.

In 1961 it was still 10 years before the term 'informal sector' would be first used in academic currency — and in fact would be coined of the informal economy of Accra by Keith Hart (1973); but it is evident that Foster knew well the extent of the informal, indigenous apprenticeship system in West Africa, and saw it as a possible basis for relevant upgrading of vocational and technical skills:

> …a considerable amount of road transport in West Africa is serviced and maintained not by highly trained operators but by 'bush mechanics' who themselves have very little formal instruction. Upon this basis has developed a burgeoning system of informal apprenticeship; though most of the instruction is extremely rudimentary, here is an expanding base which can be built upon (1965a: 156).

Before we leave Foster's first sample,[14] and turn to his larger national sample, there is a further point that is worth making. This middle school

---

[13] For the handful of fourth year middle school (i.e. non-selective post-primary) students who did succeed in reaching selective secondary, they would require no less than 15 years of schooling, in all, before they had the option to compete further for entry to their A level in the small number of senior secondary sixth forms.

[14] The middle school sample is discussed in very similar terms in both of Foster's 1965 publications under review here. In neither case is any more known of the detail of what they were asked than the two questions about their 'completely free' choice of job and then the job they actually 'expected' to get.

sample is drawn from the final years of nine so-called 'academic-type' schools in Accra. Although it is almost certainly the case that these lower status post-primary schools did mimic the academic orientation of the selective secondary sector, their centrally laid-down curriculum was meant to have been diversified, and they were meant to have included 'housecraft and woodwork', 'arts and crafts', and 'gardening' along with the academic subjects. Whether they did or not, and whether they were seriously taught, given the distraction of the middle school leaving examination, cannot now be known for certain for these nine schools. But the reason for underlining it is that we shall see later, in our own 1998-1999 questionnaire data, that the particular track, stream or type of diversification does seem to make quite a difference to the pattern of pupils' career choices.

It is particularly tantalising not to know a little more about these nine schools, and what was actually taught in their different curricula, when what is probably the purple passage of 'The Vocational School Fallacy' article is written about these schools, and not about the national sample of 2 years later. Given what this passage asserts about curriculum, it would still have been good to know in some more detail what curriculum was in fact provided to these pupils:

> The operative fact here is not that graduates [of schools] will not accept certain types of employment but rather that the schools (irrespective of what they teach) have been shrewdly used as the gateway into the 'emergent' sector of the economy. The schools themselves can do little about this. So long as parents and students perceive the function of education in this manner, agricultural education and vocational instruction *in the schools* is [sic] not likely to have a determinative influence on the occupational aspirations and destinations of students. Aspirations are determined largely by the individual's perception of opportunities within the exchange sector of the economy, destinations by the *actual* structure of opportunities in that sector (emphasis in the original 1965a: 151).[15]

This very strong version of the case against the 'vocationalisation' of the curriculum we shall return to in the 1990s when the Government of

---

[15] He re-emphasised the point very vividly a couple of pages later: "… It follows, therefore, that no amount of formal technical, vocational or agricultural instruction alone is going to check the movement from the rural areas, reduce the volume of unemployment, or indeed necessarily have any effect on the rate of economic development" (1965a, 153).

Ghana had introduced a whole series of agricultural, vocational and commercial subjects in the curriculum of the regular senior secondary schools.

3. A national sample for 'the vocational school fallacy'

Two years later, in 1961, Foster drew a national sample of secondary school pupils in their fifth year from 23 highly selective academic secondary schools. Actual responses amounted to 963 cases, or 45.8% of all enrolled boys, and 45.4% of all girls, in the fifth forms of the day. These high percentages concealed the fact that of the 963, no less than 775 were boys, and only 188 girls. This disparity was probably one reason why it was decided that only the male data should be used for the 'Vocational School Fallacy' article, though in the much longer monograph, the two key chapters (on achievement, selection and recruitment; and on aspirations) do deal with both male and female data.[16]

His purpose in this national investigation of selective secondary education was by no means concerned with an examination of the VSF; indeed the term does not even appear in *Education and Social Change in Ghana*.[17] Rather the data allowed him to consider the role of the key secondary school sector and its possible reflection of and impact on patterns of social stratification. Despite considerable evidence of differentiation in levels of achievement measured by examinations, even the very selective secondary schools were successfully drawing on a relatively wide segment of the Ghanaian population. Foster concluded that recruitment into selective secondary education was from a very broad basis indeed, and because of the key allocative role of the high status schools in determining access either to the emerging sixth forms or to higher education, he was able to affirm that there can be no doubt "that the schools operate as extraordinarily effective channels for occupational and social mobility" (1965b: 258).[18]

Although this concern with the socio-economic background of pupils was not the principal focus of the VSF article, it does in one way provide

---

[16] Though Foster could show that selective secondary schools recruited from a surprisingly broad spectrum of the Ghanaian population, the striking inequality was in patterns of female recruitment. In 1961, girls in secondary school in Ghana were drawn from a much more restricted segment of society than boys.

[17] There is a good deal of discussion, however, of the failings of the various technical and vocational schemes of the colonial period.

[18] The only exception to this generalisation would be the Northern region. But otherwise, there were even in the most prestigious secondary schools significant numbers of pupils from entirely uneducated rural parents (1965b, 246).

an important backdrop to considering now the occupational aspirations of this group of young people in Ghana. The schools, despite their high degree of selectivity, were operating in a relatively meritocratic way. Therefore the sample that Foster used is by no means the voice of second and third generation educated families, but includes a substantial number of young people from rural backgrounds, and with markedly low levels of parental education. The knowledge that a significant proportion of the aspirations we now examine are of first generation children of farmers and fishermen must be borne in mind when we revisit Foster's data a little later.

There were three dimensions of aspirations that Foster was concerned to explore:

1. pupils' perceptions of occupational status and income;
2. pupils' vocational aspirations and expectations; and
3. their hopes and expectations of further academic and vocational study after basic secondary education.

To provide a basis against which to judge their own aspirations for employment, it will be useful to look at some features of pupil perceptions of occupational status and income, and in this to pay particular attention to the jobs that are central to the debate about vocational orientation. Foster provided a list of 25 occupations, across a wide range, but including no less than four different kinds of teacher (from primary to university), several professional and artisan positions, a few unskilled, and also one or two traditional occupations such as chief.

In many ways the results of the Ghana study were not dissimilar to other studies of this kind, but Foster made much of the fact that these secondary school students did not rank farming at the bottom of the occupational hierarchy (despite what was often alleged of student attitudes to farming). It came in at 16th in prestige rankings, and no less than 10th (out of 25) in perceived income.[19] Foster commented: "Even among these advanced students farming is still rated moderately high" (1965a:151) in prestige and income, though only 1% of these students wished or expected to become farmers themselves.

With the benefit of hindsight, it is perhaps a pity that Foster did not treat the term farmer — which, he acknowledged, was a very heterogeneous group — as he had treated teacher. By breaking the latter into

---

[19] It should be noted that these ratings are for male students only, except where stated otherwise. It was explained above that only male figures are provided in the VSF article.

four distinct categories, he achieved four very different prestige ratings — from second (university teacher) to sixth (secondary teacher), to 18th and 19th for middle school and primary teacher respectively; and in terms of their perceived income, the range was even greater: 2; 5; 16 and 21, respectively.[20]

We shall note later, from our own survey data, that farmer and other terms such as businessmen benefit from being differentiated into wider categories. By contrast, the other clear artisanal or skilled jobs — motor car mechanic and carpenter — were placed far below the perhaps artificially high position of farmer — at 20th and 23rd in status (just above farm labourer and street cleaner) and at 19th and 22nd in respect of income (1965b: 269-272).

Foster's treatment of these perceptions of income and status in an occupational hierarchy allowed him to make the point that, for most jobs, status is very closely related to the reward structure, and thus any attempt to use the curriculum to try and change the attitude towards, say, carpentry or motor mechanics, through a more diversified curriculum is likely to be "ineffective and economically wasteful" (1965b: 275).

We shall return to look more closely at this position, with the benefit of our own data, but first it will be important briefly to examine what were the vocational aspirations and expectations of this highly selected group of secondary school pupils. Data on pupils' ideal occupations and then their more realistic expectations were collected through the same contrast that was mentioned at the beginning of this paper with middle school pupils in their fourth year of post-primary education. The results were dramatically different. Compared with the 51% of these middle school boys who had had artisan and skilled work as their ideal, this highly selected secondary school sample had 26% of boys aspiring to go into scientific and technological careers, and some 22% of girls into similar fields. The next most common aspirations were for medicine (17 and 16%, respectively) and then secondary school teaching (15 and 16%). What Foster found intriguing about these results was that they did not confirm the stereotype of African pupils obsessed with merely

---

[20] University teachers in Legon or Kumasi today will wonder at university incomes being ranked second in the hierarchy of occupations, when it is commonplace for lecturers now to have to find additional sources of income to make ends meet. Differentiating teachers was straight-forward and non-controversial as the categories are given. Doing the same with richer and poorer (cocoa and subsistence) farmers was carefully considered by Foster but eventually dropped because of the implied link with income which could have prejudiced other responses (Foster to King, personal communication 11th September 2000).

government administrative roles in the civil service (1965b, 275-9). Only some 7% of boys aspired to this kind of job.

When these young people were obliged, next, to say what they would *expect* to do if they were unable to continue their studies beyond their present form 5 (in another question no less than 97% of the boys had aspired to continue with full time schooling after form 5), the picture changed radically. There were now no expectations of joining medicine, law, and the higher administrative services; and there were only small groups expecting to join scientific and technological careers. No less that 34% of boys expected to have to join middle school and primary teaching; and 50% of both boys and girls now expected to take government or other clerical positions.

It is difficult to be completely confident about what is going on in the pupil reactions to this contrast between ideal job and realistic expectation. Arguably, a somewhat artificial 'choice' is created by pre-specifying that the pupils' realistic option must exclude further than form 5 education. What may then happen is a rather mechanistic enumeration of jobs that do not need form 6 and further certification as opposed to a 'realistic' second best. Be that as it may, it is intriguing that even in the conditions of very constrained choice, it would appear that no selective secondary students identified artisanal or skilled careers as a realistic option; and yet 51% of the low status secondary (middle school) pupils chose this route as their ideal.[21] We shall comment further on attitudes to skilled work in our own surveys.

Foster's chapter on "The aspirations of secondary school pupils" included a valuable attempt to look at patterns of where earlier form 5 leaver cohorts had actually gone — as compared with where this 1961 group aspired or expected to go. And it ended with a very powerful affirmation of the extraordinary importance of income expectation in influencing the vocational choice of Ghanaian pupils in secondary schools, and an equally powerful assertion that the socio-economic background of pupils seemed to have had 'relatively minor influence' on their aspirations and expectations.

Before turning now to look 40 years later in Ghana at some of

---

[21] Primary school teacher was clearly still an acceptable outcome in the early 1960s for secondary school students; whereas skilled work was probably seen as leaving the security of government jobs. The detailed questionnaire is only available for the national sample, and not the earlier group of middle school pupils; so it is not possible to compare the precise wording – apart from the two questions mentioned in the text (1965b: 206).

Foster's concerns, there are a few methodological observations that may be made on what has been analysed from these two samples so far.

First, and perhaps most important, there is, as we said earlier, remarkably little attention to curriculum-as-taught in these two publications that have taken such a robust line on the inefficacy of curricular influence on aspirations and expectations. Both the nine middle schools and the 23 selective secondary schools are said to be academic, but there is no detail on what was actually covered in the five years of selective secondary or the 4 years of middle school. We have mentioned already that, on paper, there was meant to be an element of craft and practical work in the middle schools, but it would be important to know if in fact there was any. Equally in the secondary schools, it would be worth emphasising that there really was no technical or vocational orientation of any kind in these schools.[22] We underline this because it will be noted later from our own data that different streams or tracks do seem to have some direct influence on the pattern of occupational aspirations.

Second, although Foster does disaggregate his selective secondary schools into low status and high status, and does explore the differences in social composition and academic achievement in these different segments, and even at the individual school level, he does not examine whether there are different patterns of career aspiration within the different segments of secondary. It could well be that, because of his important finding about the similar social composition of both high and low status secondary education, there might be little differentiation in aspirations. On the other hand, when pupils appear to know well that a minority of secondary schools dominate access to sixth form and thus higher education, it would have been tempting to see if their aspirations were any different both within schools and between schools.

The only disaggregation in the aspirational data is that between the unselective middle schools and the selective secondary, in which it will be recalled that half of the middle school pupils aspired for artisanal and skilled work, in their ideal option, and apparently no selective secondary pupils aspired for these skilled trades in their ideal preferences. What could be driving the differences between these two distinct types of post-primary provision, and especially when one group elects for the very

---

[22] According to those who taught in the elite secondary schools at the time of Foster's main survey, there were no vocational subjects on offer (Bennett to King, 18 July 2000).

vocational trades that are at the heart of the VSF, and the other not at all?[23]

The third and related issue is of course that there were no technical or vocational schools in either of these two samples. It would indeed have been difficult to cover this possibility since there was only one public secondary–technical school (in Takoradi) operating at the time of Foster's investigations and in 1959 "only some 1 per cent of all persons enrolled in formal educational institutions were receiving instruction in vocational, technical or agricultural subjects" (1965a: 144). But again if there had been a desire to look at aspirations at the disaggregated, individual school level, it would have been fascinating to have seen whether this single exemplar of secondary technical education produced any distinct school effect in its pattern of aspirations.

We thus have the rather paradoxical situation that this well-known article on the vocational school has itself no data on contemporary vocational education or the admittedly very limited vocationalised curricular options that existed in Ghana in the early 1960s.[24]

4. The aspirations and expectations of secondary school pupils in the late 1990s

In September 1998 and July 1999, it became possible to revisit the continuing relevance of some of Foster's path-breaking work on aspirations and expectations and on the perceptions of status and income amongst secondary level pupils in Ghana. There was a good deal of evidence that the wider economic context in which the schools found themselves in 1998 and 1999 had changed markedly from those first heady years after independence. The very terms 'emergent' sector and 'exchange sector of the economy' had made way for terms like the formal sector, but much more important than the changing terminology was a possible change in attitude towards what Dore (1976) had termed 'real jobs' in the formal sector of the economy. In the era of structural adjustment, there had been downsizing of jobs even in the once secure formal sector, and, much worse, it was widely felt that the salaries that

---

[23] In point of fact, these two groups of pupils are never compared directly in respect of this most intriguing distinction.

[24] The 'Vocational school fallacy' did comment on the late 19th and early 20th century efforts in the Gold Coast to establish agricultural schools and provide technical and vocational education, but there is no information in the article on what was offered in the 1960s. That Foster had observed some agricultural classes in formal schools is evident from his noting: "No one acquainted with agricultural teaching in West African schools can fail to be impressed by the apathy of the students, which is matched only by that of the teacher" (1965a: 159).

could accrue from being a government clerk, or a university teacher — let alone a primary school teacher — were not sufficient for more than a part of the month. In other words, it had become even more essential for many so-called formal sector workers to have at least two jobs, and often the second and third jobs were in what has come to be termed the informal economy. In the 1980s, many young people saw leaving Ghana as their first choice[25] and the adjustment measures had had a very differential impact on different careers:

> The structural adjustment medicine has not had the same effect across the economy, and its impact has differed significantly over the last decade and more. Arguably, with the lifting of price controls, with privatisation and export orientation, merchants, shopkeepers and traders have benefited, as have the privatised gold mining, and individuals with large export-oriented cocoa farms. [26] Overall, agriculture has declined in importance and the service industries have become the largest sector in the economy (Stephens, 2000: 37).

In revisiting the occupational hierarchy and approach used by Foster, it was important to retain as many as possible of his own categories and questions, but, given the changes in the wider economy and in school curricula, it was also important to find a way of allowing pupils to comment on some of the newer career options that had, possibly, become much more commonplace for pupils to begin to consider in the late 1990s. It was also vital to bear in mind, in analysing these new data, that central tenet of Foster's VSF — that schools and their (vocational) curricula can have little determinative influence on student perceptions of opportunities, occupational aspirations or destinations. But in revisiting their attitudes, we wanted to be able to look at whether the new vocational streams and tracks appeared to have any influence on pupil orientations.

We were aware that without a longitudinal design in which pupils could be surveyed at the beginning, middle and end of their senior secondary schooling, it would be difficult to reach firm conclusions about school influences; and even an experimental design would have to take

---

[25] Nicholas Bennett, who was involved through the World Bank in some of the major education reforms of the 1980s, has mentioned that through a number of informal surveys he had realised that for several categories of students (from vocational to university) the first career option was in fact to leave the country (personal communication 17.7.2000)

[26] However, saturation of markets has squeezed many petty traders, and, of course, the prices of gold and cocoa have fluctuated wildly (personal communication, Paul Nugent). Two books are available from James Currey Publishers on the adjustment experience of Ghana – see Aryetey et al. (2000) and Hutchful (2002).

account of the fact that pupils' attitudes to careers do change anyway as they mature. All we could hope to show was whether there was an indication that schools were contributing some element to the larger mix of factors behind career aspirations and expectations.

5. The new realism: attitudes towards self-employment

Foster had been able to show that there had been something of a 'white collar myth' surrounding the alleged determination of pupils to seek safe government jobs. Forty years later, we felt it might nicely parallel his concerns to look at pupil attitudes towards self-employment; it would be an appropriate litmus test of pupil realism and of their appreciation of the changing labour market.

Accordingly, additional questions, both closed and open, relating to jobs and to self-employment, were included, first of all, in a pilot questionnaire that went to 220 final year pupils in five Accra senior secondary schools in September 1998.[27] It seemed valuable deliberately to include amongst these five schools a substantial variety, with two of the highest calibre schools in Accra, a third which had originally been a middle school, a fourth which was a secondary technical school, and finally a private secondary school.[28] But with the importance of understanding more about the outlook of those in vocational schools, most of whom would have completed at minimum the three years of junior secondary school, it was decided also to include four vocational institutions, two run by government and two run by NGOs (a total of 105 young people).[29]

Apart from re-using many of Foster's questions, we also asked: "Would you be interested in becoming self-employed and working for yourself?" While this is perhaps a leading question, no less than 89% of the combined secondary school and vocational students said they would, and then went on to illustrate and confirm this by detailing the particular

---

[27] In Foster's 1961 survey of secondary schools, he selected those in the final year of the selective five-year secondary schools, and not those in the even more selective emerging sixth forms. In the subsequent reform, secondary education was divided into three years of junior and three years of senior secondary.

[28] Because of the growing importance of private secondary education in Ghana, Foster had wished to include the private sector within his national sample, but the schools at the time had not been enthusiastic.

[29] A big difference from Foster's day is the huge number of vocational training schools (mostly private/NGO) that exist now and that did not exist then in the early 1960s, related to informal and semi-skilled opportunities – We owe this insight to Nicholas Bennett of the World Bank.

character of that self-employment.[30] At first sight this would seem to support Foster's position — regardless of school type, pupils were signalling an interest in considering self-employment, presumably because of the changes they saw in the economy around them.[31] In other words, one of the things that seems to have changed most dramatically is the *organisational setting* in which pupils say they would prefer to work.[32]

The very high proportion of those ready to consider working for themselves is parallel to the even higher figure which responded to Foster's query "Do you hope to continue your full-time education after you have completed your secondary school course?" This produced no less than 97% of pupils who aspired to do so. But it was precisely these very high figures that led Foster to probe the realistic expectations of these young people. We did the same.

This very high apparent interest in self-employment was therefore explored further in a second, larger survey of secondary schools nine months later, including four of the same five Accra schools that had been used the previous year, and then three new schools in Volta Region (two in Ho, the regional capital, and one more rural). The total size of this second survey was 522. This time, amongst other things, we were anxious to follow up our earlier query about self-employment, and oblige pupils to think about this further in a variety of different ways. On the one hand, we were keen to take cognisance of the fact that many young people might have become aware of 'straddling' (being in both a formal sector job and another position, possibly in the informal sector); hence to ask them to select just one out of a list of work options might also produce a misleading response. On the other hand, procedurally, we suspected that if we asked pupils to indicate the range of what they would accept before obliging them to choose amongst these, we might get a more interesting and revealing response.

So, after asking them an open choice question about their ideal job — almost identical in phrasing to Foster's question — we then went on to probe as follows:

If you were free to choose, who would you like to work for? Please

---

[30] It is interesting to note that there was virtually no difference in this high level of interest in considering self-employment, amongst the different schools and technical training institutes.

[31] It is interesting to note that in a national sample of 2,000 surveyed in July 1999 by Michigan State University, no less than 86% agreed that individuals should pursue good business ideas, even if they must invest savings or borrow to make a business succeed (Bratton et al., 1999: 23).

[32] We are grateful to Tony Somerset for a discussion of the importance of the organisational setting.

tick ALL those you would consider (see Table 1)

Table 1: Work and self-employment preferences of senior secondary pupils in Ghana (multiple choices: N=522)

For yourself (self-employed)	62%
For your family	30%
For the government, or a government-run organization	57%
For a private firm	66%
Other, please specify	5%

When pupils were able to choose more than one, by far the three most popular categories were: working for a private firm, then self-employment, and then for government or parastatal organisation. The results very powerfully confirmed the positive indications from the pilot about self-employment. But, having established that self-employment was certainly attractive when pupils were asked to select ALL they would consider, the key question now was whether self-employment would still be selected by many pupils when they could select ONLY ONE of five possibilities:

And who would you MOST like to work for? Please tick ONLY ONE (see Table 2)

Table 2: Work and self-employment preferences of senior secondary pupils in Ghana (single choice: N=522)

For yourself (self-employed)	30%
For your family	6%
For the government, or a government-run organization	31%
For a private firm	31%
Other, please specify	2%

It was remarkable that, presented with a situation where they could only choose one, the self-employment option remained as strong with this group of senior secondary students as working for government or the private sector. This seems a very suggestive, even robust, finding, and it must be remembered that it is not derived from a group of low status secondary schools (to use Foster's term), but from a very diverse group, which included two of the most prestigious schools in the whole of Ghana — Achimota (co-educational) and Presbyterian Boys.[33]

What was also very remarkable, however, was the range of inter-school variation in preferences for self-employment, as well as for government/parastatal employment, and for private firms. Earlier, in the discussion of Foster's work, the importance of disaggregation amongst schools was mentioned. The following example will illustrate such substantial differences at the level of the individual school that it may well suggest that school character, tradition and location, as well as social composition (and family background) are playing some part. One other intriguing element in the chemistry of aspirations may well be what has been termed the effects of school 'chartering' whereby the unique characteristics of particular schools can actually confer on pupils both higher and lower aspirations than are justified by their educational performance (Somerset, 1974).[34]

For instance, Achimota had no less than 53% of its 129 sampled pupils actually preferring self-employment, while the most rural school, Awudome (in Volta Region) had only 8% of its 41 sampled pupils selecting this option as first choice. The other high quality Accra school, Presbyterian Boys, recorded 25% of its 106 sampled pupils choosing self-employment as their first preference. What could be driving these very different numbers?

One of the biggest contrasts through this school-level disaggregated data is that between preferences for government work versus working for a private firm. By far the highest preferences in two of the three regional schools (in Volta) are to work for Government. The most rural school, Awudome, registered no less than a 78% preference for government employment, and one of the other two schools, in the regional capital, Ho, registered a 42% preference for government work.[35] By contrast Achimota had as few as 9% of its pupils electing for government work as their first

---

[33] These two very high prestige schools in Accra were responsible for no less than 235 of the 522 in the second questionnaire.

[34] We are indebted to Tony Somerset for reminding us of the relevance of the schools' 'chartering' effects, and also for suggesting that there could be school effects linked to the presence or absence of career guidance programmes. We have unfortunately no data on the latter in Ghana.

[35] The Ho sample may be skewed. Ho is singular because it has never been a town of great commercial significance. Its success rests very heavily on being the Regional (and District) capital. For pupils in Ho, there is likely to be a heightened expectation of getting a job in the regional administration or in one of the state corporations that have their headquarters there (Paul Nugent, personal communication).

choice.[36]

The other angle on this is the attitude towards working for a private firm. There is again a large range, with more than three of the urban schools having 40% or higher, and the most rural school having as low as 11%. These patterns might seem to suggest that being educated in a city school in the midst of a range of private sector initiatives is one of the factors influencing this, as compared to a rural school with little evidence of large-scale formal enterprise in the vicinity. In other words, this would support Foster's assumption about the determining effect of the economy. But then comes the surprise: the only private secondary school in our sample, Harvard College in Central Accra, which has a strong emphasis on business studies, registered the second highest preference of all schools for government work (at 50%), and had a relatively low score for private firms (11%).[37]

This sheer variation amongst schools, therefore, suggests that there could well be a significant set of school level factors operating on pupil choice, in addition to whatever influence the economic environment and parental background may bring to bear. We shall return to look at this in more detail in a moment when we examine more specific job choices in different kinds of schools.

But, first, it may be timely to try and get behind what pupils are thinking of when they mention an interest in self-employment, for it is clear that they are making these choices against an economic environment that has shifted markedly since Foster's day. It was assumed that like the occupations of 'farmer', 'businessman' or 'teacher', this category of 'self-employment' would cover a substantial range, but that in the minds of some of the most highly selected pupils in the country it might include examples that linked income and status, as Foster had shown for the employment choices of his sample. Here, from the 1998 survey, are just a few illustrations of 'self-employment' from one of Presbyterian Boys

---

[36] We are indebted to Terry Allsop of DFID for suggesting that over the last 40 years the parental background of Achimota pupils may have shifted from government service to successful private sector careers, and thus changed as much as pupil perspectives (Allsop to King, 8th August 2000). A similar point has been made by a group of JICA-sponsored teacher training tutors in Hiroshima on 14th September 2000: that to the parents and children of poor farmers in the area around Awudome, a government job will still look like a secure option, while to the pupils of the best urban schools, the government jobs will appear a very poor alternative to private business.

[37] Dela Afenyadu has suggested that Harvard College whose catchment area includes some of poorest urban communities in Accra, will be reflecting, in part, in its pupil preferences for government jobs the social status, present occupation, and lower ambitions of the parents (Afenyadu to King personal communication 14 August 2000).

Secondary School's science streams:

> Open a private clinic (6)//my own architectural firm//Writing and publishing//setting up a computer firm//car mechanic//leisure artwork and painting//a firm to do construction and development projects//setting up a fast food chain or a hotel//fashion designing// electrical and electronic repair firm//seller of chemicals//music studio//computer programming//large scale farming of cash crops (2)//developing a research institute//pilot training school//lucrative barbering//small animal production//large scale bee-keeping//small scale poultry//cash crop farm//private tuition in science and computing//small scale pig farming//manufacturing local, natural soap// lucrative shoemaking// (1998 survey data; numbers in parentheses indicate the numbers of pupils making this choice).

We suspect that Foster would be delighted with this list of some 30 pupils' aspirations for what we might call entrepreneurial self-employment, because of the range of their interests and also the strong scientific and technological (and even agricultural) emphasis. Equally it probably shows some shrewd insight into the way that doctors, in particular, are known to be setting up private clinics in Ghana, and it almost certainly reflects on some of the income possibilities associated with their own parents' work.

And then by way of contrast, some of the self-employment suggestions made by girl pupils in O'Reilly's Secondary School, also from the 1998 survey. It can be immediately seen that there is a very different feel to this range of self-employment aspirations by girls from the visual arts and home economics tracks:

> Book binding (2)// graphic design (2)// fashion design (3)// computer aided design (2)// printing// snack bar (2)// catering (5)//hotel management (4)// craft products// restaurant owner (3)// small scale enterprise/trader (3)// design and dressmaking (3)// nutritionist// food stalls (1998 survey data; numbers in parentheses indicate the numbers of pupils making this choice)

Part of this difference may be explained by the fact that these pupils were girls, which may have given less of a technological and scientific feel than the options from one of the best science streams in the country. And it should be remembered that there is a very dynamic tradition of female enterprise in Ghana which could also have been influential, and to this we shall return in a moment. But there still remains the key issue of whether beyond the influence of family and the impact of the changing opportunity structure outside the schools, there is some kind of *school influence* in these very particular patterns of self-employment aspiration. There is already some suggestion of this in the substantial school-level differences in aspiration for self-employment and government versus private employment, but to look a little closer at a possible school effect, it is necessary to note some of the major curricular changes in both junior (JSS) and senior secondary schools (SSS) which came into effect from 1987.

Afenyadu (1998: 14) puts these changes from the old middle and secondary schools succinctly. It can be seen that the curricular additions are some of the very items at the heart of the VSF debate:

> Apart from English language, local language, general mathematics and general science, which have been retained from the middle school system, new courses such as life skills, vocational skills, technical skills and technical drawing, social studies and cultural studies have been introduced into the JSS curriculum.
>
> At the SSS level, apart from English, mathematics, agricultural science and Ghanaian languages, which have been retained as core courses (from the old secondary school system), elective courses introduced in the new system have been grouped under business management, home economics, general, arts and science. Home economics students study food and clothing and textiles. Business students either study costing, accounting and business management as a set of electives or study clerical office duties and typing. Some selected schools offer technical drawing and technical studies and/or visual arts as electives. Computer skills are being introduced gradually into many schools.

These curricular changes mean that, unlike the 775 secondary school pupils in Foster's national sample in 1961 who were, apparently, undifferentiated by track, our circa 742 secondary pupils in 1998 and 1999 can be identified with the following very specific tracks, options or streams.[38]

---

[38] Nicholas Bennett, of the World Bank, who was one of the key architects of the overall education reform in Ghana, has mentioned that the government, in 1990-1991, actually wanted senior secondary schools completely diversified by type as compared to the package of programme options that was finally agreed (Bennett to King, 26 January 2000).

Achimota:	General Arts (2); General Science; Agricultural Science; Visual Arts; Home Economics
Presbyterian Boys:	General Science (2); General Arts; Business
O'Reilly:	General Arts; Business; Visual Arts; Home Economics
Kaneshie Secondary Technical:	Metalwork; Building Construction
Harvard College:	Business (2)
Awudome:	General Science
Ola:	Business
Mawuli:	Technical; General Science

(survey data, 1998–1999. Figures in parentheses indicate numbers of streams sampled).

The possibility of a school influence or effect was explored further in several different ways. The first was to examine pupils' perceptions of their two most valuable school subjects "that may help you in the work you want to do". It was thought entirely possible that there would be a major emphasis by pupils on the importance of English and maths, regardless of the specialisation by track. Again, it was crucial to review this at the disaggregated school level; at the aggregate level, not a single subject except maths (8%) got more than 4% of total pupil responses. The results were quite remarkably consistent once we looked at what was happening in the individual school: pupils almost always picked out as most valuable the very subjects that were at the heart of their specialisation (and at the centre of the VSF debate):

Presbyterian (science):	93% of valuable subjects were accounted for by maths, physics, biology and chemistry (English was not even mentioned)
Harvard (business):	86% of valuable subjects were accounted for by accounting, business management, economics, and key board skills (English 4%; maths 5%)
O'Reilly (visual arts):	82% of valuable subjects were accounted for by graphic design, textiles

O'Reilly (home economics):	80% of valuable subjects were accounted for by clothing and textiles, general knowledge in art, management in living and home economics
Achimota (agricultural science):	78% of valuable subjects were accounted for by agricultural economics, general agriculture, core science, and horticulture
Achimota (general arts):	82% of the valuable subjects were accounted for by government and history (English getting only 3% and maths 6%)
Kaneshie (metal and building):	75% of the valuable subjects were covered by building construction, engineering science, metal technology, technical drawing (English 3% and maths 5%).

These are surprising and yet extremely consistent results, in which a sample of highly selected secondary school pupils identified their specialised stream subjects as the most valuable, and when asked whether there were subjects that were missing from their curriculum, they merely added further technical and practical subjects, as well as subjects like French, presumably because of its vocational use.

This school-level variation in attitude to different subjects was paralleled by very clear evidence of different preferences for self-employment by school track. Thus when we put together all the different schools and looked at the variation by track, there were again some very suggestive patterns towards self-employment, as opposed to working for the family, government or a private firm (Table 3).

Table 3: Preferred employer by school track -
Who would you most like to work for? Please tick one.

Preferred employer	School track				
	Vocational/ technical	Science	General arts	Business	ALL
Self	46%	32%	25%	24%	30%
Family	7%	4%	6%	7%	6%
Government	24%	38%	25%	34%	31%
Private	23%	22%	43%	35%	31%
Total*	100%	100%	100%	100%	100%

* Column totals may not sum to 100% due to exclusion of 'other' responses.

It can be seen clearly that those who are in the more vocational and technical tracks, such as Visual Arts, Home Economics, or technical studies, do appear to have a much stronger preference for self-employment (46%) than those in other tracks. But even here there are exceptions. For instance, in Achimota's science stream, an astonishingly high 71% of the pupils said they would prefer to work for themselves.

There would certainly appear to be some kind of school or curriculum effect at work here. But to pursue it further, the ideal career aspirations of pupils in these individual schools were examined. Again, there was a very strong correlation between the particular track and the occupations most desired. In other words, there was no such thing as an Achimota response to our questions; it differed by track and stream. Thus in Achimota which was the top academic school (along with Mfantsipim) in Foster's sample, its agricultural science stream had an extraordinary variety of preferred agricultural careers mentioned, as a first choice — including agricultural economist, agricultural scientist, agricultural engineer, horticulturist, landscape architect, soil scientist, veterinary officer, livestock farmer, poultry, vegetable and fruit specialists, large scale animal and livestock farmer, large scale fruit farmer. Whereas in its general arts stream which had regarded government and history as its key subjects, there turned up the following very different shape of vocational aspirations: lawyer; judge or solicitor (52% of replies); administrator (10%); diplomat; legal secretary; company owner; factory owner; tourism civil servant; architect; customs and excise officer — and — for good measure — President of the Nation! (1998 survey data)

Table 4: Who do you think you will work for? Please Tick One

Expected employer	All pupils
Self	14%
Family	7%
Government/parastatal	40%
Private firm	38%
Other	1%
Total	100%

Following Foster, we pursued these ideal aspirations of 1998 and 1999 by a probe into their *realistic expectations* of what they thought they would be doing after finishing their education, and who they thought they would, in fact, most likely be working for. And again there seemed to be a clearly different pattern — not just by school but by stream and track. Thus, the 30% of the entire 1999 sample who, we had noted, would have preferred self-employment as their first choice, now fell dramatically to 14%, and many of those who still stuck to their guns, and expected to be self-employed had adjusted downwards the level of their ambitions. This is entirely rational since pupils know that entering self-employment often requires work experience, some capital and connections (Table 4).[39]

Obliged to be more realistic, it is interesting to note that almost half of the pupils in the established urban schools looked to private firms, and then to government jobs, while as many as many as 80% of the pupils in the most rural school still looked to the government as their expected employer.

The 14% who expected to be self-employed do not only comprise those who, earlier, aspired to self-employment. Indeed more than a third of this group had originally aspired to another employer, with over 20% aspiring to work for the government.

This mismatch between aspiration and expectation is greatest for those who aspire to self-employment. While only 26% of those who had aspired to self-employment really expect to be self-employed after school, the corresponding figures for those aspiring to work for a private firm is 65% and for the government 75%. What can this mean? The career

---

[39] This realistic approach to self-employment still differed a good deal by school and by track. The most notable was Harvard College where as many as 30% now expected to enter self-employment. But given what we have said above in footnote 36, this 'realistic' self-employment may be much more of the subsistence than entrepreneurial variety.

trajectories of those wanting to be self-employed are apparently not so fixed or so linear? Or that the meanings of self-employment are markedly different in different schools?

The answer may in part lie in the difference that the particular career makes to the nature of pupils' aspirations and expectations. In other words, self-employment as a private doctor, accountant or engineer would be rather different from self-employment as a seller or trader, in the sense that pupils might well aspire to run their private clinics, engineering or accountancy firms, but might recognise they would probably need to start by working for government or another employer first. This was exactly the pattern that emerged when we looked at the organisational settings that pupils aspired to for these three most popular careers (doctors, engineers and accountants). No less than 28, 22 and 33% *aspired* to be self-employed in these three careers respectively, but when obliged to be more realistic, these fell to 9, 16 and 11% (and the overall numbers also fell substantially).

Realistically, many of these would-be medics, accountants and engineers thought they would in fact be working for the government instead of for themselves (68, 36, 47%). Professional builders were a somewhat different case, almost certainly because of the character of the job. No less than 62% in this career had aspired to be self-employed (with no one aspiring to work for government), but likewise both the overall numbers and the percentage expecting to be self-employed had fallen when asked to be realistic (25%), but the expectation had been more to work for the private sector than for the government. A similar pattern was evident for careers like catering, designing and business owners. High aspirations towards self-employment (45, 56 and 56%, respectively) tended to be converted into expectations of working more in the private sector.[40]

For all these careers mentioned, the numbers of those aspiring had fallen — often quite substantially — when obliged to be more realistic. At the other end of the spectrum were a few careers like teaching, or small-scale selling and trading, where the numbers of those aspiring had been very small, but realism had encouraged a change of heart. Thus only 14 out of a total of 522 had actually *aspired* to teaching, but as many as 34 eventually thought they might find themselves in this career. And

---

[40] Overall numbers in these three careers (11, 16 and 16) are so very much smaller than those who had aspired to be medics, accountants and engineers (106, 107 and 64) that we cannot be as sure of the trends.

similarly with trading, only a handful had wanted to be traders, but no less than 36 expected they might be. Here again, the organisational setting is important, since self-employment as a teacher is much more problematic than a lawyer or doctor. Hence, logically, we find those expecting to be teachers are located in the government or the private sector, rather than in self-employment.

6. Occupational rankings

In this challenge of sorting out the school influences from the impact of the surrounding economy, it was finally thought to be useful to compare our pupils' perceptions of income and of status with almost the same 25 occupations that Foster had used 40 years earlier. It might provide an insight into what had happened to the status and income of jobs over the adjustment era. We made a few changes. Where Foster had broken down 'teacher' into four levels (from university to primary), we retained it as one, but we broke 'farmer' and 'businessman' into large-scale and small-scale. We also included some newer careers, such as fashion designer, restaurateur, NGO/Community worker and engineer. The results from the pilot survey (of 1998) were quite strikingly different from the main survey of the following year, and for a reason that had not been anticipated. Where Foster had asked about the high and low 'respect' and 'prestige' of these jobs, we first asked (in 1998) about their 'importance' in Ghana and then (in 1999) about their 'high and low respect' and their 'status'. The quite extraordinary difference between the 'importance' and 'respect' of particular jobs made it very clear to us that our respondents were very sensitive to nuances of meaning. Certain jobs were 'important' in our pupils' eyes, but they had very low 'respect' or 'status'.

In fact, as Table 5 demonstrates, certain jobs were regarded by secondary pupils as 'important' but low 'status' — for example, teachers, large-scale farmers, nurses and policemen, while others were seen as high status but not particularly important, for example, politician, restaurant owner and chief. On the whole, pupils linked status to income, and differentiated both from importance.

This table with its data from two slightly different surveys allows of a rather 'non-Fosterite' interpretation. As we had noted earlier, Foster had argued that, for most jobs, status is very closely related to reward structure; hence there is little purpose in trying to use the school or the curriculum to change perceptions. But Table 5 might suggest that the close linkages amongst income, status and aspiration are not the whole story, or that the story is not so simple. Clearly, many pupils do not only see rewards in terms of status and income. Some aspire to jobs that are important (to the nation or to themselves) even if their status is low. The role of the school in ordering and influencing these attitudes is also likely to be rather complex.

Further, before looking at Table 5, it might be interesting to see just two of a large number of comments by pupils who thought that low status jobs were very important:

> If I am free to choose any that I wanted, I'd prefer to be a teacher because without teachers, the country will not develop (Harvard College, male, Arts Stream 1999 Survey Data).

> Students are mostly trained academically, and not in creative works which will help to develop our skills. These students end up doing only white collar jobs, hence leaving precious resources which could be utilised to generate income and develop the idle economy (Ola, female, Business Studies, 1999 Survey Data).

In this occupational ranking, doctor remained No. 1 (as with Foster), but both in importance and in status. No. 2 in terms of 'importance' was our undifferentiated teacher but in terms of status and respect, the teacher tumbles to No. 17 (very close to primary teacher in Foster). Nurse is another job that is regarded as important to Ghana but has relatively low status, and policeman is similar. Engineer — one of our new categories — comes out as No. 3 both in importance and status, and large-scale farmer, at No. 4, is seen perhaps surprisingly as important but low status. But what is clear in these rankings is that some of the recognised 'skilled' jobs, such as motorcar fitter, carpenter, small scale farmer, small scale businessman and petty trader are all relatively or very low in importance and status.

Table 5: Occupational Rankings by importance, status and income

	Importance (1998 survey)	Status/respect (1999 survey)	Income (figures in parentheses from 1998 survey)
Doctors	1	1	3 (1)
Teachers	2	17	19 (21)
Engineers	3	3	2 (2)
Large scale farmers	4	14	9 (8)
Pastor	5	6	13 (16)
Nurses	6	13	16 (12)
Journalist	7	8	8 (10)
Large scale businessmen	8	7	5 (4)
Policeman	9	20	20 (20)
Lawyer	10	2	1 (3)
Miner	11	12	10 (9)
Soldier	12	11	12 (11)
Factory worker	13	19	16 (15)
Civil servant	14	18	18 (17)
Fashion designer	15	10	7 (6)
NGO	16	22	22 (22)
Motorcar fitter	17	25	23 (23)
Carpenter	18	24	24 (24)
Politician	19	5	5 (7)
Restaurant owner	20	9	4 (5)
Office worker	21	15	17 (13)
Chief	22	4	11 (14)
Small scale businessman	23	21	21 (19)
Small scale farmer	24	26	26 (26)
Actor	25	16	14 (18)
Petty trader	26	27	27 (27)
Shop assistant	27	23	25 (25)

But when it comes to ranking some of these occupations in income terms, there are many more dramatic changes than in Foster's day. Our undifferentiated teacher falls to 19th from being second in importance, and the carpenters and fitters fall right to the bottom of the income hierarchy. But it is an interesting perception of several of our new jobs, many of which could be self-employed as much as employed, that fashion designers and restaurateurs moved up towards the top of the income scale along with large-scale businessmen. In fact, it could be argued that the majority of jobs in the top ten for income, including lawyers and doctors, as we heard from the pupils, could involve working for oneself as easily as being employed.

Methodologically, the case for the disaggregation of certain job categories is plain. Foster had shown the wisdom of this with the term 'teacher' which our surveys had left undifferentiated.[41] But he had made much of the fact that in his survey 'farmer' had been 16th in prestige ranking and 10th in income. Whereas we have seen, by dividing farmer into large and small, that the small-scale farmer is right at the very bottom of importance, status and income, while large-scale farmer has a much more significant ranking.

But even here, it would be valuable, if there were space, to sift out how these hierarchies change at the individual school level. However, it was already plain that there were significant differences between the school responses and the vocational institutions we had included in the 1998 pilot survey. Just one example: carpenter was rated 18th in importance by secondary school pupils but ninth by pupils in specialised vocational institutions. So again, it looks like there might be an institutional effect behind some of these differential rankings.

7. Concluding observations and continuing challenges

Foster's original monograph and article did a great deal more than provoke one of the longest-running debates on the politics of the manipulation of schooling in the developing world that there has ever been; he established that the social composition of what were in fact highly differentiated forms of selective secondary education were remarkably similar, and that there was a powerful belief that such schools were "open to all individuals of talent, irrespective of their origins" (1965b: 239). We can argue something supportive of this position. Already from our 1999 sample it is quite clear what secondary school pupils believe are "those things which people have said are important to being successful, in the job you hope to do". Indeed, challenged to say what single thing was more important to being successful than all the rest, pupils were in no doubt that it was intelligence (37%), then, interestingly,

---

[41] We had considered breaking teacher into several categories, but with the constraints of space felt it more important to do this with 'farmer' and 'businessman' which Foster had had as single categories.

honesty (20%) and only then certification (14%). A *belief* that Ghana remains a meritocratic society seems still to be alive today as in Foster's time, and in some respects perhaps more so.[42] However, the reality may be that the parental background and social composition of the high and low status secondary schools may have been widening over these 40 years.[43]

When it comes to pupil assessment today of how well schools prepare young people for the world of work, there is again a clear first emphasis on the importance of their certifying role, but, intriguingly, this is followed both by creativity and then by 'practical skills'. Again, pupils seem to be pointing to something that looks like a curriculum effect, though more analysis would need to be undertaken at the school level to verify the variety of positions taken on these key school factors in later success.

The debate about practical subjects in primary and secondary school remains highly relevant today in several countries. In Kenya, there has just been a national commission reviewing the 8-4-4 system which has had a strongly practical emphasis since the reform of 1985, and there have been powerfully competing interpretations of the results (Afenyadu et al., 2001).[44] And in South Africa a similar debate has been developing as it seeks to reform its basic education curriculum towards a series of core skills, including practical income generating activities (Afenyadu et al., 2001; King and McGrath, 2002).

One reason the issue remains in the foreground of contention, even in the new century, is that clearly pupils are directly affected by their perceptions of the opportunity structure outside the schools — whether in the post-independent Ghana of 1959-1961 or in the very different economic milieu of 1998-1999. But equally, it seems undeniable from our data, that there is some persistent form of school or track effect. This is not

---

[42] The position of chief was rated as fourth in status terms in Foster's sample and eighth in terms of income. By 1998/9, it was being rated as low as 22nd from the top in terms of importance, but was still 4th in status and respect and between 11th and 14th in income.

[43] The gap may be even greater between our sample of schools as a whole, and the large new group of Community Secondary Schools that have been developing with World Bank support in the late 1990s.

[44] In a rather provocative finding from March 1999, Nishimura and Orodho (1999) found that no less than 78% of secondary school students in Kenya thought that vocational and technical subjects in formal schools were "very necessary and very important or necessary and important"; and yet 86% of their teachers thought exactly the opposite. Equally, Kerre and Oketch (1999), as part of the larger DFID study, found that at secondary school level 63% of respondents expressed satisfaction with the way schools had provided preparation for self-employment, as compared to 66% for regular employment.

so obvious when the data is aggregated, but it shows up very strongly with disaggregation.

Of course, there will continue to be debate about whether in school systems that have tracks, it is the tracks that attract particular pupils with these specific career orientations rather than the tracks themselves that influence attitudes to work and to jobs. Without longitudinal studies, these questions cannot probably be finally resolved, and even these would be challenging because of pupil maturation in school.

There is a further factor that certainly plays a substantial role in the complex chemistry of career orientation which we have alluded to at various points, and that is the influence on pupils of their parents' involvement in particular work. This is especially important but difficult to disentangle in Ghana where there is a continuing very strong tradition of women engaging in trade and business, at all social levels. In our 1999 sample, from Achimota to Harvard, there were very high proportions of mothers engaged in such activities. [45] Here again, the influence on attitudes towards enterprise and towards different kinds of self-employment of this home experience is difficult to discount.

Foster's message today as in 1963 remains relevant for any attempts to use schools to deliver massive changes in attitude and aspiration in the absence of any parallel initiatives in the larger economic environment. His doctrine was an unpopular and necessary corrective in an era that had often a naive trust in the transformational potential of formal schools.[46] But we hope we may have said enough to suggest that influence on attitudes and expectations is not an either-or dichotomy between school and society — rather a complex compound of both, and of family backgrounds. Schools may well turn out to add to or mitigate the influence of society. But the continual weakening of teacher quality and of teacher salaries are bound to put at risk many positive school effects in the bulk of ordinary schools (King, 2001).

At the turn of the 20th century, Foster's work retains its relevance in so many ways. Nor is this famous article only about *vocational* fallacies;

---

[45] If we put together the various categories of business involvement, we have the following proportions of mothers involved in enterprise in our seven schools: Achimota (61 of 123); Presbyterian Boys (50 of 107); O'Reilly (59 of 75); Ola (26 of 41); Mawuli (39 of 86); Awudome (22 of 36); and Harvard (34 of 37).

[46] It should not be surprising to learn that Foster (1969) was one of the first to be highly critical of Nyerere's ambitious social goals for the schools of Tanzania in *Education for Self-reliance* (Nyerere, 1967). But for a useful commentary on Foster's critique of this reform, see David Court (1972). Court reaches the interesting conclusion "Critical scrutiny of this (Foster's) analysis gives a number of grounds for the view that schools are not entirely powerless to contribute to social change" (p. 10).

rather it is about any attempt to manipulate a single element of education and training to produce an economic effect out of school. Today, it is not impossible if Foster were to examine the rapidity with which an international, political consensus has emerged in the last 10 years around the centrality of basic education to the eradication of poverty that he would be tempted to write instead on the dangers of "a basic education fallacy in pro-poor growth".

But we should end this account with Philip Foster himself. He has, because of the VSF, been assumed to be hostile to all forms of vocationalisation in schools. Which is not the case. And students of today who only read this single article, and not the 17 other substantial publications he completed between 1962 and 1968, could be forgiven for thinking that this theme was something that Foster specialised in.[47] Which was not the case either. Philip Foster's own comment on the VSF is where we must leave this ongoing debate for the moment:

> Having said this, I must add that I personally am in favour of attempts at more diversified types of curriculum and school systems for *pedagogical* and *educational* reasons. Don't expect such changes to influence the realities of the labour market, however, as George [Psacharopoulos] found out in his Discus project evaluations.[48] Moreover it is simply hypocritical to talk about more 'practical' training in African schools when most are so poor that they can't even afford a few nails and hammers at best! Moreover, as you well know, I am hostile to elites in poor countries that propose reforms while sending their own kids to elite academic institutions. Funny about the 'vocational school fallacy' — I wrote it in a few days as a 'spin-off' from my own major interest in education, class formation and stratification in LDCs. You never can tell what's going to sell as the ad men say! (Foster to King, personal communication, 3 September 1999).

---

[47] Of these many publications, none is explicitly concerned with the vocational element in schooling, though see Foster (1964) "Secondary school leavers in Ghana: expectations and reality".

[48] George Psacharopoulos and William Loxley (1984) in the World Bank carried out a study in Tanzania and Colombia to try and ascertain the cost-effectiveness of diversified secondary education schemes (in the wider DISCUS research project).

Acknowledgements

This work was made possible by the support of the Department for International Development, and by the Moray Endowment. Neither DFID nor the Moray Endowment is of course responsible for what is said in this article. The authors should like to thank a variety of people for commenting on this. These would include: Philip Foster; Jon Lauglo; James Micklem; Terry Allsop; Hefasona Acheampong; Dela Afenyadu; Paul Nugent; Anthony Somerset; Nicholas Bennett; David Stephens; Gordon Mwangi; David Court; and Simon McGrath. The draft profited from discussions with a group of JICA-sponsored teacher trainers from Ghana who were studying in Hiroshima in September 2000, and especially the staff and students of our survey schools in Ghana. Any faults are, however, our responsibility.

References

Afenyadu, D., 1998. *Changes in practice and students' aspirations in the era of globalisation*. Papers on Education, Training and Enterprise, No. 16. Centre of African Studies, University of Edinburgh.

Afenyadu, D., King, K., McGrath, S., Oketch, H., Rogerson, C., Visser, K., 2001. *Learning to compete: education, training and enterprise in Ghana, Kenya and South Africa*. Education Research, Serial No. 42. Department for International Development, London.

Anderson, A., Bowman, M.J. (Eds.), 1965. *Education and economic development*. Aldine, Chicago.

Aryetey, E., Harrigan, J., Nissanke, M. (Eds.), 2000. *Economic reforms in Ghana: The miracle and the mirage*. James Currey, Oxford.

Bening, R., 1990. *A History of education in Northern Ghana 1907-1976*. Ghana Universities Press, Legon.

Bratton, M., Lewis, P., Gyimah-Boadi, E., 1999. *Attitudes to democracy and markets in Ghana*. Afrobarometer Paper No. 2, Michigan State University Working Papers on Political Reform in Africa. Political Science, MSU, East Lansing.

Callaway, A., 1963. Unemployment among African school leavers. *Journal of Modern African Studies* 1(3), 351-371.

Court, D., 1972. *The social function of formal schooling: the views of Foster and the experiences of Tanzania*. Discussion Paper No. 128. Institute for Development Studies, University of Nairobi, Nairobi.

Dore, R., 1976. *The Diploma disease: Education, qualification and development*. Allen and Unwin, London.

Foster, P., 1964. Secondary school-leavers in Ghana: Expectations and reality. *Harvard Educational Review* 34(4), 537-558.

Foster, P., 1965a. The vocational school fallacy in development planning. In: Anderson, A.A., Bowman, M.J. (Eds.), *Education and economic development*. Aldine, Chicago.

Foster, P., 1965b. *Education and social change in Ghana*. Routledge and Kegan Paul, London.

Foster, P., 1969. Education for self-reliance: a critical evaluation. In: Jolly, R. (Ed.), *Education in Africa: Research and action*. East African Publishing House, Nairobi.

Government of Ghana, 1995. *Ghana vision 2020*. Government Printer, Accra.

Hanson, J.W., 1980. *Is the school the enemy of the farm? The African experience*. African Rural Economy Paper No. 22, Michigan State University, East Lansing, pp. 1-97.

Hart, K., 1973. Informal income opportunities and urban employment in Ghana. *Journal of Modern African Studies* 11 (1), 61-89.

Hutchful, E. (2002) *Ghana's adjustment experience: The paradox of reform*. James Currey, Oxford.

Kerre, B.W., Oketch, H., 1999. *The influence of schooling on career plans and ambitions among graduates of the Kenyan school system*. Papers in Education, Training and Enterprise, No. 19. Centre of African Studies, University of Edinburgh.

King, K.J., 1971. *Pan-Africanism and education: A study of race, philanthropy and education in the Southern States of the USA and East Africa*, Oxford Studies in African Affairs. Clarendon Press, Oxford.

King, K.J., 1977. *The African artisan: Education and the informal sector in Kenya*. Heinemann, London.

King, K.J., 1989. *Training and structural adjustment: Images from Ghana and Nigeria*. Occasional Paper No. 29, Centre of African Studies, University of Edinburgh.

King, K.J., 1991. *Aid and education in the developing world*. Longman, Harlow.

King, K., 2001. Africa's informal economies – 30 years on. In: *SAIS Review* (Paul H. Nitze School of Advanced International Studies) XXI (1):97-108.

King, K., McGrath, S., 2002. *Globalisation, enterprise and knowledge: Education, training and development in Africa,* Symposium Books, Oxford.

Lauglo, J., Narman, A., 1987. Diversified secondary education in Kenya: the status of practical subjects, and effects on attitudes and destinations after school. *International Journal of Educational Development* 7(4): 227-242.

Nishimura, M., Orodho, J., 1999. *Education, vocational training and employment: Designing projects that link education and vocational training and employment in Kenya.* Japan International Co-operation Agency, Nairobi.

Nyerere, J., 1967. *Education for self-reliance.* Government Printer, Dar es Salaam.

Psacharopoulos, G., Loxley, W., 1984. *Diversified secondary school curriculum study (Discus).* World Bank, Washington DC.

Somerset, A., 1974. Educational aspirations of fourth-form pupils in Kenya. In: Ghai, D.P., Court, D. (Eds.), *Education, society and development: New perspectives from Kenya.* Oxford University Press, Nairobi.

Stephens, D., 2000. Girls and basic education in Ghana: a cultural enquiry. *International Journal of Educational Development* 20(1): 29-47.

UNESCO and UNECA, 1961. *Final report. Conference of African states on the development of education in Africa,* 15-25 May 1961. (UNESCO/ED/181) UNESCO, Paris.

Further reading list

Foster, P., 1962. Ethnicity and the schools in Ghana. *Comparative Education Review* 6(2): 127-135.

Foster, P., 1963. Secondary schooling and social mobility in a West African nation. *Sociology of Education* 37(2): 150-171.

Meyer, J.W., 1970. The charter: conditions of diffuse socialisation in schools. In: Scott, R.W. (Ed.), *Social processes and social structures.* Holt, Rinehart and Winston, New York.

Commentary from Philip Foster

I was delighted to be asked to write a short commentary on this article for two reasons. First, it constitutes a major contribution to the literature: how many other examples exist of replication studies undertaken after an interval of almost 40 years? This outstanding piece enables the authors to confirm and in other instances legitimately question some of the conclusions reached in my original study.

Second, I am grateful to King and Martin for emphasising that the "Vocational School Fallacy...." constituted a spin-off from a far more ambitious scheme first delineated in my *Education and Social Change in Ghana* and in a series of articles written in the ensuing decade. Over that period I was attempting to provide a more general perspective on the relationship between educational development and socio-economic change that would be applicable to a wide range of post-colonial states. Unfortunately, a rather catchy title only too often attracted a readership that was largely concerned with what it perceived to be the immediate policy implications of the piece without any concern for the caveats it included nor the theoretical assumptions that undergirded it. Perhaps a few scholars might be persuaded to examine the corpus of that literature after reading the present piece.

To turn to the present article, one observes that two major changes have taken place in Ghana since the early 1960s. First, although economic development has been halting, the Ghanaian economy has become more diversified, thus generating a range of occupational opportunities that were not open to the students of my generation. Second, this has been paralleled by the creation of a much more diversified structure of post-primary education which has provided a much greater variety of curricular offerings than was available in 1960. At that time, the education system was essentially monolithic and, in practice, offered virtually no curricular alternatives at either the middle school or selective secondary levels.

The present study clearly shows how the occupational inspirations and expectations of students have altered in response to those changes. This is what I would have expected and students exhibit the same rationality in their responses to a *changing* economic environment as they did in 1960. In short, I don't think that King and Martin would disagree with my earlier conclusion that it is essentially the structure of occupational opportunities that determines student attitudes.

However, where we might disagree is over their cautious contention that the school curriculum itself might operate as an independent causal variable in the formation of occupational attitudes. This may be so but I must observe that the type of cross-tabulations that they advance cannot factor out "school effects" and, as they themselves suggest, alternative explanations can be made (causation may flow in the opposite direction from that which they posit). We are all agreed, however, that the ultimate questions concerning the nexus between social background, educational experience and occupational destination can only be answered by longitudinal studies currently beyond our time and resources.

I must conclude by noting that our authors more generally do well to emphasize that education is only *one* of the factors associated with *economic* development. Over the last 30 years a formidable body of evidence has been generated to emphasize that it plays a major role. But I would contend that education is *not* the "prime mover" in economic change but it is a powerful accelerator *given an appropriate structural and institutional environment.*

This caveat is absent from much of the current policy-oriented literature some of which exhibits the same kind of naiveté that characterized the writings of 30 years ago. Hence I am obliged to concur with our authors' observation that "I might be tempted to write on the origins of a basic education fallacy in pro-poor growth." Of course, the long-run effects of educational investment are undeniable, but I am troubled by the extent to which research findings are often currently translated into unrealistic educational policy prescriptions.

Chapter 7

The opportunity to maintain contact with Kenya's informal, *jua kali* sector over almost 50 years has made it possible not only to produce two monographs, *The African artisan* (1977) and *Jua kali Kenya* (1996), but also to contribute to major meetings and edited books and journals. One of the more influential of these edited books, during the 1980s, was produced by the International Labour Organization (ILO) and entitled *Training for work in the informal sector* (ILO, 1989). I wrote a chapter on 'Training for the urban informal sector in developing countries: Policy issues for practitioners' (King, 1989). The article reproduced here is from 2001, 30 years after the term 'informal sector' had first been used. Over that period, the early focus on the urban informal sector had shifted to acknowledge the very widespread presence of the rural informal sector.

There had also been a readiness to review the old distinctions between the so-called formal or modern sector and a separate informal sector. It began to become clear that the informal sector was actually present within the formal sector, exemplified in the very large number of casual workers within 'formal' firms. Equally important, it became evident especially during the structural adjustment era in much of Africa that formal sector workers were taking on second and third jobs in order to gain sufficient incomes. Often these second or third incomes were informal in the sense of not being declared or taxed. This informalisation of the formal sector had major implications for many careers, including teaching and many positions in the civil service.[1] It had led to the saying in Kenya that 'we are all *jua kali* nowadays' (King, 1996: 25).

Kenneth King (2019): *Education, Skills and International Cooperation: Comparative and Historical Perspectives*. Hong Kong: Comparative Education Research Centre (CERC), The University of Hong Kong, and Dordrecht: Springer. © CERC

[1] The scale and variety of forms of shadow or supplementary education are such that at the informal end of the spectrum large numbers of teachers provide tutoring, after school or at weekends. In many countries the recipients of the tutoring are commonly the same students that the teachers instruct during official school hours. For the larger picture
, see Bray, 2017.

© Springer Nature Switzerland AG 2019
K. King, *Education, Skills and International Cooperation*, CERC Studies in Comparative Education 36, https://doi.org/10.1007/978-3-030-29790-9_7

This article captures some of the significant shifts in the period of 30 years. It is taken from a special issue on 'Whither formality?' in the *SAIS Review: A Journal of International Affairs* (2001).

References

Bray, M. 2017. 'Schooling and its supplements: Changing patterns and implications for comparative education', *Comparative Education Review*, 62, 3, 469-491.

King, K. 1977. *The African artisan: Education and the informal sector.* Heinemann, London.

King, K. 1989. 'Training for the urban informal sector in developing countries: Policy issues for practitioners', Fluitman, F. (Ed.) *Training for work in the informal sector*, ILO, Geneva, 17-38.

King, K. 1996. *Jua kali Kenya: Change and development in an informal economy,* James Currey, London.

King, K. 2001. 'Africa's informal economies: Thirty years on', *SAIS Review: A Journal of International Affairs*, XXI, 1, 97-108.

Africa's Informal Economies:
Thirty Years On[2]

It is almost exactly 30 years since the term *informal sector* emerged from Keith Hart's fieldwork in Accra, Ghana, and was internationalised by the work of the World Employment Mission to Kenya in 1972. The term itself has been much criticised, but it has proven remarkably robust in French, English, Portuguese, and Spanish; and it has also taken on all kinds of local meanings in different languages.[3] On the eve of the 30th anniversary of the term, it may be useful to examine some of the principal developments in the knowledge of the informal economy in Africa. In particular, this article will explore the special character of the informal sector in the countries of sub-Saharan Africa. Ghana and Kenya, two of the countries where the term was first used, will be examined in detail, but illustration will also be drawn from elsewhere, including South Africa and Tanzania. The article will also look at the ways in which the self-employment potential of the informal sector appears to have influenced other sectors, such as education and training systems. Some of the most stubborn problems that continue to surround this area will be discussed, and a set of agenda items for the future will be offered.

The Evolution of the Informal Economy: From an Isolated Artisanal Sector to a National Phenomenon?

The earliest work on the informal sector focused on the towns and cities of Africa. Its appearance was a very welcome antidote to fears about the consequences of emerging large-scale urban unemployment so shortly after many African countries had achieved independence from colonial rule in the 1960s. Later, the existence of the informal economy in rural areas was also recognised, although scholarship in this area tended to concentrate on the non-farm productive activities of rural dwellers rather than on subsistence or cash-crop agriculture. During the 1980s and early 1990s, the disruptive impact of structural adjustment measures on the formal sector led to widespread factory closures and to a reduction in

---

[2] This chapter derives from King (2001), 'Africa's informal economies: Thirty years on'.

[3] One of the better known terms is now *jua kali*, which is used in Swahili in Kenya to cover many different aspects of informal work, including the original group of workers who toiled, without premises or shelter, under the hot sun (*jua kali*). See King, Kenneth, *Jua kali Kenya: Change and development in an informal economy 1970-1995* (Oxford: James Currey, 1996).

once-secure government and parastatal employment. Economic growth rates were low or often negative, and foreign direct investment was minuscule.

Our understanding of the informal sector has changed from something limited to particular artisan groups in many Third World cities to something that cuts across entire economies. This transformation has resulted significantly from the continuing fragility of the formal sector of the economy in many African states. As a result, public-sector wages have proven to be inadequate, and large numbers of so-called formal sector workers have taken on additional informal income-generating activities. In one way, this development parallels the multiple wage-earning activities that have characterised rural areas of Africa for a very long time. Just as rural workers have for decades combined subsistence and cash-crop agriculture and non-farm microenterprise, so it has become common-place for teachers, office workers, police officers, and many other formal sector employees to have more than a single source of income. The old certainties of being a full-time pastor, primary school teacher, or government clerk have been replaced by a new world in which many individuals switch back and forth between a main job and other types of work.

The Informalisation of the Formal Sector
Although the majority of these second or third jobs often go untaxed, they are not necessarily considered illegal activities. In a number of countries, including Tanzania, spending leisure time on informal productive activities has been formally endorsed in the 1990s at the very highest level. In Kenya, the government formally allowed civil servants to combine their public-service jobs with other sources of work. Instances such as these amount to the informalisation of the formal sector, as the second and third "jobs" begin to affect the first, main job. Many of the important obligations of the original full-time job cease to be fulfilled as the income-generating demands of the additional jobs erode the time available for the first job. This has important consequences for many crucial professions.

There are accordingly two parallel developments relating to the formal and informal sectors. First, there has been longstanding policy concern about capturing the best elements of the informal sector, its productivity and innovation, for the benefit of the larger economy. Attempts to gradually formalise the informal sector focus on encouraging the use of contracts, licenses, and taxation. Second, the recent process of informalisation of formal work has occurred alongside this desire to formalise the informal sector, as large numbers of formal employees begin to seek informal (and untaxed) income opportunities.

Eating from One's Job

"...One of them was narrating an encounter with a City Council employee, a parking attendant, who had urged him not to pay the Sh50 parking fee to the Council. 'Why pay the Council fifty bob when they are not paying salaries? Give me a pound (Sh20) and I will look after your car', the employee suggested. Whereupon the motorist asked: 'You people are always going on strike because the council is not paying you. If you keep stealing from them, where will they get the money to pay you'?"

Source: article by Magadha McGwire in Nairobi's *The Sunday Nation*, September 10, 2000.

This growing incidence of "eating from one's job", as Kenyans call the use of one's formal job as a source of additional untaxed and irregular income, enervates the rule of law and the good governance that are necessary for the development and expansion of both the informal and the formal sector. For example, if police officers, inspectors, tax officials, and civil servants begin to treat services that should be fairly provided as a new but routine way of getting additional income, then corruption will impede informal sector growth. If every application for a plot, license, or loan, and every bid for a government contract become informal income opportunities, then the notion of incorporating the informal sector into the formal economy takes on a different, negative connotation.

Nor is it just a question of whether petty corruption may hinder informal sector expansion. At a much higher level, trade or land policy may be conducted in ways that directly undermine the hard work and innovation of emerging informal sector entrepreneurs.[4] In such situations, it is hard not to sympathise with new informal businesses that decide to remain entirely outside the state tax and licensing system. As a result, the

---

[4] An example of higher level corruption could be taken from the second-hand clothing sector. It is often said that those behind the massive import of second-hand clothes avoid full payment of import duties. The presence of such low-cost clothing across the country directly threatens the jobs of both the tailors in the informal sector and the modern sector firms that make new clothes. This makes it entirely possible that the devastating fire that destroyed the largest concentration of second-hand clothes in Kenya on Wednesday, September 6, 2000 was not accidental. See *The Sunday Nation*, September 10, 2000, p.8.

potential tax income for the government is dramatically reduced;[5] which in turn makes even the maintenance of public sector salary levels problematic. Hence, the vicious circle of seeking informal and untaxed supplemental income continues.

Informal Income Generation in the Education Sector

Over the last 30 years, more has been written on the traditional urban artisan side of the informal economy than on the informal side of public sector employment. Though there are few detailed studies analysing these new combinations of formal jobs and informal work, there should be no doubt about the impact of this development on many different forms of employment.[6] This essay examines the education sector to explore the interaction of the formal and informal economies in more detail.

The public education system in African countries typically provides irregular and insufficient remuneration. As a consequence, primary school teachers, who are so central to the achievement of equitable education in one of the least educated regions of the world, are now combining teaching with many other sources of income. Private tuition is one example of this phenomenon. On the positive side, the possibility of earning extra income from private sources is possibly keeping many teachers in the profession; on the negative side, tuition can have a direct and hugely inequitable effect on ordinary schools. Teachers may divide regular school children into groups according to the ability of each child's family to pay additional fees.[7] The quality of basic education can therefore very easily be undermined by the multiple income-generating schemes of teachers. Indeed, Stephen Kerr has concluded that "the term 'improper economy' could be used to describe the effects that the different ways in which teachers obtain money, goods, and services are having on Tanzanian education."[8]

---

[5] Among the most successful of the enterprises revisited by King (1996) were some that had no intention of paying taxes as long as the government itself remained so corrupt.

[6] In Tanzania, Stephen Kerr carried out doctoral research on teachers' livelihoods for the University of Edinburgh. This provides the first detailed insight into what the phenomenon of multiple sources of income may imply for teaching and school quality. See Kerr, Stephen, "Teachers' Sustainable Livelihoods," Ph.D. dissertation, University of Edinburgh, 2006.

[7] In one East African country, it was at one point the case that only children who paid extra fees could get their regular homework corrected. It is worth noting that private tuition is not straightforwardly a function of poor salaries; the nation with the best-remunerated teachers in the world, Japan, also has extensive private tuition. See further, Bray (2017).

[8] Kerr, Ibid.

At the other end of the educational spectrum, the impact of alternative income requirements on higher education has been equally devastating in many countries. Of greatest concern has been the retreat from research and graduate supervision in favour of consultancy income. Few professors without long-term external research support have been able to resist the fragmentation of their university careers by the persistent need for additional income. Only a handful of universities, such as Makerere in Uganda, have managed to develop innovative ways of turning the informal income needs of their staffs to the institutions' advantage. [9] These universities have succeeded in inviting fee-paying students into regular classes and developing the opportunity for urban fee-paying workers to enrol in evening classes.

Educating Future Informal Workers

Beyond these wider concerns, there is an additional paradox in the relationship between education and the informal sector. On the one hand, employees at different levels of the education system are actively searching for additional income opportunities. On the other hand, there have been many examples over the last few decades in which ministries of education have sought to ensure that the entire education system is orienting young people toward self-employment. Countless schemes, from Nyerere's well known *Education for Self-Reliance* in Tanzania in the late 1960s to the Kenyan or Ghanaian reforms of the 1980s, have sought to use school curricula to change young people's attitudes toward work, and particularly toward engaging in self-employment rather than waiting for a formal sector job. [10]

Education has thus become a dual site for research on the informal sector. Many teachers now straddle the informal and formal sectors, and in so doing are probably seen by parents and pupils as engaged in desirable alternative forms of income generation. At the same time, students are being encouraged, often indirectly because insufficient resources are devoted to the teaching of practical subjects, to consider options other than what Dore has called "real jobs" in the formal sector of the economy. In other words, education for the informal sector and for

---

[9] Court, D., "Makerere: The Quiet Revolution," joint report for Rockefeller Foundation and World Bank, *Financing Higher Education in Africa* (Washington DC: The World Bank, 2000).

[10] Although policymakers may use the terms *self-employment* and *informal sector* interchangeably, it is clear that some self-employed, e.g., medical and legal professionals, are in the formal sector. Similarly, there are large numbers of workers in the informal sector who are actually wage-earning employees of microenterprise owners.

self-employment is being promoted as part of official school curricula by teachers whose own livelihoods depend on informal work.

As early as 1965, Philip Foster warned against attempts to stem unemployment crises through shifts in educational curricula in Ghana. Terming such activity the "vocational-school fallacy in development planning,"[11] he argued that schools are very limited vehicles for large-scale social engineering; they cannot, on their own, arrange the employment of young people or reorient their aspirations toward particular kinds of jobs. Inclinations toward particular careers are most substantially affected by the surrounding economy, not by special vocational or self-employment-oriented curricula.

Even though academics and some development agencies, including the World Bank, have heeded this warning, national governments have given it less attention. The latter have often continued to reorient their national curricula toward a greater degree of practical, agricultural, or vocational content on the grounds that young people can use these skills for either formal employment or self-employment. The attempt to use schools for encouraging productive work outside of the formal economy was most evident in Nyerere's *Education for Self-Reliance*,[12] but there have been many other examples, including the relatively recent curriculum reform in South Africa, which included elements specifically aimed at promoting income-generating experiences for young people.

It is understandable that policymakers faced with the reality of few well-paid job opportunities for young people should turn to the "vocationalisation" of schools as a possible route toward the diversification of career aspirations for young people. On the other hand, current evidence on small-scale start-ups suggests that new entrepreneurs need much more than poorly-supported vocational school courses to prepare them for the marketplace.

Educational and Societal Influences on Self-Employment

Estimating the influence of schools and their curricula on the attitudes and final destinations of young people will continue to pose methodological challenges to policymakers, especially when the nature of work and employment is changing in the ways that we have suggested earlier.

---

[11] Foster, P., "The vocational school fallacy in development planning," in A.A. Anderson and M.J. Bowman, eds., *Education and economic development* (Chicago: Aldine Publishing, 1965).

[12] Nyerere, Julius, "Education for self reliance," in Nyerere, J.K., *Ujamaa: Essays on socialism* (Dar es Salaam: Oxford University Press, 1967).

Recent research in Ghana has raised some intriguing questions about young people's increasing interest in self-employment. In brief, it shows that levels of aspiration toward self-employment are as high as those toward employment in the government or in private firms, particularly among pupils in some of the most renowned academic schools in the country.

Below is a listing of some of the careers that were mentioned as ideal by students in their last year of secondary school at one of the best-known boys' schools in Ghana, as we saw in chapter 6. The numbers in brackets indicate the number of pupils making this choice.

Open a private clinic (6)//my own architectural firm//writing and publishing//setting up a computer firm//car mechanic//leisure artwork and painting//a firm to do construction and development projects//setting up a fast food chain or a hotel//fashion designing// electrical & electronic repair firm//seller of chemicals//music studio// computer programming//large-scale farming of cash crops (2)// developing a research institute//pilot training school//lucrative barbering//small animal production//large-scale bee-keeping//small-scale poultry//cash crop farm// private teaching in science & computing//small-scale pig farming// manufacturing local, natural soap//lucrative shoemaking//[13]

Such data suggest another crucial dimension of current informal economies in Africa. There exists a growing awareness in Ghana and perhaps in other countries that the old attraction of government jobs is receding. In its place, a very strong appreciation of the private sector and of self-employment careers is emerging.

It is not easy to tease out all the different strands in these new perceptions of employment, but essentially it would seem that many educated professionals have turned to new kinds of careers as the economies in which they work have become progressively free of government control. Instead of straddling the formal and informal sectors in the manner outlined above, significant numbers of professionals have entered into full-time private businesses, such as import-export or running a private clinic or private school. These aspirations are in turn passed on to children and become a crucial element in the complex

---

[13] King, K. and Martin, C. "Revisiting the Vocational School Fallacy: Education, Aspiration and Work in Ghana, 1959-2000," *International Journal of Educational Development,* reproduced as chapter six of this present volume.

chemistry of pupils' career orientations.

It is clear that the career aspirations observed in these renowned schools are not for low-level informal sector jobs or for traditional public sector employment. Rather, students seek opportunities that can offer substantial income and perhaps avoid the kind of hand-to-mouth multiple roles mentioned in this essay. This new interest in entrepreneurial self-employment is actually growing in certain African countries, and may have an equity dimension attached to it. This orientation toward private sector and full-time self-employment is much more evident in high quality schools and much less obvious in poorer urban and rural secondary schools, where new job opportunities are sparse and where parents in subsistence self-employment may continue to point their children toward the relative security of government jobs.

Beyond parental influence, it would appear that the role of the school and its specific curriculum also play some part in this mix of attitudes. Even within the same school, where parents presumably have quite similar backgrounds, different kinds of career aspirations are found. These aspirations would seem then to be influenced in some measure by the particular track that pupils are following within their schools.

What this means for our present understanding of the informal sector and education in Africa is that schools, by themselves, are likely to be a rather blunt instrument for orienting young people toward self-employment. The evidence suggests that vocationally-oriented schools may give some pupils new ideas about careers, even if a lack of adequate resources prevents them from teaching the necessary skills.[14] In addition, the large education schemes associated with the International Development Targets of the OECD/DAC (Development Assistance Committee), which aim to provide all young people in Africa with basic numeracy and literacy by 2015, should encompass much more specific targets for post-basic education and skills training if they are to prepare pupils for sustainable livelihoods.[15]

Outstanding Challenges for Africa's Informal Economies

Thus far we have pointed to the complexity of the relationships between

---

[14] This might suggest that the development of effective career services for schools would be as valuable a policy as striving to provide a series of vocational streams.
[15] The International Development Targets of the DAC seek to synthesise a whole series of minimum goals for education, health, poverty elimination, etc. that have emerged from world conferences during the 1990s.

the so-called formal and informal sectors and the multiple influences on aspirations for self-employment. There are several other important challenges that need to be addressed before concluding this review of the current situation. These issues relate much more to the traditional view of the informal sector, i.e., to those involved in productive work or commerce on their own account rather than to those in the public sector who work in the informal sector on the side.

Avoiding the Dualism of the Formal and Informal Sectors
After 30 years, the study of the informal sector still seems to be saddled with a dualistic approach toward work and jobs. The continued use of the terms formal and informal economies reinforces this view, even though the developments described above make their separation problematic. However, this dualist approach can be overcome, as the new skills-development programme in South Africa shows. It attempts to be a single national system that includes the whole span of skilled work for each of the 12 economic sectors, from the individual multipurpose mechanic in the rural areas to the most specialised technician in the mines.[16] The Department of Labour intends to use the new Skills Levy on medium and large-scale firms to subsidise skills training in what would have been neglected in other countries – the microenterprises and rural non-farm enterprises. It will be extremely interesting to see how these ambitious skills-development objectives are implemented.

Racial and Ethnic Tensions
A second enduring issue affecting the informal sectors in many parts of sub-Saharan Africa, including South Africa, has been the lack of a satisfactory subcontracting relationship between microenterprises and the medium- and large-scale industrial sector. The ownership of industry and a great deal of large-scale commerce by multinational or local white, Indian, or Lebanese capital has meant that, unlike other regions such as East and South Asia or Latin America, subcontracting possibilities in much of Sub-Saharan Africa have a distinctly racial dimension.[17] This is

---

[16] King, Kenneth, "Policy Coherence   in Education, Training and Enterprise Development in South Africa: The Implementation Challenge of New Policies," in W. Morrow and K. King, eds., *Vision and Reality: Changing Education and Training in South Africa* (Cape Town: UCT Press, 1998).

[17] The sheer complexity of large-scale formal versus less formal sectors is illustrated by Kenya's recent ban on the import of the 25,000 to 30,000 second-hand cars that come annually from Japan. These imports put employment in the few large scale car assembly

not to say that there have not been cordial and even collaborative relations in several countries among enterprises and business communities of different sizes, but the continuing absence of large-scale African-owned formal sector enterprises has been a major problem for the next layer of African microenterprises. It has meant the lack of relevant role models for aspiring entrepreneurs, as well as the lack of high-level African representation in the chambers of commerce and industry.

Some countries face the additional problem of the historical domination of informal sector enterprises by particular African communities and sometimes by expatriate African entrepreneurs, as in some parts of South Africa. This inter-community competition, combined with political hesitation about allowing particular African groups to profit from parastatal divestiture, have certainly delayed access to large-scale opportunities. Political factors have often hindered emerging African business communities that have a comparative advantage in a specific economic activity. The debate encouraged by the international development agencies and particularly by the World Bank about the need for Africa to diversify industrially and to compete internationally is often conducted with scant attention to these crucial racial and ethnic factors.[18]

Informal Sector Business Associations

Emerging communities of informal sector entrepreneurs can be assisted by specific indigenous trade and business associations. These associations have been more evident and successful in west Africa than in east Africa or southern Africa, and they speak to the need for a degree of formalization of informal sector expertise. As before, however, in a situation where there are established chambers of industry and commerce representing the interests of the large- and medium-scale non-African industrialists, it is difficult for informal sector associations not to appear like some part of a mirror universe.

Conclusions

Although this brief article has mentioned some of the major structural questions facing the two sides of the informal sector, we should certainly

plants at risk, but the ban may also threaten the tens of thousands of informal sector mechanics who work to resuscitate older cars. See "Kenya bans Japan's junk to save jobs," *The Japan Times*, September 19, 2000: p.12.

[18] The World Bank's *Can Africa claim the 21st century?* (Washington DC, 2000) had virtually no discussion about the pattern of ownership in its proposals for diversification and for the promotion of exports.

underline the progress that has been made in the last 30 years in the original (artisanal) informal sector. As tracer studies in Kenya have shown, very significant changes and technological developments have occurred in many different professions within the so-called informal sector.[19] These transformations are substantial, and they need to be supported by evidence from other countries. Microenterprises have registered success in many different ways, from technological development to import substitution and business and employment expansion.

Nevertheless, few micro-entrepreneurs in sub-Saharan Africa will not feel that they have succeeded almost entirely on their own. In many cases in the 1980s and 1990s, external forces, including the IMF and the World Bank sought to encourage laissez-faire regimes in Africa, which have precluded the kind of developmental state so necessary to the sustained encouragement of small- and microenterprises (SMEs).

It is perhaps time to look again at the opportunities for formalizing the informal sector that suit the national interest. Considering the international apathy about investing in Africa, this effort will need to be based on a new African confidence about African development. SMEs could play a major role in this vision, which Mkandawire describes below:

> The point here is that it will be prudent for African policymakers to work on the assumption that capitalist accumulation will be largely national for much of Africa. Indeed, given Africa's very tarnished image, confidence by Africans in the continent's future will be of prime value in resuscitating investment. The small enterprises can serve both as a seed bed of such a capitalist class and can provide some of the political support to capitalist accumulation in Africa. This will require that the efforts of individual enterprises are embedded in a broad development effort with fairly coherent object-tives...and strategies for SMEs. More specifically the state will have to play more than a merely regulatory or custodial role by assuming clearly developmental tasks. There is nothing either in African economic and political history or the experience of other development states that makes it inherently impossible for African states to play such a role.[20]

---

[19] King, K., *The African artisan* (1977); King, K., *Jua kali Kenya* (1996).
[20] Mkandawire, T., "Developmental State and Small Enterprises," in K. King and S. McGrath, eds., *Enterprise in Africa: Between poverty and growth* (London: IT Publications, 1999), p.47.

Chapter 8

Targets, goals and their indicators have become central to the international discourse on education and jobs. The setting of the Sustainable Development Goals (SDGs) is the latest and arguably one of the most inclusive UN processes of consultation (Naidoo, 2016). But national governments, and particularly those with planned economies, have participated in target-setting from the middle of the 20th century, and even earlier in the case of Russia, other parts of the USSR, and Turkey (King, 2016).

Target-setting in education has been a key element in what Jonathan Jansen has termed the 'politics of performance'; and whether led by international agencies or by national governments, it has tended to have a negative impact on educational quality (Jansen, 2005). In the case of Kenya, which illustrates powerfully the effects of quantitative targets on qualitative outcomes, the government promoted the goal of 500,000 new jobs annually, and this was doubtless connected to the calculation that there were 500,000 youngsters entering the labour market each year. To make this target-setting in education more complicated, free primary education had been promised as the first manifesto commitment of the new government in 2003. Following this declaration, no fewer than 1.4 million additional children appeared in government primary schools.

Interrogating the meanings and consequences behind these iconic numbers in Kenya is vital to teasing out the consequences of target-setting for schools, training institutions and the labour market. While the goal of 500,000 new jobs annually may have been highly attractive in election terms, the reality that the great bulk of all these jobs would have to be found in Kenya's informal, *jua kali* sector would not have appealed to the electorate if this had been clarified earlier.

Kenneth King (2019): *Education, Skills and International Cooperation: Comparative and Historical Perspectives*. Hong Kong: Comparative Education Research Centre (CERC), The University of Hong Kong, and Dordrecht: Springer. © CERC

© Springer Nature Switzerland AG 2019
K. King, *Education, Skills and International Cooperation*, CERC Studies
in Comparative Education 36, https://doi.org/10.1007/978-3-030-29790-9_8

The same calculation applies to the political appeal of 1.4 million additional children in government schools. How many of these children had left low-cost fee-paying schools in order to have free primary education? And how many children who had already been in government schools left to attend fee-paying schools because of the massive over-crowding in the state schools?

These are just a few of the illustrations of what can actually happen once the 'numbers game' of targets for schools, skills and jobs gets underway. Universal primary education, for instance, can mean many things, including universal access, universal completion and universal achievement of an agreed level of learning. Those who created the suggestions about countries setting 'their own targets' following Jomtien were very clear about the need for all three: access, completion and achievement:

> Universal access to, and completion of primary education (or whate-ver higher level of education is considered as 'basic') by the year 2000;
>
> Improvement in learning achievement such that an agreed percentage of an appropriate age cohort (e.g. 80% of 14 year-olds) attains or surpasses a defined level of necessary learning achieveme-nt. (UNESCO, 1990: 3)

It is worth underlining that the authors of the *World Declaration* and *Framework for Action* at Jomtien sought to avoid a set of global targets for basic education. But Jomtien's suggested dimensions for country targets were soon turned into global ones. It is also worth underlining that the original draft of the *Framework for Action* deliberately avoided a target date. However, one of the four convening agencies insisted that there be a target date – of 2000.

The material for the chapter on targets in Kenya which follows was first presented at a section of the 2003 Oxford Conference convened by the United Kingdom Forum for International Education and Training (UKFIET). Papers from this section became a special issue of the *International Journal of Educational Development (IJED)*. It was entitled *International or national targets for education: Help or hindrance?* (Rose and King (eds.), 2005).

References

Jansen, J. 2005. 'Targeting education: The politics of performance and the prospects of "Education for All"', *International Journal of Educational Development*, 25, 4, 368-380.

King, K. 2016. 'The global targeting of education and skill: Policy history and comparative perspectives', *Compare: A Journal of Comparative and International Education*, 46, 6, 952-975.

Naidoo, J. 2016. 'Education by 2030: Ambitious targets require a community united to succeed', blog of 29 June 2016 for *Deliver2030.org* (ODI) http://deliver2030.org/?p=7007 accessed 24 October 2017.

King, K. and Rose, P. (eds.) 2005. *International or national targets for education: Help or hindrance?* Special issue of *International Journal of Educational Development*, 25, 4, 361-476.

UNESCO 1990. *Framework for action to meet basic learning needs*. UNESCO, Paris.

Re-targeting Schools, Skills and Jobs in Kenya: Quality, Quantity and Outcomes[1]

Introduction

The private sector is the engine of growth and prosperity. It is our responsibility as a government to create the enabling environment for the private sector to create wealth and generate employment for millions of our youth.

The *jua kali* sector and other micro-enterprises are expected to play a crucial role in the creation of jobs in Kenya. However, we recognise that the sector's growth potential is inhibited by several constraints. These include poor access to markets, lack of credit and a poor policy environment. My government will soon be presenting to the House a Sessional Paper on the development of micro and small enterprises for poverty reduction and employment creation.

My government promises to reverse the current negative economic trends. To this end we shall start by creating a National Economic and Social Council. This will advise on proper management of our economy. It is our intention to grow at 7% per annum in order to create 500,000 jobs per year. This will progressively eradicate poverty through wealth creation. We have initiated and will implement an Economic Recovery Plan aimed at creating employment. (Kibaki, 2003)

The new President of Kenya, Mwai Kibaki, specifically mentioned the *jua kali* – the Swahili term for Kenya's informal economy – in his Opening of Parliament speech in February 2003, as one of the areas where there would be substantial policy change. Indeed, it would appear that growth in the *jua kali* sector is expected to play a significant part in achieving the government's high visibility target of half a million jobs to be created annually. Whether it is coincidental or not, it is intriguing to note that the target of 500,000 is exactly the same as that used for the total number of young people annually entering the labour market and looking for jobs or work in Kenya (Johanson and Adams, 2003, p.18). Increasingly, from 2003, the education level of this group entering the workforce will be raised as the impact of the new government's first manifesto target – free

---

[1] This chapter is taken from King (2005), 'Re-targeting schools, skills and jobs in Kenya: Quantity, quality and outcomes' *International Journal of Educational Development* 25, 1.

primary education (FPE) for all – begins to affect the schooling composition of the school-leavers.

This paper examines some of the relationships between these two targets. On the education side, the target of FPE was clearly felt to be something that should and could be acted upon immediately the new government came to power. The declaration translated into an additional 1.4 million children in the primary cycle within a few months of the schools opening on the 6 January 2003 (Gichura, 2003). In quantitative terms, this expansion was quite dramatic, just as it had been with Uganda and Tanzania a few years earlier.[2] But the implications for quality of achieving these quantitative targets remain extremely worrying, as we shall see.

By contrast, the targeting of 500,000 new jobs is a very different matter. In the sphere of the Ministry of Education, a presidential declaration can have the effect of bringing hundreds of thousands of young people, regardless of age, into school within days or weeks. In the sphere of the Ministry of Labour, even a presidential declaration can be of little avail when it comes to direct job creation. This is perhaps one of the main differences in the targeting of education and employment goals – that with schools direct action by government can result in marked progress towards universal primary education (UPE) goals, whereas with employment and jobs, it was the creation of an enabling environment for the private sector that President Kibaki expected would produce economic growth and hence, indirectly, increased employment.

But there is a third area – skills development – that lies between the goal of FPE and the goal of employment generation. Arguably that area has been the Cinderella of development agencies for almost two decades, and in a number of sub-Saharan African countries it has also become a low national priority, both in its school-based, and post-school manifestations. There are some indications that this may be changing, certainly on the donor side, and also in several countries. But, interestingly, few targets have been set in this domain by the Government of Kenya.

In the early 2000s, Kenya had become an intriguing test case of the interplay of these three fields, education, skills development and employment, just as it had done on a number or earlier occasions, including the Kericho Conference (1967), the Kenya World Employment

---

[2] In Uganda, the expansion had been more than dramatic – from 2.3 million in primary schools in 1996 to no less than 7.3 million in 2003 (Okuni, 2003a, b).

Mission (1972), the Gachathi Commission (1976) and Koech Commission (2000). But as far as the new world of targets and development goals is concerned, *internationally* it has been UPE for all – and gender equity therein – that alone have been the focus, while skills development and job creation have not at all been part of the global target-setting consensus. Skills and jobs do not appear either in the International Development Targets (IDTs) or in the Millennium Development Goals (MDGs). By contrast, at the *national* level, we have noted Kenya's recent focus on targeting both primary education for all and jobs.

Concerns about education, training and self-employment: The historical context

There is a certain cyclical feeling about the intersection of these three areas in Kenya, as there may well be in other countries. And it is worth noting that these are rather long cycles. It is just 36 years since the first great wave of primary education expansion after Independence in 1963 led to the first acute, political and research concern in Kenya about the primary school leaver crisis. And in turn this led directly to the report of the National Christian Council in Kenya, *After school what?* (NCCK, 1967), and to the creation of the Village Polytechnics which were intended to offer skills development for self-employment, especially in the rural areas.[3] They now represent a network of some 650 institutions, now termed Youth Polytechnics, nation-wide.

In the mid-1970s, a similar concern lay behind the targeting of self-employment through the school system, as NCCK had pursued through post-primary training. The Gachathi Commission strongly emphasised this requirement, but it was almost 10 years before the school system was reformed in 1985 to accommodate this, in the new 8-4-4 structure, which was examined in chapter 4 above.

It is important to mark the difference between these two approaches to targeting skill development for self-employment. The first, associated with the Village Polytechnics, originally saw skills development as an alternative to secondary schooling, and frankly targeted rural self-employment and not urban formal sector employment. The second did not separate out skills as an alternative to schools, but argued that sufficient orientation to practical, business and agricultural skills should

---

[3] It is interesting, comparatively, to note that Uganda, after a really major expansion of primary education already referred to, has determined to build no less than one low-cost accessible community polytechnic in every sub-county (Okuni, 2003b).

be required for everyone in the general school system, both primary and secondary. The latter was politically attractive for two reasons; it explicitly made a target of skills-for-all – and reached very large numbers with the idea of a curriculum that could in some way help with job creation. And, second, it offered some version of skills in the regular educational mainstream, and not as a second chance for those who could not afford to stay in secondary education. It was admittedly a minimalist version of practical and vocational arts that was on offer, but it did reach the entire school cohort in one way or the other.

Kenya's version of the 'vocationalisation' of primary and secondary education lasted for almost 20 years before it was virtually scrapped, in an uncoordinated way, and without any full evaluation. Paradoxically, it was evaluated on a small scale by Kilemi Mwiria as part of a World Bank review of skills development in 2002 but this was done after most of the practical subjects had already been summarily removed from the curriculum in the middle of a school year. Mwiria was to find himself as assistant minister for education in the new Kenya government in December 2002, just a few months after he had concluded, as an educational consultant, that 'the wholesale withdrawal of industrial education courses, typewriting with office practice and computer studies from even those schools that are well equipped to teach them is a somewhat unfortunate development' (Mwiria, 2002, p.47).

There are clearly many things still to be learned from this lengthy episode in the national targeting of a weak version of skills for self-employment. Not the least problematic and intriguing is that very large numbers of students continued to feel that their curriculum had given them a good preparation for self-employment, despite the very patchy provision of technical and vocational facilities (King et al., 2002).

The third element in the targeting of skill and self-employment relates directly to the informal economy itself. Surprisingly, though the concept of the informal sector was internationally disseminated from its central role, as a very new concept, in the ILO Kenya Employment Mission Report of 1972 (International Labour Organization, 1972), it took a further 14 years till the notion became centre stage in the Kenya policy environment with the publication of the Sessional Paper No.1 of 1986 *Economic management for renewed growth* (Kenya Government, 1986). This acknowledged the crucial role of the informal sector in creating jobs and was the first really significant national policy document which urged that it be recognised as a dynamic force. Six years later, in 1992, there was a further Sessional Paper, probably the first in Africa, which focused solely on the potential of the informal economy: *Small enterprise and jua kali development in Kenya* (Kenya Government, 1992). Though in some ways this was a remarkable document, it arguably targeted everything possible that was related to the informal sector, and urged all ministries to take a whole series of specific actions. The record on implementation was very meagre.

The single biggest difference in the government's targeting of self-employment via schools, training institutions and the informal sector is that substantial government action was actually taken in relation to schools in respect of vocationalisation and to youth polytechnics. By contrast, the quite dramatic developments of self-employment in the informal economy over the last 30 years are scarcely an achievement that the government can claim. They appear to have taken place before there was a government policy in place, and even when there was a policy, there was virtually no government intervention or action, or if there was, it tended to be negative, such as harassment or the destruction of premises.

Here then, over these past several decades, have been just some of the cycles in which education for all, skills for all, and self-employment have been targeted. The historical record would be much more complex if the international targets are added to the national picture, including the Addis Ababa (1961), Jomtien (1990) and Dakar (2000) agreements, along with whatever apparatus was put in place (see Jansen, 2005), with external encouragement, in order to facilitate compliance with these.

Quantity, quality and outcomes in the domains of schools, skills and employment
Beyond the numbers' game: The main challenge of free primary education
One of the main tasks in interrogating these politically rounded figures – 500,000 young people, mostly school leavers, entering the labour market annually in Kenya – and 500,000 jobs to be created annually – is to try and see more clearly what they imply for the various stakeholders. What might this number of young people imply for the skills development and training system? And what of the jobs that are to be created? Where will they be found? And in what sense will they be 'created'?

Much has been made in all three East African countries, Kenya, Tanzania and Uganda, of the sheer numbers entering primary school as a result of the new policies on free access; and the press is full of discussions about the huge budgetary and teacher requirements for satisfying the enormous numbers of new entrants (1.4 million in the case of Kenya). But much less is said, or widely known, about the levels of competency in language, maths and science, as well as in other social and practical skills that are acquired in the course of the cycle of basic education. Yet, clearly, the process of labour market absorption will be much easier if there is serious attention to the quality standards of those leaving the basic cycle of education.

But here there are very major concerns emerging from all three East African countries. Scholar after scholar, as well as policy makers, pinpoint challenges to quality as having been the accompaniment of dramatic expansion (see *NORRAG News* 32 passim). Detailed analysis of quality is just beginning, but if recent research in Uganda is anything to go by, then the quality crisis that has developed is certainly as serious as the quantitative deficit in enrolment that the governments have been addressing. Ugandan research reports that 'Pupils' performance in the different tests strongly suggests that at both lower and upper primary, literacy attainment is very low. A vast majority of the children in the sample lacked proficiency in English and, sadly, in their mother tongue' (Kyeyune, 2003, p.45). Kyeyune concluded that there was a real question about what pupils were actually gaining in seven years in primary education. The evidence we have suggests a similar level of concern for Kenya, though hard data are not yet in the public domain (World Bank, 2004).[4] There is similar evidence from Malawi which has had a longer period of experience of FPE (Kadzamira and Rose, 2003).

A different angle – but equally worrying – on the whole targeting of UPE in quantitative terms is that apparently the well-trodden assertions about the higher returns to primary are no longer so securely in place. In fact, it had always been one of the weaknesses of the 'returns' literature that the many claims about the monetary and non-monetary returns to primary education tended to be made without any serious reference to quality. Now, the international case on the superior returns to primary education does continue to be made in some quarters, though admittedly with more qualifications (e.g. UNESCO, 2002). By contrast, the World Bank, which once championed the returns to primary schooling, is now turning out country studies for Rwanda and Ethiopia which document the low return (World Bank, 2003, 2004). In the countries themselves,

---

[4] The World Bank's 2004 report on Kenya has, perhaps not surprisingly, no detail on whether and how the extra million children in primary schools have impacted on the primary school leaving results.

there are increasingly voices asserting that the labour market reality for those who only have primary education is very bleak:

> One of the major concerns currently is the issue around the allegedly zero economic return rates on primary education. In most of our countries, school leavers with only a primary education are not really better off in securing a job than those who never went to school at all. (Villet, 2003, p.77)

Though many parents in Kenya have certainly felt this for 20 or 30 years – hence the extraordinary waves of self-help financing of *harambee* secondary schools and tertiary colleges – the apparent weakening of the research case for the economic returns to primary certainly cannot be used to argue that initial school access for all children and the improvement of school quality are not politically important.[5] But what is politically crucial is to recognise that parents continue to see primary school as a stepping stone to secondary schooling or further skills development. In this connection, it would be fascinating to know more about the motives and ambitions of the parents of the 1.4 million new children who entered Kenya primary schools since January 2003. In all likelihood, they had been obliged to be selective in the past about which of their children to put into primary. Now that there is FPE, a greater number of their children could be able to compete in due course for the crucial secondary entrance examination.

Recognition of this crucial parental (and pupil) factor in education investment underlines the reality that the discourse of targeting tends to be a state and external agency discourse. The latter two perspectives will increasingly need to take account of beneficiary views of the educational process if the planning for full access and inclusion in primary is not to run counter to parental demands for post-primary schooling, training and work.

If one of the main concerns of parents and pupils about primary education is that it should *not* be terminal but should lead directly to secondary schooling or skills training, then one of the key questions for most parents about FPE will be about outcomes: what proportion of the FPE cohort is going to succeed in securing good quality training or secondary education? In other words, the main consumers of basic education – the parents and the pupils – steadfastly see not just access for

---

[5] There have been non-agency voices critical of the primary school returns literature for years; see King, 1989 and Bennell, 1996.

all to primary school as their target; they will also be very aware of the quality of the new openings to UPE, and conscious about the possibilities for continuation. But there is already some concern emerging that FPE has actually widened the gap between poorer and richer families in their access to schooling (Mwiria, December 2004); and there is no evidence that the continuation to secondary has become any easier for poor, bright children. Secondary school fees remain a huge barrier, and there are no clear pathways for the talented children of poor families to get access to secondary, as there were just before and after Independence.[6]

Targeting access, achievement and placement in skill development
If the targeting of FPE seldom covers our three markers of quantity, quality and outcomes, how much more is this the case for the domain of skills development. At least with primary education, there are a small number of quantitative indicators that can be reported – gross and net enrolment ratios, repetition, drop-out, and transition ratios – not to mention exam scores. But in the area of skills development what are the figures that can be counted upon? Even the most basic quantitative dimensions do not appear to exist. Of the 500,000 young people annually said to be entering Kenya's labour market, what proportion might have acquired some job-related training? Where would that training be located, in the public, private and NGO sectors? And what do we know of its quality, not to mention its outcomes?[7]

The answer is very little on any of our three counts. By comparison with UPE where there is a single ministry covering most of the provision, there are a multitude of post-primary training providers. This makes even getting a sense of the quantitative coverage much more difficult. The new Kenya Government inherited a situation where there was no national technical and vocational training policy, and hence there are only the beginnings of a debate about the rights of young people to training, and a discussion about the training needs of a country (Kenya Government, 2003c, d).

In the absence of persuasive national documentation about quantitative coverage, some of the most recent evidence for Kenya and the rest of sub-Saharan Africa can be derived from the World Bank's

---

[6] MPs have been given special funds for bursaries, but concerns remain about their utilization.
[7] There was a 'Rapid Appraisal' of TVET in Kenya done by the Ministry of Education, Science and Technology and the GTZ, but this has not so far led to a programme of action (MOEST and GTZ 2003).

current study of skills development (Johanson and Adams, 2003). This suggests that the total capacity for training in Kenya reaches less than 7% of labour market entrants each year, not counting the backlog of those already in the labour force' (Johanson and Adams, 2003, p.81). This is almost certainly an underestimate of the total provision, if a full account were to be taken of the range of training in the NGO sector, the 'back street' and 'main street' training worlds of the principal towns, and the series of public sector institutions.[8] There is also informal apprenticeship training in the *jua kali* sector (on the job) which the Bank study judges to be 'responsible for more skills development than the offerings of all other training providers combined' (Johanson and Adams, 2003, p.82).

Unlike for the UPE domain, therefore, we seem to have few of the key numbers that would be valuable for the planning of the skills development challenge in Kenya. Ideally, we should have available the following four figures:

1. an institution-based training sector figure (both public and private);
2. a figure for formal training in formal sector enterprises, whether large, medium, small or micro;
3. a figure for informal training in informal sector enterprises, mostly very small scale;
4. a figure for those entering work, formal and informal, with no training, as casual or day labourers.

At the moment, we do not have a good sense, for Kenya or for Sub-Saharan Africa, of the size of the group of school leavers who do get some post-basic training, whether in public or private sector, formal or informal training institutions. But the World Bank study implies that this is a rather small segment of the entire cohort, perhaps as small as 5-10%, and it is argued that the bulk of this small percentage is private or non-government provision.

As for the issue of training targets, there seem to be none.[9] And certainly there is nothing as firm as in South Africa where there is an explicit and formal commitment by government to provide so many of their new learnerships (apprenticeships) by certain target dates, and for

---

[8] In the countries where the Bank study did investigate the size of the NGO and private training worlds, it found them substantially larger than the public provision.

[9] Kenya's draft Education Sector Strategic Plan, 2003-2007 does have a section on Objectives for TIVET, with indicators and targets, but only 1 of the 16 targets is quantified and none of them has a timeline before 2007 (Kenya Government, 2003d).

workers in different kinds of firms to have guaranteed access to certain level of training.

If there is simply nothing approaching a discourse about an obligation to train, let alone any debate about a training policy regime that would prepare Kenya for its ambitions of 7% growth annually, there is equally an absence of data on the quality of what little there is available. But both the Ministry of Labour (quoted in Haan, 2001) and the research community (e.g. Ngome, 2003) are united in condemning the very low quality of much that is offered.

As to outcomes, again the picture is dismal and extremely sketchy. Even the recent data in the World Bank report suggests that, of that small fraction of school leavers who actually do manage to get training only a very small fraction find that translates into a formal sector job (14% for Tanzania) (Ngome, 2003, p.34). The figure for Kenya is higher at 27.4% (World Bank, 2004, pp. 5-6). This also makes it less surprising that the graduates of the skills development institutions find it extremely difficult to secure formal sector jobs. But the result, as the World Bank report points out constantly, is that 'most entrants to the labour market (in Sub-Saharan Africa) have no choice but to seek work in the informal economy' (Johanson and Adams, 2003, p.15). Employment in the informal sector in Kenya was as high as 72.6% in 2001 (World Bank 2004, p.6). It is a point we return to when we consider the government's pledge of making 500,000 new jobs for young people annually.

We reach a rather disappointing lack of a conclusion when we apply our three markers – quantity, quality and outcomes – to the domain of post-basic training. There are no reliable numbers on the scale of training; there are very major concerns about quality – but virtually no evidence; and there no acceptable data on outcomes – beyond the rule of thumb logic that because there are few jobs in the formal sector, young people must be getting absorbed by the informal economy. Beyond this depressing record, there is available no nationally agreed policy on skills development, and no discussion on what steps might need to be taken if the ultimate Government target of industrial transformation by 2020 was going to come within reach.

There was some targeting of self-employment via schools and training institutions as far back as the Gachathi Commission (1976) which was reinforced by the 8-4-4 School Reform of 1984. But we have already noted that targeting self-employment via schools has been close to abandoned; meanwhile, the 1976 encouragement, reinforced in 1986, that all technical training should aim at employment *and* self-employment has also been dropped. The World Bank Review of 2003 (p.37) makes it rather clear that in Sub-Saharan Africa formal sector training should be oriented much more to the informal sector, but it admits that many of its own country reform programmes of skills training during the 1990s, including its recent project for Kenya, have failed because of the fierce opposition of the training institutions to their re-orientation to support preparation for work in the informal sector.

The ultimate target – productive work

We come now to our third and last domain – and arguably the most crucial in the eyes of pupils, parents and politicians – whether there are jobs and work at the end of the FPE and skills development tunnels. Here the Government has given itself a double target – a 7% growth rate and the creation of 500,000 new jobs annually. These are certainly ambitious goals. And it will be recalled that in the President's speech they were actually connected: 'It is our intention to grow at 7% per annum in order to create 500,000 jobs per year.'

Also, unlike FPE or even skills development, where government action can dramatically create pupil or trainee numbers, the provision of sustainable numbers of new jobs on an annual basis is not an arena where the government alone can take very effective action.

It may be worth noting the sheer scale of what these targets suggest before turning to examine in more detail their implications for the informal economy of Kenya. First, as of 1998-1999, Kenya's growth rate was 0.5% (*World Development Report* for 2000-2001, quoted in Haan 2001, p.24); so the 7% goal was not going to be easy to reach – even if there had already been some improvement prior to the change in government, and it had reached 2.4% in late 2004. As to the 500,000 new jobs, it will need to be recalled that Kenya's formal sector labour market is not large. For example, that part of the entire formal sector which is in the category – Trade and Industry – has only 300,000 jobs (Kenya, 2003), while one of the largest groups of government employees – teachers – numbers just 230,000. In addition, that part of the formal labour market which the government most controls – the public sector – is actually under major pressure to shed jobs, as must the parastatal industries. So where are the 500,000 jobs going to be found?

It should not perhaps be surprising that by the time the new

Government had done its calculations about squaring economic recovery with its jobs and growth pledges, in June 2003, it was honest enough to admit that it would be through the *jua kali*, informal economy that these, their main targets, would be met:

> Since it is unlikely that the formal sector will annually create 500,000 jobs over the medium term, the bulk of employment creation will continue to be in small enterprises. **Therefore the policy focus during the recovery period will increasingly be on the small business enterprises.** Over the period 2003-2007, a total of 2,636,130 jobs are expected to be created, out of which 12 per cent will be from the formal sector and the balance of 88 per cent from small enterprises. (Kenya Government, 2003, p.8 [emphasis in original])

This example illustrates rather well the politics of the numbers game in targets. There is little doubt that to the ordinary, uninformed listener the manifesto pledge of half a million jobs annually might well have been thought to mean that the new government would itself be in the business of hiring very large numbers of people, if returned at the polls. The reality behind the figures in the *Economic recovery strategy for wealth and employment creation* is that there will only be a little over 10% of the new jobs found in the formal sector of the economy, and logically perhaps about half of those, at the very most, in the public sector. It would have sounded very different in the pre-election days to have said that the Government was expecting the public sector only to grow by about 25,000 jobs annually!

When we turn now to look in more detail at how the government intends to create some 450,000 jobs annually in the informal, micro- and small enterprise (MSE) sector, we need to remind ourselves that over the 30 years since the terminology of informal sector became accepted both internationally and nationally in Kenya, there have been few if any government spokesmen bold enough to claim that the ingenuity, dynamism and competitiveness of the *jua kali* sector owe anything at all to government. Quite the reverse, the government has traditionally been seen by the MSE sector as corrupt and rent-seeking, as well as directly harassing the sector in respect of location, licensing, and under-cutting local production through illegal imports. If there have been jobs created in the *jua kali* sector over the last 30 years, this has been done without any government help or support.

But how does the job creation target for the informal sector look in the face of the existing magnitude and structure of the sector? In brief, the total non-agricultural, informal sector contains about 1.3 million firms and some 2.4 million people. So the government's plans, on its job pledge, amount to creating about as many jobs again as the entire non-agricultural informal economy within 5 years. It should also be noted that 2/3 of all these current MSE jobs are in the rural areas, while only 17%, or 400,000 MSE jobs, are to be found in the two largest cities – Nairobi and Mombasa (Central Bureau of Statistics, ICEG and K-REP, 1999). So, again, the job pledge would mean reproducing something like 5 times the entire *jua kali* population of Nairobi and Mombasa over the quinquennium. This would not, of course, be the intention of government even if it were feasible. Ronge et al. (2002, p.1) are possibly correct to point out that it has been 'the lack of enthusiasm by policy makers to encourage the growth of the informal sector in urban areas' that 'may explain the poor implemen-tation record in the MSE sector'. This is an attitude that can also be picked up in the *Economic recovery strategy* where the Report notes with approval the recommendation in the CBS baseline survey that 'policy and programme attention or priority should increasingly be targeted towards rural-based enterprises' (Kenya Government, 2003b, p.35). But it goes further, and betrays an additional reason for targeting the rural informal economy:

> One important spin-off of focusing policy interaction on the rural based MSEs is the advantage of stabilising migration and hence reducing stress on urban environment and infrastructure. (Kenya Government, 2003b, p.35)

This emerging rural focus of the Government's interest in the informal economy is given some further support – from a very different angle – by the latest drafts of the 'Sessional Paper on the Development of MSEs for wealth creation and employment generation' (Kenya Government, 2003a; Kenya Government, 2004).[10] Though it has been traditional to talk of the informal sector as non-farm or off-farm, the Sessional Paper argues strongly that 'small farms are also small businesses' (Kenya Government, 2003a, p.2). In an important break with tradition, the latest draft of the Sessional Paper boldly redefines the sector finally to cut across the farm/ non-farm divide: 'The definition of the MSE sector is therefore expanded in the Paper to include all enterprises, both farm and non-farm,

---

[10] The first draft of the paper was available in mid -2003; a second went to Cabinet in late 2004, and would be published and discussed in Parliament early in 2005.

employing less than 50 persons' (Kenya Government, 2004, p.2). As the bulk of all work and employment in Kenya is in the rural areas, this redefinition of the *jua kali* sector massively increases the size of Kenya's MSE sector to 'over 74.2% of the total number of persons engaged in the country' (Kenya Government, 2004, p.6).

We are not arguing against the reclassification – indeed it has been an anomaly for over 30 years that the *jua kali* sector has been classified as off-farm or non-farm, in a country where so much of the total employment is in the rural areas. But we are merely noting that the government's measures to create new opportunities for work and for jobs would be located primarily in rural areas and would be in the MSE sector. Again, a good thing, but if the jobs pledge had been initially presented as principally a rurally focused initiative in the informal economy, it might have had a rather different political resonance than it did.

In terms of implementation of the jobs pledge, it became clear rather early on that the way the Government was going to fulfil its mandate was not at all by large rural or urban work creation schemes; indeed, it was not going to create jobs directly at all. It would be the private sector that would actually create the jobs – and the Government's responsibility would NOT be to intervene directly but to create the enabling environment 'for the private sector to create wealth and generate employment for millions of our youth' (Kibaki in Kenya Government, 2003a, p.1). This clarification, of course, means that it becomes immensely more complicated to judge whether the Government is actually on target with its 500,000 jobs, since it is the private sector which is now responsible, and of course the private sector, as we have said, includes both the rural and urban informal economy. Statistically, it will be hugely problematic to determine whether the private sector has actually created new jobs because of specific changes to the national environment or because of wider global changes in the investment climate or the terms of trade.

On our other marker, quality, it will be impossibly difficult to make a judgement about whether the tens and hundreds of thousands who are entering the labour market each year are acquiring a particular quality of what the ILO terms decent work. Without any Government action, the enormous majority of those entering the *jua kali* sector may find themselves engaged in subsistence self-employment.

But leaving aside the challenge of assessing whether the target is actually being achieved, what other evidence is there of how the Government may be trying to change the environment in which this particular element of the private sector – the *jua kali* – is operating? Here there are several important indications of intended changes in Government policy, and there are also a number of very specific interventions by the Government in the activities of the *jua kali* in urban Kenya that need to be briefly discussed.

First, the Government is clearly interested in the removal of the barriers between the informal and formal sector (Kenya Government, 2003a, p.2). There are two sides to this; on the one hand, MSEs remain informal because the costs of complying with the regulations, licenses, etc. are too high. But, equally, small firms remain informal in order to stay outside the tax net. Here, the first draft of the Sessional Paper was more explicit than the final draft:

> By staying informal, MSEs forego the advantages of formalisation (which include less vulnerability to harassment and the payment of bribes, and better access to financial services and government contracts) while the government is deprived of tax revenue which could be used for better public services. (Kenya Government, 2003a, p.3)

> Mechanisms will be put in place to ensure that the MSE can pay a tax that allows them to fulfil their tax obligation and to thrive at the same time. (Kenya Government, 2004, p.44)

It is hard to estimate the impact on employment of any substantial success in persuading the most profitable parts of the informal sector to start paying tax, but almost certainly, in the short term, it would reduce employment in the *jua kali* sector. Formalisation would likely diminish the numbers of young people working on very low and irregular wages for long hour. But part of the challenge to the tax authorities would be to judge who to target in tax terms – the MSEs proper – or the very large number of civil servants, as well as teachers and other professionals, who have a second or third (informal) job from which income is tax-free, and who therefore are straddling the informal and formal sectors. Even some of the anti-corruption measures which are going to oblige junior civil servants and parastatal employees to declare their wealth (much of it from these side-jobs) may actually reduce employment in the short term.

If it is too early to say what the new regulations from the Public Officers' Ethics Act passed in early 2003 will mean for employment and 'enterprise', there have been some much more controversial interventions by Government ministries in some very public parts of the urban informal sector. Apart from the early initiatives to remove street children from the city centre of Nairobi and provide them skills through the National Youth Service, there were also, in mid-2003, substantial demolitions of street traders' kiosks in many different parts of Nairobi, as well as elsewhere. Various ministry rationales were available to justify these actions, including the need to prevent encroachment on road reserves country-wide. But it is worth noting that these very public destructions of property (and obviously of jobs) took place – not in the enormous outlying *jua kali* areas of Nairobi, where the formal – informal boundaries are almost impossible to determine, but right in the heart of Nairobi's modern streets and avenues. Whatever the rights and wrongs of these first major acts of harassment of the *jua kali* sector of Kenya by the new Government, many thoughtful analysts of the MSE sector saw it as a public relations disaster for a Government that had pledged to create an enabling environment for the private sector to operate.[11]

In late 2004, the jury was still out on what the Government's policy and practice will be in respect of this enormously diffuse and diversified sector of the economy. There is an emerging Sessional Paper, but it will not be out before early 2005. It contains a whole host of policy targets for the development of the MSE sector including setting aside market space for traders, and allocating vacant spaces and public halls or some streets on some days for use by MSEs. There will be physical planning in both urban and rural areas for the MSE sector. Of course only a handful of Kenyans have seen this document; while hundreds of thousands have seen the demolition of substantial numbers of the workplaces of the *jua kali*.

In respect of the quantity, quality and the outcomes of the Government's targets for job creation, the conclusion must be very tentative for the moment. Unlike the Skills Development domain, there is an actual target number (500,000), and there is shortly to be a national policy. But it will be extraordinarily difficult for the Government or civil society to monitor whether jobs are or are not created, and especially if most of them – almost 90% – are to be created in the informal economy – and most of these in the rural areas.[12]

---

[11] If the demolitions had been part of a planned concentration of the *jua kali* into new market areas, it would have been very different.

[12] Predictably, the Government has claimed to be on target with the creation of almost 1 million jobs in its first 2 years – a claim roundly dismissed by opposition and other critics.

Conclusions on targeting school, skill and work in Kenya

We have examined the presence or absence of targets in FPE, skills development, and employment. Of the three areas, there can be little doubt after 2 years of the new Government that the greatest impact politically was derived from FPE – getting 1.4 million additional children into school. But the provision of FPE could turn into a poisoned chalice, if there is insufficient attention to quality, or to the continuation and job outcomes of being in primary school for eight years.

By contrast with the target of universal primary, there is no target of any kind for the skills domain, or any national policy. But the much greater diversity of provision in the area of skills development, and the opportunity for skills to be delivered in schools, in training institutions, and in the workplace itself, underline the fact that there cannot readily be a simple (simplistic) 'Skills for All' development goal. The inability to construct a single slogan for the whole skills arena does not mean that the business of planning and of setting priorities should be abandoned. In a way, the IDT and MDG process may have contributed to the necessarily complex planning processes of governments and ministries, and asserted the primacy of just a handful of super-targets.

The skills domain desperately does need a whole series of intermediate goals and targets if it is to play a role in the country's modernisation, as the Government's manifesto declared, and not least if it is to encourage its MSEs to be more regionally competitive, and its larger industries to forecast the skills needed for industrial transformation.

Finally, in the realm of work and employment, we have used the target of 500,000 jobs to illustrate just how distracting and ultimately meaningless a simplistic target or an undefined goal can be. We have argued that this particular target fails all our three tests: it cannot be measured in quantitative terms; there is no discussion of the type or the quality of the jobs being aimed at – formal, informal, casual or permanent. And finally, the target is not embedded in any agricultural or industrial or commercial context. At best, it may be quietly forgotten; at worst it might, for a time, get in the way of elaborating an agricultural and industrial set of strategies that is relevant to Kenya's recovery.

References

Bennell, P., 1996. Rates of return to education: does the conventional pattern prevail in Sub-Saharan Africa? *World Development* 24 (1), 183-199.

Central Bureau of Statistics, ICEG, K-REP, 1999. National micro and small enterprise baseline survey 1999. Nairobi.

Gichura, S., 2003. The turning point: free primary education in Kenya. *NORRAG News 32*, August. Centre of African Studies, University of Edinburgh.

Haan, H.C., 2001. *Training for Work in the Informal Sector: Fresh Evidence from Eastern and Southern Africa.* International Training Centre, International Labour Organization, Turin.

International Labour Organization, 1972. *Employment, Incomes and Equality: a Strategy for Increasing Productive Employment in Kenya.* ILO, Geneva.

Jansen, J.D., 2005. Targeting education: The politics of performance and the prospects of education for all. *International Journal of Educational Development* 25(4), 368-380.

Johanson, R., Adams, A., 2003. *Skills development in Sub-Saharan Africa.* The World Bank, Washington DC.

Kadzamira, E., Rose, P., 2003. Can free primary education meet the needs of the poor? Evidence from Malawi. *International Journal of Educational Development* 23, 501-516.

Kenya Government, 1986. *Economic management for renewed growth.* Sessional Paper No.1 of 1986. Government Printer, Nairobi.

Kenya Government, 1992. *Small Enterprise and Jua Kali Development in Kenya.* Government Printer, Nairobi.

Kenya Government, 2003a. Sessional paper on the development of micro and small enterprises for employment creation and poverty reduction, draft of May 2003.

Kenya Government, 2003b. *Economic recovery strategy for wealth and employment creation, 2003-2007.* Government Printer, Nairobi.

Kenya Government, 2003c. *Report on rapid appraisal on the status of Technical and Vocational Education and Training (TVET) in Kenya.* Ministry of Education, Science and Technology, September, Nairobi.

Kenya Government, 2003d. Technical, Industrial, Vocational and Entrepreneurship Training (TIVET) Reform symposium, theme: reforms for employment and industrial prosperity report of a symposium held 2-5 November 2003. Nyeri, Kenya.

Kenya Government, 2004. *Development of micro and small enterprises for wealth creation and employment generation.* Sessional Paper No. 3 of 2004. Government Printer, Nairobi.

Kibaki, M., 2003. *Speech at the Opening of Parliament.* Nairobi.

King, K., 1989. Primary schooling and developmental knowledge in Africa. *Studies in Science Education*, 17, 29-56.

King, K., McGrath, S., Oketch, H., 2002. *Learning to Compete in Kenya: A Challenge to Education, Training & Enterprise. A Synthesis Report.* Centre of African Studies, University of Edinburgh, Edinburgh.

Kyeyune, R., 2003. *Basic education for what? Literacy skills deficiencies in primary schools. NORRAG News* 32, August. Centre of African Studies, University of Edinburgh, Edinburgh.

Mwiria, K., 2002. *Vocationalisation of Secondary Education: a Kenya Case Study.* World Bank, Washington, DC.

NCCK, 1967. *After school what?* National Christian Council in Kenya, Nairobi.

Ngome, C., 2003. Overview of skills development in Kenya: constraints and prospects. *NORRAG News* 32, August. Centre of African Studies, University of Edinburgh, Edinburgh.

NORRAG News 32, August. Special issue on critical perspectives on education and skills in Eastern Africa at basic and post-basic levels. Centre of African Studies, University of Edinburgh, Edinburgh.

Okuni, A., 2003a. Quantity-quality trade-offs after UPE: prospects and challenges of universal access in Uganda. *NORRAG News* 32, August. Centre of African Studies, University of Edinburgh, Edinburgh.

Okuni, A., 2003b. Basic education for what? Low transition rate to secondary education and the challenge of technical and vocational skills provision. *NORRAG News* 32, August. Centre of African Studies, University of Edinburgh, Edinburgh.

Ronge, E., Ndirangu, L., Nyangito, H., 2002. Review of government policies for the promotion of micro and small-scale enterprises in Kenya. Discussion Paper DP/20/ 2002. Kenya Institute for Public Policy Research and Analysis (KIPPRA), Nairobi.

UNESCO, 2002. *EFA Global Monitoring Report 2002: Is the world on track?* UNESCO, Paris.

Villet, C., 2003. EFA: quantity-quality trade-offs after access to UPE: the challenges of universal access in the SADC region. *NORRAG News* 32, August. Centre of African Studies, University of Edinburgh.

World Bank, 2003. *Education in Rwanda. Rebalancing Resources to Accelerate Post-Conflict Development and Poverty Reduction.* A World Bank country study. World Bank, Washington DC.

World Bank, 2004. *Kenya: Strengthening the foundation of education and training in Kenya: Opportunities and challenges in primary and general secondary education.* Africa Region, Report No. 28064-KE. World Bank, Washington DC.

World Bank, 2005. *Education in Ethiopia: A World Bank Country Study.* World Bank, Washington DC.

Further reading

Jones, P., 1992. *World Bank financing of Education.* Routledge, London.

Kenya Government, 1996. *Industrial transformation to the year 2020.* Sessional Paper no 2 of 1996. Government Printer, Nairobi.

Kenya Government, 2003a. *Education sector strategic plan, 2003-2007.* Draft, September 2003. Ministry of Education, Science and Technology, Nairobi.

Kenya Government, 2003b. *A policy framework for education, training and research: meeting the challenges of education, training and research in Kenya in the 21st Century.* Draft of October 2004, Sessional Paper No of 2004. Ministry of Education, Science and Technology, Nairobi.

King, K., 2003. The international steering of education systems: the case of the World Bank in the fields of work, education and occupation. In: Oelkers, J. (Ed.), *Futures of Education.* Essays from an Interdisciplinary Symposium II. Work, Education, and Occupation. Peter Lang, Bern.

National Rainbow Coalition, 2002. Manifesto for the National Rainbow Coalition.

Samoff, J., Carrol, B., 2003. Pathways of influence and congruent interests: the World Bank and higher education in Africa. Paper to Oxford Conference on The State of Education: Quality, Quantity and Outcomes, 9-11 September. New College, Oxford.

Sheffield, J.R. (ed.), 1967. *Education, Employment and Rural Development.* University of Nairobi, East African Publishing House, Nairobi.

Chapter 9

This chapter reviews what happened to a particular commitment after it had been included in the final wording of an international set of EFA Goals at Dakar in 2000. In effect, this became almost 'sacred text'. Once Jomtien's 'essential skills required by youth and adults' had been turned into 'appropriate learning and life skills programmes' in Dakar (UNESCO, 2000: 8), it became very difficult for the EFA Global Monitoring Report (GMR) teams to monitor it. The term 'life skills' had been successfully lobbied by one of the core agencies in the Dakar World Education Forum, and had been preferred over terms such as work skills, livelihood skills or vocational skills. The lack of attention to these latter dimensions of skills development had not been helped by the Millennium Development Goals, also in 2000, focusing only on UPE and gender parity in the sphere of education.

This situation resulted in almost a decade of discussion by the GMR teams about the difficulty of monitoring this commitment to life skills. There were major problems of definition and lack of data. Only in 2010 did the GMR finally decide to treat Dakar's Goal 3 on life skills as skills development (King, 2011a). Doubtless this shift to consider skills development rather than life skills was aided by the wider international climate. The British Council had organised a major report and conference and report on skills, UNESCO had agreed a strategy on technical and vocational education and training (TVET), and the Swiss-supported Working Group for International Cooperation on Skills Development had arguably played a role too. The OECD was also turning its attention to a skills strategy. Finally, there was to be a whole GMR dedicated to skills development in 2012.

However, when the GMR team came to dedicate an entire issue of its valuable report to skills in 2012, it divided skills into foundation skills,

Kenneth King (2019): *Education, Skills and International Cooperation: Comparative and Historical Perspectives*. Hong Kong: Comparative Education Research Centre (CERC), The University of Hong Kong, and Dordrecht: Springer. © CERC

© Springer Nature Switzerland AG 2019
K. King, *Education, Skills and International Cooperation*, CERC Studies
in Comparative Education 36, https://doi.org/10.1007/978-3-030-29790-9_9

transferable skills and technical and vocational skills (UNESCO, 2012). Though this meant that technical and vocational skills were finally considered as part of the monitoring process, there was a tendency to focus more on foundation and transferable, soft skills than on technical and vocational skills. And within this sphere, the focus was much more school-based than on the many versions of post-school skill – whether in further education colleges, vocational training institutes or industrial training centres. Having waited a long time for a complete volume to be dedicated to skills, many actors were disappointed that it had a rather narrow lens on TVET.

As for my own involvement in these processes, I had been asked by the British Council to do a report on the global monitoring of skills development (King and Palmer, 2008). This was carried out along with a colleague originally from Edinburgh, Robert Palmer, whom I have mentioned before (introduction to Chapter 5). The same year, 2008, UNESCO asked me to help develop a TVET skills strategy. And a little later, Robert Palmer and I completed a volume in the IIEP Fundamentals of Educational Planning series on TVET (King and Palmer, 2010). I also contributed a background paper for the GMR on skills under the title of 'Eight proposals for a strengthened focus on TVET in the Education for All Agenda' (King, 2011).

This was a time when there was a heightened interest in skills development and its relations with work in a number of international agencies. It meant that the EFA GMR 2012 on skills appeared at a very opportune moment.

The particular chapter which follows takes the skills story from Jomtien to Dakar and on through the first 10 GMRs (King, 2011a). It anticipates the GMR on skills in 2012 but was published before the GMR appeared. For a detailed analysis of the skills GMR, there is an article in *Prospects* (King, 2014).

References

King, K. 2011a. 'Skills and Education for All from Jomtien (1990) to the GMR of 2012: A policy history'. *International Journal of Training Research*, 9, 16-34.

King, K. 2011b. 'Eight proposals for a strengthened focus on TVET in the Education for All Agenda', background paper for the Education for All Global Monitoring Report 2012, UNESCO, Paris.

King, K. 2014. 'Youth, skills development, and work in the Education for All Global Monitoring Report 2012: Learning from Asia or for Asia?' *Prospects,* 44, 2, 141-158

King, K. and Palmer, R. 2008. *Skills for work, growth and poverty reduction: Challenges and opportunities in the global analysis and monitoring of skills.* British Council, and UK National Commission for UNESCO, London.

King, K. and Palmer, R. 2010. *Planning for technical and vocational skills development,* Fundamentals of Educational Planning No.94, International Institute for Educational Planning, UNESCO, Paris.

UNESCO, 2012. *Youth and skills: Putting education to work. Education for All Global Monitoring Report 2012,* UNESCO, Paris.

WEF (World Education Forum), 2000. *The Dakar framework for action: Education for all: Meeting our collective commitments.* World Education Forum, 26-28 April 2000, Dakar.

Skills and Education for All from Jomtien (1990) to the GMR of 2012: A Policy History[1]

Introduction

This article reviews, over a 20 year period, the place of different aspects of skill in the literature associated with the very influential world conferences of Jomtien and Dakar. It then looks at the particular history of the treatment of skill within the global monitoring reports (GMRs).[2] The GMR was one of the key mechanisms set up, with the support of development agencies, to assess progress on the six Dakar goals, one of which, goal 3, was concerned with skills (for Dakar goals, see Table 1).

Table 6. The Six Dakar goals

1. Expanding and improving comprehensive early childhood care and education, especially for the most vulnerable and disadvantaged children;

2. Ensuring that by 2015 all children, particularly girls, children in difficult circumstances and those belonging to ethnic minorities, have access to and complete free and compulsory primary education of good quality;

3. Ensuring that learning needs of all young people and adults are met through equitable access to appropriate learning and life skills programmes;

4. Achieving 50% improvement in levels of adult literacy by 2015, especially for women, and equitable access to basic and continuing education for all adults;

5. Eliminating gender disparities in primary and secondary education by 2005, and achieving gender equality in education by 2015, with a focus on ensuring girls' full and equal access to and achievement in basic education of good quality;

6. Improving all aspects of the quality of education and ensuring excellence of all so that recognised and measurable learning outcomes are achieved by all, especially in literacy, numeracy and essential life skills.

Source: World Education Forum, 2000a, p.8

---

[1] This chapter is taken from King (2011a) 'Skills and Education for All from Jomtien (1990) to the GMR of 2012: A policy history', *International Journal of Training Research*, 9, 16-34. A first version of this paper was presented in London as part of King and Palmer (2008) *Skills for Work, Growth and Poverty Reduction*, a commissioned paper for the British Council and UK National Commission for UNESCO, to be discussed at an international conference in London in that month.

[2] The GMRs are developed within UNESCO by an independent team supported by external funding as well as by UNESCO.

This policy history of the role of skills development within the Education for All (EFA) movement underlines the critical importance of text, or perhaps 'sacred text' would be more accurate. Once skills had been defined as 'life skills' in the Dakar process, it became very difficult for some agencies and governments to relate to the term. And hence the process of reaching agreement on a treatment of goal 3 became a major challenge. But this is only one part of an intriguing insight into agency policies and their influence over the international agenda. Arguably, the architecture of many global conferences, texts and reports is not truly global, but is powerfully influenced by the leading donor countries and the donor agencies (King, 2007a; *NORRAG News 43*). This paper details for the first time the particular agency policy origins of the Jomtien and Dakar texts, and the crucial role of the independent GMR process after UNESCO had attempted to carry out the first EFA Monitoring Report in 2001. In this whole historical process of over 20 years, detailed attention to particular discourses and texts has proved necessary to illuminate the shift in policy on skills.

From Jomtien to Dakar

Skills within basic education at Jomtien

The debate about skills takes place in 2010 in a very different global environment from Jomtien in 1990 or even Dakar in 2000. 1990 marked the formal launch by key multilateral agencies, but particularly the World Bank and UNICEF, of a much needed and long overdue global campaign to focus attention on the 100 million children with no access to school, the 100 million children who failed to complete school, and the 960 million adults who were illiterate. It was also focused on a third of the world's adults who had no access to 'new skills and technologies'. The concept adopted to pursue these massive and urgent needs was 'the expanded vision of basic Education for All' (WCEFA, *Framework for Action*, 1990a, pp.15, 17). This carefully chosen term was used to cover early childhood education, primary schooling, adult literacy, and skills development. The drafters of Jomtien did not use the words 'secondary education' at all in the *Declaration* or the *Framework for Action*, but judicious phrasing kept a place for secondary education within the expanded vision;[3] and, equally,

---

[3] One of the key suggested dimensions for national target-setting was 'Universal access to, and completion of, primary education (or whatever higher level education is considered as 'basic') by the year 2000' (WCEFA, *Framework* for Action, 1990a, p.3).

higher education and research were noted as vital to any sustainable environment for basic education. That the key concepts in Jomtien were basic education and basic learning needs can be judged by the fact that the term 'basic' was used 166 times in just 37 pages, whilst 'primary' was used just 13 times, 'skills' 11 times and 'literacy' 9 times.

This is not to say that the Jomtien documents were somehow sidelining the contribution of primary schooling. Indeed, they made it quite clear that *'The main delivery mechanism for the basic education of children outside the family is primary schooling'* (WCEFA, *Declaration*, 1990a, p.6 emphasis added), but they went on to make it equally clear that there was, in addition to primary school, a whole other world of learning: *'The basic learning needs of youth and adults are diverse and should be met through a variety of delivery systems'* (ibid. emphasis added). And it is this other world of learning that they principally illustrated with the word 'skills', whether acquired in the household, the firm, or the farm.

The Jomtien *Declaration* and *Framework for Action* used 'skills' in a series of different ways, which is entirely possible in English, but is not necessarily as straightforward in other languages. In a single, crucial paragraph, illustrating the diverse basic learning needs of youth and adults, they could refer to 'knowledge, skills, values and attitudes' which cover potentially a whole range of cognitive skills and competencies. They could also talk about 'essential knowledge and skills' which contrasts knowledge with skill. In addition, they could recognise that 'Literacy is a necessary skill in itself, and also the foundation of other life skills'. But they could distinguish between these several uses of skill and another meaning linked to training, by going on immediately, in the same paragraph, to note that: 'Other needs can be served by: skills training, apprenticeships, and formal and nonformal education programmes in health, nutrition, population, agricultural techniques, the environment, science, technology, family life...' (WCEFA, *Declaration*, 1990a, p.6).

It is interesting also when it comes to the *suggested* goals and targets of the World Conference, and to the target which is of closest interest to many readers of this paper, 'skills' is used in this target along with the term 'education and training' in the context of improved 'employment and productivity' (see item 5 in the Table 2).

Thus, the World Conference used the word 'skills' in many of its different possible senses. Given its combining of 'skills training, apprenticeships, and formal and nonformal programmes', it should be clear that its approach to this suggested target covered not just formal institution-based skills, and not just non-formal skills, but both. In other words, its usage of skills was quite close to the notion of 'skills development' today, even though that term was not yet in common usage in 1990. Equally, its use of the relatively new term, 'life skills', but in the phrase 'life skills training for youth and adults' is more suggestive of livelihood skills than some of the interpersonal uses of life skills (WCEFA, *Framework*, 1990a, p.4). But all of these uses of skill were clearly felt to be essential parts of Education for All.

Table 7. The Six Dimensions of EFA Targets at Jomtien

- expansion of early childhood care and development activities, including family and community interventions, especially for poor, disadvantaged and disabled children;

- universal access to, and completion of, primary (or whatever higher level of education is considered as 'basic') by the year 2000;

- improvement of learning achievement such that an agreed percentage of an age cohort (e.g. 80 per cent of 14 years olds) attains or surpasses a defined level of necessary learning achievement;

- reduction of the adult illiteracy rate (the appropriate age-group to be determined in each country) to, say, one half its 1990 level by the year 2000, with sufficient emphasis on female literacy to significantly reduce the current disparity between male and female illiteracy rates;

- expansion of provision of basic education and training in other essential skills required by youth and adults, with programme effectiveness assessed in terms of behavioural change and impact on health, employment and productivity;

- increased acquisition by individuals and families of the knowledge, skills and values required for better living and sound and sustainable development, made available through all education channels including the mass media, other forms of modern and traditional communication, and social action, with effectiveness assessed in terms of behavioural change.

Source: WCEFA, Framework 1990a, p.3

What should be underlined is that those responsible for framing the expanded vision of Jomtien were innovative in including some key dimensions of livelihood skills and of training within their holistic approach. The deliberate use of the phrase 'education and training' in several places in the Jomtien documents makes the crucial point that training is part of basic learning needs. Or in other words, the expanded vision of Jomtien includes training. Significantly the document ends with this dual emphasis: 'This effort will require a much greater and wiser investment of resources in basic education and training than ever before' (WCEFA, *Framework*, 1990a, p.50).

Since Wadi Haddad, the Executive Secretary of the Jomtien Conference, played such a key role in elaborating the central concepts in both the *Declaration* and the *Framework*, it may be useful to note, from a paper in which he revisits Education for All almost 10 years later, how strongly he reinforces the joint importance of general education and skill training, for gaining 'advanced knowledge and skills'. In this valuable reflection, there is, significantly, no use of the term 'life skills' at all:

> While it is important to strengthen general education and skill training, **providing opportunities for acquiring advanced knowledge and skills must be pursued concurrently** in order to advance development of the economy and harness new technologies. Technological capacity – the ability to assess, select, adapt, use and develop new technologies – is becoming a critical determinant of a country's competitiveness prospects. Institutions of higher education and training must be first-class to equip individuals with the advanced knowledge and skills required for positions in govern-ment, business, industry, and the professions. (Haddad, 1999, p.7 emphasis in the original)

There can be little doubt, therefore, that one of the principal architects of Jomtien saw the development of knowledge and skills as equally crucial at all levels, and he would later regret the way that the world community narrowed his vision down to an artificial focus on only the very basic level of education and training:

> Jomtien, by making the case for basic learning needs, has created in the minds of some a false dichotomy between basic and higher levels of education. The diversified economic, social and political demands on education leave countries with no choice but to invest in building the whole structure of knowledge and skills. With such profound changes in technology and the economy, a country foregoes the opportunity for advancement when it focuses on one level to the disadvantage of others. The workforce of the future will need a whole spectrum of knowledge and skills to deal with technology and

the globalization of knowledge. (Haddad, 1999, p.6)[4]

A word on the emerging locations of skills development

Although in this paper we shall be focusing on the way that essential skills and life skills training have been conceptualised in Jomtien, in Dakar and in the Global Monitoring Reports, it will also be important, from time to time to relate this to the different locations of skill identified by the international agency skills constituency. For instance, just a year after the Jomtien World Conference, the World Bank produced a highly influential, if controversial, policy paper on *Vocational and Technical Education and Training (VTET)* (World Bank, 1991). Interestingly, it was developed under the ultimate leadership of Wadi Haddad, the then Division Chief at the World Bank, for two years prior to Jomtien. Very much better resourced, and drawing on a much wider base of expertise than either the Jomtien or Dakar documents, it succeeded in substantially reconceptualising the range and scope of vocational and technical skills locations in a pattern that has influenced many subsequent reports. It dealt with public school-based VTET,[5] public training or centre-based VTET, enterprise-based VTET in both the formal and informal sectors, private for profit and private non-profit training. Interestingly, there was no mention of life skills at all. These six locations of skills were powerfully revisited in the Bank's *Skills development in Sub-Saharan Africa* (Johanson and Adams, 2004), in *Skill development in India* (World Bank, 2008b), in the Asian Development Bank's (2004) *Improving technical education and vocational training: strategies for Asia*, and in DFID's *Technical and Vocational Skills Development* (2007).

Eliminating skills, early childhood education, adult literacy, and quality in the MDGs

We shall not elaborate here how this judicious, if innovative, coverage of skill within an expanded vision of basic education and training was

---

[4] The key background document for Jomtien, and for understanding the meanings intended for 'essential skills required for youth and adults' is *Meeting basic learning needs: a vision for the 1990s* (WCEFA, 1990b). It establishes a clear distinction between 'essential learning tools', such as literacy, numeracy and problem-solving, and basic learning content as an array of knowledge and skills organized to meet the basic needs of learners, both as individuals and as actors in the contexts of the family, the work place, and the community (ibid. p.63).

[5] For reasons not explained in the text, the Bank used the terms Vocational and Technical Education and Training (VTET) instead of the commonplace TVET or VET.

eliminated by the OECD Development Assistance Committee's framing of the International Development Targets (IDTs) in 1996, which were in turn largely converted to the Millennium Development Goals (MDGs) in September 2000. This has been covered elsewhere.[6] By contrast, UNESCO sought to maintain its commitment to the broad spirit of Jomtien, through the mid-term review of progress towards EFA in 1996 in Amman. This potentially major review was far from a success, however, as Sauvageot has argued persuasively:

> To evaluate and monitor the objectives drawn up in Jomtien in 1990, the five organisations that organised the [Jomtien] conference defined 18 indicators. It is regrettable that they did not do so until 1996, following a fairly disastrous conference intended as a mid-term review, but which, in the absence of reliable indicators, was unable to evaluate anything.[7] These 18 indicators were used to evaluate Dakar follow-up. Additional indicators are currently being validated. (ETF, 2007, p.15)

Preparing the end of decade EFA Assessment (2000) without any data on skills

Learning from the Amman experience, these 18 indicators were used to develop the individual country assessments of progress towards EFA that would be needed for presentation in the Dakar World Forum on Education for All in April 2000. But they did not attempt to collect any data on the provision of 'essential skills for young people and adults'. The *Technical Guidelines* for preparing the Assessment had a perfectly reasonable and well-argued account of the data that *might* be assembled under the heading, 'Training in Essential Skills' (UNESCO, 1998, p.24), but none of the 18 indicators actually chosen was relevant to capturing formal and non-formal essential skills.[8] As the foreword by Denise Lievesley, the then Director of the UNESCO Institute for Statistics (UIS),

---

[6] See for example 'Multilateral agencies in the construction of the global agenda in education' (King, 2007a) and 'What room for skills development in 'post-primary education'? (King, 2007b). See also Gustafsson, formerly of Sida, and formerly Chair of the GMR Editorial Board, 'As you and I have noted several times 'the Expanded Vision' at Jomtien has been played down or disappeared in practice' (Gustafsson to King, 03.4.08).

[7] Neither the *Working Document nor the Statistical Document* from the Mid-Decade Meeting made any attempt to capture progress on 'other essential skills for youth and adults'; see UNESCO, 1996a, 1996b.

[8] Indeed, the terms, 'skills' and 'life skills training', did not appear in the otherwise very useful glossary of the Technical Guidelines.

admitted in the *Statistical Document,* two years later:

> In addition, the indicators selected to assess progress were themselves only a subset of the indicators needed to have a complete picture of the current situation. (Lievesley in UNESCO, 2000)

The result of not attempting to cover the areas of essential skills and life skills training for this crucial statistical document that sought to summarise the 167 country reports[9] prepared for the Dakar World Forum is that the countries obviously did not provide any data on skills, and in turn the *Statistical Document* prepared for the *Education for All 2000 Assessment* only covered early childhood education, primary education, teacher qualifications and literacy.[10] Seven years later, Sauvageot, the Editor of the *Statistical Document,* would reflect on the missing indicators for the objectives and goals of Jomtien and Dakar:

> It is noteworthy that no indicator has been defined for Dakar objectives 3 and 6, in the same way that none was defined for two of the Jomtien objectives.[11] Admittedly the task was not easy, but this deficiency will make it difficult to evaluate initiatives for these two objectives. (ETF, 2007, p.16)

Entering the Dakar World Forum without any data on skills

The Dakar World Forum, therefore, sought in April 2000 to revisit the Jomtien objectives of ten years earlier but without any adequate preparatory coverage of what had been agreed in Jomtien, on the 'provisions of basic education and training in other essential skills required by youth and adults' (WCEFA, *Framework for Action,* 1990a, p.3).

---

[9] India for example produced a whole series of substantive reports as their response to the EFA 2000 assessment, which was published as a book by OUP India. But there is no coverage of skills or life skills. See Govinda (2002).

[10] The Executive Summary neatly captures the inadequacy of what was attempted, in its inaccurate synthesis of Jomtien: 'In 1990, delegates gathered at the World Conference on Education for All in Jomtien, Thailand, to set the global agenda for education and literacy. They identified several goals, including universal access to primary education for every child, improved access to early childhood care and development programmes and the reduction of adult illiteracy. And they pledged to reach these goals by the year 2000' (UNESCO, 2000, p.8). It should be noted that though the Statistical Document did not collect data on essential skills, it did collect data on teacher qualifications and on primary education financing, despite these not being explicit Jomtien objectives.

[11] The second missing Jomtien objective was education, skills and values obtained through all education channels including mass media.

It should not be surprising then that the drafters of the Dakar *Framework for Action* and the later *Expanded Commentary on the Framework for Action* should have found it difficult to reach a consensus about goal 3 (or indeed goal 6).[12] No relevant data had been collected on these two areas in preparation for the Forum, either in the country EFA assessments or in the key *Statistical Document*. Indeed, the document did not even include 'skills' or 'life skills training' in its 6 page appendix of 'Key terms and definitions'. This omission is all the more surprising given that UNESCO had just played the principal role in organising in April 1999, in Seoul, the Second International Congress on Technical and Vocational Education.[13]

As with Jomtien, we shall look particularly at what happened to the relation between the basic education coverage in Dakar and the conceptualisation of skills, both formal and non-formal. In particular how did Dakar end up with a goal relating to skills which was, in the view of one seasoned bilateral agency commentator, 'frankly a mess'?[14]

This was the goal whose aim was intended to re-affirm the suggested Jomtien Target of:

> Expansion of provisions of basic education and training in other essential skills required by youth and adults, with programme effectiveness assessed in terms of behavioural changes and impacts on health, employment and productivity. (WCEFA, *Framework for Action*, 1990a, p.3)

In Dakar the new version of this Target merely read as follows:

> Ensuring that the learning needs of all young people and adults are met though equitable access to appropriate learning and life skills programmes. (WEF, 2000a, p.2)

Where Jomtien had suggested, by referring to training, skills, employment and productivity, that these other essential skills could be secured in formal and non-formal settings, but certainly included 'work skills' or 'livelihood skills', Dakar's adoption of the term 'life skills' alone left the

---

[12] 12 Only the Dakar *Framework for Action* (6 pages) was agreed at the Forum, while the *Expanded Commentary on the Framework for Action* (16 pages) was done by the World Education Forum drafting committee, during the month *after* the conference had ended.

[13] We are grateful to Tang Qian for reminding us of the short time between the Seoul and Dakar conferences (Tang to King, 07.08.08).

[14] Bilateral agency official to King, 26.10.07

scope extremely uncertain. In the absence of any data on skills from the EFA Assessment at the country level, the field was open for lobbying around this skills goal. Just as with the construction of the International Development Targets by the OECD DAC, so it was again one of the key multilateral agencies at Dakar which forcefully lobbied to have goal 3 use the language of 'life skills'.[15] Despite the very recent Seoul International Congress on TVE, the technical and vocational educators from UNESCO Headquarters were not present in Dakar; nor apparently were the relevant people from ILO.[16]

The replacement of 'essential skills' by 'life skills'
From the viewpoint of a number of UN agencies, the translation of the Jomtien concept of skills into life skills was probably viewed positively. There had, after all, just been a United Nations Inter-Agency meeting on Life Skills Education held in the World Health Organization (WHO) headquarters in Geneva in 1998, just two years before Dakar. In the view of one multi-lateral UN agency commentator, Amaya Gillespie, this meeting and its subsequent report (WHO, 1999) were critical to the promotion of life skills:

> For the development of the life skills concept, at UNICEF and many other UN agencies, a major milestone was an inter-agency meeting organized by the WHO Dept. of Mental Health in 1998: http://www.who.int/mental_health/media/en/30.pdf[17]

Like the term 'basic' in Jomtien which was used 166 times in the 37 pages of the *Declaration* and the *Framework*, the term 'skills' was used 160 times in just 17 pages in this WHO paper. Naturally, given the focus of the meeting, most of these usages were concerned with life skills. But the consensus at the meeting was that life skills were essentially 'psychosocial': 'Keywords used to describe psychosocial skills were: personal, social, interpersonal, cognitive, affective, universal' (WHO, 1999, p.3).

This usage of course is very different from 'work skills', 'livelihood

---

[15] '(Life Skills) would have focused on the skills (and attitudes, behaviours, and values) required to maintain a healthy life – physically and emotionally' (Shaeffer to King, 26.06.08).
[16] The author is grateful to Tang Qian for information on the disconnect between Seoul and Dakar, (Tang to King, 07.08.08).
[17] Amaya Gilllespie to King, 28.02.08.

skills', or 'entrepreneurial skills'. Indeed, the Inter-agency meeting made it absolutely clear that life skills were very different from such work-related skills:

> There was also a clear consensus *that livelihood skills such as crafts, money management and entrepreneurial skills are not life skills,* although the teaching of livelihood skills can be designed to be complementary to life skills education, and vice versa. (WHO, 1999, p.4, emphasis added)

In the light of this approach to life skills, it should not be surprising that this Inter-agency meeting did not include the ILO, despite its being held in Geneva.[18]

The 'sacred text' versus the expanded commentary on the Dakar Framework for Action

Even though it was just 'life skills' that made it into the Dakar goal 3 (as well as into goal 6),[19] it is nevertheless important to pay some attention to what else is said about skills in the rest of the *Framework*, as well as in the *Expanded Commentary*. We should also remember that there is nothing sacred about the text of these six Dakar goals; they were essentially man-made, often the result of lobbying and special pleading amongst the key drafting agencies, as we have noted above.[20] So the fact that life skills had replaced skills should not mean that we have to be narrowly focused on the lens of psychosocial life skills, in considering how to interpret or monitor the goal. Life skills can also cover orientation to sustainable futures, to livelihoods, and skills to 'navigate' through life.

The text surrounding the goals certainly also needs to be taken into account, and especially as goal 3 on its own has proved apparently so difficult to interpret in the subsequent eight years. Surely, it should be the spirit of Dakar rather than the letter that should be followed. For instance, just a few sentences before the six goals are laid out in the Dakar

---

[18] The UN agencies represented were: UNHCR, UNAIDS, UNICEF, UNFPA, and WHO.

[19] Dakar goal 6: 'Improving all aspects of the quality of education and ensuring excellence of all so that recognised and measurable learning outcomes are achieved by all, especially in literacy, numeracy and essential life skills'.

[20] Just as the MDGs were actually hammered out after the Heads of State had left the Millennium Summit, so also the bulk of the Dakar World Forum agreement was drafted, as we have said, in the weeks after the participants had left Dakar (see further King, 2007a).

Framework, there is the following use of 'skills' which suggests much more of a skills-for-work orientation than just psychosocial awareness:

> ... the quality of learning and the skills fall far short of the aspirations and needs of individuals and societies. Youth and adults are denied access to the skills and knowledge necessary for gainful employment and full participation in their societies. (WEF, 2000a, p.2)

However, the *Expanded commentary on the Framework* added some further important layers of meaning to this particular goal, which made it reminiscent of Jomtien's insistence on the need for higher education to complement basic education. In the key paragraph explaining goal 3 in more detail, three comments are made which may help to put the goal into a more operational perspective. First, and very importantly, it is stressed that all young people and adults should be given the opportunity to gain 'the knowledge and develop the values, attitudes and skills which will enable them to develop their capacities to work, to participate fully in their society, to take control of their own lives, and to continue learning' (WEF, 2000b, p.13). This will require, for all countries, that a certain proportion of their work force completes secondary education. 'In most countries this requires an expansion of the secondary system' (WEF, 2000b, p.13). This first comment on the implications of goal 3 is intriguing, therefore, by its very strong link of goal 3 to secondary education expansion.

By contrast, the second comment, which is principally about the risks and threats to young people from unemployment, conflict, HIV & AIDS, pregnancy, drugs etc might seem to reflect the psychosocial coping and awareness 'life skills' of the WHO text, but these threats to the young are in fact used to argue for 'youth-friendly programmes' providing 'information, skills, counselling and services needed to protect them' from such risks (WEF, 2000b, p.13).

But it is the third comment on goal 3 which links its application particularly to 'those who drop out of school or complete school without acquiring the literacy, numeracy and life skills they need' (WEF, 2000, p.13). It suggests there should be a range of options for continuing their learning, and to 'help them become active agents in shaping their future and develop useful work-related skills' (ibid). It is interesting that the term 'work-related' is preferred to 'life skills'.

In other words, the discussion in the surrounding text of the *Framework*, as well as in the three comments specifically on goal 3, all include a wider discourse on skills as well as on life skills, and suggest that the range of options for the goal are much closer to the spirit of Jomtien's 'other essential skills' than the bare letter of the Dakar goal by itself would first suggest.

One other factor may have influenced the use of life skills rather than work skills in the Dakar text. Life skills could, like the other goals, be seen as an entitlement, or as rights-based, falling in line with the supply-side orientation of Dakar as a whole. If work skills, or education and training in essential skills, more generally, had been included, it would have raised issues about training provision, as well as about the labour market demand. Life skills were therefore attractive to some agencies to include, but, as we shall see, they would prove much harder to monitor and assess than work skills.

The Treatment of Skills in the Global Monitoring Reports, 2002-2010

Having teased out some of the meanings of skill in the Jomtien world conference (1990) and the Dakar World Forum (2000), and noted the failure to incorporate skills in the preparatory assessment for Dakar, we shall now turn to examine how the domain of skills, including in its new garb of life skills, gets treated in the series of global monitoring reports that started in 2002. As we proceed through these, there will be an opportunity to reflect on the changing definitional issues relating to skill, as the GMR teams grapple with how most appropriately to conceptualise skill, and then how most effectively to monitor it. We note here again that they appear to do so without drawing on the new policy work of the World Bank on skills development in Sub-Saharan Africa that was already available in draft (Johanson, 2002), as the GMR process began.

Before passing to this series of impressive scholarly, yet strategic, policy volumes (the GMRs), we should recall that initially UNESCO sought to carry out this monitoring of the EFA goals and Dakar commitments on its own resources. It had been charged to do so by the Dakar forum, and the first result of this UNESCO monitoring attempt was available by October 2001 (UNESCO, 2001).

This volume was executed within the regular if constrained resources of UNESCO, and consisted of just 43 pages of text, and a few pages of appendices. Its statistical tables were six pages long, and covered only a handful of the EFA Dakar dimensions, such as pre-primary,

primary and adult literacy. (The subsequent GMRs were ten times longer at ca. 430 pages.) There were no tables relating to skills or life skills.

In the key chapter on progress towards all the EFA goals, much more attention was given to the 'Goals with a deadline' – UPE [2015], adult literacy [2015] and gender parity [2005] – than the others. Compared to the 10 pages allocated to these, the other goals such as early childhood and life skills had two pages; and the focus of our attention in this paper, the acquisition of life skills, was covered in just four sentences, saying nothing of any significance (UNESCO, 2001, p.23).

To be fair to this rather meagre report, it was operating with the same group of 18 indicators which had been put together after the problematic mid-term 1996 Amman conference – indicators, which, it will be recalled, do not cover skills or life skills at all. Indeed it only covered 13 of these 18 in its own tables. It was clear, however, that for the monitoring task to be continued, much more would need to be done:

> To perform this task successfully, a major priority must be the development and sustained production of reliable indicators relevant to current EFA goals and targets (UNESCO, 2001, p.24).

It is not certain what would have happened to this EFA monitoring process, if it had been left to UNESCO alone. It does not appear from the text that regular annual monitoring was even assured as the volume was described by its author as 'the first in a **possible** series of annual reports' (UNESCO, 2001, p.12, emphasis added). What we can say with complete certainty, however, is that this slim report did nothing at all to progress the understanding of Dakar goal 3.

The independent global monitoring reports get underway

1. GMR 2002: the challenge and the promise
By early 2001 those external donors concerned with EFA had decided that the monitoring of Education for All was too important to be left to UNESCO alone, and a process was rapidly underway to produce the first of the global monitoring reports.[21]

The first of these GMRs (UNESCO, 2002) had to be produced at an unprecedented speed, and a new team had to be assembled, and procedures and approaches independent of UNESCO had to be

---

[21] As the report of the first High Level Group meeting on EFA makes clear, donors, including particularly DFID, wanted a more substantive EFA report, independent of, but under the auspices of UNESCO (bilateral donor agency representative to King, 31.03.08)

negotiated and established. It should not be surprising, therefore, that this was not the GMR that would break new ground in the treatment of goal 3. But the report looked forward to doing so in future years:

> The monitoring of this Dakar goal presents major conceptual and methodological challenges which this Report is in no position to address. Nevertheless, it is important to identify some of the issues to which future reports will need to respond. (UNESCO, 2002, p.56)

The GMR 2002 did not focus narrowly on teasing out the meaning of the bare text of the goal itself, but judged that the wider discussion of young people and adults' entitlements to develop their capacities to work and participate fully in their societies was what the Dakar Forum had intended for this goal. Thus the treatment of the goal was headed up as 'Learning needs of all young people and adults' (UNESCO, 2002, p.56).

Even though the Goal was judged to present major methodological and conceptual problems, it is important that when it came to analysing the monitoring challenge, it was felt that these methodological problems were not unique but were 'akin to those … on early childhood care and education' (ibid, p.58). Indeed, the first Director of the GMR team, Christopher Colclough, has since confirmed and expanded upon the alleged conceptual challenges of this goal, as follows:

> I don't think that the conceptual issues involved are any more challenging than those surrounding quality, gender or ECCE. Some people think that the wording of the goal is not tight enough, and that some problems surrounding the meaning of the goal were unresolved. However, I don't personally find that a constraint to dealing with it in GMR. (Colclough to King, 20.2.08)

That said, the GMR 2002 nevertheless managed in a few pages to give a taste of the 'rich conceptual debate' about the meanings of skills and around the search for indicators (UNESCO, 2002, p.56). It gave a flavour of the sheer range of the skills domain, and the possibilities of different approaches, covering the diversity of usage of life skills, the potential of a human capabilities lens on skills, livelihood skills, psychosocial and interpersonal skills, generic and context-specific varieties.[22]

Looking ahead to the monitoring challenge, it sketched out an

---

[22] It is however debatable whether, on its own, the psychosocial focus of life skills would really allow for this rich conceptual discussion around skills to evolve.

ambitious agenda for future action:

> there is a need to get a better understanding of exactly what is taking place in terms of programme provision. A comprehensive picture of who is doing what in support of the learning needs of adults and young people requires well developed typologies that include coverage of programme theme, objectives, duration, frequency and delivery methods. (UNESCO, 2002, p.58)

Meanwhile on the monitoring side, a whole range of possibilities were noted that could assess access and participation in situations where there were multiple providers in different locations, including large numbers of young people gaining their skills in the informal sector. It was suggested that household surveys could be valuable, as well as new instruments associated with the Adult Literacy and Life Skills Survey, then in progress (OECD & Statistics Canada, 2005).

2. GMR 2003/4: Engaging with skills and life skills

This report engaged with what GMR 2002 had termed the rich debates about skills in a serious way; it also made some judgments about how best to proceed with monitoring the skills goal, in conjunction possibly with the adult literacy goal 4, with which it judged goal 3 to have some very substantial overlap. Indeed, the report treated goals 3 and 4 together under the umbrella title: 'Learning programmes for life skills and literacy' (UNESCO, 2003, p.84 ff).

In particular, this GMR reflected critically on life skills in a special box that covered an entire page. This was a valuable but very preliminary exercise that put down a marker that life skills would require some serious analysis in any more in-depth study of skills. By this point, in 2003 when the GMR was being actively prepared, there were many strands of the life skills discourse that had emerged, apart from that linked to the UN Inter-agency meeting of 1998 to which we have already referred. There was the OECD's Definition and Selection of Competencies (DeSeCo); there was UNICEF's Life Skills Based Education; and there was a series of context-specific life skills approaches such as Skills-Based Health Education Including Life Skills (WHO, 2003). In addition, a background paper, 'Understanding life skills' had been commissioned to the UNESCO Institute of Education (UIE) in Hamburg (Singh, 2003).

Interestingly, in April 2003, at the very time that the GMR team was engaging, in this very provisional way, with life skills and its links to literacy, there was being held a crucial meeting of the Working Group for International Cooperation in Skills Development (WGICSD), the main donor agency body charged with discussing and disseminating new ideas and good practice in skills development.[23] Its focus, in this particular meeting at the UNESCO UNEVOC Centre in Bonn was, coincidentally, on *Skills for Life and Work;* and within a few weeks the 54-page report of this Working Group meeting was available (WGICSD, 2003). Many of the main strands of the life skills discourses were represented there, including the OECD DeSeCo, the Adult Literacy and Life Skills Survey, and the life skills dimension of the Dakar Framework.

But the Working Group had an additional crucial dimension on life skills that was still absent from the few pages of the GMR 2003/4 that were dedicated to goal 3; and this was the link to work skills. The Working Group meeting and the subsequent publication of its working paper 8 brought together these two discourses, through presentations from the World Bank, the European Training Foundation and the ILO. The potential synergy between the life skills and work skills discourses was ably captured in McGrath's subsequent overview introduction to the working paper: 'Life and work skills and their contribution to education and training debates'.

This key paper captured effectively the synergies between life and work skills, and persuasively demonstrated where the life skills discourse in particular had derived from, including how the health promotion strain in the discourse of life skills had found its way into Dakar goals 3 and 6. It also critically addressed the potential importance of life skills, and commented on the challenges for providers of such core skills programmes. But, in terms that could have been relevant to the GMR's monitoring concerns, it raised issues about the assessment of these skills:

Experiences to date also raise concerns about modes of assessment. It

---

[23] See Working Group, Paper 8, 'The Group has chosen to use the notion of vocational and technical skills development rather than technical and vocational education and training. This reflects a concern to take notice of the move away from a focus on the large, homogenising institutions of the state in favour of more varied modalities of skills development which prevail in many countries' (Working Group, 2003, p.53). Though the meetings of the Working Group are comprised primarily of agency personnel, the staff work on the Working Group was provided by academics linked to the then Graduate Institute of International and Development Studies in Geneva and to NORRAG in Edinburgh. See further: www.norrag.org/resources/publications. The WGICSD operated from 1996 to 2008, supported mainly by Swiss Development Cooperation.

is not always clear how the development of these skills is to be demonstrated. Most existing systems for measuring such skills or competencies have proved highly complex, bureaucratic and expensive. The notion of life/work skills is closely related to the rise of lifelong learning across formal, non-formal and informal settings. This points to the need for functioning systems of recognition and accreditation of prior learning if the full range of such skills is to be acknowledged. However, such systems have proven very difficult to put into operation. This has meant that the advantages that such programmes were intended to bring in terms of equity and access have remained primarily rhetorical. (McGrath, 2003, p.11)

Failure of the global skills development discourse sufficiently to influence the GMR approach to goal 3

We have underlined the coincidence of the main donor agency group concerned with skills development discussing this very topic of life skills at the precise time that it could have been of very direct assistance to the GMR team. This is not merely to argue that the Working Group could have been directly beneficial to the GMR team solely in the latter's preliminary work on life skills. But, with the benefit of hindsight, it could more generally have been of critical support to the GMR team, which has arguably lacked capacities in the domain of skills development over its entire period of 6 years so far.[24]

As an illustration of the apparent disjunction between the global skills development discourse and the discussion of literacy and life skills in GMR 2003/4, it is interesting to note that this GMR introduces, for the first time, tables (and some discussion) about technical and vocational education and its share in total secondary enrolment. But this is not in relation to goal 3 but to an assessment of goal 5 – 'Eliminating gender disparities in primary and secondary education' (UNESCO, 2003,

---

[24] The GMR team is not alone in this regard; many donor agencies have shed their reliance on vocational educators over the period of increasing interest in EFA since Jomtien 1990. Now, as skills development becomes dramatically more salient in many government agendas, there are major gaps in agencies' skills development capacities. Both DFID and the World Bank are acting sharply to increase their staff's awareness of TVET. See British Council (2008) *Rethinking TVET for Education Development*. It should be noted, however, that the GMR team does not contain expertise on several of the other Goals; thus, expertise had to be brought in for early childhood education and for adult literacy. This would be the same for any Skills GMR.

pp.72-73).[25]

As it was, the GMR 2003/4 was more interested in the links and overlap between literacy and life skills, and for its background paper on life skills it went to a body, the UNESCO Institute for Education (UIE), now the UNESCO Institute for Lifelong Learning (UIL), concerned primarily with literacy and adult education rather than to members of the Working Group for International Cooperation in Skills Development. In addition, this was not the moment when it would have been possible to have had a direct impact on the GMR 2003/4, apart from nuancing and developing what was said on life skills. The main theme of this volume had already been decided as the goal concerned with gender parity and gender equality. And indeed the next volume, on Quality, had also been decided upon.

Although ultimately the GMR's linking of goal 3 and 4 (skills with literacy) was probably prejudicial to any holistic analysis of skills, GMR 2003/4 was certainly realistic in judging that progress could be made on both goals by focusing on the monitoring of access rather than outcomes. Hence it was argued that the following indicators could be a first priority – whether for skills or literacy acquisition:

- demand for, enrolment in and target groups of these programmes;
- providers (e.g. government, communities, NGOs, private providers), initiators and longevity of the programmes;
- duration, costs and fees;
- content, learning objectives and themes. (UNESCO, 2003, p.86)

We shall not deal with indicators here; but these few pages in this GMR 2003/4 were the closest the GMR process had reached in dealing with skills development, and understandably it focused principally on teasing out how life skills related to the conceptualization of other core skills, whether generic or contextual. Apart from this valuable, preliminary conceptual work, skills could not really become a major priority in the first three reports, as these had already been agreed as – UPE, Gender Parity, and Quality. But, arguably, skills could have figured in the 2006 or 2007 GMR, if there had been stronger 'skills voices' pressing the case for such a treatment. This scarcely happened at all.[26] As it was, the early

---

[25] According to Tang, the inclusion of this TVET data was a delayed effect of the 1999 Seoul TVE Congress, (Tang to King, 7.8.08).

[26] The author is grateful to Steve Packer, formerly of the GMR team, for this (Packer to King, 14.03.08).

childhood and adult literacy voices were much more prominent, and hence the first three GMRs were followed by Adult Literacy and then by Early Childhood Care and Education.

3. GMR 2005: Literacy and skills development continue to share a bed

We have already mentioned that this GMR was to be on Quality; hence there was only minor attention to skills development. Again, skills development found itself in the same bed as literacy, under the rubric 'Literacy and Skills Development' to the latter's disadvantage. There turned out to be a great deal more that needed to be said about literacy (seven pages) than about skills development (three pages). In fact, while it was a positive move, in this volume, to adopt the more general terminology of skills development rather than life skills, the entire 3 pages (UNESCO, 2004a, pp.133-5) was taken up with summarising the results of a single four-country research study on *Skills development to meet the learning needs of the excluded* (Atchoarena and Nozawa, 2004). This was, in fact, a salient study and it sought to make the case from its approach 'so that a more or less standardised instrument emerges for the monitoring of goal 3' (UNESCO, 2004a, p.133). There were no funds forthcoming to allow this to happen, but it may still be worth noting the dimensions of skills development which were pursued:

- Who are the target groups?
- What skills are relevant in specific contexts?
- What is the existing skill development provision in formal and non-formal settings, within and outside the public sector?
- What training modalities work best in specific circumstances (centre-based versus community-based, use of distance modes...)?
- What are the respective roles of government and NGOs?
- Who are the trainers? How can they be better recruited, trained and supported?
- What languages should be used?
- What financing sources and mechanisms are suitable for skills development?
- What are the needs for monitoring and evaluation of skills development strategies and programmes? (UNESCO, 2004a, p.133)

4. GMR 2006: Good analysis of why goal 3 has not yet been tackled, but no progress report on skills

At this point in the series of GMRs, the Director of the GMR team changed from Christopher Colclough to Nicholas Burnett. A decision to make literacy the subject of GMR 2006 had already been taken before the change-over. But one of the most valuable and frank discussions of the challenge of pursuing goals 1, 3 and 4 (on early childhood, life skills, and literacy) is contained in this GMR 2006.

This GMR starts by admitting that goals 1, 3 and 4 have been 'relatively neglected' since most attention has been dedicated to the improvement of formal elementary education systems. This neglect is accounted for in a number of ways. First, these three EFA domains all come under multiple institutions and ministries, and hence don't fall neatly under the remit of the Ministry of Education. Second, the 'unfounded idea that primary education is more cost effective than youth and adult literacy programmes' was compounded by the MDGs only focusing on two EFA Goals, and the Fast Track Initiative equally being restricted to UPE (UNESCO, 2005a, p.28). One result of this global focus and priority on primary education was to reduce further both the national and external financial allocations to these other 3 areas. Third, these neglected goals have been difficult to define, and hence to monitor. Furthermore, the previous three GMRs have in particular interpreted goal 3 (and the second part of goal 4)[27] in different ways in the different reports, as there clearly are many possible understandings of these goals.[28]

Despite these challenges, the good news for the large constituencies, both in government and agency, concerned with these neglected goals and in particular goal 3 was that they were definitely going to be tackled:

the Report team intends to develop appropriate ways to monitor these important but imprecise goals, consistent with growing interest in this goal among developing countries. (UNESCO, 2005a, p.29)

Already when this was written, Adult Literacy had been tackled in depth for the GMR 2006; and an agreement had been reached with the GMR's Editorial Board to deal with Early Childhood Care and Education the following year, in GMR 2007. So it looked like Skills and Life Skills would

---

[27] The second half of Goal 4 reads as follows: 'and equitable access to basic and continuing education for all adults'.

[28] The process of privileging UPE over other EFA Goals and Targets goes back to the Jomtien conference, where before the end it was already clear that certain agencies, such as the World Bank and UNICEF, were going to prioritise support to primary education. See *NORRAG News 8*, downloadable at www.norrag.org

soon also be dealt with in its own volume, in order to complete the series.

Surprisingly in the light of this explicit undertaking, nothing was said about skills/life skills in chapter 2 which had been used in all the previous reports to cover EFA progress across all the goals. In this GMR, there was an update on all the 6 EFA goals except goal 3.

5. GMR 2007: from skills and life skills to non-formal education

This is only the second GMR so far that had sought seriously to revisit the conceptual challenge of goal 3 (along with the second part of goal 4). But again, as so often in the whole series of GMRs, this has been attempted in a couple of pages. Thus, paradoxically, the allegedly most challenging goal has been given the least systematic and sustained attention. We have suggested that this failure to see that the Jomtien and Dakar objectives were arguably as much about skills as life skills, and as much about formal skills development as non-formal learning, derives partly from the linking of life skills to literacy in the early GMRs, and partly from a focus on the psychosocial dimension of life skills rather than on the livelihood, entrepreneurial or work-related life skills. Again, in the GMR 2007, the team went back to the interpretation of the Inter-Agency Working Group on Life Skills which had, as we saw earlier, preferred the health promotion rather than the work promotion approach to life skills (UNESCO, 2006, p.71 fn).

Similarly as the Report cast about for an approach to possible monitoring, it turned to educationist perspectives as in the Adult Literacy and Life Skills Survey, and in the non-formal education management information system (NFE-MIS) rather than to the kind of work associated with the World Bank's policy studies on skills development in Sub-Saharan Africa or in India (Johanson and Adams, 2004; World Bank, 2008b[29]).

Hence despite recognizing that the clients for goal 3 could be 'adults or out-of-school youth re-entering basic education, or they may be young people needing basic education, life skills or livelihood skills' (UNESCO, 2006, p.71), the GMR ended up by recommending that 'A first step in monitoring learning and life skills programmes is to investigate elements of provision, participation and access to non-formal learning activities at national or sub-national level' (ibid).

It also looked forward to 'a more systematic assessment of progress

---

[29] First drafts of this India report were readily available in 2006.

in meeting the learning needs of young people and adults' in the GMR of 2008. By the time this was written, however, it had already been decided that the next GMR would not be dedicated to learning and life skills after all, but instead there would be a mid-term review of the EFA process, as 2008 would be about half way to the deadline (for 3 of the goals) of 2015.

6. GMR 2008: Not a more systematic assessment of progress in meeting the learning needs of young people and adults?

Despite this expectation of a serious assessment in 2008, in point of fact there was more discussion of the monitoring approaches and options for goal 3 in GMR 2007 than there turned out to be in GMR 2008. There was disappointingly little coverage of goal 3 in the GMR 2008. In the *Summary* volume, for example, there were just four paragraphs on the assessment of goal 3 (UNESCO, 2007b, pp.15-16), and just 2.5 pages in the relevant chapter of the full report out of a total of no less than 62 pages for the other 5 Goals (UNESCO, 2007a, pp.59-61). The message of the GMR 2008 was simple: 'EFA goal 3: the hardest to define and monitor' (UNESCO, 2007a, p.60). Despite this admission, surprisingly little serious analysis of life skills, let alone skills, was actually undertaken in this 434 page stock-taking volume.

Following the suggestion of the GMR 2007, the GMR team looked at the non-formal arena in late 2006 and early 2007. They had already decided to focus particularly on the most disadvantaged young people, and also on programmes that fell outside those covered by the International Standard Classification of Education (ISCED). They also asked the UNESCO Institute of Life Long Learning (UIL) to carry out some of the essential background work for the forthcoming GMR. Not surprisingly given the focus of the UIL on adult education and literacy, the some 30 case studies commissioned at the country level covered more literacy-related non-formal education (NFE) than work or skills-related NFE.[30] At the end of a very brief discussion about some dimensions of NFE programmes, the GMR 2008 again reached its, by this time, well-worn conclusion that much more needed to be known about these learning activities:

The EFA agenda calls for a comprehensive approach to learning in

---

[30] The UIL has been distinguished for its work on literacy and adult education, while the UNEVOC Centre in Bonn has been specialised in the field of technical and vocational education and training.

which non-formal education is an essential and integrated part. While a great variety of structured learning activities for youth and adults take place outside formal education systems, the extent to which this supply corresponds to demand is largely unknown. Improved monitoring of the supply and demand for non-formal education is urgently needed at the national and international levels. (UNESCO, 2007a, p.61)

Earlier in the volume, the GMR 2008 had commented that goal 3 was 'woefully undocumented' and 'particularly neglected' (ibid: 33). We would judge that the skills development constituency must bear some responsibility for this sad situation at the end of six major volumes of EFA monitoring. They, including the WGICSD, ought to have done a great deal more to bring the insights from research and monitoring on skills development to the attention of the GMR team. But it would also have to be said that the skills' domain remained 'woefully undocumented' now, eight years on from Dakar, because there had been so little sustained analysis of learning and life skills for young people and adults within the GMR process.

7. *GMR 2009: Skills 'still stymied by problems of definition and lack of data' (UNESCO 2008: 91)*

The GMR 2009 was the first of the volumes under the direction of Kevin Watkins, and it was a very powerful GMR, making the case that there was massive and growing inequality in education systems, rich and poor, and that governance mattered. But in respect of any commitment to the skills area, goal 3 was still mixed up with the second half of goal 4 ('equitable access to basic and continuing education for all adults'). Lack of definition and of data were still said to be the problem, but at least a commitment was made 'to explore these issues as part of an overarching theme' in a future GMR (ibid). As usual, only a very small area (1.5 pages) of the large chapter of 86 pages on the 6 goals was dedicated to goal 3 and the second half of goal 4.

8. *GMR 2010: Goal 3 and skills development finally recognised*

After 8 years of the GMR teams failing to deal with goal 3, finally in 2010 the situation changed dramatically, and there was a full and thoughtful analysis of skills development in the key chapter two of the 2010 Report which deals with the 6 Dakar goals. This was certainly the result of Kevin Watkins, the new director of the GMR, taking a personal interest in ensuring that Goal 3 was put on the agenda. There were no less than 17 pages in this key chapter as compared to the usual 2-3 paragraphs, and it is likely that for much of this Kevin Watkins was directly responsible. The discussion of the need to analyse skills development as a priority finished with the following: 'What is clear is that no government can afford to ignore the importance of skills and learning in supporting economic growth, combating poverty and overcoming social marginalisation' (UNESCO, 2010, p.93). The result is that 'Skills development: expanding opportunities for marginalised groups' will be the subject of the GMR 2012.

Other factors may well have influenced the decision to go ahead with a GMR on skills. Amongst these would be the major report and conference on the global monitoring of skills organised by the British Council and the UK National Commission for UNESCO, as well as the new priority for TVET in UNESCO, and the adoption by UNESCO of a TVET policy paper (UNESCO, 2007d). Doubtless, NORRAG's support to the donor Working Group for International Cooperation in Skills Development also played a role. In other words, the global treatment of skills had rapidly changed so that it suddenly seemed to make eminently good sense to plan for a GMR on skills.[31] As the GMR team stated: 'Globalisation, the transformation of labour markets and the ongoing financial crisis are increasingly bringing the need for skills development to the attention of policy makers' (UNESCO, 2011a, p.1).

9. GMR 2011: 'A policy focus on overcoming the marginalisation of low-skill workers in developed countries' (UNESCO, 2011b, p.57)

What is intriguing about the treatment of skills development in the GMR 2011 whose main theme is Armed Conflict and Education is that the principal policy focus (for 8 out of the 11 pages in the Youth and Adult Learning Needs section of the chapter reporting on the 6 goals) is on the problem of skills in *developed, industrialised* countries. This makes a crucially important point – that the EFA Dakar goals are not to be thought of only for the poor, developing countries. The section is almost entirely concerned with the mismatch between skills and jobs, and with a variety of mechanisms and initiatives for overcoming the skills divide, in the OECD countries. What this suggests is that when we finally reach GMR

---

[31] See papers on skills development in the GMR team meeting in November 2010 (UNESCO, 2011a), including by Adams (2010) and King (2010).

2012 and the treatment of skills development in a whole GMR volume, it will be a genuinely global report. Indeed we can anticipate this from the Concept Note for the next GMR.

One of the threads is precisely this:

> Concern over learning and skills deficits is as marked in rich countries as in poor countries. The global recession has generated a renewed impetus for investment in skills training programmes in developed countries, partly in response to rising unemployment. (UNESCO, 2011a, p.1)

10. GMR 2012: Skills development: expanding opportunities for marginalised groups

Thanks to the Concept Note just mentioned, we do know just a little about some of the main threads that are likely to be tackled in the GMR 2012 on skills. First of all, this is certain to be the GMR that will interrogate the relations between education, training and the world of work; the linkage between skills and employment will be under the microscope. We already know that although there is still a focus on marginalised groups, the Report will look at the lessons from economically dynamic and socially inclusive societies. We also know that there will be a concern with 'learning and skills deficits' in both rich and poor countries. We can moreover anticipate from the Concept Note that there will be a review of the role of skills development in the large informal sectors of many developing countries. Interestingly, there is a clear intention to examine relevant experience from the so-called new donor countries, including those that have registered high economic growth, in part due to investing in skills.

Finally, the GMR 2012 will seek to address some of the oldest questions of all, but ones where there is often no clear answer. Should skills be supply-led or demand-led? Who should provide skills, and who pay for this provision? What about the assessment and certification of skills? What is the scope for complementary and second-chance skills training? These are just a few of the challenges that lie ahead during 2011.

Concluding Comments

Hopefully, it has been valuable to have documented over the period of almost exactly 20 years since Jomtien what have been the challenges to analysing what Jomtien judged to be the crucial area of 'education and training in other essential skills' for young people and adults, 'with programme effectiveness assessed in terms of behavioural changes and impacts on health, employment and productivity' (WCEFA, *Framework for Action*, 1990a, p.3). Jomtien's concerns about the impact of education and training in skills on health, employment and productivity are worth recalling. They make the point that skills development is not just an entitlement like primary education or early childhood education, but is seen to be a key connection with the labour market and productivity.

Over these 20 years, national developing country concerns about the role of skills in their global competitiveness have risen dramatically as strategic priorities. This skills' dimension of globalisation has been articulated very forcefully by Nicholas Burnett, the former director of the GMR, and the former Assistant Director-General (ADG) for Education in UNESCO:

> One of the issues globalisation is raising in almost every country is: what sort of specific skills do people need, what is the balance between specific and general skills? We need to help countries come to their own answers. (UNESCO, 2007c)

If indeed the GMR 2012 goes ahead as now planned, a whole range of key issues for skills development will be addressed: skills for poverty reduction; skills for growth; skills for competitiveness; skills for the disadvantaged and marginalised. But not least, skills that are essential for all young men and women to acquire as they move through basic and further education and training towards work and towards employment. Arguably the coalition of forces encouraging a thorough treatment of skills in the influential GMR series is much more widely based now than the small group of agencies that determined the text of Goal 3 in 2000. But after ten years of waiting for the GMR on skills development, the expectations are correspondingly very high.

References

Adams, A.V. (2010) 'The role of skills development in overcoming social disadvantage', Paper to meeting of the GMR team on Expanding opportunities for the marginalised through skills development. Draft agenda, BMZ, Bonn, November 3-4, 2010.

ADB [Asian Development Bank] (2004) *Improving Technical Education and Vocational Training Strategies for Asia*, Asian Development Bank, Manila.

Atchoarena, D. and Nozawa, M. (2004) 'Skills development to meet the learning needs of the excluded', Background paper, EFA Global Monitoring Report 2005.

Banks, J. (2011) *Encyclopaedia of Diversity of Education*, Sage, Thousand Oaks, CA.

British Council (2008) *Rethinking TVET for Education Development: Transferable Lessons from the UK*, World Bank Course, British Council, London, June, 2008.

DFID [Department for International Development] (2007) 'Technical and vocational skills development: a DFID briefing paper', DFID, London.

ETF [European Training Foundation] (2007) 'Euromed observatory function guidelines for developing indicators on technical and vocational education and training', by Claude Sauvageot, Methodological Notes, MEDA-ETE Project, ETF, Turin.

Govinda, E. (2002) *India Education Report: A Profile of Basic Education*, Oxford University Press for NIEPA, New Delhi.

Haddad, W. (1999) *Education for All for the 21st Century. A Discussion Paper*, Knowledge Enterprises Inc, Washington DC.

Johanson, R. (2002) 'Vocational skills development in Sub-Saharan Africa: Synthesis of phase I of a regional review', draft of June 15, 2002, World Bank, Washington DC.

Johanson, R. and Adams, A. (2004) *Skills Development in Sub-Saharan Africa*, World Bank, Washington DC.

King, K. (2010) 'Some modest proposals for a strengthened focus on technical and vocational education and training (TVET) in the Education for All (EFA) agenda', Paper to meeting of the GMR team on *Expanding opportunities for the marginalised through skills development*. Draft agenda, BMZ, Bonn, November 3-4, 2010.

King, K. (2007a) 'Multilateral agencies in the construction of the global agenda in education', *Comparative Education*, 43(3), 377-391

King, K. (2007b) 'What room for skills development in 'post-primary education'? A view from the development agencies', Background paper for the meeting of the *Working Group for International Cooperation in Skills Development*, Paris, November 13-15, 2007. Now available within Working paper no. 13, downloadable from: www.norrag.org/resources/publications

King, K. and Palmer, R. (2008) 'Skills for work, growth and poverty reduction', A commissioned paper for the British Council and UK National Commission for UNESCO, to be discussed at an international Conference in London in October 2008.

McGrath, S. (2003) 'Life and work skills and their contribution to education and training debates', in *Skills for Life and for Work. Debates in Skills Development,* Working paper no. 8, Working Group for International Cooperation on Skills Development (WGICSD), Swiss Development Cooperation, Bern.

NORRAG News No. 43 (February 2010) Special Issue on *A World of Reports? A critical view of global development reports with an angle on education and training,* www.norrag.org

NORRAG News No. 40 (May 2008) Special issue on *Education for Sustainable Development? Or the Sustainability of Educational Investment?,* www.norrag.org;

NORRAG News No. 8 (1990) *What happened at the World Conference at Jomtien?* www.norrag.org

OECD and Statistics Canada (2005) *Learning a Living: First Results of the Adult Literacy and Life Skills Survey,* OECD and Statistics Canada, Paris and Ottawa.

Singh, M. (2003) 'Understanding life skills', Background paper for the *Education for All Global Monitoring Report 2003/4 Gender and Education for All: The Leap to Equality,* UNESCO, Paris. http://portal.unesco.org/education/en/file_download.php/32f065862b89709d9c0575839f1d959c Understanding+life+skills.doc [accessed 8/2/2011]

UNESCO (1996a) *Education for all: achieving the goal. Working document,* UNESCO, Paris.

UNESCO (1996b) *Education for all: achieving the goal. Statistical document,* UNESCO, Paris.

UNESCO (1998) *Education for All. The Year 2000 Assessment. Technical Guidelines.* International Consultative Forum on Education for All, UNESCO, Paris.

UNESCO (2000) *Education for All 2000 Assessment: Statistical Document,* UNESCO, Paris.

UNESCO (2001) *Monitoring Report on Education for All,* UNESCO, Paris.

UNESCO (2002) *EFA Global Monitoring Report 2002. Education for all: is the world on track?* UNESCO, Paris.

UNESCO (2003) *EFA Global Monitoring Report 2003/4. Gender and education for all: the leap to equality,* UNESCO, Paris.

UNESCO (2004a) *EFA Global Monitoring Report 2005. The Quality Imperative,* UNESCO, Paris.

UNESCO (2004b) *Report of the Inter-Agency Working Group on Life Skills in EFA,* 29-31 March 2004, UNESCO, Paris.

UNESCO (2005a) *EFA Global Monitoring Report 2006. Literacy for Life,* UNESCO, Paris.

UNESCO (2005b) *NFE-MIS handbook: Developing a Sub-National Non-Formal Education Management Information System,* UNESCO, Paris.

UNESCO (2006) *EFA Global Monitoring Report 2007. Strong Foundations.* Early childhood care and education, UNESCO, Paris.

UNESCO (2007a) *EFA Global Monitoring Report 2008. Education for all by 2015: Will we make it?* UNESCO, Paris.

UNESCO (2007b) *EFA Global Monitoring Report 2008. Education for all by 2015: Will we make it?* Summary. UNESCO, Paris.

UNESCO (2007c) 'From education for all to all of education', Interview of the newly appointed Assistant Director-General for UNESCO's Education Sector, Nicholas Burnett, by Ariane Bailey and Sue Williams (UNESCO), *The UNESCO Courier,* No.8.

UNESCO (2007d) *A UNESCO Strategy for Technical and Vocational Education and Training,* Executive Board, 179 EX/49, 27 February 2008, UNESCO, Paris.

UNESCO (2008) *EFA Global Monitoring Report 2009. Overcoming inequality: Why governance matters.* UNESCO, Paris.

UNESCO (2010) *EFA Global Monitoring Report 2010. Reaching the marginalised.* UNESCO, Paris.

UNESCO (2011a) 2012 EFA Global Monitoring Report: Skills development: expanding opportunities for marginalised groups [One page concept note for on-line consultation of 4-25 February 2011], GMR team, UNESCO, Paris.

UNESCO (2011b) *EFA Global Monitoring Report 2011. The hidden crisis: armed conflict and education.* UNESCO, Paris.

World Bank (2008b) *Skill Development in India: the Vocational Education and Training System,* Report No. 22. South Asia Human Development Sector, World Bank, Washington DC.

World Bank (1991) *Vocational and Technical Education and Training: a World Bank Policy Paper,* World Bank, Washington DC.

WCEFA [World Conference on Education for All] (1990a) *World Declaration* and *Framework for Action*, International Consultative Forum, UNESCO, Paris.

WCEFA (1990b) *Meeting basic learning needs: a vision for the 1990s. Background Document*, Inter-Agency Commission, UNICEF, New York.

WEF (World Education Forum), 2000a. *The Dakar Framework for Action, Education for All: Meeting our Collective Commitments*, adopted by the World Education Forum, April 26-28, Dakar, Senegal, UNESCO, Paris.

WEF (World Education Forum), 2000b *Education for All: Meeting our Collective Commitments. The Dakar Framework for Action* and *the Expanded Commentary on the Framework for Action*, UNESCO, Paris.

WGICSD [Working Group for International Cooperation in Skills Development] (2003) *Skills for Life and for Work. Debates in Skills Development*, Working paper no. 8, Swiss Development Cooperation, Bern, downloadable from http://www.norrag.org/resources/publications

WHO [World Health Organization] (2003) *Skills for Health: Skills Based Health Education Including Life Skills: An Important Component of a Child-Friendly/Health-Promoting School*, Information Series on School Health, Document 9, WHO, Geneva.

WHO (1999) *Partners in Life Skills Education: Conclusions from a United Nations Inter-Agency Meeting*, Department of Mental Health, WHO, Geneva.

Chapter 10

The Introduction to this book noted the substantial change in focus during my career associated with moving in 1978 from research, teaching and supervision in a university to working in a development agency, the IDRC, dedicated to supporting research in the South. It brought a fundamental shift from the development of knowledge through personal research to the development of projects that would generate knowledge by Southern institutions. But one of the commonest discussions in the agency world continued to be about the widespread setting of knowledge priorities by agencies in the North. I have already shown how the first education commissions to Africa arrived with their own priorities for Africa already set. I have also noted in Chapter 3 the very substantial amounts of knowledge generated by development agencies as part of their own project cycles.

Even if IDRC as a small research funding agency had a different agenda, it was hugely important to understand how other agencies, and particularly the World Bank, were beginning to set agendas for development aid in education. This tendency was already obvious in the Bank's education sector papers in 1971 and 1974, but once the Bank had built its own research capacity in the late 1970s, its 1980 *Education: Sector working paper* was much more dependent on its own research findings than its earlier sector papers (World Bank, 1980).

The Bank's growing analytical capacity during the late 1970s and 1980s allowed it not only to review the education situation in most of Sub-Saharan Africa, for example in its *Education in Sub-Saharan Africa* (World Bank, 1988), but also to bring out education policy papers on primary education (1991a) and on vocational and technical education and training (1991b). The Bank's influence was also evident in the co-convening of the World Conference on Education for All in Jomtien in

Kenneth King (2019): *Education, Skills and International Cooperation: Comparative and Historical Perspectives*. Hong Kong: Comparative Education Research Centre (CERC), The University of Hong Kong, and Dordrecht: Springer. © CERC

© Springer Nature Switzerland AG 2019
K. King, *Education, Skills and International Cooperation*, CERC Studies
in Comparative Education 36, https://doi.org/10.1007/978-3-030-29790-9_10

1990, already referred to in Chapter 3. Those responsible for bilateral education policy in countries such as Sweden, Denmark, the UK and Germany engaged critically with the growing influence of the World Bank in education, illustrated in many commentaries and conferences on aid priorities (e.g. Hawes and Coombe, 1986).

In the UK, this desire to become involved more deeply in the analysis of both international and national trends in aid policy was one of the reasons behind the formation in 1990-1991 of the UK Forum on International Education and Training (UKFIET) – now also called the Education and Development Forum. A critical influence in encouraging the hitherto scattered British education resource to come together as UKFIET was Beverly Young of the British Council, and in the summer of 1991 UKFIET organised the first of its major biennial international conferences on education and development.[1] Its interest to pool and network the expertise within the UK was to prove a key dimension of the later agency-wide preoccupation with knowledge management (Dyer and King, 1993). It is illustrative of UKFIET's concern with the role of international aid that the title of its first conference was: 'The external agenda of aid in internal educational reform', and that plenary speakers came from UNICEF (Richard Jolly) and the World Bank (Steven Heyneman) [King, 1991].

The major impact of the World Conference on Education for All in 1990 was in part due to the drawing together of a great deal of relevant research in the valuable *Background document: Meeting basic learning needs: A vision for the 1990s* (UNESCO, 1990a). It was also due to many agencies and national governments bringing to Jomtien their latest policy papers on basic education (King, 1990). However, the follow-up by UNESCO of Jomtien's *Framework for Action* (UNESCO, 1990b) was disappointing. Even though the Conference had promoted a very wide vision of basic education, key agencies narrowed that to primary education in their own programming (King, 1990). A somewhat lack-lustre mid-term review of the *Framework*'s pledges was held by UNESCO in 1996 in Amman, but for the high ground on education and other targets the baton passed to the OECD's Development Assistance Committee (DAC) in that same year. In an ambitious exercise that synthesised their view of what had been the core lessons learnt in the whole series of seven world conferences during the first half of the 1990s, OECD-DAC proposed just six targets which

---

[1] A history of the formation of the UKFIET is presented by Dyer and King (1993).

could be 'aspirations for the entire development process, not just for co-operation' (OECD-DAC, 1996: 9).

In four years' time, these international development targets would become the core of the Millennium Development Goals (MDGs) after the Millennium Summit in 2000. Even though the international education community had suggested six possible targets in Jomtien, and developed these into six Education for All goals in the World Education Forum in Dakar in April 2000, it was the development knowledge summarised by OECD-DAC which prevailed about education. Just universal primary education and gender parity in education were decided upon in Paris for the global agenda, and without the presence of the developing countries. Both these international education targets which became the education MDGs were explicitly supported by research. It was a powerful illustration of the role of knowledge in constructing the world's agenda in education (King, 2007).

From development to knowledge agencies
Chapter 3 showed that long before the OECD-DAC had demonstrated very sharply that development agencies were *Shaping the 21st century* (OECD-DAC, 1996), the multilateral and bilateral agencies – as well as the international NGOs – had become massive repositories of knowledge about development. It was coincidentally in that same key year, 1996, that the new President of the World Bank was looking for a big idea that could define his presidency, and he found it in knowledge: 'We need to become, in effect, the Knowledge Bank' (Wolfensohn, 1996, quoted in King and McGrath, 2004: 38).

Within two years, the *World Development Report 1998-9* was entitled *Knowledge for development*, and the Bank was soon turning itself into a Knowledge Bank; and where the Bank led, other agencies were following. Simon McGrath, my former doctoral student, and at that time a post-doctoral fellow in the Centre of African Studies in Edinburgh, suggested that we should study the process both in the Bank itself and in three very different bilateral agencies. We selected the UK's Department for International Development (DFID), the Swedish International Development Agency (Sida, formerly SIDA), and the Japan International Cooperation Agency (JICA). We wanted at least one agency whose traditions and culture had been formed outside the Western world. Also, at the time, Japan was still the world's largest bilateral donor.

There was another reason for selecting Japan. At the time of publishing *Aid and education in the developing world* (1991), I had not spent time in Japan, and there was, unfortunately, almost no mention in the book of Japanese aid, or, for that matter, of Chinese or Indian aid. So part of the chapter on 'Experience, experts and knowledge in Japanese aid policy and practice' is included in what follows. The rest can be found in the book by Simon McGrath and myself: *Knowledge for development: Comparing British, Japanese, Swedish and World Bank aid* (King and McGrath, 2004). An analysis of Japanese aid was made much easier by three months in 2000 in Hiroshima University's Centre for the Study of International Cooperation in Education. It was organised by Nobu Sawamura, a colleague with whom I shared a long-term engagement with research on education in Kenya. He also had done an MPhil under my supervision in Edinburgh.

Work on knowledge for development, initially from Japan, made me wonder whether the construction of knowledge agencies was really 'a new way of working or a new North-South divide' (King, 2000: 23). But it also made me aware that Japan had its own culture and context for thinking about its aid – something I captured years later in the term 'Japaneseness' in development cooperation. The term had been suggested to me by Kayashima Nobuko, a JICA colleague whom I had first met in a meeting preparing for Jomtien in 1989 (King, 2016).[2]

References

Dyer, C. and King, K. 1993. *The British resource on international training and education: An inventory*, Department of Education, University of Edinburgh.

Hawes, H. and Coombe, T. (Eds.). 1986. *Education priorities and aid responses in Sub-Saharan Africa*, Overseas Development Administration (ODA), Her Majesty's Stationery Office, London.

King, K. 1990. 'What happened at the World Conference in Jomtien', *NORRAG News 8*, University of Edinburgh.

King, K. 1991. *Aid and education in the developing world*. Longman, Harlow.

King, K. 1992. 'The external agenda of aid in internal education reform'. *International Journal of Educational Development*, 12, 4, 257-263.

---

[2] Kayashima Nobuko spent many years in JICA, and later moved to the JICA Research Institute (JICA-RI).

King, K. 2007.'Multilateral agencies in the construction of the global agenda on education', *Comparative Education*, 43, 3, 377-391.

King, K. 2016. *Lenses on 'Japaneseness' in the Development Cooperation Charter of 2015: Soft power, human resources development, education and training*, Working Paper no. 135, JICA Research Institute, Tokyo.

King, K. and McGrath, S. 2004. *Knowledge for development: Comparing British, Japanese, Swedish and World Bank aid.* Zed Books, London.

King, K. 2000. 'Towards knowledge-based aid: A new way of working or a new North-South divide', *Journal of International Cooperation in Education*, 3, 2, 23-48.

OECD-DAC. 1996. *Shaping the 21st century: The contribution of development co-operation*. OECD-DAC, Paris.

UNESCO. 1990a. *Framework for action to meet basic learning needs*. UNESCO, Paris.

UNESCO. 1990b. *Meeting basic learning needs: A vision for the 1990s. Background document.* World Conference on Education for All, 5-9 March 1990, Jomtien,

World Conference on Education for All, 5-9 March 1990, Jomtien, Thailand, UNESCO, Paris.

World Bank. 1980. *Education: Sector working paper,* World Bank, Washington DC.

World Bank. 1988. *Education in Sub-Saharan Africa: Policies for adjustment, revitalisation and expansion*, World Bank, Washington DC.

World Bank. 1991a. *Primary education: A World Bank policy study,* World Bank, Washington DC.

World Bank. 1991b. *Vocational and technical education and training: A World Bank policy paper,* World Bank, Washington DC.

World Bank. 1998. *World Development Report 1998-9: Knowledge for development*, World Bank, Washington DC.

Experience, Experts and Knowledge in Japanese Aid Policy and Practice[3]

This chapter confirms that the new discourse on knowledge management (KM) and knowledge sharing (KS) is powerfully affected by the particular context, culture and tradition of these agencies. This study will be conducted against the background of wider policy interests in knowledge-based aid (King 2001). Whilst a primary focus of the chapter will be on sketching the development of what we have termed knowledge projects and policies in very recent Japanese aid thinking, we will also examine some of the deeper attitudes in Japan towards both Japanese and Western expert knowledge on international development. The attitudes are very much embedded in the culture and bureaucracy of Japan, and, it will be argued, these older traditions of thinking about expertise and professional knowledge are likely to impact upon and influence in some measure the newer mechanisms for knowledge sharing. We shall especially underline the role of personal expertise as one of the major sites of knowledge. The belief in person-to-person transfer of skills, technologies and attitudes seems to be the Japanese parallel to learning and capacity development in other agencies.

In particular it might even be argued that one element in the current predominantly Western discourse about knowledge sharing was originally derived from an analysis of what made for success in Japanese firms – including the ways that workers shared their insights about improving the quality and effectiveness of their specific operations. The knowledge discourse is by no means, therefore, a discussion that has been restricted to the West (McGinn 2001); one of the better-known management texts is by Nonaka and Takeuchi (1995), *The knowledge-creating company: How Japanese companies create the dynamics of innovation*. Interestingly, there has been little evidence of the Japanese public sector learning from the corporate sector in the way that seems to have happened in Sweden and Britain, and also with the World Bank. Indeed, we shall suggest that the adoption of knowledge management in the case of the Japan International Cooperation Agency (JICA) – Japan's lead implementing agency for official development assistance (ODA) –

---

[3] Extracted from King, K. and McGrath, S. (2004): *Knowledge for development*. London: Zed Books. King was responsible for this chapter on Japan.

appears to have been derived from the example of the World Bank (itself directly influenced by corporate America, which in turn had in part learnt from Japan) rather than sourced from the Japanese private sector.

Here, we shall explore the salience of the knowledge discourse in Japanese co-operation, and see to what extent it is becoming expressed in different products, policies and practices. But right at the outset we must note that the explicit discussion of knowledge management and knowledge sharing began only in 2000 in JICA, and it was not until mid-2002 that it was impacting at all visibly on a selected number of JICA staff.

Thus, by contrast with the World Bank's visibility as the pioneer of knowledge-for-development – in its 1998-99 *World Development Report* and in its many other knowledge initiatives, which are very accessible on the World Bank's website – JICA gives very much less salience to a knowledge strategy in its formal mission statements and in its leading discourse, whether on paper or on its website. Indeed, knowledge activities are not at all currently foregrounded on its website, nor have members of JICA or associated analysts of Japanese aid played any part in the on-line network discussions of 'Knowledge management for international development organisations'. Neither the lack of a strong web presence nor the absence from relevant knowledge management debates on-line are reliable pointers to whether Japan considers knowledge to be central to development. Rather they suggest that the current and explicit discourse about 'knowledge agencies' does not sit easily with those responsible for the public face of JICA. Though change is afoot, as we shall see, much of JICA's public documentation and its website continue to illustrate the separate time-honoured schemes through which its assistance has been traditionally provided. These, taken in their entirety, suggest that a different lens is needed to focus on Japanese development priorities.

Japan's own experience for development

Instead of knowledge, or capacity development, one of the key concepts in Japanese aid philosophy appears to be 'experience'. A strong concern with Japan's own historical experience may be seen in this chapter to be in some creative tension with the newer knowledge activities associated with knowledge management. This Japanese experience is manifested in many different ways which it may be useful to tease out here. But it is worth considering, at the outset, that on a spectrum from global universal knowledge at one end to very context-specific knowledge at the other, clearly an experience-based approach will be much closer to the contextual and local.

First of all, there is a very clear sense in much official aid discussion of how important Japan's own direct historical experience of development may be to its ability to offer insights to others. At one level, it frequently rehearses its own post-Second World War history of transformation to make a number of fundamental points about this experience. For example, Japan can claim 50 years of being an aid donor, if the reparations to East and South-East Asia are counted as an early form of economic cooperation, from 1953, along with the formal start of economic assistance through Japan's participation in the Colombo Plan in 1954. This makes Japan one of the earliest bilateral donor countries.

But this very lengthy experience of being an aid donor is often discussed in parallel with the experience of being an aid recipient. Although it has become commonplace for Japan to refer to the responsibilities associated with its being the largest bilateral aid donor since 1991, it is also intriguing to note how much significance as a donor it attaches to having been an aid recipient: 'Japan has the experience of being the world's largest recipient country of humanitarian aid, from 1946 for six years after World War II, receiving aid in forms of food, clothing, medicine, and medical supplies' (Kato 2001: 205). Nor was this only short-term humanitarian aid; Japan is very conscious of having had direct experience of receiving loans from the World Bank for the construction of its transport network, roads, power stations, automobile industry, ship-building and steel plants. It remained a recipient of such loans until 1966. Nor is this something that might be hidden away, or even regarded as a matter of shame. Rather there are stories senior aid officials tell about how Japan experienced early attempts at what would later be called 'conditionality' in the negotiation of these loans, but how it managed to get its own way, because it was convinced of its own priorities, for example, for high-speed trains over air transport. In other words, there was an early emphasis on the ownership of the development process whatever the challenges from the donors or lenders of the time.

This extended historical episode has had a powerful symbolic value in Japanese thinking and official writing about its development experience. Arguably, its own record has contributed to its thinking about the crucial importance of self-help. It has also justified the appropriateness of loans to a country that is sure of its development priorities. But as politically significant as any of these is the sense that this special history has conferred a measure of solidarity between Japan and its own current aid recipients, particularly in East and South-East Asia. Again note the key term 'experience' in the following quotation: 'Such a rare position in the donor community, experience as an aid recipient country, has enabled Japan to understand all the more the importance of extending co-operation with due respect for the partner's situation' (Kato 2001: 205).

It could be argued, therefore, that many of the central elements in Japanese thinking about aid had been acquired early in the period of being a donor-cum-recipient: the crucial importance of self-help; the priority of country ownership; the recognition of the role of loans; South-South co-operation (including when Japan itself was part of the South)[4]; and a focus on the relevance of its own experience in some measure of solidarity with other nations. It should be underlined that this cluster of approaches which we term experience is also shot through with an awareness of the key role of attitude. In other words, Japan's approach to aid is not just in the cognitive domain, but, like much in East Asian economies, draws on convictions about the role of effort, achievement and determination, whether in individual development and schooling or in development and transformation at the national level (Cheng 1994).

There is another historical element that has almost certainly played a salient role in fashioning some of the principles behind Japanese aid approaches, and that lies a good deal earlier, in the period of the Meiji Restoration from 1868. This was one of the most planned examples of rapid 'modernisation' in the nineteenth century, and involved a very deliberate selection by Japan from Western knowledge, Western technology and Western institutions. Interestingly, it involved a form of technical co-operation but, again, on Japanese terms. Foreign nationals from several different nations were invited, from both public and private sectors, and reached a maximum of some 850 personnel at the height of this process (Kato 2001: 206). The precise manner in which Westerners were incorporated into Japanese institutions would be worth pursuing further, but what is already clear is that this whole episode was symbolic of successful borrowing and adaptation, or of what would later be called technology transfer. What is also intriguing is that this experience is even today quite explicitly thought of as being relevant to an understanding of Japanese aid.

According to Sawamura, the Japanese axiom that sums up this kind

---

[4] Japan became a member of OECD in 1964.

of deliberate borrowing of knowledge and technology from elsewhere, which is potentially so relevant to current development thinking, is *wakon yosai* – Japanese spirit, Western knowledge. He argues that 'The Japanese have been sensitive and selective in adopting foreign institutions and systems, because they believe that no knowledge is completely free of the culture from which it came, and that seldom is knowledge globally applicable (Sawamura 2002: 343). But just as the lesson for Japan had been that their own spirit (and priorities) must determine what was borrowed in the 1870s or in the 1950s, so in their role as modern donor it would follow that Japan might expect today's recipients to be as clear about what they wanted to borrow Japanese funds for as they themselves had sought to be. Japan had been very selective about Western knowledge; hence borrowers would need, in turn, to be critical of the wholesale borrowing of both Western and Japanese knowledge. The emphasis on 'Japanese spirit' may be taken to stand for the cluster of attitudinal concerns that are so central to ownership and self-reliance.

If this principle might help to explain a Japanese diffidence about promoting wholesale their own knowledge-for-development, two other dimensions are worth noting briefly. One is that Japan is the only major donor country that has not been associated with some form of extended missionary promotion of Christianity in the developing world (See Orr, quoted in Sawamura 2002); indeed it had itself been the object of missionary attention both before its extended period of deliberate isolation and after the Meiji Restoration. The conviction and the certainties associated with Western evangelism were often found in parallel with a 'civilising mission'. Second, this record and potential advantage of its official aid not being seen as in some sense a continuation of missionary aid – which would distinguish Japan from other donors such as the USA, UK, Germany, Sweden, Switzerland, and so on – could have been compromised by the period of Japanese colonialism, especially in the inter-war years. However, the experience of having been a colonial power would appear to have made the Japanese determined no longer to be involved with the sort of interventions in education and the social sectors with which they had been associated in Korea and elsewhere. In other words, the colonial episode and the consequent sensitivities in Asia seem to have confirmed a Japanese preference for their aid to support technical and infrastructural areas and not the so-called softer fields, such as human resource planning and governance.

Cross-ministerial vs. specialist agency experience of development

We have emphasised that there were some unique features of Japanese aid history which were influenced by aspects of its own transformation, both in the nineteenth century and in the period after the Second World War. These have entered the canon of aid philosophy in Japan and continue to provide a rationale for certain forms of co-operation.

Arguably, the Japanese emphasis on the relevance of their own experience for their development assistance to others is only a version of what once was historically a very widespread bilateral aid tendency – to focus on the comparative advantage of what particular industrial countries felt they had to offer to developing countries. We shall suggest shortly that one of the key differences with Japan is that it has been less ready than other bilaterals to shift from this focus on its own comparative advantage and its own experience – expressed in project aid – to a focus on policy, expressed in policy-based lending and sector grants carefully coordinated with many other donors.

However, even the delivery of this traditional bilateral project aid has been powerfully influenced by the ODA system in Japan. Unlike the other principal OECD bilateral donors, Japan does not rely on a single ministry or single executing agency for the delivery of its aid. Even though four bodies – Foreign Affairs (MOFA), Finance (MOF), Economy Trade and Industry (METI) and Economic Planning (EPA) – are the main players in economic co-operation, in principle all ministries have access to the aid envelope. In practice, this does not mean that all have such access to anything like the same extent, but it does mean – unlike almost all other Western donors – that there is a substantial international co-operation agenda within such ministries as health, education, agriculture, forestry and fisheries, labour, and construction. This tradition of as many as seventeen different ministries being involved in development co-opera-tion has been changing in the most recent period, as the government has sought to restructure and rationalise the number of ministries and public corporations. Nevertheless there remains a much wider basis of official involvement in ODA than in any other OECD country, with the possible exception of Portugal.

What this means for Japan's knowledge or experience of inter-national development is worth exploring briefly, as it is directly related to our overall topic. Where regular bilateral implementing agencies such as Swedish Sida, Canada's CIDA, Germany's GTZ, Denmark's Danida and ODA/DFID have traditionally sought to maintain smaller or larger in-house bodies of sectoral competence (for example, on education, health, small-scale industry, or agriculture), JICA historically did not need to have its own advisers on these or many other sectors since the responsible line ministry would have taken this role through second-ments of its own experts to JICA or to JICA's project development activities overseas. The result of this dispersed ODA involvement could mean that the knowledge base on international co-operation within the Japanese government is very much more diffuse than elsewhere; it may also have meant that the emergence in a single agency of a cadre of people with specialist expertise on the developing world has been less of a priority for Japan than the utilisation of personnel in temporary development roles whose primary knowledge has been of developments in agriculture, health, education or industry in Japan itself.

It is worth remarking here that this particular pattern of dispersed personnel use for development tasks is much more likely to reinforce the notion of the relevance – in all the different sectors – of Japanese experience than the more common bilateral model of a single agency with responsibility for all development assistance. The Japanese model could well make for a more symmetrical discussion about agriculture, forestry, health or education, involving expertise from Japan's line ministries and their counterparts in Indonesia, China or elsewhere, than in the more common bilateral model, which always runs the risk of there being seen to be some specialist knowledge about development priorities on which it is the responsibility of a single development agency to dispense its convictions. JICA could never have rapidly drawn from its own ranks the expertise that could produce some equivalent of DFID's nine sectoral target strategy papers. Rather, JICA has traditionally been a synthesiser of other ministries' expertise, and this has primarily been expertise on Japan and not on 'development'. It makes it, then, a fundamentally different kind of agency from the World Bank, with its claim to be a 'unique reservoir of development experience across sectors and countries'.

Experts and generalists in development co-operation
If the range of ministries (not to mention other corporations and private sector bodies) involved in Japanese aid were not already sufficiently complex, the challenge of identifying the special character and features of Japanese development aid is made more demanding by the two very distinct categories of personnel involved. Both in JICA and throughout government, there is a major difference between staff on permanent

(lifetime) employment, who are termed 'staff' or 'generalists' (*shokuin*), and those who are 'development specialists' or 'senior advisors' (*senmonin*), who may sometimes have higher salaries but have less security of employment.

The great majority of the 1,200 professional employees in JICA, for instance, are generalists, while a significant number of JICA's development specialists (of whom there are just under 90) are associated with JICA's Institute for International Co-operation (IFIC) in Tokyo, and are seen as 'life-work technical experts' – that is, dedicated for life to a particular technical field such as education or industry. This cadre of senior advisers are the closest in character to the DFID advisers. But unlike their DFID counterparts, JICA's numbers in any field are so small that they routinely need to draw in expertise from outside for most of their regular reports and studies. By contrast, the generalists move every 2-3 years, following a pattern that obtains across all ministries, and, with almost no exception, they hold all the senior positions, including the directorships of JICA departments and divisions.

This differentiation between generalists and specialists obviously has some bearing on the precise nature of JICA's expert knowledge, since the organisation is essentially run by generalists, and even those coming on secondment from other line ministries will usually be generalists, though with a technical bent in some cases. But it is possible to exaggerate this dichotomy between types of staff, because, over the last decade and longer, generalists have been encouraged to develop a degree of specialisation, and in some departments of JICA (for example, mining and industrial development, or health) a good number of the 'generalists' will have had common engineering or medical backgrounds. However, it remains the case that with the regular rotation system none of the generalists can focus throughout their careers on what may have been their primary disciplinary interest.

Nevertheless, the formal situation seems to be that those with the deepest sectoral expertise in a particular field such as education are seldom in a position where they can affect policy directly. But then even this must be qualified, for in JICA as a whole, it must be remembered that overall policy making lies with the Ministry of Foreign Affairs; so neither generalists nor development specialists in JICA are in policy making roles *per se*, though it is widely accepted that JICA does have a substantial measure of policy autonomy under the overall umbrella of MOFA.

The status of Japanese experience and expert knowledge is thus becoming more complex than where we had reached at the end of the previous section. We had noted that responsibility for development aid is distributed much more widely in government within Japan than in most other OECD countries, and that the major development agency, JICA, has traditionally drawn on the expertise of many different ministries, thus pulling into the development field a potentially rich vein of experience of Japanese development from as many as 17 (now 13) ministries. However, it then appears that these secondees are normally not themselves experts but are generalists with administrative experience of a number of sectors, like the majority of their hosts in JICA.

Consequently, at many different stages of the different project development processes, these regular staff, whether from JICA or from other ministries, need to have recourse to other specialist expertise. Our provisional conclusion is that JICA, like other government agencies and ministries, has a wealth of administrative and procedural expertise, but depends on other sources of expertise for a great deal of its technical and scientific input. We can thus anticipate that the challenge of knowledge sharing within JICA or other Japanese agencies concerned with development aid may be rather different from the kind of knowledge sharing, for example, in the thematic groups of the World Bank, among staff with similar professional concerns about a sector or a cross-cutting issue. But it is possible that JICA staff will increasingly need to face both the sectoral challenge and the larger changes to their roles that shifts in development co-operation itself are producing.

Japan's multiple external sources of development expertise

In a situation where the core, generalist staff in JICA are relatively few in number for one of the largest technical co-operation programmes in the world, it should not be surprising that there are many modalities for JICA to access technical expertise through a variety of routes, to ensure careful project design, implementation and evaluation. The sheer scale of the specialised knowledge and expertise upon which JICA depends must be underlined if we are to understand the sense in which JICA is a knowledge agency. This is not to argue that some other bilateral agencies do not also have large numbers of experts; they clearly do. What seems different is that Japan publicly presents these sources of their own expertise as being at the very core of its development co-operation. The main categories of this diverse expertise are the following.

Kenneth King

Despatch of project-type technical co-operation experts
In this project modality, which usually lasts five years but is often re-newed, the despatch of experts is one important element of an integrated package, along with counterpart training and equipment. The source of the experts is normally the other line ministries which duly second staff to JICA. Traditionally this opportunity for placing experts in projects overseas had been restricted to these other ministries, but in 2001 there was the beginning of competitive bidding for these openings on a trial basis. The procedures for identifying the almost two thousand such experts in any one year are quite complex, involving partner govern-ments, JICA, MOFA and then the line ministries. Almost 50 per cent of experts in 2001 were drawn from the regular employees of these min-istries and associated organisations. It would seem that ministries differ considerably in their capacity to provide experts, with Agriculture, Forestry and Fisheries having a surplus of experts, and others, such as Education and Science, drawing on national universities for their secondees.

Despatch of individual experts
This category is different from the above, since it involves a response to a whole series of different requests by partner governments for individual expertise outside the project framework. The numbers here in any one recent year are rather large, running at 1,750 in fiscal 1999. The actual identification of these experts is carried out with the involvement of JICA's regional departments, but also by MOFA consulting the line ministries who will be the source of these experts. Again, it must be assumed that the scale is such that the line ministries will in turn identify many of these experts from outside their own ranks but, unlike other bilateral agencies, these will tend not to be from the consulting or the private and for-profit sectors.

It should be noted that the recruitment of experts is actually expand-ing (JICA 2000a: 122), and the two categories so far discussed have, since January 2000, been handled by a new Human Resources Assignment Department. It is interesting to note that this new department is described as a 'personnel bank for the recruitment of experts by JICA' – perhaps an unconscious resonance with the 'knowledge bank' of the World Bank, but one which underlines that it is personnel, experience and expertise that are at the heart of Japanese ODA and not its own codified knowledge in policy papers.

Senior overseas volunteer programme (SOVP) and JOCV

Though not strictly regarded as an expert despatch programme, there is little doubt that this senior version of the long-running Japanese overseas co-operation volunteer (JOCV) programme for younger people is drawing very directly on 'the skills and knowledge' needed by developing countries, but also on those attributes that had supported Japan itself during its period of high-level growth. The description of this cadre, which has grown rapidly in the few years since it started, and measured 758 in 2002, underlines their 'outstanding skills and plentiful professional experience' (JICA 2000a: 14). This certainly suggests that a proportion of these senior volunteers would be regarded as similar to the senior advisers or development specialists if they were working in the ministries. The SOVP, if added to the 2,500 JOCV in the field at any one time, produces a significant number of volunteers.

These three categories alone, in fiscal 2000, involved a substantial number of Japanese experts and volunteers (about 7,000) being requested, recruited, trained and marshalled for overseas work. Beyond these, there are significant numbers of Japanese consultants working directly on the different studies which underpin most Japanese development assistance. The main categories of these are also worth noting because of their sheer scale.

Development studies

In its Japanese usage this term describes a wide range of studies carried out as an integral part of project identification, design, support and follow-up. They include master plans, which are comprehensive, long-term sectoral development documents for a country or a region, as well as feasibility studies. In fiscal 1999 alone, they numbered over 250, and routinely they would have used Japanese consulting firms which in turn could have drawn in 'international' consultants for up to half of the team members. The number of expert personnel working on these was no less than 2,974 in this single year. Though not formally termed 'experts', these consultants are recruited through competitions organised by JICA's development study department. The JICA staff involved in this selection process are likely to be generalists, and yet they will have to carry out this process as well as receive up to five reports for each development study project. This is probably one of several procedures where generalists have to turn to external expertise for assistance – just another reason why in-house sector expertise is becoming more compelling.

Kenneth King

Basic design studies for general project grant aid
This category of grant aid is for infrastructure and facilities – from school buildings to bridges and roads. But for our current concern with expert knowledge, it should be noted that basic design studies are critical to this category of grant aid. These are handled by Japanese consultant firms, as are the development studies, but on completion they are reviewed and recommended to MOFA by JICA's grant aid management department. Again, there is likely to be a review process by generalist staff of design studies which are of a technical nature. This too is a very major activity, with no less than 240 projects and their associated basic design studies being completed within fiscal 2000.

These are only two of the no less than fifteen categories of study teams that routinely go out from Japan to all the regions where there are possible projects to be developed. The sheer scale of this analytical work can be judged by the fact that in fiscal 1999 alone there were almost 9,000 individuals associated with this series of more than 1,500 study activities.

Thematic and country evaluations
This is a third major area of consultant use. Again, in some of these, the competitive bids amongst Japanese firms can include international consultants for up to 50 per cent of the proposed team. For other mid-term and end-of-project reviews, Japanese firms can be requested to assist in implementation. In the regular evaluations carried out by the evaluation division, there are substantial numbers in any one year; in 1999, for instance, there were two hundred evaluations done, and this includes just the completion, post-project, and post-project status evaluations (JICA 2000a: 154-8; JICA 2000b). Taken together, these will have involved very considerable amounts of development expertise, and again a good deal of the review of the results will have been undertaken by staff inside JICA.

As in other bilateral agencies, it will have been commonplace for evaluations to have been carried out by consultants, but in Japan this exercise seems likely to have involved more varied expertise than other OECD countries because of the multiple sponsorship of evaluations by JICA, MOFA and JBIC.[5] All in all, it would not be surprising if some 4,000 consultants were occupied across all three evaluation categories in any one fiscal year.

---

[5] The Japan Bank for International Cooperation became a part of the New JICA in 2008.

The scale of the Japanese expert, study team and evaluation presence
Putting this together with our estimate of formal expert personnel being recruited for work overseas, we reach a figure of around 7,000 for short- and long-term experts (along with senior and regular Japanese volunteers), and study-team personnel in all the different categories of almost 9,000, and a significant number of further personnel involved in the JICA evaluations. It would appear that as recently as fiscal 1999, there may have been between 16,000 and 20,000 Japanese engaged in these overseas expert, analytical and evaluative activities.

Japanese expertise in international perspective
The continuing – and perhaps growing – presence of all these very visible sources of Japanese expertise in their bilateral development co-operation activity comes at a time when there is a major UNDP-led rethinking of technical assistance and technical co-operation (Fukuda-Parr et al. 2002). There is clearly still a great deal of questioning of the old paradigm of North-South transfer of expertise, and a concern to explore new and more symmetrical ways of building and networking knowledge and capacity in the North and the South.

It would appear that perhaps unlike some other donors, where there has been a sharp criticism of technical assistance personnel, Japan has seen a rise in the use of these, and an expansion to include new categories of civil society and local government expertise, even, possibly, during the recent years of cuts to the overall aid budget. It would be intriguing to explore further whether the new paradigm for capacity development, as articulated by UNDP, which highlights notions such as 'scan globally, re-invent locally', may not already be accepted in the *wakon yosai* (Western knowledge, Japanese spirit) conception of expertise we have analysed above.

Indeed, for the World Summit for Social Development (WSSD) in South Africa in September 2002, Japan, significantly enough, chose to highlight and confirm its faith in technical co-operation in spite of the criticisms; and, again, it is interesting to see the reference in Johannesburg to Japan's own development experiences:

Japan International Co-operation Agency (JICA) places importance on the following aspects in providing technical co-operation to developing countries and supporting their capacity development.

- respecting ownership of the developing countries

- sharing knowledge and technology through working together with developing countries
- establishing human and institutional relationships between Japan and developing countries
- utilising Japanese experiences in her development process (JICA Programme for WSSD, 30 August 2002, 2 September 2002).

Direct exposure to Japanese experience through overseas training
At the same time, the other key dimension of technical co-operation - participant training in Japan or overseas – has also been growing over the last decade, whilst the training programmes of several other OECD donors have been drastically cut since the end of the Cold War. The specifically JICA component of this involved some 7,700 participants coming to Japan in fiscal 1999 for short-term training, while a further 8,000 received training in developing countries, including a very significant number in third countries. In this single year, when all the different training categories are compounded, almost 18,000 trainees were involved, in Japan or overseas. Added to this is a new component of long-term degree-level training to be provided by JICA.

JICA's is of course only one part of the Government's response to international student mobility; a much larger programme is the one designed to bring 100,000 to Japan in any one year. This is the responsibility of the Ministry of Education and Science, and although there has been some slippage from the overall goal of 100,000 by the end of the twentieth century, this is still the target of the ministry for implementation as soon as possible (Shibata 2001).

Behind this powerful emphasis on increased overseas training is the same concern with the direct exchange of expert knowledge *in situ* that is evident in the dispatch of experts to developing countries. This is why the technical training of overseas participants is judged to be 'the most fundamental "human development" programme implemented by JICA' (JICA 2000a: 111). Running through the justification is the crucial exposure, once again, to Japanese experience:

From the standpoint of technical co-operation there are several advantages in implementing this programme in Japan. These include the following: i) participants are motivated by seeing how new technology and ideas not yet available in their own countries are used; ii) Japan's experience is transmitted to the world at large; and

iii) participants have the chance to exchange ideas and experience with colleagues from other countries facing similar issues as themselves. (JICA 2000a: 111)

In case it is concluded that face-to-face contact exclusively with Japanese expertise is the foundation of its aid policy, it should be recalled that JICA is probably the foremost agency protagonist of South-South co-operation, whereby a group of 'pivotal countries', such as Thailand, Brazil, Chile and Singapore, are encouraged to make the transition to donor status by engaging their own experts in technical co-operation to developing countries, through funding from Japan. At the moment, this modality is increasing and is changing its shape, but it certainly can be thought of as a mechanism for transferring Japanese experience and technology through a third party (Miyoshi 2001). It could be argued that both the use of third-country experts rather than Japanese, and the use of third-country training rather than in-Japan or in-country, are aspects of South-South co-operation that Japan takes very seriously.

Conclusions on the expert experience

Given the great importance, nevertheless, that is attached to Japanese expert knowledge in development assistance, there is not a great deal of analysis – at least not in English – that seeks to capture the nature of this learning transaction. The salience of this modality, as a key form of knowledge sharing, needs to be pieced together from different sources. On the one hand, there are clear references in the discussion of experts to the way they represent the best in the Japanese on-the-job training system. In other words, in a small way, experts illustrate some of the facets of the Japanese traditions of learning within the firm for the aid project or programme. For instance, they are clearly seen to be in the business of sharing both knowledge and attitudes, and these attitudes are frequently illustrated by the fact that the Japanese experts are actually to be found in the paddy field or on the project site itself. Unlike British or German expatriates, who may have often been attached to key policy advisory positions in particular ministries, the Japanese experts have typically been middle-level practitioners rather than high-level policy people. The joke about the Japanese expert being called 'Mister Like This' points out the frequency with which Japanese experts might not be able to explain in excellent English but could show how something should be done by actually doing it, 'Like this!'

The emphasis has been on practitioner knowledge rather than on policy knowledge, on people-to-people transfer of skills and technology. Some pride is taken in the difference between many Japanese experts, who are there in the developing world for this particular task, and the number of much longer-term expatriates who work as experts for some of the other donor agencies. Just as the Japanese company has less status distinctions between workers and management, so it is possible that Japanese experts do not immediately fall into the expatriate community in developing countries. Former JICA president, Kimio Fujita, now working as a senior overseas volunteer in Samoa, put this Japanese perception of their difference from Western expatriates sharply:

> For most donor countries and organisations outside Japan, the central theme of capacity building is how to reduce dependence on the expatriate policy advisors who have occupied the central positions in the policy-making agencies of developing countries. Their position is the opposite from that of Japan, which has mainly dispatched specialists to the organisations responsible for implementation in developing countries and is only now looking into ways of sending them to policy-making agencies as well. (Fujita 2001)

Japanese commentators, however, are quick to admit that the success with which experts were able to work in Asia has not been secured as easily in Africa, partly because of skill gaps, and partly because of attitudinal differences.

It is clear from the way that experts are discussed in JICA official documents that along with overseas participant training, they constitute 'the core of co-operation in the field of human resources development in developing countries' (JICA 2000a: 120). But Japanese experts also proved politically valuable to the aid constituency in the late 1990s and early 2000s, when politicians, faced with recession in Japan, began to talk up the importance of 'aid having a clearly visible profile' (a translation of *'nihonno kaoga mieru'* – aid with a Japanese face). The political requirement for Japanese aid to be more visible may have the effect of pushing the expert out of the paddy field and into the ministry, as is argued on the JICA website.

These sections on the philosophy and history of Japanese aid, and on the particularity of Japanese approaches to expertise and to experience in relation to development, have been an essential prelude to any discussion of what phrases such as 'knowledge-based aid' might mean for JICA and for the other agencies in Japan involved in development assistance. In a word, it could be said that the Japanese discourse about development has made little explicit use of the language of knowledge for development, preferring to talk of sharing skills, technology, know how and experience in all the ways that have been analysed above. There are, nevertheless, a small number of knowledge initiatives which we shall turn to shortly; but first it may be worth looking at the ways in which Japanese aid has been associated with particular expressions of policy. It will be seen that though there is a series of lead documents expressing policy on development co-operation, there continues to be a major reliance on an established canon of positions and attitudes towards development.

Sources of policy knowledge in Japanese development assistance

What we are arguing is that although there is some documentation on development policy, which we shall briefly review, the core values of development seem to have been already set and are to a considerable extent embedded in a long-standing culture of development assistance. These typically include a concern with aid as a means of helping those who help themselves (Nishigaki and Shimomura 1996: 153). Central issues such as this focus on self-help – and all that flows from this – are also reinforced in the ODA Charter of 30 June 1992. This in turn has been elaborated in the Medium Term Policy for Overseas Development Assistance of 1998 (which runs for five years). The relation of this domestic aid policy development process to the series of new aid approaches that have emerged in OECD DAC, the World Bank and in some other donors over the last ten years is worth noting. In a number of important ways this domestic agenda has come into conflict with the aid paradigm associated with the World Bank.

Clearly there has been a desire within the aid policy community in Japan to achieve greater clarity about their own aid philosophy, especially since it came to be the largest bilateral aid donor in 1991. We have said enough above to suggest that there is a rather widespread set of convictions about what Japanese aid approaches consist of, but these have not been powerfully promoted outside Japan. Nishigaki and Shimomura capture this well in some of their discussion about the 'special features of Japan's ODA': 'It is only natural that societies with different historical and religious backgrounds should have different views on aid. What is needed is an awareness that Japan, too, has its own aid philosophy'

(Nishigaki and Shimomura 1996:153).

One of the first instances of the desire for a distinctive Japanese approach surfaced over continued Western support for structural adjustment policies, especially in Africa. Although Japan had given support for these in earlier years, there has been marked evidence since the early 1990s of concern with the assumptions underlying, and the impact of, adjustment measures (Stein 1998). Further evidence of a desire to promote a different model of development aid was to be seen in Japanese funding of the *East Asian Miracle* study through the World Bank in 1993 (see World Bank 1998). This study, Stein argues, was intended by Japan to move the Bank away from its dogmatic neo-classical position and make it more appreciative of state-led development along Japanese lines. This did not happen: 'The result was somewhat disappointing since the report did little to affirm the Japanese view of policies responsible for their own development' (Stein 1998: 17).

If the *East Asian Miracle* study was one of the first substantial attempts to get Asian (and specifically Japanese) development history acknowledged internationally, a second occasion was provided by the OECD-DAC report *Shaping the 21st century: the contribution of development co-operation* (1996). Arguably, Japan took very seriously the discussions that led to this report. While the targets themselves do not particularly reflect anything that could be called a Japanese approach, the background text provides much evidence of Japan's priorities, not least the frequent emphasis on the need for 'locally owned strategies'. JICA also produced a three-volume study on the OECD-DAC's new development strategy (NDS) (JICA 1998), which underlined even more clearly how closely aligned they felt the assumptions of the DAC report were with their own development assumptions.

At the heart of the Japanese belief is self-reliance, and it is interesting to see how powerfully this message from their own experience is confirmed in their commentary on the DAC report:

> Drawing general conclusions from progress that has been made in the development arena, the NDS declares that development assistance can do no more than complement the efforts made by the citizens, organisations, institutions, and governments of developing countries, and that ownership by developing countries will accordingly be of the utmost importance to the achievement of sustainable development. This emphasis on ownership effectively reaffirms the assistance philosophy that Japan has cultivated through

years of experience. (JICA 1998: 79)

The role of Japan in shaping key aspects of the DAC report is further confirmed by Fumiaki Takahashi, deputy director-general of the economic co-operation bureau of MOFA in November 1997. He argues that one of the three key principles of the DAC report is the ownership of their development by developing countries: 'One example is the dramatic economic growth in East Asian countries. This example has made clear that first comes the ownership of developing countries and donor countries should act to assist their efforts as equal partners' (Takahashi 1997: 13). Japan's influence on and pride in the DAC report's philosophy itself is made very clear: 'Japan played a leading role in shaping this strategy because she wanted to share her own experience with the other partners – the experience of her post-war reconstruction to become a donor country from a recipient' (Takahashi 1997: 13).

A third example of Japan's seeking to emphasise its own approach to development would be evident in its independent sponsorship of the series of Tokyo International Conferences on African Development (TICAD). These took place in 1993, in 1998 and 2003. In Takahashi's words: 'The main theme of the TICAD process is the importance of self-help efforts of African people and the co-operation between Asia and Africa' (Takahashi 1997: 15).

In contrast to these three examples, which illustrate Japanese involvement in getting some of its own development knowledge accommodated in the international discourse about aid, there are other examples of new aid developments, such as the Sector-Wide Approach (SWAP), the Comprehensive Development Framework (CDF) and the Poverty Reduction Strategy Paper (PRSP), where the Japanese have not been convinced that the modality fits with their own aid and accountability traditions. One reason for some hesitation about these new modalities is a Japanese preference in their own aid priorities for the country-specific approach, worked out bilaterally between their own experts and a particular self-reliant government (or in a South-South medium). By contrast, all the new aid approaches imply very consider- able degrees of donor co-ordination around a nationally owned programme. Furthermore, there is a worry that new approaches are being tried out in the developing world that, unlike their own tried and tested schemes, have not really yet been validated carefully. An example of this caution comes from MOFA comments on SWAPs, but it might be extended to other new aid paradigms of the late 1990s and early 2000s:

SWAPs are just being tried out at the moment, and we don't know whether they are going to prove effective or not. We ought to take our time to judge whether their approach is effective. Certainly, using developing countries as 'experimental sites' for new aid methodologies is something we shall need to be cautious about. (Ministry of Foreign Affairs, Japan, Summary, 2000: 11 [original in Japanese]).

Knowledge-sharing initiatives in a culture of valuing experience

We mentioned at the outset of this chapter that a number of agencies have in different ways followed the lead of the World Bank in exploring some dimensions of what it might mean to be a 'knowledge agency'. These have taken very diverse routes, whether in DFID, Sida or CIDA, affected by traditions of organisation and aid philosophy as well as wider movements in Northern governments. It might be assumed that Japanese explorations of knowledge-based aid would also be coloured by some-thing of what we have considered in the previous sections.

We shall first examine briefly a number of knowledge-based activities relating to Japanese aid, and then look in somewhat more detail at a project that is explicitly concerned with knowledge management and knowledge sharing. In doing so, we shall note some tensions between what we have been examining – the experience-based knowledge that is embedded in a particular context and history, and is often largely tacit – and the new initiatives deliberately to construct a more explicit sharing of knowledge, including across embryonic sectoral approaches.

Knowledge via sector work and sector studies

Earlier, we mentioned that there were very few explicit discussions about Japan's policy knowledge, but there are a great deal about Japan's experience. One of the reasons for this relative scarcity, despite the few important illustrations given above, is that the organisation of Japanese co-operation by a series of schemes (for example, dispatch of experts, overseas technical training, project-type technical co-operation) means that what would, in other agencies, be sector concerns – with education, small enterprises, and so on – are dealt with by a whole set of different schemes. It is often said, for instance, that the field of education is actually covered by no less than twenty different divisions in JICA. It has accordingly been difficult traditionally to conceive of how an education sector paper could actually be done organisationally within JICA. And it must be remembered, in addition, that education policy is a prerogative not of JICA but of MOFA, where all macro-level policy is determined, Even that is not the end of the story, for the key role of other ministries in aid policy would certainly require that the education ministry be consulted in an education sector initiative.

Thus, producing a JICA-wide account of education or of other key sectoral issues would have been a really major organisational challenge. One illustration of this challenge to the development of policy knowledge on key sectoral issues can be seen in the division concerned with global issues. There are just seven of these and they cover major fields such as environment, education, gender and WID, poverty, population and HIV-AIDS. It is the intention that they should produce guidelines for each of these major topics, but, so far, the useful little pamphlets that have been produced on each global issue merely exemplify how that topic is being dealt with across the various traditional schemes mentioned above. We shall shortly note how the new knowledge management scheme seeks to build on these global issues by its sectoral approach to a whole series of new 'development issues'.

Knowledge via dissemination of evaluation summaries

One of the forms of information disclosure on aid outcomes that has been of apparent interest to the Japanese public is the publication of evaluation results of all projects. This has happened since 1995, and since 2000 the full text of every evaluation has been available on the JICA website. Also since 2000 a very substantial document synthesising all evaluations in the particular year covered has been published in attractive format. The rationale for this degree of dissemination is 'to provide accurate in-formation on JICA projects to the people of Japan', and 'to increase the understanding of the people toward ODA'. It also reinforces the concern that aid should have a clearly visible (Japanese) face, since the evaluation summaries have plentiful photographs illustrating Japanese experts at work, or trainees experiencing Japanese expertise at first hand.

'Intellectual support' as a new element in expert policy

The development of this modality in recent years has signalled an interest in exchange of experience going beyond the technical. It has tended to be used for expertise connected with institutional and or oganisational development, especially in transition countries, and often in such allegedly 'soft' fields as legal, administrative and parliamentary systems.

By its very existence as a separate concept, it affirms that the bulk of support hitherto has been for 'hard' technical and technological areas. There is an intriguing parallel here with Sida's identification of their concerns with capacity building at the individual/professional, institutional and organisational levels (See Sida 2000a). JICA describes it thus:

> Intellectual support ... aims at establishment of institutional and legal systems, support for policy making, and improvement of operational capability. In this sense, it is different from just simple transfer of existing technology or skills, as has been done so far. More precisely put, it is the form of support that requires high level intellectual supporting activity, while taking fully into account the economic and social conditions of the recipient country. To help personnel of the recipient country think together and come up with optimum solutions is one example. (JICA 2000c: 4)

The term 'intellectual support' signals an important shift in JICA towards a more explicit approach to policy knowledge in those very sectors such as democratisation and trade liberalisation where Japan had traditionally been very diffident about intervening. It leads Japan into sector support and not just project support, and it suggests a new and interesting example of people-to-people co-operation in the more demanding sphere of policy knowledge:

> The 'Medium-Term ODA Policy' ... placed greater emphasis than ever before on intellectual co-operation ... JICA is being required to change over from an approach based on individual projects to one based on programme units covering the whole of a sector. (JICA 2000a: 24)

An early challenge to 'Knowledge for Development in Japan'
We have said how little explicit writing there is about knowledge for development, or knowledge discourse, at least in English, apart from the knowledge management initiative to which we shall turn in a moment. There is, however, a curiously anonymous document on this very topic produced by FASID (Foundation for Advanced Studies on International Development) as early as March 1998 entitled *Realities and issues of Knowledge for Development in Japan*. Thus, it was published several months before the *World Development Report* of 1998-99, *Knowledge for Development*, was made public in September 1998, although work on that WDR would have been initiated in 1997. What is especially intriguing about the FASID

report is that there is no reference to the World Bank's knowledge interests, but reference is made instead to the knowledge for development activities of DFID, NORAD, Sida, USAID and IDRC. Yet clearly these agencies were reviewed before any of them had developed any explicit knowledge sharing or knowledge management initiatives.

The document as a whole – just 24 pages – is a valuable commentary on the way that Japan and other bilaterals use knowledge. It examines the use of knowledge in the different phases of project development and implementation. Amongst a wide range of insights and suggestions, it sees scope for Japan to develop its unique experience of foreign aid into a more knowledge-based theory. This would be a healthy counterweight to the current approaches, which are dominated by North America and Europe.

Its most persuasive analysis relates to how agencies might best construct bodies of knowledge jointly with developing countries. For this, experience is crucial, and so is theory, but the third element that is essential is trust. One of its main conclusions is that establishing mutual trust with the recipient country and taking part in a joint effort to compile a body of knowledge is essential (FASID 1998: 23).

Although there is a good deal more in this paper, this particular emphasis on 'a joint effort to compile a body of knowledge' is very relevant to our purpose and resonates very much with the approaches of SAREC and Sida. Coming a year or two before agencies seriously began to consider how they should become 'knowledge agencies', it is refreshing in its assumption that knowledge development should probably encompass a shift away from the tradition of delivering specialised knowledge and towards the joint development (with the South) of new knowledge.

Knowledge management in JICA: A new approach

With this much background, we leave the only explicit knowledge management project in JICA, which has been actively in the making since 2000. Its origins lie as far back as 1996 when Koichi Miyoshi, later to become a key member of JICA's Planning and Evaluation Department, and then Senior Advisor in IFIC, was posted to the JICA office in Washington. Subsequently, one of the earliest identified publications by JICA on knowledge management was commissioned by the Washington office of JICA. It was a consultancy to examine knowledge management in USAID and the World Bank (Fillip 1999). It argued that JICA should follow its own organisational needs.

For detail on the working out of JICA's knowledge management project, see remainder of Ch. 7 in King and McGrath (2004).

References

Cheng, K.M. (1994). 'Quality of education as perceived in Chinese culture', in Takala, T. (ed). *Quality of Education in the Context of Culture in Developing Countries*, Tampere: University of Tampere, Department of Education.

FASID (Foundation for Advanced Studies on International Development). (1998). *Realities and issues of knowledge for development in Japan,* Tokyo: FASID.

Fillip, B. (1999). 'Knowledge management for development agencies: A comparison of World Bank and USAID approaches and some implications for JICA', Washington, DC: JICA.

Fujita, K., interviewed in Nov 2001 *Japan Economic Review*, downloaded from JICA website, 26.8.02 [jica.go.jp]

Fukuda-Parr, S., Lopes, C. and Malik, K. (eds.). 2002. *Capacity for development,* London: Earthscan/UNDP.

JICA. (1998). *The OECD/DAC's New Development Strategy: Report of the issue-wise Study Committee for Japan's Official Development Assistance,* Tokyo: JICA.

JICA. (2000a). *Japan International Cooperation Agency Annual Report 2000,* Tokyo: JICA.

JICA. (2000b). *Annual Evaluation Report,* Tokyo: JICA.

JICA. (2000c). *Report on Intellectual Support for Electric Power Sector Development Committee for the Promotion of Cooperation on Intellectual Support for Electric Power Sector,* Tokyo: JICA.

JICA. (2002). Programme for the World Summit on Sustainable Development, Johannesburg August 2002, London: attachment from JICA Office London.

Kato, K. (2001). 'Knowledge perspectives in JICA'. In Gmelin, W., King, K. and McGrath, S. (eds.) *Development knowledge, national research and international cooperation*, Bonn and Edinburgh: Centre of African Studies/German Foundation for International Development/NORRAG.

King, K. (2001). 'Knowledge agencies: making knowledge work for the world's poor?'. In Gmelin, W., King, K. and McGrath, S. (eds.).

Development knowledge, national research and international cooperation, Bonn and Edinburgh: Centre of African Studies/German Foundation for International Development/NORRAG.

Ministry of Foreign Affairs, Japan. (2001). 'Annual evaluation report on Japan's economic cooperation: summary', Tokyo: Ministry of Foreign Affairs, Economic Cooperation Bureau.

Miyoshi, K. (2001). 'Toward the promotion of support for South-South cooperation, to build an effective framework of international cooperation', Tokyo: JICA, unpublished paper.

McGinn, N. (2001). 'Knowledge management in the corporate sector: implications for education'. *Development knowledge, national research and international cooperation,* Bonn and Edinburgh: Centre of African Studies/ German Foundation for International Development/ NORRAG.

Nishigaki, A. and Shimomura, Y. (1996). *The economics of development assistance: Japan's ODA in a symbiotic world,* Tokyo: Long Term Credit Bank International Library Foundation.

Nonaka, I. and Takeuchi, H. (1995). *The knowledge creating company,* Oxford: Oxford University Press.

Organisation for Economic Co-operation and Development, Development Assistance Committee. (1996). *Shaping the 21ˢᵗ century: The contribution of development cooperation,* Paris: OECD.

Sawamura, N. (2002). 'Local spirit, global knowledge: a Japanese approach to knowledge development in international cooperation', *Compare: A Journal of Comparative Education* 32, 3, 339-348.

Shibata, M. (2001). 'Whatever happened to the 100,000 students-to-Japan target?', *NORRAG News 27,* 9-10

Stein, H. (1998). 'Japanese aid to Africa: Patterns, motivation and the role of structural adjustment', Chicago: Roosevelt University, unpublished paper.

Takahashi, F. (1997). 'Japan's ODA and the challenge of development', paper presented at the *Financial Times* Seminar, 'Japan's Official Development Assistance: The dynamics of development', November, London.

World Bank. (1993). *The East Asian Miracle: Economic Growth and Public Policy,* Washington DC: World Bank.

World Bank. (1998). *World Development Report 1998/9. Knowledge for development.* Oxford University Press, Oxford.

Chapter 11

The despatch of African students to USA had been one of the outcomes of the two Phelps-Stokes Commissions, but the intention of Jesse Jones, the Commissions' director, had been to ensure that such students were exposed to the Hampton-Tuskegee spirit. This meant a cooperative attitude in race relations, and a capacity to resist more radical, Pan-African approaches towards the colonial situation in Africa. In the words of Aggrey, they were intended to be 'good Africans' (King, 1971: 232).

It could be thought that this fear of 'radicalisation' might not occur in independent Africa, but for example in the Cold War years, students who went from Africa to China or the Soviet Union were viewed on their return as possibly critical of the successor regimes to the French, British and Portuguese rulers. Indeed, some of the first Kenyans who went to China in the early 1960s were sent there by Vice-President, Oginga Odinga. As one of them said on his return, his time in China 'had all been about Kenyan politics' (see chapter below).

China, in the 10 years of the Cultural Revolution from 1966 accepted few African students, but even after the Opening-Up that commenced in 1978, China had first to contend with the earlier image of its being politically and ideologically radical. A second hurdle facing African students in China in the 1980s was racial prejudice. Indeed, there were riots against African students in Nanjing in the year of Tiananmen Square protests, 1989.

China sought radically to change this image from 2000 with the launch of the triennial Forum on China-Africa Cooperation (FOCAC). In the 'Programme for China-Africa Cooperation in Economic and Social Development' at this first FOCAC conference, one of the pledges was for more African students to study in China; and the delegates advocated encouragement to both sides to study Chinese and African civilisations

Kenneth King (2019): *Education, Skills and International Cooperation: Comparative and Historical Perspectives*. Hong Kong: Comparative Education Research Centre (CERC), The University of Hong Kong, and Dordrecht: Springer. © CERC

© Springer Nature Switzerland AG 2019
K. King, *Education, Skills and International Cooperation*, CERC Studies
in Comparative Education 36, https://doi.org/10.1007/978-3-030-29790-9_11

(FOCAC, 2000: 15.1.1.). Shortly, resource bases in Chinese universities would be granted for the promotion of different dimensions of education, including higher and distance education, basic education and agricultural education. The several existing centres of African studies in Beijing and Shanghai received greater attention, and new centres were established.

At every FOCAC conference, the number of scholarships pledged by China to Africa rose, and had reached 30,000 by the time of the sixth FOCAC meeting in Johannesburg in 2015. But over the period since the first FOCAC in 2000, the attraction of China as a destination of choice by African students had changed dramatically. Indeed, there are now many more African students paying their own way to study in China than there are on Chinese scholarships. Teasing out the reasons for this extraordinarily rapid shift is one of the themes running through the chapter that follows.

References

FOCAC. 2000. 'Programme for China-Africa Cooperation in Economic and Social Development', First Ministerial Conference of FOCAC, Ministry of Foreign Affairs, Beijing, downloaded from http://www.focac.org/eng/ltda/dyjbzjhy/DOC12009/t606797.htm

King, K. 1971. *Pan-Africanism and Education*, Clarendon Press, Oxford.

African Students in China: Changing Characteristics, Contexts and Challenges[1]

African students are clearly a key foreign policy issue for China. Indeed, as noted by the Chinese government, "Exchanging students between China and Africa is one of the oldest forms of China-African cooperation" (China, MOE, 2005: 12). In the White Paper on *China's Foreign Aid* they are mentioned as having been part of the aid agenda since the 1950s. The total number of students trained by 2009 is mentioned precisely as 70,627, and the total number on China scholarships in 2009 was 11,185 (China, 2011a: 14).

Students from Africa were not referred to as a category in Zhou Enlai's eight principles of foreign aid, enunciated in early 1964 in Accra on his African tour (China, 2000), but they are routinely claimed as an element in China-Africa education cooperation. Thus in the volume published in 2003 in conjunction with the Forum on China-Africa Educational Cooperation, the theme of 'Exchanges of Students' took by far the largest part (40 pages) of the seven modalities of educational cooperation used by China for Africa. Again, there was a special concern shown for the history of this particular mechanism, stretching back to the first students, at least in modern times, who came from Egypt to China in 1956. But there was also a powerful ethical claim made about this category of educational cooperation, especially in regard to the great care to be shown them, the respect due to their cultures and customs whilst in China, and to their prospects on their return:

> The majority of African students work hard and score great achievements in their schoolwork. African students who return to their homelands have played positive roles in their nations' politics, economics as well as cultural development respectively. (China, 2003: 17)[2]

---

[1] This chapter is from King (2013), *China's aid and soft power in Africa: The case of education and training.* Kenneth and Pravina King jointly carried out all the interviews for this chapter.

[2] Dr. Mulatu Teshome is used as an illustration of this in the celebratory volume; at the time of its publication he was Speaker of the Ethiopian House of Federation; and by 2010 was Ethiopia's ambassador to Turkey. He had spent nine years doing bachelors, masters and doctorate in Peking University (King, 2011a).

There are two main dimensions of this capacity-building cooperation according to *China's African Policy* (China, 2006). One is the training of African personnel, many of whom already have jobs but who have been coming to China for short-term courses under the auspices of the African Human Resources Development Fund since the early 2000s. The other dimension is the continuation of the exchange of students between China and Africa (ibid.: 7).

In what follows, we shall see that there is not an abundance of sources on either of these two training modalities, short-term or long-term. But the few sources that do exist are much more concerned with the longer-term scholarship students from Africa than with the short-term training awards. We shall note that several of these sources are preoccupied with the problems of racist perceptions of Africans by Chinese students, and African student awareness of these attitudes, and to some extent also inadequacy of scholarship funds. In other words their focus is a challenge to the claim made above by the Chinese authorities. The issue of racial characterisation of African students appears to be sharply different, however, at different periods over the last 50 years.

On the other hand, we shall see that there is a tendency in several of the Chinese sources,[3] both government and academic, to focus on the quantitative dimension of African students and trainees. This emphasis is if anything increased with the formation of the Forum on China-Africa Cooperation (FOCAC) in October 2000. Particularly following the FOCAC meeting of 2003 in Addis Ababa and the Beijing summit of 2006, the African student and trainee modalities become principally represented as quantitative targets to be reached over the following triennium. There is still reference to the importance of encouraging more exchanges and closer cooperation between institutions of higher learning on both sides (China, 2006: 12). But the core message for instance in Beijing FOCAC III was the increase in government scholarships from 2000 awards in 2006 to 4,000 awards by 2009, and to a total of 6,000 by 2015. A similar commitment was made for the short-term training of African professionals from 10,000 to 30,000 in total over that same period from 2006 to 2015.

What is missing in this quantitative approach to students and trainees by the Chinese government is some sense of who these students

---

[3] The Chinese sources consulted have been primarily in English such as FOCAC, but one of the key texts on China-Africa education cooperation is only available in Chinese. This has been translated for the author by Zhang Zhongwen then in the Centre of African Studies, University of Edinburgh.

are, where they come from, what their aspirations are, why they chose China as a destination for study. Apart from the brightly coloured pages of exchange students enjoying their classes in China, in the celebratory volume on *China-Africa Education Cooperation,* there is very little in the public domain that gives any sense of the quality of this experience of three, four or more years of study on scholarships in China.

Even though African students have been coming on government scholarships for over five decades, there has not been any formal evaluation of the individual, institutional or societal impact of this major training initiative. Intriguingly, the Commonwealth Scholarship scheme has also been going for over 50 years (since 1959), and in that period some 16,000 scholars alone have come to the UK.[4] Over that same time frame double the number of Africans have come to study in China on government support.[5] However, for the 16,000 scholarships held in the UK, a major review of this experience is available, and an attempt to assess impact in key development priority areas (CSCUK, 2009).[6] China is not alone in not having sought to assess the impact over time of their training provision in this area;[7] other major middle-income scholarship providers such as Brazil and India have not done so either.

Accordingly, in this chapter we shall seek to put some flesh on the skeletal African numbers for this long-standing major education scheme of the Chinese Government.

Changing attitudes of Chinese and African students?

We shall start by examining the sources that document the apparently very negative feelings of African students about their reception and treatment in China. Firstly, we shall take note of a very personal account by a Ghanaian student, John Hevi, who came to China in 1960, and presented his experience under the title *An African Student in China* (Hevi, 1963), and also of two Canadian scholars, Sandra Gillespie, who

---

[4] The total number of scholarships across the Commonwealth, e.g. to India, Malaysia, Canada etc was 26,000 by 2009.
[5] The figure was 12,384 African scholars to China by the end of 2002, since when there have been FOCAC triennial pledges of 1,500, 4,000, 5,500 and 6,000 respectively in 2003, 2006, 2009 and 2012.
[6] Of the total of 16,000, 6,000 were traced by 2009, of which 2,400 took part in the survey. 61% of the survey respondents were from Commonwealth Africa.
[7] In the case of the short-term training this would be the responsibility of the Ministry of Commerce (MOFCOM) and for long-term students on government support, it would be the China Scholarship Council (CSC) under the Ministry of Education which would be ultimately responsible for any such analysis.

examined the experiences of African students almost 40 years later, in 1997, in a book called *South-South transfer: A study of Sino-African exchanges* (2001), and Barry Sautman who published a critical article in *China Quarterly* in 1994 on 'Anti-Black racism in post-Mao China'. We should also acknowledge the pioneering work of Frank Dikötter on the long history of racial stereotyping in China, and the adoption by some Chinese intellectuals in late 19th and early 20th century of some of the 'scientific' racism of the West towards Africans (Dikötter, 1992).[8]

Interestingly, both Hevi and Gillespie discussed similar numbers of African students as part of their investigations; Hevi's book concerns the 118 students who had been brought from 11 African countries in 1961-2 to study Chinese initially at the Institute of Foreign Languages in Beijing. He records dramatically that within nine months of being in China, 96 of the 118 had returned to Africa. Allegedly, this vote with their feet against China was the result of 'undesirable political indoctrination', 'language difficulty', 'poor educational standards', 'social life', 'hostility', 'spying', and 'racial discrimination' (Hevi, 1963: 117-136, see also Gillespie, 2009: 212). For Hevi, racial discrimination is 'the first item on our list of grievances' (ibid.: 183).[9]

Gillespie's fieldwork in 1997, some 34 years later, also found that racial tension was a key lens for understanding the African student experience in China. From 1979 through to 1989 there was what she characterized as a 'decade of conflict across campuses' (ibid.: 213). This culminated in the 'Nanjing Anti-African protests' of 1988-9 in which some 3000 Chinese students maintained a week-long anti-black student protest which also included wider concerns on human rights and democracy. Gillespie sees the Nanjing anti-African protests as heralding, four months later, the pro-democracy movement of 1989, 'as Chinese "democrats" used the anti-African sentiments to direct protest against the party regime (Sautman, 1994, p. 426)' (Gillespie, ibid.).

Although there were no more protests over the next almost ten years, by the time Gillespie did her fieldwork in 1997, she still felt it was possible to present 'colour and money' [i.e., discrimination and allowances] as 'the essential elements in the lives of Africans today' (ibid.: 223). She surveyed

---

[8] See also on the early history of Africans in China, Wyatt, 2010. *The Blacks of Pre-modern China.*
[9] Snow's unique historical account of*China's Encounter with Africa*(1988) draws on Hevi's book and comments that 'Its appearance rang down the curtain on a brief and catastrophic experiment' (ibid.: 199). Snow's analysis of the next 20 years of African student experience in China is invaluable. See particularly his account of the anti-African upheaval in Tianjin in 1986 (ibid.: 202).

133 students from 29 countries, studying in four major cities, Nanjing, Beijing, Hangzhou and Shanghai.[10]

In the very first section reporting on the fieldwork interviews, the first seven sentences are a series of critical comments about Chinese racial prejudice towards black Africans from students from seven different countries. The rest of the report on the interviews is unremittingly negative. A whole series of terms are used by the African students and the counsellors in African embassies to capture the anatomy of the discrimination in China towards Africans: black devils, dirty, stupid, non-human, ugly, alien, poor and much else. So far from this being a win-win exchange as in China's rhetorical discourse reviewed in earlier chapters of *China's aid and soft power in Africa*, the Africans are seen to come to China empty-handed. They fail to make friends because 'you can never have a Chinese friend'. Relations between African men and Chinese women are impossibly difficult; hence abstinence or resort to prostitutes are the only options.

As if open discrimination was not enough, the great majority of the African students who were interviewed (71%) found that their 'so-called scholarship' from China was 'woefully inadequate' in terms of covering costs. Further, there was no way that they could make up for the inadequacy of their scholarship by part-time jobs, even during the holiday periods. Such jobs were said to be not allowed.

The paradox therefore was that at a time when China was growing dramatically wealthier, the African students felt increasingly poor, and not least because they were as a group perceived to come from a continent that had fallen behind and had lost China's respect. This picture from Gillespie's research has no lighter side; there is nothing positive said about China's attitudes towards these particular students. Nothing at all.

Gillespie's was not the only account of sharp racial prejudice against the African students in China. She drew also on an earlier article and survey by Sautman (1994) who had analysed educated Chinese attitudes both towards Africans in general and towards the Chinese peasantry. This survey, carried out five years before Gillespie, in 1992, covered no less than 461 individuals, the majority of whom were students and

---

[10] Gillespie also carried out more qualitative interviews with five African students (two undergraduates and three postgraduates), four graduates, and three Counsellors from African embassies in Beijing.

intellectuals.[11] The survey was unusual in asking the Chinese respondents to rate seven groups of foreigners, including Africans, on ten attributes, and also to rate the Chinese peasantry, intellectuals and entrepreneurs on the same basis. The 10 areas of inquiry covered: cultural level, intelligence, industriousness, behaviour, role models from which one can learn, attractiveness, interest in education, honesty, capacity to manage their own political affairs, and interest in economic development (Sautman, 1994: 429).

There were many similarly disparaging comments made by respondents both on Africans and on Chinese peasants. But for our present review, it was the Chinese university student comments on Africans that were the most 'vitriolic':

> Africans were said to be undisciplined, wild, ignorant, uninhibited, primitive, uncivilized, lazy, foolish, ugly, weak, rude, incapable, back-ward, troublemakers, nuisances, not welcome, and the least intelligent tribe of black apes. They were held to lack the strength to resist suppression, to project a bad impression and lack a capacity for progress. A few students remarked that Africans are honest, but also simple and backward. Unambiguously positive characterizations were strikingly absent. (Sautman, 1994: 434)

It must be noted that the respondents were not being asked specifically about African students but about Africans as a group in comparison with Indians, Western Europeans, Japanese, etc. Nevertheless for most of the roughly 160 student commentators, their only direct experience of Africans would have been of them as students.

However, within just over a decade and a half, in 2008, Sautman and Yan carried out a survey of some 300 African students in the various universities of the city of Tianjin. Their findings on attitudes of these students towards China and the Chinese were generally rather positive:

> the [results] generally showed that African students had overall positive attitudes toward China and Chinese, not substantially different from those of African students in Africa.[12]

---

[11] There were also high school students, People's Liberation Army recruits in a 'Norma 1' university, staff of two research institutes, also from a municipal planning office, a trade mission, as well as technical and managerial staff from a factory.

[12] Sautman and Yan (2009) carried out a study in nine African countries of some 2000 students and faculty regarding their perspectives on the Chinese and on China's developments in Africa.

Many had experienced occasional street-level experience while in China; that is, they overheard negative remarks about them made by Chinese as they passed them on the street, but no institutional racism and fairly positive interaction with Chinese faculty and students (Sautman to KK, 22.10.2011).[13]

How could this be? Had something happened to government and university policy on Africa in just over a decade to explain such a radical shift? The West has become used to very rapid and dramatic changes in values and orientations in China. Could this really be another example? Had there been any major policy change on China-Africa in this decade? Had there been any significant changes in the Chinese universities' connections with, and awareness of, Africa since the late 1990s? Were the African students coming to China with different perceptions of China as a destination for study than in earlier decades? We shall review some of the possible influences on changing attitudes towards Africa and African students in China in what follows.

Interestingly, Sautman and Yan's Nigerian research assistant for this Tianjin survey was less sure about the claimed change in attitudes: 'If I would rate or summarise the attitude of African students towards China on a scale of positive, slightly positive, indifferent, slightly negative and negative, I will say NEGATIVE' (former student to KK, 9.11.2011). We shall return to this apparent contradiction later in this chapter.

Significantly, by the time Gillespie actually published her findings in book form in 2001, the Forum on China-Africa Cooperation (FOCAC) had just been established (in October 2000). This proved to be an invaluable Pan-African mechanism for China to engage with Africa. The series of FOCAC's triennial meetings had started, in which, as we have said, the quantitative targets for African students and trainees to come to China became a regular dimension of their Action Plans, at least from 2003. That summit offered 10,000 short-term training awards through the African Human Resource Development Fund, and 1,500 scholarships, over the next triennium.

FOCAC did not therefore immediately or dramatically alter African scholarship numbers. Indeed, scholarships were not even mentioned in the FOCAC 2000 Summary of Commitments (Taylor, 2011: 43). Nevertheless, over the 1990s the total number of African students in China had reached 5,569, doubling from the 2245 who had been in China during the

---

[13] Survey data conveyed to KK by Sautman.

1980s (He, 2006). Even when the third FOCAC summit in Beijing in 2006 doubled African scholarship numbers from 2,000 to 4,000 by 2009, it must be remembered that the figure of 4,000 is the total number of African scholarship holders in China, of all years, by that date. It was not a commitment to 4,000 per annum; the actual figure for new scholarships each year would have been closer to 1,000.

In other words, it would be difficult to argue that between Gillespie's fieldwork in 1997 and Sautman and Yan's in 2008, there had been a dramatic rise in African scholarship student numbers. The number of privately funded African students was certainly on the rise since 1989 when they were first allowed, and there had been a sudden rise, since 2003, in the arrival of the FOCAC-sponsored short-term trainees. Over the five years to 2008, probably some 17,000 such African professionals had come to China, and the majority would have received their training in the new resource centres based in the universities. Indeed, one of these centres, for the training of African professionals in vocational education, was in one of the universities in Tianjin.

By 2008 (the time of the Sautman/Yan survey), FOCAC had certainly put Africa on the aid policy map of China, and progressive academics with international interests could see that Africa could bring visibility and policy influence to their universities. Thus, Yunnan University set up its Centre for Afro-Asian Studies in 1999; Shanghai Normal University established its African Studies Centre in 2000; Zhejiang Normal set up China's first Centre for African Education Studies in 2003, along with Tianjin University of Technology and Education's Centre for Aid to African Vocational Education, just mentioned. At the same time, other universities such as Beijing Foreign Studies, and Beijing International Studies, were offering instruction in Hausa, Arabic and Swahili. They would be followed by others such as Tianjin Normal University, offering Swahili from the mid-2000s. Chinese scholars also began much more extensive publishing about Africa (China, 2003: 106-117). Relatively large research grants began to become available to carry out research in Africa. Doctoral candidates began to do fieldwork in Africa.

Illustrating the speed with which institutional change is possible in China, Zhejiang Normal University had moved from setting up a very small Centre for African Education Studies in 2003 to launching a full-blown Institute of African Studies in August 2007. Some twenty new staff were hired to work on Africa, and a first set of masters students in African studies had started in 2008. For almost the first time, staff were travelling to Africa to undertake research, and it became possible even for masters students to contemplate carrying out some fieldwork in Africa.

But the changing awareness of Africa was not just taking place in universities with named centres or institutes of African Studies. Following the setting up of the first Confucius Institute in Seoul in November 2004, a series of African universities, literally from the Cape to Cairo, began to follow suit. In 2005, the University of Nairobi was the first to open a Confucius Institute, its Chinese partner university being Tianjin Normal University. Soon there were 30 other African universities (including Cape Town and Cairo) which were forging close links with their sister universities in China for the development of Confucius Institutes. But much earlier than the Confucius Institute partnerships with China, some 25 Chinese universities from Peking to Chang-an, and from China Agricultural to Beijing Language University, had developed links with partner universities in Africa in order to provide scientific laboratories. Many of these long-term partnerships from the mid- to late-1990s were formalised when the 20+20 scheme was announced in the Fourth FOCAC meeting in 2009. This again linked 20 Chinese universities more closely to 20 of their African partners.

But this growing awareness of Africa in the Chinese universities was not dependent only on institutional links. African celebrities such as President Nelson Mandela were to be heard addressing large audiences in Peking University just a year after South Africa initiated diplomatic relations with China in 1998.[14] Other heads of state from Africa such as the late Meles Zenawi of Ethiopia were recognised as the Co-Chair of the Second FOCAC summit in Addis Ababa in 2003. Beijing itself was the site of the largest meeting on Africa ever held outside Africa in November 2006, when almost 40 heads of state from Africa assembled in the capital for the FOCAC III summit. Beijing transformed itself into a celebration of Africa, from massive photographs of Africa in the metro to huge replicas of African wildlife in the best known shopping area. Banners and the media proclaimed 'Amazing Africa', and no fewer than one million ordinary citizens volunteered to be helpers and provide additional security on all street corners (King, 2006).

2006 was also the year in which China declared its *African Policy* (China, 2006). And 2006 was widely hailed in the Chinese media as the Year of Africa. In terms of deliberate orientation of the press and the

[14] President Hosni Mubarak of Egypt was awarded an honorary doctorate by Peking University in April 1999, and Mandela accepted one in May 1999.

media towards Africa, this year of the Beijing Africa Summit was seen as a useful preparation for the even larger event of the Olympic Games two years later in August 2008.

The question we return to now, however, is whether the scale of these new developments relating to Africa, many of them affecting the universities in China, could have been responsible for a change in orientation towards Africa of the kind reported in Sautman and Yan's survey of African students in Tianjin's universities. Interestingly, no less than three of Tianjin's major universities had been drawn into substantial African partnerships in the decade before their 2008 survey. This included Tianjin Normal, Tianjin University of Technology and Education, and Tianjin University of Traditional Medicine which had links with Kenya, Ethiopia and Ghana respectively.

However, a further critical factor that could have made for a change in attitude towards China between the 1990s and the late 2000s was the dramatic alteration in China's status as a world power, with many of its universities aspiring to be world class, especially from May 1998.[15] Many Chinese universities, including Zhejiang Normal where the new Institute of African Studies was based, literally transformed themselves during the 2000s with massive investments in libraries, research facilities, student and staff accommodation. Deliberate internationalisation was part of this transformation, and the African elements in this process were a small part in a much greater movement to embrace a wide-ranging reorientation in higher education (Adamson et al., 2012; King, 2012).

Recognition of these changes in China's universities was evident in many of the countries sending students to China; hence the worldwide interest in foreign universities partnering with Chinese universities through the Confucius Institutes when this became possible from late 2004. The change in status also meant that Chinese universities began to become destinations of first choice for a number of countries, including in Africa. Thus in Kenya, for example, sources in the Ministry of Higher Education recognised China as a priority destination along with Germany when it came to the popularity of its scholarships. This could well mean that there were different kinds of students drawn to Chinese universities from Africa during the 2000s than there had been in the 1990s. The internationalising changes in the Chinese universities and in the type of

---

[15] Jiang Zemin's centennial speech at Peking University that year is widely taken as a launch point for China's world class university initiative (Li, J. 2012).

international students aspiring to come to them could translate into different attitudes towards their hosts by African students in the later 2000s and vice versa.

Be that as it may, it is now time to turn from speculations about the impact of internationalisation in general on African students coming to China, to the specific insights of Africans currently studying in China, and the perceptions of those who have studied in China but returned to Africa. We shall first look at a range of Kenyan students who have studied in China and returned, and then examine the insights of a number of African students studying in China from 2010.

In most of the discussions with Kenyans, one of the key issues that emerged was what could be learned from China for the improvement of work back home. There was often a particular comparative interest shown by the Kenyan students on China's work style, discipline and the quality of the working environment in China.

Kenyans study in China

These discussions with Kenyans who have studied or hope to study in China were principally held in July 2009 except where otherwise mentioned,[16] and they covered a wide range of graduates of Chinese universities in the last 25 years. But the history of Kenyans studying in China goes a lot further back.[17]

We do know that Kenya was one of just five countries which had one or more students in China during the 1950s (He, 2006: 3). Intriguingly, the other four countries were Egypt, Cameroon, Uganda and Malawi (Nyasaland). We do also know that two Kenyans were amongst the 118 Africans referred to in Hevi's account of *An African Student in China*, which was mentioned above, and they were amongst the 96 who decided to leave prematurely in 1962 (Hevi, 1963: 116). In addition, what we do know now for certain is that some of the other earliest Kenyans to travel to China in 1964 for a study tour were recruited personally in Makerere University in Uganda by the then vice-president of Kenya, Oginga Odinga. There were six of them, four Luo and two Kalenjin. Odinga's

---

[16] Except where mentioned otherwise, all the direct quotations are from July 2009.

[17] Although the tradition is that one of Chinese Admiral Zheng He's fleets reached the current areas of Lamu and Mombasa on the Kenya coast in the 1400s, with some Chinese sailors settling after shipwreck, it was not until the celebrations of the 600th anniversary of this exploration, in 2006, that a Kenya-China training dimension developed from this early safari; Shariff, a Kenyan girl with claimed Chinese ancestry, was sent on a China government scholarship to spend seven years in Nanjing University of Traditional Chinese Medicine (PRC Ministry of Culture, n.d.).

purpose was apparently to demonstrate to a number of well-educated Kenyan students that 'communism was not all that bad' and perhaps even better than the capitalist road being promoted by President Kenyatta. One of these six, interviewed in November 2011, has given us one of the earliest sets of comments by a Kenyan on the lessons from China:

> Overall, Mutai said he was impressed by the Chinese authorities' management of human capital in terms of total employment of the population with corresponding provision of welfare services to everybody on an equal basis. (Kipkorir to King, 11.11.2011)[18]

In due course it would be valuable to know a little more about these earliest impressions, coming from even before the Cultural Revolution. But as far as any impact of this safari to China was concerned, Mutai had the following to say: 'When we came back we forgot all about it – it had all been about Kenyan politics.'

An early vocational safari with a comparative perspective on Kenya
Our earliest direct interview was with someone who is now a senior medical officer in Kenya. He had hoped to study medicine in Nairobi University but did not get admitted on his first try. Instead of spending a year preparing to re-sit, he was advised to try Poland or China. It is interesting to note that the choices available to him, back in the early 1980s when he went to China, were Poland, still within the Soviet bloc, and China. At that time there were ten scholarships offered by China to Kenya, and he was one of three who went to pursue medicine. He entered Sun Yatsen Medical University in Guangzhou.

The key lessons from China for him were quite clear. Time management; if someone was late by two minutes, then repeat the job. The university syllabus was completely clear insofar as what was to be studied, prepared for and discussed; the system was transparent and if there was any problem on marks or grades, it was possible to go straight to the top and have it sorted. The machines related to medicine were

---

[18] Dr Ben Kipkorir has mentioned that the party of six Kenyans who had been students in Uganda were offered a very special experience in Shanghai. In China, the Kenyan party were taken to many places including the Great Wall; and even when the visitors had become too tired of travel, their hosts still had another surprise for them: a visit to Shanghai where they were invited to meet a factory worker whose hand had been severed by a machine but had been rejoined by Chinese surgeons who claimed that that was the first such medical procedure in the world, accomplished thanks to the great leadership of Mao (Kipkorir to King, 11.11.2011).

already excellent. But when he had gone back to China fifteen years later the transformation was quite dramatic, 'an eye-opener'.

The contrast with Kenya was stark: 'Overall in China, while they are developing, we are deteriorating. Our discipline is bad. Our consultants come in, in the morning, but then go off to make money in private practice. Management is bad. In terms of promotion, there is a lack of merit. Even corruption.'

This set of comments is crucially important for seeking to understand one of the common threads of the debates about the advantages of overseas scholarship. The impact upon the individual is one thing, but the impact on the institution to which the scholar returns is something that is of great interest to many of the scholarship funding organisations. An indication of this kind of institutional impact is that this particular alumnus successfully managed to take a whole team of Kenyan doctors to China in 2000.

Identifying different kinds of institutional impact is what the survey of 50 years of Commonwealth Scholarships to the UK sought to establish. Thus they were able to claim that 'High numbers of respondents reported being able to introduce new practices or innovations at their workplaces' (CSCUK, 2009: 18).

An early Kenyan female student in China; surprise at China's ignorance of Africa
Our next Kenyan student in China went 10 years later, in 1993, to what was then called Shanghai Textile University. She was one of very few black women in the city at that time, and faced a good deal of harassment which she put down to ignorance and because they had been 'closed in by their government for so long'. She had expected they would be fascinated but it was rather different:

> They would block my way, so they could look at me with a closer view and of course would say things I didn't understand. But when I started understanding Chinese, then I heard SOME of the NASTY things they said. "Black devil" was a very common term. When they crowded around me they would try to touch the skin and hair to see if it was really dirty-and if their hands would get dirty after touching. Can you imagine trying to ward off many little hands from you as you would flies or other insects? I didn't take it all negatively because I thought they were ignorant and not exposed to a world outside theirs. They would, for example, ask if I came to China from Africa on foot or by bicycle, and if I told them I walked up to their

capital where I was given a bicycle, they appeared to believe me.
(Former student to KK, 20.11.11. caps in original).

She had gone there for technical expertise, which she received. But she
was not impressed or influenced by their culture or work ethic although
she recognised that they were 'workaholics and followed the rules'. In fact
she felt the Kenyans were more culturally advanced even if China was
making more technological progress. She did note that when the African
students had had to learn Chinese, there was more interaction with the
Chinese students; she was in the first batch that studied in English. And
the 'Chinese contact with foreign students in my university was limited or
even prohibited'.

Returning from China critical of Kenya
Another Kenyan who went to China in 1996 and stayed for over a decade
registered 'huge disappointment' and 'lack of incentive' on his return.
Kenya, he felt, by contrast with China, lacks opportunities, has poor
equipment and facilities in the public sector; and hence there is the
attraction of the private sector, especially in medicine. But there is also,
again, the work and governance culture:

> The people here are idle; they don't come in and work. And they lack
> the discipline. What could be brought in from China is good
> governance of the institutions; also of student behaviour. The
> students monitor each other and look after each other.

This doctor had been able to take additional jobs in China in order to
supplement his CSC allowance. But for him the paradox was that the very
apolitical character of student life in China had had a powerful effect on
his return to Kenya: 'There is no politics in Chinese universities; yet you
come back from China more critical of the Kenyan situation.' But he
retained an overpoweringly positive view of the Chinese people, as good,
honest and straightforward.

Admiration for China's culture including its culture of work
A further Kenyan who went to China, in 2003, on a provincial Chinese
scholarship rather than one from the China Scholarship Council, was very
clear about the lessons to be learned from China. He was very aware of
the direct impact of China on his own outlook, ethics and approach to
work:

The greatest impact was in understanding more of other cultures, including China's.

It helped me to change the way I looked at something. The Chinese always look at the bright side. They have a can-do approach. They are very hardworking. And this affected me. At the weekend, all the Chinese went off to do part-time jobs. So I did likewise.[19] When it came to improving their English, they would go off and volunteer to teach English in middle school, to sharpen their practical skills. I did the same.

All in all it had a very positive impact on my keeping time and doing the right thing. They were very time conscious and target driven. What I learned was to do things ahead of schedule or right on time. No excuses about missing targets. I can't remember any occasion when a Chinese student came late. So I came back to Kenya with these attitudes.

This perspective on what can be learned from study in China, we shall note in other interviews, is rather commonplace. The recognition that there is a very powerful work ethic found in both teachers and students in China is seen as something very positive by many overseas students on scholarships or awards in China. The belief that hard work and effort (*nuli* in Mandarin) are crucial to academic achievement is very widespread in China and in several other East Asian societies.[20]

Fascination with the Chinese language and culture, plus a desire to teach it in Kenya

Another dimension of Kenyan interest in studying in China is less vocational but derives from an enthusiasm to learn this very different language. In the case of a student from the Rift Valley in Kenya, it was the direct impact with Chinese workers constructing buildings in an educational institution that lit the spark. This was followed by some eight months of part-time study of Chinese in Egerton University, and then suddenly there was the chance to compete for a scholarship to China. It is noteworthy that it was his very strong desire to teach Chinese on his

---

[19] This is in contradiction to what the students were saying in Gillespie's survey about not being able to work.

[20] 'Teachers in China tend to believe that with due effort, a child should always be able to achieve the expected standard. They believe that genetic factors are always secondary, so long as pupils are trying hard. The motto "diligence compensates for stupidity" is seldom challenged' (Cheng, 1990: 165). See further, King, 2007c.

return to Kenya that probably improved his chances of getting a scholarship in 2001.

As far as the impact on his own approach to work is concerned, it was a similar story to what we have just heard:

> They are such hard workers. 24 hours a day! Very different from Kenya. On the subject of hard work, they have proverbs about this.[21] But they pay more attention to these proverbs about hard work making for success than we do in Kenya.[22] I was really impressed by their hard work; they worked perhaps twice as hard as we did. But I was also impressed by their sports, their strong family ties as well as their study. I noticed this when I was invited to their homes for some three weeks at a time.

On his return to Kenya two years later, there were already no less than five public or private colleges offering Chinese in Nairobi alone, and in a year's time the Confucius Institute would start in the University of Nairobi, right in the centre of the city. It was easy therefore to put into practice his ambition to teach Chinese. Soon he was teaching classes of twenty students. His longer term aim, in order to continue teaching Chinese more effectively, was to pick up a degree part-time in Nairobi, and then go back to China and get a Masters in teaching Chinese as a foreign language.

On the issue of racism towards Africans in China which we have focused upon in the earlier sections of this chapter, it is worth noting his rather balanced approach:

> Yes, there was some stereotyping of Africans, and perhaps some teachers gave less attention to African than to other international students. But this was a question of individuals. And don't forget, we Kenyans stereotype the Chinese! The Kenyans readily say that the Chinese are eaters of dogs, snakes and frogs. And they also say that the Chinese can't see properly!

---

[21] Amongst the many illustrations of this emphasis on the crucial importance of effort and determination is the story told by Li Bai, the poet of the Tang dynasty, about the old granny grinding an iron pestle on a stone in order to turn it eventually into a needle. After the granny had explained that this could be done if she ground it every day, Li Bai thought: 'She's right. There is nothing that cannot be accomplished by perseverance. The same is true with learning' (King, 2011b: 4).

[22] For a rather similar set of proverbs about the role of effort in Kenya's Central Province, see Marris and Somerset (1971).

Learning Chinese in a changing, enabling environment in Kenya

The interest in learning Chinese and in studying in China is inseparable of course from an environment in Kenya where there are encouragements and incentives to become interested. This environment will differ greatly from country to country in Africa, and even within countries will differ from the capital city to rural and provincial towns. But already in Kenya in the mid-2000s, it was possible to access TV from China through CCTV9, the international channel. Also, China Radio International (CRI) had set up first a national centre in 1991 and a regional centre in 2006. Starting in 2008, this was broadcasting 58 short lessons in Chinese; and Xinhua, the official Chinese news agency, had set up its regional headquarters also in Nairobi. By the end of 2012, there were no less than 70 African professionals in the Nairobi office alone, with about 50 Chinese colleagues, and another 15 correspondents across the continent (Peter Wakaba to KK, 3.12.12).[23] Finally, *China Daily Africa Weekly* became available for the first time on the newstands across Eastern Africa from 7 December 2012 (Wekesa to KK 15.12.12).

These resources played their part in encouraging a number of young people to become interested in China and in studying Chinese. In the case of the sister of the Kenyan teacher of Chinese just mentioned, these multiple resources drew her to the study of China, but equally there was an awareness of China's success and its growing role in the world:

> My brother had gone to China in 2001. But I used to look at CCTV9 and listen to CRI. I admired China. I admired its culture. I got very positive images. So immediately after secondary school, in the gap before university, I studied Chinese intensively with the teacher attached to Egerton University. I did six hours a day for one and a half years. Looking ahead, after my BA, I am planning to study in China and get a chance to teach there. For me, doing Chinese is the key, and my parents are in favour.

Another factor which is likely to encourage similar responses to what are noted here with her is the start of teaching Chinese, as a pilot programme, in the primary schools of the Western Kenya city of Kisumu. This is the

---

[23] See also Wu Yu-shan (2012) on China's state-led media dynasty in Africa.

result of a request to the Chinese Embassy in Nairobi from the Kisumu East MP, Shakeel Shabir (King, 2010: 493).[24]

Switching from OECD countries to China?

Kenya is not alone in having examples of students who were in USA for their undergraduate degree deciding that they should do their masters or doctorate in China. There is an example of another African student (from Senegal) who was actually enrolled in a Canadian Business Studies course deciding to abandon his studies and move to the Shanghai University of Finance and Economics for both cultural and professional reasons.[25] This is not to suggest that higher education China is simply easier to access than some of the OECD countries. At least for the China Scholarships offered to Kenya, there is now stiff competition. According to the Minister of Education in Kenya in July 2009 it is necessary to have an upper second in one's first degree to be considered. Ministry staff indicated that the largest providers of scholarships in that year were Germany, China and India, and that first choices of destination, of the countries that relied on the Ministry to do the selection, tended to be Germany and China, as we mentioned above.

For the Kenyan student who elected to switch his host country from the USA to China in medicine, in 2008, one deciding factor, as a prospective engineering student, was that he had discovered, after a little research, that a great deal of the machinery in the Kenyan hospitals had come from China. An additional issue that students like him needed to bear in mind when competing to come to China on a government scholarship is that success usually means that the whole first year is dedicated to becoming sufficiently fluent in Chinese to cope with the terminology of a science degree. And it is primarily in the applied sciences that China's government scholarships are provided.[26] Hence the

---

[24] Wekesa, a Kenyan doctoral student from Western Province, has confirmed that Mr Yu was the Chinese teacher who came first, and who is still there; two further Chinese teachers have joined him, and other MPs are clamouring to repeat the initiative (Wekesa to KK, 12.09.12).

[25] 'There are more personal reasons that counted in his decision to move to China. He had for a long time an interest in this country and, even in Canada he continued to read a lot on its culture and its emerging as an economic power. Since he is studying business, he considers that China is already counting and will continue to play an important role in this globalized world. So he decided to move there with the advantage of learning Mandarin and to continue his studies with a major on Chinese Business. He plans to do business with partners in China who target Africa for their business. Two of his friends from Dakar have decided to join him in Shanghai' (Father of student to KK, 1111.2011).

[26] In 2009, the disciplines prioritised were: medicine, surgery, aeronautical, aerospace, systems engineering, computer studies, telecoms, and megatronics.

challenge is to reach the level of HSK 5 in Chinese which is the condition set for foreign students undertaking any science degree in China.

The wider picture for this student who elected to move from the West to the East is that there is a lot that Kenya can learn from China:

> We are not the same as China; we are the Third World. We accept aid and we say 'Let them come and help us'. But we should be more self-reliant. We should not rush to be helped. Unlike China, we look at some jobs and say they are dirty jobs; we don't do them. The most important lesson is that China has developed. We need to learn from here and go back to Kenya.

The advantage of this immersion year in Chinese is that it offers a real opportunity to become part of another country's culture, like the best experience of the ERASMUS exchanges across the European Community, but even more intensive. The result is that this particular Kenya student found that '… he spent most of his time with Chinese students; they tell me that I am one of theirs.' This, of course, is in direct contrast with what the Gillespie survey had found much earlier.

Self-sponsored Kenyans studying in English in China

It is worth mentioning that apart from the China Scholarship Council (CSC) students whose degrees are in Chinese and who study alongside Chinese students, there are a growing number of Kenyans recruited by organisations such as China Information and Culture Communications (CICC) which has been operating in Kenya since 2006, and intending to open branches also in Uganda and Zambia. Within two years, it was sending 40 students to China to no less than eight different well-known universities, where courses were also in English. It has not been possible to secure a figure for the total number of self-sponsored students in China, but with fee levels, in 2008, of as little as US$2,750 for tuition, accommodation and insurance even in a field such as medicine, few other countries may appear equally competitive as degree destinations.

In Chongqing Medical University (CMU), for instance, there were some 20 Kenyans in the first and second years alone. Two of these were would-be women doctors in their third year in 2009. They had checked out that CMU was certified by the WHO and was recognised in Kenya. They found that there were no fewer than 200 international students in their year. But the great difference from CSC students was that they were studying, in English, in classes which had no Chinese students at all.

These were in effect separate classes made up exclusively of international students. But would this mean that the work ethic which other Kenyans have mentioned as a major influence in their time in China would be missing? Apparently not; the Chinese teachers 'kept encouraging us and saying "Work hard and you will reap what you sow"'.[27] In addition classes were compulsory, and they were well aware of the effort the Chinese students were putting into their parallel medical studies in Chinese medium.

One last Kenyan student, who already was working in the media, before going to China in 2010, illustrates the fact that expertise and experience of China may now be regarded as a comparative advantage in the competitive media business:

> The first thing I did was to look up the programme and the information provided on the website of Communication University of China; it fitted the bill for me – media literacy, theory of communication, communication research methodology, etc. – these were courses I'd wanted to undertake and I reckoned China was now a global power and therefore media studies would be thorough-going – I was not unduly worried about China-bashing as working on the government newspaper had exposed me to the positive side of China's meteoric economic growth. Plus, I increasingly became convinced that an oriental perspective would be important as there were already many Kenyans who had studied in the West – a competitive advantage existed, I thought. I put in my application, the rest is history. (Wekesa to KK, 24.9.2012)

We shall return to the issue of whole groups of African students and professionals being separately taught from their Chinese counterparts when we review the Ministry of Commerce (MOFCOM)-sponsored Masters courses. But for now, it may be useful to draw together some of the threads that have emerged from examining this group of Kenyan students and trainees who have been in China at different times over the last 25 years, or 45 years if the earliest recruits to China by Odinga are included.

First, of these students who have been in China (or are planning to be in one case), the theme of racial discrimination discussed in the first section of this chapter did not emerge as a critical issue. One reported that

---

[27] For the widespread belief amongst teachers in East Asia that effort will lead to successful achievement by the majority of students, as mentioned above, see Cheng (1990) and King (2007c).

ten years ago some of the children they encountered in Beijing had never seen a black person; they wanted to touch to see if the colour came off. In another case, in a provincial university city, the children had wanted to know if their skin was black because of the heat of the sun in Kenya. Two others had been aware that there was some stereotyping of Africans by the Chinese but they were equally aware that there was similar stereotyping of the Chinese by Kenyans. There was little evidence at all that this group of Kenyans had found it hard to mix in China; indeed the reverse was true, and was much helped by having good Mandarin. One or two had maintained their links with Chinese friends after returning to Kenya.

Second, China has rapidly become a destination of choice for Kenyan students, and in the view of the Kenyan ambassador in Beijing in 2010, it had replaced India as a destination because of the readiness of the Chinese to transfer their knowledge and technology. This is not to say that many Kenyans might still prefer London or USA; but that might change, as in the case of the Kenyan who actually decided to switch to China from the USA. Some evidence of this growing popularity can be seen in the embassy's estimate of there being some 500 Kenyan long-term students in China. There were strong clusters in Nanjing where there have been links with Kenya's Egerton University since the 1990s and in Tianjin where there has also been a link forged through the Confucius Institute partnership. Despite these numbers, there was not yet an Association of Kenyan Students in China, although there is a plan for one. However, apparently, there was already a Kenya Alumni Association of former graduates who had returned home (China, MOE, 2005: 21).

Third, since the Beijing Summit of 2006, the annual allocation of CSC awards to Kenya has been running at about 40, which over a five-year period would produce a figure of about 200-plus scholarship holders on central government scholarships. We have noted already that there are provincial scholarship holders as well, and we would add that through the Confucius Institutes there is a wide array of Kenyans coming for language and culture awards of varying length. Others too have been coming through the MOFCOM Masters scheme. But overall it probably means that there are about equal numbers of scholarship and self-funded Kenyan students in China.

Lastly, the dominant thread in the Kenyan student experience of China has been the exposure to a very powerful and influential work and study ethic. This theme is picked up and echoed by the Kenyan Embassy in Beijing. It is possibly reinforced by the relatively slow pace of the liberalisation of Chinese society; hence there is not to the same extent a whole range of activities outside the classroom like civil society, the churches, and so on. According to the Kenyan students, very little time is taken up in the discussion of politics as it would be in Kenya. In contrast to these Kenyan students with experience of China, there were in 2009 just one or two Chinese students in Kenya on Kenya Government scholarships. Discussion with one of these pursuing a PhD on the political thought of Thabo Mbeki revealed many problems with the award, the accommodation, access to the library, and even allocation to the most suitable department in the University of Nairobi.

Other African students in China's universities

Apart from using a Kenyan lens to analyse some dimensions of student experience in China, it was thought valuable to look at the view of African students in one of the universities which has prioritized links with, and studies of, Africa in the last decade and longer. We had already mentioned Zhejiang Normal University (ZNU) above, as an example of a provincial institution in China which had dramatically changed its international orientation including towards Africa in a very short time. Its first contact with Africa, with Cameroon, only goes back to 1996, linking with the International Relations Institute of the University of Yaounde II.[28] The first African student came to ZNU from Cameroon shortly afterwards. But within ten years, ZNU had a full-blown Institute of African Studies as described earlier. There were more than 70 African students by 2011, drawn from 29 different countries, and unlike several of the African studies centres in the UK, these students were drawn from Arabic-speaking North, Francophone West and Central, as well as Anglophone Africa. Here we shall consider in some detail two from Ghana and Nigeria respectively, two from Egypt, and through these students, several others from Ghana, Cameroon, South Africa and Nigeria.[29]

While considering these ZNU discussions in August 2010, with some of the same issues as before with Kenya, we shall pay more attention to the relations with the university itself and to the role of African student associations. Like the debate above on whether African views of China

---

[28] See further on the relationship, Nordtveit (2010a: 102).
[29] Unless otherwise mentioned, all interviews with ZNU students took place in August 2010.

are positive or negative, so here too there is some controversy over the quality of educational experience of African students. Nor of course are these debates about quality restricted to African students in ZNU. The journal *Nature* has raised questions about the quality of China's degrees in science especially because of their allegedly being pursued in a Chinese medium at the same time as the language is being acquired.[30] This is not of course the case; on the other hand it is certain that many African students on CSC awards continue formally to study Chinese after their initial immersion year of Chinese language training.

Switching from French to Chinese language teaching
In our discussion of the Kenyans, we had talked of examples of students switching from studying in OECD countries to studying in China. With the first of our ZNU students, the original intention had been to study at the Masters level in French in order to become qualified as a French teacher in Ghana. She had then heard about the Chinese scholarships and about the possible development of a Confucius Institute in one of the major universities in Ghana. Indeed, Chinese had begun to be taught in her university even before a decision had been taken on a Confucius Institute, thus illustrating the key role of the enabling environment for the spread of Chinese;[31] so she had come on a CSC award to ZNU, specifically to help build up Ghanaian capacity in teaching Chinese. Surprisingly, she had failed to be allocated to the masters on teaching Chinese as a foreign language for the whole of her first year, but this was sorted out in her second year. That aside, the facilities in ZNU were good; the computing very good. Also accommodation and food were fine. Shortly, there was a completely new hostel for international students, but again that would be separate from the Chinese students.

Beyond her professional development in Chinese, she had also thrown herself very actively into the seminars and workshops for African teachers who come to the resource base in ZNU for short courses in

---

[30] 'Other researchers argue that China's efforts aren't always tailored to Africa's needs. For example, China already sponsors long-term training programmes for African students, who move to China for several years, taking language courses while they study science in Chinese. Students see the experience as a good career move, but once they return to Africa, "the calibre of such scientists is very low", says Chinsembu, a molecular biologist at the   University of Namibia, noting that the students struggle to assimilate scientific concepts in a foreign language. "Most cannot pass local examinations here in African universities"' (Cyranowski, 2010: 477).

[31] It was reported that an agreement had been signed between the Chinese Language Council in Beijing and the University of Ghana for teaching Chinese language and culture from the 2008/9 academic year. http://www.modernghana.com/news/160374/1/legon-teaches-chinese.html

education. She had undertaken a study with one of the Institute of African Studies' staff of other African students in ZNU. Further, she had planned to write a joint research paper with a Chinese doctoral student working on China's aid to Africa. She had begun to think about China-Ghana cooperation and more broadly, China-African cooperation. Here her preliminary conclusion was that China's aid was different from other aid; it was win-win economic cooperation and not colonisation. On the other hand, she recognised that the Chinese clearly knew what they wanted. But she was not so sure that the Africans had worked out what they wanted from the relationship with China.

Country unions and scholarships in support of African students in China
Perhaps because of the presence of an Institute of African Studies in ZNU, several of its students were aware of the place of African student associations.

Issues such as students being placed on apparently inappropriate courses in China raise the question of whether national associations of African students can play a role in sorting out such anomalies. Very few African countries with students in China have such associations, however. Those which do, such as Cameroon, Sierra Leone and Ghana, do not claim to have national coverage in China. Thus, the international branch of the National Union of Ghanaian Students (NUGS) in China is said by its current President to have about 1,000 members, and although every Ghanaian student, public or private, in China is automatically a member, only 250 have actually registered, of which 122 are active.[32] There are currently eleven branches in different cities on the Mainland. Interestingly, the eleven branches do not include either Hong Kong or Macao. There is an annual Congress, most recently on 24 October in 2012.

It is interesting to note that the current President of NUGS-China is not aware of the existence of any more general African students' union (ASU) or association in China. This says something about its visibility; and one of the other executives of NUGS-China has said:

> I have not heard of ASU. I don't know how strong it is. If it were in Wuhan I would have heard of it by now. The association probably exists but is not very active, because China is still warming up to the

---

[32] See the active and well-developed website for the National Union of Ghanaian Students-China: http://nugschina.com/

idea of associations and gatherings; so they might be keeping a low profile.

In fact, there is just one known branch today of an Africa-wide association in China and that is the General Union of African Students in Tianjin (GUAST).[33] Earlier on, we know from Gillespie (2001) that there was a General Union of African Students in China (GUASC) which had played an active role in 1996 on the living allowances of those on CSC awards. We also know that the GUASC was involved in defending African students in the China-Africa Nanjing riots in early 1989.[34] It seems likely, however, given the year of these Nanjing riots, that the authorities would have discouraged the continuation of Africa-wide unions or associations.

It would be valuable to have a full tally of the active national student associations or unions in China. As mentioned, we are presently aware of just three West African unions, Ghana, Cameroon and Sierra Leone;[35] there are also an Egyptian, a Tanzanian and a Ugandan student association in China. Perhaps not surprisingly, there is no Nigerian students' union of students in China, given the sensitive nature of China-Nigeria relations which we shall come to below. But there is an association called Young African Professionals and Students (YAPS).[36] This non-profit organisation only dates from 2009 but it is not clear from its website how active or widespread it is. Its most recent site visitors were many weeks earlier.

The other issue that surfaces is the overall composition of Ghanaian students in China. According to the current President of NUGS-China, about 95 per cent of them are said to be privately funded, and most of these are doing medicine. The small minority are on China government scholarships, or on Ghana government scholarships, or on both.[37] This last category raises an issue which appears to be of importance particularly to a number of Francophone African countries; there it is the government policy that, if students secure a China Scholarship Council (CSC) award,

---

[33] Over the last 12 years it has had presidents from Tanzania, Cameroon, Gabon, Mali, Nigeria and Sierra Leone.

[34] See the LA Times on the mention of the President of the Nanjing chapter of the GUASC being detained at the time of the riots: http://articles.latimes.com/1989–01–04/news/mn-140_1_african-students.

[35] For the Sierra Leone Students Union in China which was established in 1993, and which has a current membership of 121 members, on all of which there is full detail of university affiliation and discipline on the website, see http://www.slsuc.com/

[36] This is referred to in an interesting article by Ferdjani (2012).

[37] The president of the NUGS-China, for instance, is on both a China and Ghana government scholarship.

they are automatically eligible for a counterpart scholarship from the national government. Amongst the countries which have adopted this policy are Gabon, Benin, Chad, Senegal and Mali. Of course, what this suggests is that the CSC award is not sufficient to cover the costs of being in China, although CSC stipends for international students are more generous than local Chinese awards.

In the case of the Cameroon, for instance, this 'top-up' of China Scholarship Council awards is almost mandatory. Indeed, a great deal of the activity of the Cameroon Students Association in China (CSAC), which counts 200 members, is concerned with trying to ensure that the Government of Cameroon pays these allowances.[38] This issue is very visible on its website. Currently, the sum involved is some $US 160 a month from the Cameroon Government. This is said to be particularly important for postgraduate students in the sciences where there are additional costs of laboratory work.

Some of the most common issues faced by these national unions or associations, according to the President of the National Union of Ghanaian Students in China, are, first, transfer to another university in order to pursue a more appropriate course. Insisting on a transfer can incur a fine of some US$ 160 and the possible cancellation of the student visa. A second issue is the importance of pursuing practical training back in Africa, whether in medicine or in teaching Chinese. It is sometimes difficult to arrange this because of cost or of the absence back home of parallel equipment as is found in Chinese medical faculties. Third, a continuing issue for students on CSC awards, despite many Africans being very good at second, third or fourth language learning, is whether one year of immersion in Chinese is really sufficient to deal with an undergraduate or graduate course taught entirely in Chinese.

Egyptians studying Chinese and Chinese studying Arabic: a more equal partnership?
Unlike the start of teaching Chinese in the University of Yaounde II in the late 1990s, in Nairobi from 2005, and in University of Legon in Accra from 2008, Ain Shams University in Egypt was teaching Chinese from 1958. It has been joined by four other universities since 2000, and there are now some 1,000 students studying Chinese in Ain Shams alone (Nordtveit,

---

[38] See the website of the Cameroon Students Association in China: http://www.camerchine.com/ home.php. CSAC was founded in 1996 and it too has a regular annual congress.

2010b: 62).[39] Also, the provision of scholarships is more symmetrical, with Egypt providing 20 to Chinese students and China providing 50 to Egypt. It is not yet known if these arrangements have changed since the fall in 2011 of Hosni Mubarak. He had been a firm friend of China over many years, having visited there some ten times, and having hosted the Fourth FOCAC Summit in Sharm El Shaikh in November 2009.[40]

One of the Egyptian students pursuing the Masters in Teaching Chinese as a Foreign Language in ZNU said that this could be done instead of military service. Again, this may have changed. As far as the teaching and learning environment in ZNU was concerned, it was much superior to Ain Shams, even though the university was in a provincial city rather than the Chinese capital. There were no less than 10 Egyptians including himself following this same masters and two pursuing doctoral studies from their own university but in ZNU. His interest was vocational, as he had already worked for two years in a Chinese firm in Egypt, and now wanted to improve his language skills.

By contrast, the second Egyptian had already been studying Chinese for four years in Ain Shams. His interest was very different; it was in languages themselves and especially Asian languages. It is too easily assumed that foreign study is entirely vocational; so it is refreshing to recall that there are intrinsic rationales for study as well:

> My interest was in the way languages function – the mystery. For me it was like a moth to a flame – a magnet. So I am not sure that I came here for work or for jobs, but rather for interest, to learn more about the language.

Ideally, he would have liked more time to study Chinese literature, go to films and read books. But he found he was studying the whole time. 'The Chinese religion is hard work!'.

This intrinsic delight in the Chinese language and literature was shared by another student from Cameroon, who was deliberately taking a second BA, this time in East China Normal University in Shanghai, in order to understand Chinese literature. This is an aspect of China-Africa

---

[39] There is good deal of detail in *China-Africa Education Cooperation* on the dramatic growth of interest in Chinese in Ain Shams University, and in 2005 there were in the Department of Chinese Language: eight associate professors; 18 lecturers, and six assistant lecturers. These are all Egyptian, but China had sent some 50 Chinese lecturers to Ain Shams since 1954 (China, MOE, 2005: 60-62).

[40] On his arrival for the FOCAC Beijing Summit in November 2006, he had declared: 'For me, visiting China is like going home. Egypt sees China more as a brother than as an ordinary friendly nation.' (Hosni Mubarak, former Egyptian President, 1.11.06) See further, King (2006b).

cooperation that is too often neglected in the emphasis on win-win economic cooperation. In fact, cultural cooperation and exchange is also an integral part of *China's African Policy*.[41] The student explained his own position further:

> Since China is very positive about the African Union I thought it was important to know more about who the Africans were dealing with. The politicians know the politics, but the culture is so deep I thought I could be a bridge between China and Africa. [42] Like many Cameroonians, I had liked martial arts in Cameroon. Then I had studied history, world history, and Chinese history which is the oldest in the world. Right now I am focusing on the literature of China – novels, poems, *The Dream of Red Mansions*, Lu Xun, Ba Jin, – the evolution of Shanghai society. I know about Peking opera and the special dialect it is sung in.

In his view, there was however something profoundly unequal at the moment in this cultural exchange and cooperation between China and Africa. China was promoting its language and culture worldwide, including in Africa, through the Confucius Institutes, cultural centres and scholarships. But how many Chinese students and scholars were there in Africa studying the diversity of its cultures? He did not believe that Chinese had nothing to learn from Africa's cultures and history. On the side of African governments, he had noted that they had not promoted a single African cultural centre in the whole of China.[43] His own personal contribution to this cultural exchange was to be involved in writing a book, in Chinese, on African tales and wisdom.

A last issue raised by this thoughtful Cameroonian student of Chinese literature was that there was still quite a large gap between many of the OECD student destinations and China. In many of these OECD countries, students who can manage to stay on and get work over a period of years can eventually secure citizenship, whether of Canada, USA, Sweden or another country. This is not possible in the case of China,

---

[41] China will implement agreements of cultural cooperation and relevant implementation plans reached with African countries, maintain regular contacts with their cultural departments and increase exchanges of artists and athletes. It will guide and promote cultural exchanges in diverse forms between people's organizations and institutions in line with bilateral cultural exchange programs and market demand' (China, 2006: 8).

[42] He was able to fulfil this bridge role by acting as compere in Mandarin to introduce the African musical groups to the Chinese audience at the Shanghai Expo in 2010.

[43] By contrast there are three Chinese cultural centres in Africa, in Mauritius, Benin, and Egypt. Gontin (2009) has also argued that 'The continent is culturally absent in China.'

and the same is true of Japan. Effectively, he argued, this reduces the brain drain out of Africa as far as China is concerned.

Nigerian students in China: the promise and the challenge

Our last discussion with a ZNU student was appropriately with a Nigerian. After a Bachelor's degree in education at Ibadan, he had taught, and then become involved with the private educational institutions (both university and secondary school) associated with the former president, Obasanjo. The company's intention had been for him to study higher education administration in China. However, he was allocated a scholarship to teach Chinese as a foreign language. As Obasanjo Holdings was also involved with the Chinese in packaging and in agro-allied activities, business Chinese would have been a better alternative. Still, there were always possibilities perhaps of using his language degree should a Confucius Institute become linked to his university of technology in Nigeria.

His own considered view of his first year in China was positive; he felt he was well received in China and in ZNU in particular. If there were negative perceptions about Africa, he felt that on the whole these derived from lack of exposure to Africa; so he found the ordinary Chinese people had no problem with Africans. There was however a serious problem at the higher policy level *vis à vis* Nigerians in China. Because some Nigerians had been involved in criminal activity in China, there had been a tendency to generalise suspicion to all Nigerians. Thus, even in ZNU, his wife had not been allowed to study Chinese, though he had been ready to pay fees, and she had had to renew her visa much more frequently than would be the case with other Africans and their families.[44]

It is paradoxical that when it was Obasanjo who was responsible for making it very easy for Chinese businesses to come into Nigeria in very large numbers, someone working with Chinese employees in Obasanjo Holdings should find his family in such difficulty in terms of staying in China. From his own small-scale research and visits to other universities in China it would appear that several universities will not consider admitting Nigerian students. Illustrative of this becoming a major problem in China-Nigeria relations is that one of his Chinese friends who was in the Study Abroad business made a special point of going to Nigeria and seeking to interest young Nigerians in considering China as a

---

[44] For additional problems faced by Nigerian migrants, see Haugen, 2012.

student destination. After a long stay in Nigeria, he could not recruit a single candidate.

The crisis is widely described in blogs and other fora on Nigeria and China; which merely intensifies the suspicions on both sides. Thus 'The situation of Nigerians in China' posted in the Nigeria Forum[45] paints a very different picture from that of the Chinese ambassador in Nigeria's speech in *This Day* newspaper in 2011 under the title of 'Good brothers, good friends and good partners'[46] or the Chargé d'Affaires' speech in August 2011 to China scholarship holders and other trainees departing for China.[47] The latter was celebrating the fact that there were over 300 officials and technicians going on short-term training seminars in China annually, and no less than 100 long-term scholars in China at any one time. Equally, he mentioned that 10 Chinese students had just completed their studies of the Hausa language in Bayero University in Kano, thus underlining that it was a two-way partnership.

It is worth noting that our former student in ZNU is now back in Nigeria and is happily involved in a joint energy venture with the Chinese. His concerns regarding the widespread suspicions about Nigerians in China have not at all affected his own working relations with the Chinese.

Former President of the General Union of African Students in Tianjin (GUAST) reflects on his experience

The former president had studied in Tianjin University between 2003 and 2009, completing his doctorate, and had returned to the University of Agriculture in Nigeria. As a Nigerian who had played a leadership role in GUAST, he was very clear that African students 'most or all of the time face prejudice from the Chinese Government and especially Nigerians, even though China has strong business links with Nigeria. The reasons are not far to seek as many Nigerians have displayed dubious or unacceptable behaviour within the Chinese community which has produced stigmatisation' (Former student to KK, 6 November 2011).

We have mentioned earlier that his personal view about the attitudes of the African students responding to the Sautman and Yan questionnaire he had administered in 2008, and from his own individual interviews was

---

[45] http://www.topix.com/forum/world/nigeria/TBGO83PK278FD
[46] http://ng.china-embassy.org/eng/xw/t794324.htm. The Nigerian ambassador to China admitted in 2009 that Nigerians were responsible for about 90% of the crimes committed by Africans in China (Taylor, 2011: 87).
[47] http://ng.china-embassy.org/eng/xw/t850456.htm

that 'the majority of African respondents were negative about their experience of the Chinese.' Indeed, some respondents had added that they felt the provision of scholarships from China was a 'second colonisation of Africa'. His own personal view on racial prejudice in China towards Africa was that some African students never saw anything good about China because of the discrimination displayed by Chinese towards Africans while there. The racial abuse he felt was directed at skin colour instead of taking account of the positive contribution of the African communities in China. Overall, as was mentioned earlier in this chapter, his own view on this sensitive issue was clear: 'If I would rate or summarise the attitude of African students towards China on a scale of positive, slightly positive, indifferent, slightly negative and negative, I will say NEGATIVE.'

In this connection, it is worth underlining that the survey he was helping to administer was not based on just a handful of Africans in one university; rather it covered Tianjin University, Tianjin University of Traditional Medicine, Tianjin Normal, Tianjin University of Technology and Education, Tianjin Polytechnic University, Nankai University, Tianjin University of Finances and Tianjin Foreign Studies University.

He was clear that one could not strictly compare attitudes gained from a survey of African students in China in 1997 (Gillespie's survey) and from 2008 (Sautman and Yan). Much had changed, including many of the university rules, the former Communist ideology, and not least the influence of the market economy. But he felt that though there had been some positive responses in the survey he had helped administer, these were because the African students were making positive statements about the marketability and acceptability of Chinese goods in Africa rather than about Chinese attitudes towards Africans and African students in China.

Furthermore, he was certain that the FOCAC process and particularly the Beijing Summit of November 2006 had helped change African leaders' mentality about Chinese prejudice towards Africa. But on the ground, he felt that if it came to any dispute between African students and Chinese authorities, it was obvious that the law was on the side of the Chinese. For this reason, he added, 'many Africans, including himself, would not want to stay in China for a long time.' Nevertheless, despite the legal and racial problems, the sheer availability of Chinese scholarships and the relatively low cost of study and of living were continuing to draw students to China.

Moving from these wider issues of racial attitude to the crucial question of the impact of studying in China on himself, he would be the first to admit that the work ethic of the Chinese students and faculty had altered his own approach to his job: 'This had really changed my attitude to work and to my lectures as a lecturer. I hardly ever come to class late or to appointments; moreover I have banished that phrase "African time" from my diction'!

From African student to African business in China and Cameroon

Almost the last of our profiles in this section is also not with a ZNU student, but with a Cameroonian who had come to China in 1998. On the racial discrimination against Africans, he had a balanced view; of course many African students had experience of racism and were bitter about it. However, there was absolutely no point in pursuing this. On the other hand, African students recognised that China was a good place to see how development was actually working out in practice. There were also powerful messages to be learned in China about the value of hard work and the importance of discipline.

Not surprisingly, given the shortage of work back home, many Africans elect to stay on in China, and they explore joint business opportunities with China. This student had started a consulting company in 2005 which specialised in providing Africans with access to China and vice versa. He had also found a role in facilitating China-Africa business development after the 2006 FOCAC summit. His knowledge of Mandarin was vital in these ventures.

A South African student in China

Although the illustrations have come from Kenya primarily, they could have been drawn from Ethiopia or from South Africa. One of the South Africans, a graduate from Stellenbosch, spent five and half years in China. It was hugely influential on his later behaviour, not least because of the Chinese impact on his own work culture:

> I was never late for class. Except once. When I came late, the only place was right at the front. I went down there and the professor offered me a cigarette, and then lit it for me. I smoked it surreptitiously but I was never late again. Being in China affected my own behaviour later on. I will never forget this episode in my whole life.

There is a view that contradicts this positive connection between the gains of education and the move into China-Africa business. Rather it argues that the social and educational environment in Chinese universities does not impress the students. Allegedly this disappointment with the educational experience obstructs the promotion of Chinese values such as those just mentioned, thus obliterating the soft power potential of Sino-African educational exchanges. It is in part this discontent with the quality of the education in China that leads to African students turning to trade instead of their studies in China (Haugen, 2012b). There are examples of this, but most of our Kenyan and other students do not confirm this view.

Aid-supported English medium Masters training in China

We have mentioned already that the mainstream government-supported scholarship scheme in China, associated with the China Scholarship Council (CSC) gives strong priority to learning Chinese in an intensive year of language training before embarking on the substantive degree. This emphasises the crucial importance of students getting inside the language and culture as well as their learning alongside Chinese students in their main years of study. However, as in many other countries providing scholarships, there is not a single highway for scholarship support in China. We have, for example earlier in this chapter and elsewhere, looked at the range of scholarships associated with the Chinese Language Council (Hanban) via Confucius Institutes in Africa (King, 2017).

Here we shall briefly mention the emergence of a very different modality, following the FOCAC IV of 2009 in Sharm El Shaikh. This was a Masters in Public Administration and it was offered in Tsinghua University and also in Peking University.[48] The aim was specifically to serve the needs of some 200 middle and senior level African officials. The medium of instruction was English and hence there was no major emphasis on acquiring Mandarin before starting the course. Although some parts of the course were taken only by officials from developing countries, there were apparently some courses that were shared with Chinese students of international public administration.

At the same time in the field of educational administration two intensive International Masters in Education degrees were also initiated,

---

[48] It appears to have started in Peking University even earlier than FOCAC IV.

one in East China Normal University (ECNU) and one in North East Normal University. These were delivered entirely in English, and the students from Africa who were on them were taught separately from Chinese students. Surprisingly for Chinese Masters degrees, the new Masters in ECNU was delivered in just one year, as compared with Masters of three years where there is a year of Mandarin as a precondition.

One of the Zimbabwean students on the ECNU masters found the course so influential that she decided to come back at her own expense but with a particular desire to catch up more on Chinese culture and language for she had not had the time during her first very pressured one-year Masters degree. She had not fully worked out how China benefits from all these students they fund, 'but one thing is certain: it is fast becoming a place where people want to be!' (Zimbabwean student to KK, 10 November 2011).

Issues for further reflection and policy analysis

This tour around some of the history of African students in China and some of the debates brought up by our discussions in Kenya as well as in China suggests a number of avenues for further reflection.

Contested perceptions on racial discrimination and prejudice

We have noted from Hevi's, Gillespie's and Sautman's analyses and studies that there are very strong comments that Chinese and African students in China have been prepared to make about each other. On the other hand, in Sautman and Yan's more recent and not yet fully analysed work, there are signs of a discernible shift. At the level of the individual African student or graduate returnee with whom we have discussed this, we have encountered a good deal of maturity about this issue, and a recognition that prejudice is often related to ignorance. The pace of internationalisation of China's universities is certain to continue to have a positive impact on the awareness of Africa. But the fact that one of the recent presidents of the General Union of African Students in Tianjin should consider attitudes towards Chinese students by Africans still to be largely negative must continue to be a source of serious policy concern.[49]

---

[49] The fact that he is a Nigerian and must be aware of the critical generalisations about Nigerian students in China may be worth bearing in mind.

Interestingly, one of the most recent publications on African students in China discusses many different issues but reserves just four lines for the issue of racial discrimination, as follows:

> We're used to it by now but it's still annoying to be a black person in China on a daily basis. We have to endure the rudeness of taxi drivers, people in public transportation, etc. And it's not really a communication problem because I speak fluent Mandarin. It's not necessarily racism. But it's ignorance! (Ferdjani, 2012: 28)

Very powerful positive impacts on attitudes and values at individual and institutional levels?
One of the constant refrains from both present and past African students in China is their admiration of the work ethic of their Chinese student counterparts. This has also led to a fascinating set of claims about the impact on the individuals of being exposed to this particular culture of work. How these influences can in turn translate into the working environment back home is a very different issue. Civil service traditions are notoriously difficult to change, unless the incentive and management systems are changed.

These challenges to the transfer of attitudes and values, as well as of knowledge, were tackled by the Commonwealth Scholarship Commission's evaluation of impact in what they called key priority areas. The intention of the survey was to find some answers to the following questions:

- Did the award benefit you in terms of your individual knowledge and skills?
- Did the award, and those skills, benefit you in terms of your employment and career?
- Have you been able to pass on those skills and that knowledge?
- Has your award increased your ability to have an impact on your place of work?
- Have you maintained links with contacts in the UK?
- Have you been able to have an impact on wider society? (CSCUK, 2009: 18)

The Commission would acknowledge that individual assessments of these questions are highly subjective and notoriously difficult to demonstrate; nevertheless the great majority of returnees were able to point to very specific illustrations of knowledge transfer and influence.

There could well be a case for research in China to carry out something parallel. There has been an equally long time frame; there have been policy shifts over this lengthy period. Certainly, there would be an interest in how graduates of Chinese universities are received back in their own public and private sectors. Many of the questions about individual, institutional and societal impact are equally of concern to the Chinese policy and academic community as they are to the Commonwealth. There would be widespread interest within comparator scholarship agencies about the results of any such survey, whether Africa-wide or restricted to four or five countries in the first instance.

Exploring impact via associations or unions of African students in China
Although we have noted that unions or associations of African students in China still have a slightly uncertain legal standing, a few of them operate vibrant websites and have good data on their coverage and branches, and even on the individual members, in the case of the Sierra Leone Union of Students in China. This might suggest that they could play a role in identifying former members of their unions or associations who had already returned home. It is not immediately clear from their websites if there is an African students' alumni association operating at the country level. In the case of Ghana, 'Alumni' are referred to on the home page menu, but this is one of the pages still under construction. It is, however, known from our student discussions that Cameroon does have an active alumni association for former students in China. The most readily accessible associations seem to be Cameroon, Ghana and Sierra Leone, with Ghana claiming, at least amongst these, to have the largest number of members in China. It should also be recalled that former Kenya students in China had formed an alumni association as early as April 2003 (China, MOE, 2005: 20).

It would also be possible to use the good offices of the General Union of African Students in Tianjin (GUAST), which appears to be well organised, but only covers a single city.

Perhaps in these days of social networking sites, alumni associations may be replaced by other mechanisms. The numbers of graduates are presumably still too small for particular universities in China to be maintaining associations in Africa in the manner of leading US and UK universities.

Exchanges of students or predominantly one-way scholarship flows and targets
China historically has preferred the language of student 'exchange', as in
its African policy rather than presenting itself simply as a provider of
scholarships.[50] The reality seems to be that there are few countries in
Africa, with the exception of Egypt, which independently send students
to China on national scholarships. Rather, we have noted that in the case
of several especially Francophone countries, their national scholarships
seem to be added on to those candidates who are awarded a China
Scholarship. They become therefore a kind of additional allowance,
topping up the CSC award.

The introduction of targets for both long-term and short-term
awards within the FOCAC framework reinforces the emphasis on
one-way flows rather than exchanges. This particular focus for the
presentation of scholarships and training awards dates from the Second
FOCAC conference of 2003 in Addis Ababa, but it caught world attention
in the Beijing Summit of FOCAC of 2006. Up to a month before the
Summit, the language in the draft declaration had been incremental:
'Gradually increase the number of scholarships for African students in
China, which now stands at 1,200 per year'. Within a few weeks, it had
become: 'Increase the number of Chinese government scholarships to
African students from the current 2000 per year to 4,000 per year by 2009'
(FOCAC, 2006a; 2006b. 5.4.4.).

The salience of target-setting in the discourse of international
education in general has been sharply criticised by Jansen in his
'Targeting education: the politics of performance and the prospects of
"Education for All"' (2005). There is a sense in which the targets become
the policy, or become a substitute for policy. The same is true for the
Millennium Development Goals (MDGs) and the whole evaluative
apparatus that has been constructed around them.

We should not exaggerate the significance of the scholarships having
become a key FOCAC target. But it does then mean that there has to be a
mechanism for determining that the target has been met. This was duly
put in place with the formation of the Chinese Follow-up Committee of
FOCAC (King, 2009). There is no parallel African Follow-up Committee
of FOCAC, presumably because it would be difficult across 50 different
African countries to track precise scholarship numbers. And in any case it

---

[50] Thus in *China's African Policy* (2006), the term 'exchange' appears no less than 18 times in just
eleven pages to describe different kinds of two-way collaboration. By the time of *China's Foreign
Aid* (2011), the term 'exchange' was only used once in 18 pages.

could be argued that FOCAC remains a bilateral mechanism with a Pan-African face. As far as scholarship numbers are concerned, short-term training awards, or any of the other pledges such as hospitals or schools, these continue to be agreed through bilateral arrangements.

In summary, although targets in education remain a valuable yardstick, in these days of agency concern with 'value-for-money', 'results' and 'impact', it would be valuable, through focused research, to be able to go beyond the merely quantitative achievements claimed in this way for education by *China's Foreign Aid* (2011:14):

> By the end of 2009, China had helped other developing countries build more than 130 schools, and funded 70,627 students from 119 developing countries to study in China. In 2009 alone, it extended scholarships to 11,185 foreign students who study in China. Furthermore, China has dispatched nearly 10,000 Chinese teachers to other developing countries, and trained more than 10,000 principals and teachers for them.

The other side of student exchange is of course the question of symmetry in Chinese students electing to take up scholarships offered to them in Africa, or electing to go on their own resources to Africa, or accepting Chinese scholarships to study in Africa. We know from the Ministry of Education's review of educational cooperation between China and Africa that sending Chinese students to Africa was seen as critical in improving China's understanding of Africa. Hence a first group of students were sent to Egypt very early on. We have already mentioned that Egypt offered on its own account scholarships to Chinese students. By the end of 2000, some 270 Chinese students had gone on Chinese scholarships to Egypt, Kenya, Morocco, South Africa, Senegal, Tanzania, Tunisia and some other countries (China, MOE, 2005: 21).

An increasing number of self-funded students from China also went to Africa. Indeed, the Chinese Ambassador in South Africa claimed that there were 1000 Chinese students in South Africa (Ambassador to KK 12 October 2012). This is not the principal focus of this chapter but it might still be insightful to note the safari to South Africa of Iris Wu, even if this is just a single enterprising, privately funded student:

> After trying three times to go to the US, she found she could go and do English for half a year in the Cape Peninsula University of Technology. She then went to the University of Port Elizabeth, but found it too quiet, and she wanted to combine study with work. So

she applied to the University of Western Cape, and was accepted in 2003, and completed honours and masters, and is now doing a PhD. In 2007, she started a Chinese restaurant in the university, and now has five staff, African, Chinese and white. The same year she started a Chinese Student Society to which any Chinese students can come. Shortly, she had organised a Chinese Education Exhibition which brought as many as 45 universities from China in 2007 and 62 in 2009 to advertise their courses, and offer scholarships to South Africa. Finally, and presumably to keep herself busy, she organised the first Confucius Classroom in the Cape Academy near Cape Town. In an opening ceremony on 2ⁿᵈ March 2010, the Chinese Consul General did the honours, and teaching of Chinese started on the 15ᵗʰ. (Iris Wu to KK 14 March 2010)

Towards a political economy of China's scholarships or a scholarship policy with Chinese characteristics

There are a number of issues that arise in the discussion of African students in China which are *sui generis*. First, there is the notion that the Chinese were the only people in the world to be free of racial prejudice (Snow, 1988: 204). This question of discrimination has been sufficiently raised in this chapter for it to be clear that there has been a continuing problem on this at different times, and at certain points this had threatened the wider political discourse about China-Africa cooperation and friendship.

Second, since the establishment of FOCAC in 2000, mentioned above, China appears to have pursued a genuinely Pan-African approach when it comes to the distribution of scholarships. Unlike some scholarship donors who focus on a particular subset of countries in Africa, China appears to offer scholarships in all of the 50+ African countries with which they have diplomatic relations. This is not to say that there is exactly the same quota for each of these but, given that there have been roughly 1,500 new scholarships per year since the Fourth FOCAC conference, the order of magnitude is approximately 30 awards annually per country. It will, however, be invaluable to know more about the distribution process. Illustrative of its working out in practice is that in a university like ZNU there are no less than 29 different African countries represented in their African student body, half of whom are on CSC or Confucius Institute awards.

Third, it has been argued that African student numbers were politicised following the events in Tiananmen Square in 1989, and that the visible absence of African government criticism of China was rewarded by doubling of scholarships (Nordtveit, 2011a: 101). On reflection, this seems unlikely given that in Nanjing, just a few months before Tiananmen, there had been large-scale anti-African protests. It would have been difficult in the wake of this event dramatically to increase African student numbers. The evidence points rather to the increases taking place in the later 1990s. Fourth, we started this chapter with a very strong ethical claim made by the Ministry of Education in respect of African students in China. These principles about people-to-people exchange, mutual benefit and friendship remain central to China's discourse about cooperation with other developing countries, even when the policy reality is that scholarships have become FOCAC targets and when there is little evidence of symmetry in terms of Chinese students going to Africa in large numbers. Arguably, however, these fundamental principles are not dependent on exact symmetry. Win-win economic, cultural or educational cooperation does not depend on precisely equal activities within the education sector but rather on a shared appreciation that the other party is an equal, and that there is mutuality across the range of both economic and social cooperation.

Lastly, there is the basic question of whether scholarships and the offer of Chinese language training, in China or in Africa, constitute soft power. The very term, 'soft power', with its emphasis on obtaining what 'one wants through cooption and attraction' (Jian, 2009) sounds very much at odds with the fundamental principles just mentioned above. Indeed, at first glance, soft power as a concept seems to sit rather outside the 'symbolic universe' of South-South cooperation which Mawdsley has proposed, based on solidarity, direct development expertise, empathy from shared experience, and the virtues of mutual benefit and reciprocity (Mawdsley, 2011; 2012). On the other hand, scholarships, whether from China, India, Brazil or South Korea, do give direct access to the development experience of countries that were until recently very poor. They may also be seen as a form of solidarity since they do not provide the host universities with very large fee incomes as UK and Australia do. Indeed, we have seen that the amount of the scholarship in China is such that some African countries deliberately top it up. As to mutual benefit and reciprocity, we have noted that there is no exact symmetry; 'student exchange' is actually more of a one-way than a two-way street. So too is cultural exchange, and especially since the development of the Confucius Institutes from 2004.

But the transfer back to Africa of some 12,000 CSC alumni or alumnae from China in the period from 2006 to 2012 alone is a substantial figure. As scholarship holders, they would have acquired Mandarin, and as we have seen in some of our student case studies, they find themselves teaching Chinese in both the public and private sectors, or getting involved in joint ventures with Chinese companies.

Assessing the reciprocity from China's point of view is complex. The explicit purpose on the China Scholarship Council website is short and applies to all international students, obviously, not just those from Africa. It is:

> In order to strengthen mutual understanding and friendship between the Chinese people and people from all over the world, and to develop cooperation and exchanges in fields of politics, economy, culture, education and trade between China and other countries. (CSC)[51]

How that ideal translates into practical action is not the responsibility of any Chinese ministry. But it obviously makes an enormous difference to the possibilities of using skills acquired in China, including the language, if there is a large and active Chinese presence back home. As compared to the pioneers who came back, and like our earliest Kenyan, might forget all about it, graduates are in some African countries returning to a situation where, as one Nigerian alumnus described it, the Chinese are 'in every nook and cranny' of his state. So the routine assessment of individual, institutional and societal impact of study abroad is very different if the graduate is returning to a unchanged or even disabling economic environment, as opposed to one where there are opportunities to use Mandarin skills as translators, interpreters, tourist guides or teachers. Thus the presence of large and growing communities of Chinese migrants is directly impacting on the utilisation of the language skills acquired abroad, not to mention other skills and knowledge.

The deliberate forging of links between graduates and China, in the manner of the Commonwealth's professional networks, has not yet happened, as far as is known. Chinese embassies in Africa tend to organise special functions when a large group of scholars or professional

---

[51] en.csc.edu.cn/Laihua/dd6ed814b3074388b197734f041a42bb.shtml

trainees is setting off for China. [52] But it would appear that active networking amongst the returned graduates has not yet happened apart from the case of Cameroon.

As far as reaching a neat conclusion about China's scholarship students from Africa is concerned, that is of course still possible, and eminently worthwhile, as it was in the case of the 2009 Commonwealth students' survey. But it needs to be remembered that it is now more than twenty years since privately funded students could apply to come to China. So whatever conclusions may be drawn about the 30 to 40 Ghanaians going annually on CSC awards to China, there are apparently around 1,000 Ghanaian students in China, as mentioned earlier, 95% of them privately funded, and many of these studying medicine. This presents suddenly a very different challenge to establishing what reciprocity between Ghana and China in aid-supported student numbers might mean. Equally, establishing the impact of Chinese study on the Ghanaian health sector would need to pay serious attention to the role of private Ghanaian students getting their medical training in China.

The same argument applies to those who would argue, as one of our case study students did in November 2011, that China is engaged in an undue degree of cultural diplomacy. He commented that, as far as China scholarships are concerned, 'some Africans are of the opinion that this is leading to a second colonisation of Africa.'

Back in 1989, the year that the South African cartoonist, Zapiro, did his famous sketch of the Fulbright scholars trekking back home with their American flags, there were no privately funded Ghanaians in China,[53] and the term soft power had not yet been used by Nye (1990). Now, just as 80 per cent of international undergraduate students in US higher education are self-funded, a similar situation is clearly true of Ghanaians in China (Belyavina, 2011: 67).

Fifty years after John Hevi, the Ghanaian author of *An African Student in China*, quit China in disgust along with 96 of the other 118 Africans whom China had brought to the Institute of Foreign Languages in Beijing, the Ghanaian students are back in China with branches of their national student association in eight cities. And unlike Hevi, the great majority are now paying to be there. More generally, of the 20,744 African students in

---

[52] See for example: en.csc.edu.cn/Laihua/dd6ed814b3074388b197734f041a42bb.shtml
[53] Self-funded students were allowed to come to China for the first time in 1989 (China, MOE, 2005: 15).

China in 2011, no less than 14,428 are privately funded and just 6,316 are on government scholarships (Gu, 2012).

References

Adamson, B, Nixon, J. and Su, F. (Eds) 2012. *The Reorientation of Higher Education: Challenging the East-West Dichotomy.* CERC Studies in Comparative Education 31, Comparative Education Research Centre, The University of Hong Kong, and Dordecht: Springer.

Belyavina, R. 2011. The United States as a destination for international student. *NORRAG News,* 45, Special Issue on the Geopolitics of Scholarships and Awards, 67-68. Accessed from www.norrag.org

Cheng, K. 1990. The culture of schooling in East Asia. In: Entwistle, N. (Ed.) *Handbook of Educational Ideas and Practices.* Routledge, London.

China, Ministry of Education, 2003. *China-Africa Education Cooperation,* Department of International Cooperation and Exchanges, Ministry of Education, Beijing.

China, Ministry of Education (MOE), 2005. *China-Africa Education Cooperation,* Peking University Press, Beijing (in Chinese).

China, People's Republic of, 2006. *China's African Policy,* 12 January 2006, downloaded from: www.gov.cn/misc/2006-01/12/content_156490.htm

China, People's Republic of, 2011. *China's Foreign Aid.* Information Office of the State Council, Beijing. Downloadable at http://www.scio.gov.cn/zxbd/wz/201104/t896900

Commonwealth Scholarship Commission in the UK (CSCUK). 2009. *Evaluating Commonwealth Scholarships in the UK: Assessing Impact in Key Priority Areas.* Commonwealth Scholarship Commission, London.

Cyranowski, D. 2010. China boosts African research links. *Nature,* 464, 25 March 2010.

Dikötter, F. 1992. *The Discourse on Race in Modern China.* Hurst, London.

Ferdjani, H. 2012. *African Students in China: An Exploration of Their Increasing Numbers and Their Motivations in Beijing.* Centre for Chinese Studies, September 2012, University of Stellenbosch, Stellenbosch.

Forum on China-Africa Cooperation (FOCAC), 2006a. *Beijing Action Plan (2007-2009)* Draft of October 2006, FOCAC, Beijing.

FOCAC (Forum on China-Africa Cooperation). 2006b. *Forum on China-Africa Cooperation. Action Plan (2007-2009),* 16th November 2006, FOCAC, Ministry of Foreign Affairs, Beijing. Downloadable from: www.fmprc.gov.cn/zflt/eng/ltda/dscbzjhy/DOC32009/t280369.htm

Gillespie, S. 2001. *South-South Transfer: A Study of Sino-African Exchanges.* Routledge, New York.

Gontin, M. 2009. China's cultural interest in Sino-African cultural exchanges, *Pambazuka News*, 31 January 2009, No.417. *http:// pambazuka.org/en/category/africa_china/53759*

Gu, J. 2012. New developments in the internationalization of higher education in China and implications for China-Africa cooperation in higher education, International Forum on Higher Education Exchange and Cooperation, 10-11 September 2012, Zhejiang Normal University, Jinhua.

Haugen, H. 2012. Nigerians in China: A second state of immobility. *International Migration*, 50 (2), 65-80.

Haugen, H. 2013. China's recruitment of African university students: policy efficacy and unintended outcomes. *Globalisation, Societies and Education*, 11, 3, 315-334.

He, W. 2006. Educational exchange and cooperation between China and Africa. In: 3rd Roundtable Discussion on African Studies, organised by African Studies Group, University of Hong Kong, 25th May 2006, Hong Kong.

Hevi, E. J. 1963. *An African Student in China.* Praeger, London.

Jansen, J. 2005. Targeting education: the politics of performance and the prospects of Education for All. *International Journal of Educational Development*, 25, 368-380.

King, K. 2006. Aid within the wider China-Africa partnership: a view from the Beijing Summit. In: China-Africa Links Workshop, 11-12 November 2006, Hong Kong University of Science and Technology, Hong Kong. King. K. 2007c. Commitment to learning: China's treasure within. In: Living Knowledge Seminar, March 2007, Jinguan Community Learning Centre, Gansu Province, China.

King, K. 2009. China's education cooperation with Africa. Meeting the FOCAC targets? In: Africa Day Workshop African Studies Programme, HKU, 25th May 2009, University of Hong Kong, Hong Kong.

King, K. 2010. China's cooperation with Africa, and especially South Africa, in education and training. A special relationship and a different approach to aid? *Journal of International Cooperation in Education*, 13 (2), 73-88.

King, K. 2011a. China's cooperation with Ethiopia. With a focus on human resources. *OSSREA Bulletin*, VIII, 1, 88-113. Accessed at: http://www.ossrea.net./images/stories.ossrea/bulletin-feb-2011.pdf

King, K. 2011b. Skills development and lifelong learning. Challenges for poverty reduction, sustainable growth and employability. In: International Symposium on Lifelong Learning January 12-13, 2011, Hong Kong Institute for Education, Hong Kong, accessed at: www.ied.edu.hk/isll/Keynote_present.html

King, K. 2012. Sino-African relations and the internationalization of China's universities. In: Adamson, B, Nixon, J. and Su. F. (eds). 2012. *The Reorientation of Higher Education: Challenging the East-West Dichotomy*. Comparative Education Research Centre, University of Hong Kong/Springer, Hong Kong, 134-147.

King, K. 2017. Confucius Institutes in Africa: Culture and language without controversy? In Batchelor, K and Zhang, X. (Eds.), *China-Africa relations: Building images through cultural cooperation, media representation and on the ground activities*. Routledge, London.

Li, J. 2012. World-class higher education and the emerging Chinese model of the university. *Prospects*. 42, 319-339.

Marris, P. and Somerset, H.C.A. 1971. *African Businessmen: A Study of Entrepreneurship and Development in Kenya*. Routledge and Kegan Paul, London.

Mawdsley, E. 2011. The changing geographies of foreign aid and development cooperation: contributions from gift theory. *Transactions of the Institute of British Geographers*, NS 2011, The Royal Geographical Society, London.

Nordtveit, B. 2010. China and Egypt: The continuation of a long friendship. *NORRAG News*, 44, 60-63; downloadable at www.norrag.org

Nordtveit, B. 2011. An emerging donor in education and development: a case study of China in Cameroon. *International Journal of Educational Development*, 31, 2, 99-108.

Nye, J. 1990. *Bound to Lead: The Changing Nature of American Power*, Basic Books, New York.

Sautman, B. 1994. Anti-Black racism in post-Mao China. *The China Quarterly*, 138, 413-437.

Sautman, B. and Yan, H. 2009. African perspectives on China-Africa links, *The China Quarterly*, 199, 749-51.

Snow, P. 1988. *The Star Raft. China's Encounter with Africa*. Weidenfeld and Nicolson, London.

Taylor, I. 2011. *The Forum on China-Africa Cooperation (FOCAC)*. Routledge, Abingdon.

Wu, Y. 2012. The rise of China's state-led media dynasty in Africa.

Occasional Paper no 117, South African Institute of International Affairs, University of the Witwatersrand, Johannesburg.

Wyatt, D.J. 2010. *The Blacks of Premodern China: Encounters with Asia.* University of Pennsylvania Press, Philadelphia.

Chapter 12

Several institutional threads lay behind the paper that follows. One of these, mentioned earlier, is that there had gradually been building over the first decade of the 2000s in many international agencies and foundations a recognition that, despite the narrow focus of the Millennium Development Goals (MDGs), technical and vocational education and training, or skills development, were crucial elements in economic growth as well as in diversified career development. The year 2012 had certainly been a very rich for those interested in the links between skills and jobs, and it had seen the launch of a number of major global reports on this topic. In May, came the International Labour Organization's *World of Work Report 2012* (ILO, 2012) and the *Shanghai Consensus* of UNESCO's Third International Congress on Technical and Vocational Education and Training (UNESCO, 2012a), as well as the new OECD skills strategy, *Better skills, better jobs, better lives* (OECD, 2012). In June, the McKinsey Global Institute's *The world at work: Jobs, pay and skills for 3.5 billion people* (McKinsey, 2012) arrived, and October saw two more: the World Bank's *World Development Report 2013* on *Jobs* (World Bank, 2012), and the long-awaited EFA Global Monitoring Report 2012 on *Youth and skills: Putting education to work* (UNESCO, 2012b).

Several more examples had been evident in the two previous years. The OECD had carried out a whole series of reviews on *Learning for jobs* (OECD, 2010). NORRAG, through Michel Carton and myself, had coordinated 10 years of reports by the Working Group for International Cooperation on Skills Development, and in particular had partnered with India's Institute of Applied Manpower Research in organizing with Santosh Mehrotra a conference and a report on *The challenges facing skills development in India: An issues paper* (IAMR, 2010). There had also been a special issue of *NORRAG News (NN46)* on *Towards a new global world of*

Kenneth King (2019): *Education, Skills and International Cooperation: Comparative and Historical Perspectives*. Hong Kong: Comparative Education Research Centre (CERC), The University of Hong Kong, and Dordrecht: Springer. © CERC

© Springer Nature Switzerland AG 2019
K. King, *Education, Skills and International Cooperation*, CERC Studies
in Comparative Education 36, https://doi.org/10.1007/978-3-030-29790-9_12

skills development: TVET's turn to make its mark (*NORRAG News*, 2011). NORRAG, furthermore, arranged a special issue on the year itself: *2012: The year of global reports on TVET, skills and jobs* (NORRAG News 48, 2013). Both these and other NORRAG special issues continued the RRAG tradition of critically analyzing a large and complex body of work and producing a sharp state of the art review on it from multiple perspectives, both South and North. This was also attempted in the article that follows on the extraordinary skills ambitions of India. Again, it was important to set India's massive skills initiative within an historical context of how skills had traditionally been acquired in South Asia, largely through training on the job and informal apprenticeships. At the same time, international 'best practice'[1] was encouraging India to explore national qualification frameworks and sector skills councils, and a great deal else in the sphere of policy transfer.[2]

References

IAMR, Institute of Applied Manpower Research. 2010. *The challenges facing skills development in India: An issues paper*, IAMR, New Delhi.

ILO, 2012. *World of Work Report 2012: Better jobs for a better economy*. International Labour Organisation, Geneva.

NORRAG News 46. 2011. *Towards a new global world of skills development: TVET's turn to make its mark*, Graduate Institute, Geneva. Accessed at norrag.org.

NORRAG News 48. 2012. *The year of global reports on TVET, skills and jobs*, Graduate Institute, Geneva. Accessed at norrag.org.

NORRAG News 37. 2007. *'Best practice' in education and training: Hype or hope*. Graduate Institute, Geneva. Accessed at norrag.org.

OECD. 2010. *Learning for jobs: OECD reviews of vocational education and training*, Organisation for Economic Co-operation and Development, Paris.

OECD. 2012. *Better skills, better jobs, better lives*, Organisation for Economic Co-operation and Development, Paris.

Sharma, A. and King, K. 2019. 'Skill India': The 'Modification' of Skill Development in India, in McGrath, S., Papier, J., Mulder, M. and Suart, R. (Eds.) *International handbook of vocational education and*

---

[1] For a critical look at 'Best practice" in education and training', see *NORRAG News 39*.
[2] What happened to these massive skills' ambitions in the following six years, including under Prime Minister Narendra Modi, can be followed up in Sharma and King 2019.

training for the changing world of work, Springer, New York.

UNESCO. 2012a. *The Shanghai Consensus: Recommendations of the Third International Congress on technical and vocational education and training.* 14-16 May 2012, Shanghai.

UNESCO. 2012b. *Youth and skills: Putting education to work. Education for All Global Monitoring Report 2012,* UNESCO, Paris.

World Bank. 2012. *Jobs: World Development Report 2013,* World Bank, Washington DC.

The Geopolitics and Meanings of India's Massive Skills Development Ambitions[3]

India is no stranger to large numbers. But its 11th Plan (2007-2012) has developed a scheme that appears to challenge even the wish lists of politicians. It has targeted increasing the proportion of formally and informally skilled workers in its total workforce from a mere 2% now to 50% by 2022, thus creating a 500 million strong resource pool. In this, it hopes to profit from a 'demographic dividend', gaining from the fact that its labour force is much younger than that in China and other competitor countries. It aims to supply the world's future skill needs for some 50 million workers, apart from satisfying its own.

The paper analyses what lies behind this extraordinary ambition. What policies have produced these proposals for skilling almost half of India? How important is the perception of China's substantial lead in skills development? How crucial has been the evidence that more than 90% of new jobs in India have been created in the informal sector? How critical has been the claim that such 'training' as has been available has been totally inadequate in terms of relevant theoretical knowledge? Equally important may be the modalities chosen for securing this skills goal. Why has the Government decided that a national vocational education qualification framework (NVEQF) could be essential to reaching its target? The paper reviews the implementation challenge with one year left in the 11th Plan. What have policy and politics achieved so far in the Plan's most ambitious goal – skills development?

The paper also asks about the meanings behind the recent dramatic rise of technical and vocational education and training (TVET) in the policy agenda of India. What are the assumptions about the existing traditions and character of India's culture or cultures of skills development? Is the massive planned expansion of skilled people in India simply more of the same, or is there a new paradigm involved? For instance, how central will be the role of the private sector and of public private partnerships (PPPs) in the new skills training environment?

---

[3] This chapter is taken from King (2012) 'The geopolitics and meanings of India's massive skills development ambitions', *International Journal of Educational Development*, 12, 665-673.

A further intriguing issue must surely be this: that India achieved almost double-digit growth for years despite having a tiny proportion of its workforce formally skilled. This might suggest that it would be difficult to persuade the private sector dramatically to change gear and invest in training. The other paradox is that although the relative wages of workers with general secondary education have been increasing, the same has not been true of workers with technical and vocational education. According to the World Bank (2006), the evidence seems to point to a decline in the demand for workers with these very same skills (World Bank, 2006: 4-5).

There is no shortage of unique conditions, therefore, in seeking to understand why the world's second largest nation in population terms (1.2 billion in 2011) should be proposing the largest ever expansion of skilled people in the next 10 years. For good measure, we may add a last issue which is that India, amongst the so-called emerging donors, appears to be promoting overseas aid to TVET at a much higher rate than any other BRICS donor, including Brazil and China (King and Palmer, 2011). But what model, if any, is it offering?

1. Origins and traditions of skills training in India and the skills mission

Prime Minister Manmohan Singh has played a key role in articulating the high priority for skills training of the Indian workforce. Back to at least 2004, there have been speeches extolling the need for 'all new entrants to the workforce' to be 'equipped with the requisite skills for high productivity and high quality work', and spelling out the implications for the modernisation of the industrial training institutes (ITIs) and apprenticeship training schemes, as well the active involvement of industry in both the public and private sector in curriculum design and management. He argued that there was much to be learnt, especially from Germany, when it came to industry's active participation in apprenticeship training (Singh reported in Planning Commission, 2007: 74).

But perhaps in identifying the skill levels of the workforce as 'an area of concern', and in arguing that 'the quality of manufacturing output and the wages paid to labour are critically dependent on the quality of labour', the Prime Minister might have said more about why industry should be expected to invest more in the quality and training of its labour. He might have explained the paradox that there appears to have been a lack of interest by employers in formally trained labour in

India despite the economy booming.

It may be worth reflecting on whether there are particular reasons within the culture and history of India's formal and unorganised sectors that have some bearing on these low enrolments in TVET just mentioned. Part of the answer is provided by a fascinating account of the 'Building of technical skills' in the Human Development Report (HDR) in South Asia 1998 (Ul-Haq and Ul-Haq, 1998: ch. 7). This provides a searing analysis of the state of skills across the countries of South Asia. The start of the chapter gives a flavour:

> The vocational and technical education programmes in South Asia are often inadequate, irrelevant, and qualitatively poor. There is perhaps no other field in education that requires from South Asian policy-makers more fundamental rethinking, sweeping reforms, and extensive change (Ul-Haq and Ul-Haq, 1998: 96).

The Report does raise the key point that many employers have a preference for on-the-job training as opposed to institution-based training, but the point is not elaborated. In fact, this goes to the heart of the problem. Across South Asia, there is a very widespread preference for training workers on the job. Typically, workers are taken on as unskilled, casual labourers, and over many years, the more promising and hard-working are sifted out, and attached to older, skilled workers. In the early years, the trainees are paid little and sometimes even nothing. Frequently, they get none of the social benefits accorded to permanent workers. Because the labour laws give great protection to permanent workers, employers go to great lengths to avoid staff gaining such status. Many workers are literally 'permanent casuals'; they sign contracts which agree to their being sacked before the deadline that would entitle them to be permanent, and they are then rehired.[4]

It is worth reflecting on whether these very different traditions of learning and training in today's India reflect the continuing influence of caste. Even though there is an account of the 'Idea of India' that holds these very different communities of religion and ethnicities together (Khilnani, 1997) with a politics of 'reservations' for scheduled and backwards classes, arguably today the India of IT Bangalore can still be contrasted with illiterate India, represented in the millions of uneducated

---

[4] See Jan Breman's work (1996) on *Footloose labour* for confirmation of these patterns in Gujarat State.

and untrained Rajasthani women working on the roads and construction sites across the country. The staggering inequalities that are found in today's India are also reflected in its training systems. Though the mass training system remains 'learning to labour' on the job, in casualised, highly exploitative conditions, even the small formal training system of the industrial training institutes (ITIs) is perceived by the middle classes as primarily suitable for lower caste youth.

If this is indeed the system and culture of labour force training that prevail in India, apart from the more progressive firms, then the challenge of getting industry involved in designing and managing training, as the Prime Minister hopes, may be huge. The point is, however, that industry is already massively involved in labour training, but in a very profitable and exploitative fashion. Thus, when the Task Force on Skills Development of the Planning Commission argues that 'There has to be a paradigm shift in the national policy on skill development with the private sector playing a lead role instead of the government, as they are the job providers', it does not acknowledge that the private sector is already playing too dominant a role in labour recruitment (Planning Commission, 2007: I, emphasis in original). When the Task Force emphasises the priority of 'a shift from a *supply* to a *demand* driven policy', it does not seem to have noticed that the present system is already very demand driven, but driven by a massive demand for using cheap, unskilled labour, and training on the job (Planning Commission, 2007: emphasis in original).[5] We shall need to be aware of this existing demand driven system as we note constant calls at the present time for India's skills system to be more demand led.

The failure to acknowledge the nature of the existing labour training system within industry may compromise the current TVET reform process. This is not to say that the private sector will not be sympathetic to initiatives where the government is offering large amounts of new funding to encourage industry's involvement with the ITIs, but it may not lead to industry abandoning its mainstream, tried and tested system of training through casual labour on the job.

---

[5] The Executive Director of Tata comes close to admitting this is the system: 'Of the 120 lakh [12 million] new entrants to the workforce, the ITIs (private and public put together) are able to handle about seven lakh [700,000] only. The rest either are fresh hands – they come into the workforce untrained or are trained by the employer on the job. Some others get trained at an unorganised local shop, but mostly they remain untrained or under-trained' (Planning Commission, 2007: 3).

Learning from the past, and from the work of previous commissions, should be important when it comes to designing skill development initiatives or national skill missions. Yet it would seem that the planning of the current skills mission has been undertaken without much interest in the work of the National Commission on Enterprises in the Unorganised Sector (NCEUS), set up in 2004, or in the work of its Task Force on Skill Formation in the Unorganised Sector set up the following year. Despite the unorganised sector being responsible for 93% of employment, the NCEUS had been closed down by 2009, and its innovative scheme for training millions of poor youth never saw the light of day (Unni, 2011).[6]

The series of steps towards the current skills mission were already underway during the deliberations of the NCEUS. Every year from the Budget Speech of 2004/2005, the Finance Minister referred to the skills priority; there was upgrading of technicians to 'world class' from 500 ITIs; already in 2004, there was enthusiastic mention of the public private partnership (PPP) model. Then in 2005/6 there was the pledge to use the PPP model to 'promote skills development programme under the name 'Skill Development Initiative' (Planning Commission, 2007: 73-74).

By Independence Day, August 15 2006, the Prime Minister had returned to his concern with India as a high growth, but low skills economy, and had moved the idea of a skill development initiative to a 'Mission mode', signalling a higher priority than a skill development initiative, but only after emphasizing the crucial importance of higher education:[7]

We will need to ensure far greater availability of educational opportunities at the higher education level so that we have not just a literate youth but a skilled youth, with skills which can fetch them gainful employment. As our economy booms and as our industry grows, I hear a pressing complaint about an imminent shortage of skilled employees. As a country endowed with huge human resources, we cannot let this be a constraint. We are planning to

---

[6] Krishna Kumar has commented: 'Nobody, it seems, wants to do something substantial or radical about the so-called unorganised or informal sector. I suppose the equilibrium will get greatly disturbed if better quality workers in the unorganised sector started expecting and asking for better wages. Where will the organised sector then get its cheap accessories from?' (Kumar to King, 1st February 2012).

[7] The Prime Minister announced the foundation of three Indian Institutes of Technology (IITs) and no less than 19 medical institutions of national standing before turning to skills.

launch a Mission on Vocational Education so that the skill deficit in our economy is addressed (Planning Commission, 2007: 74).

Following this announcement, there was set up a Working Group on Skill Development and Vocational Training to feed into the forthcoming 11th five-year plan, 2007-2012. Intriguingly, it referred no less than 200 times to the industrial training institutes (ITIs), but only five times to the unorganised sector, where the great bulk of all vocational training takes place in India, informally. Surprisingly in light of the NCEUS being already under way at the time, the informal sector was acknowledged to produce almost all new jobs and most of the national GDP, but was dismissed as not being eligible for formal training:

> The largest share of new jobs in India is supposed to come from the unorganised sector that employs up to 93% of the national workforce and produces 60% of GDP. Since small and micro enterprises are supposed to play a central role in the national employment creation strategy, they should be assisted in development of skills. The formal skill training system, because of its educational entry requirements and long duration of courses, is basically not designed to offer skills to the low-educated people [of the unorganized sector] (Planning Commission, 2006: 27-28).

The 11th Five-year Plan was unusual in dedicating no less than an entire chapter of its first volume to skill development and training. It is not the case that this Plan focused only on skill development; it was called the 'Education Plan' because it proposed some of the largest expansion of higher education that India had ever seen. But it did for the first time look at skill development seriously and it set out a number of key figures, targets and concepts that would determine the Indian discourse about skills for the next several years. The Plan effectively launched the National Skill Development Mission which the Prime Minister had, more narrowly, announced in 2006 as the Mission on Vocational Education.

Amongst these key figures and targets, it would claim that only 2% of its 15-29 year olds had received formal vocational training, and another 8% non-formal vocational training, compared to 60-90% in industrialised countries. Apart from this stark contrast with such countries, there was also the crucial comparison with China, the other 'Asian driver'. Here one of the frequent references in the policy literature relating to training is that India had relied on just a few long duration courses covering about 100 skills; by contrast, in China 'there exist about

4000 short duration modular courses which provide skills more closely tailored to employment requirements' (Planning Commission, 2008: 87). These references to China reinforce the comments made in other key policy documents on training such as the World Bank's *Skill development in India* (2006), where China not only has very many million more young people securing vocational education in school but has a very much higher ratio of firms providing in-service training (68%) than India (17%).

The quantitative review of the formal training arrangement across the country reaches the severe conclusion that only 2% of the entire workforce has had skills training, and 80% of new entrants to the labour market have had no access to such training. The qualitative audit is equally depressing. Surprisingly for such a detailed review of the nation's training system, there is almost no mention of the long-held tradition of training via casual labour on the job, which we referred to above. The nearest the Plan comes to analyzing this vast culture of training on the job without any security of employment is in its comments on the 'low-paying capacity of learners and the reluctance of industries to train workers for fear of losing them to competition' (Planning Commission, 2008: 89-90). When the Plan reviews training in the vast, informal, unorganised sector, it comments that 'By and large, skill formation takes place through informal channels like family occupations, on the job training under master craftsmen with no linkages to the formal education training and certification' (Planning Commission, 2008), but what it does not acknowledge is that this is precisely what is happening in large swathes of the so-called formal system.

What was impressive about the series of reports produced by the National Commission for Enterprises in the Unorganised Sector (NCEUS) was that it defined the unorganised or informal sector very carefully so that it included the millions in the agricultural sector, as well as the millions working informally in the organised sector. Of the total of 362 million workers in 1999-2000 in informal employment out of the total labour force of 396 million, not less than 26 million were to be found in the organised or formal sector of the economy. In other words the informal sector is to be found inside the formal sector, as in the case of the millions of workers hired informally, trained informally, and given no social security (NCEUS, 2006: para 2.9). In fact in India, almost half of the 56 million in the organised sector of the economy are effectively informally employed.

Arguably, it is these figures on the 93% of the Indian workforce in the informal sector that should have seized the attention of the 11ᵗʰ Plan with its ambition for 'inclusive growth'. But the Plan, in its concern with national training policy, failed to take advantage of the detailed work being done, in parallel, in the NCEUS, on skill formation in the unorganised sector (NCEUS, 2009). Perhaps understandably more attention was given to rethinking the fortunes of the relatively very small formal sector training institutions, and the small vocational education option in upper secondary schools. But what was missed in this focus on the formal sector was a recognition that the small size and character of the formal training system were directly connected to and explained by the size of the informal training system. The Plan's desire therefore to 'bring about a paradigm change in handling of skill development programmes and initiatives' will logically be impossible if the focus is restricted to the formal training system (Planning Commission, 2008: 87).

Before concluding this first section on origins and traditions, we should underline that much of this policy thinking is based on powerful and largely unquestioned assumptions about 'how skills can be developed into actual productive use' or how the self-employed 'can enhance their productivity' (Planning Commission, 2008: 90). The only research institute within the Planning Commission has been the Institute of Applied Manpower Research (IAMR) which has had a very long tradition of manpower planning. Arguably, the thinking around the skills development mission falls neatly into what McGrath (2012), quoting Giddens, terms productivism, the notion that the role of skills is fundamentally concerned with employability, productivity and ultimately economic growth. There have of course been other politics of skills in India's history, and none more famous that Gandhi's vision of skills-for-all in village India, as a crucial element of Indian self-reliance but also as an essential part of being human (Gandhi, 2008).

2. The numbers game

We have already noted that India's training system has some of the worst numbers in the world, and we have suggested that one reason for this is that there exists a massive shadow training system right across the country, though there may be a regional variation between the Southern states and the Northern. What is intriguing in this dire situation for skills development is that there have emerged some iconic targets for the future of skills in India. Of these none is more remarkable than the claim that India will have 500 million skilled workers by 2022. The source is claimed to be the Prime Minister though it is not clear when the target was first set.

Running through this whole section, it is important to be conscious of what may be termed the targetisation of development, or what Jansen (2005) has powerfully analysed as 'the politics of performance' in international education and training. There is a sense in which the target actually becomes the policy, just as in the world of the Millennium Development Goals the target date of 2015 has become endowed with iconic status.

When Manmohan Singh first announced the need for the Mission on Vocational Education back in August 2006, he noted that the working population was 397 million in total, and that 67% of this total was either illiterate or suffered from limited literacy. The figure of 396 million for the entire workforce, formally and informally employed, in the year 2000 is confirmed by the NCEUS in 2009, but it should be recalled that no less than 340 million of these workers were in the unorganised sector, and another 26 million were working informally within the so-called formal system of the economy. The figure of 500 million has presumably been arrived at by adding 12.8 million new recruits to the workforce annually till 2022, which is the 75th anniversary of India's independence.

But although the figure of 500 million by 2022 has become part of the stock in trade of politicians, public and private bodies concerned with skills development, and the media, it is not at all clear what it means. Thus when the Minister of Human Resource Development declares that 500 million skilled persons will be needed by 2022 to sustain its double digit growth, is he acknowledging that some 400 million are already working, the great majority of them in the informal sector? Is he not also admitting that the spectacular and sustained growth has thus far been managed without 500 million skilled people? The Finance Minister joined the chorus in October 2009, declaring that 'As against 40 million people currently who have received any kind of formal or non-formal training, the new vision envisages creation of a pool of 500 million skilled people by 2022'.[8] In other settings, the 500 million has been divided up amongst 20+ ministries and organisations, each of which has been allocated a skills target. Thus the Ministry of Human Resource Development (MOHRD) has 50 million, Labour, 100, Agriculture and Rural Development 20 each,

---

[8] http://smetimes.tradeindia.com/smetimes/news/top-stories/2009/Oct/21/fm-launches-nsdc-eying-500-million-skilled-people-by-2022.11525.html.

etc. The largest slice, 150 million, has been allocated to the new public–private body set up as part of the skills architecture, the National Skills Development Corporation (NSDC) (Sharma, 2011). Yet again, it is mentioned by the IAMR (2010) that a vision to create 500 million skilled people by 2022 has been endorsed by the Prime Minister's National Council on Skills Development, itself set up in July 2008, as another part of the skills architecture.

But whilst there is much celebration of the target figure, there is very little discussion about what the implication of such a target is. What does it mean to say that the entire working population of India will be skilled in some 10 years' time? Seeing that 238 million of the working population at the moment is in agriculture, almost entirely in the unorganised sector, why is the responsibility for just 20 million allocated to the Ministry of Agriculture, and just 20 million to Rural Development? What will they do with the 40 million, and what not do with the 200 million others? More importantly, what proportion of the targeted 500 million are already skilled?

We were told earlier that only 2% of the workforce was formally skilled, and a further 8% skilled non-formally. But has this figure really been interrogated? Can it really be the case that 90% of the labour force is unskilled? According to the 61st Round of the National Sample Survey on Employment and Unemployment (NSSO, 2006) these figures are correct. But if the actual schedule for the NSSO is examined carefully, the sample population was asked about receiving (a) formal vocational training, (b) non-formal: hereditary, (c) others, and (d) did not receive any vocational training (NSSO, 2006, schedule 10, c-4). Arguably, the great bulk of the working population who acquired their skills on-the-job, whether in large or small factories, building sites or in agriculture, would probably have said they did not receive any vocational training. This was true; their employers were not offering either formal or non-formal skills training. But tens of millions of workers did acquire substantial skills through years of working on the job. Though the 500 million figure does not appear in the influential 11th Plan, the skills chapter of the Plan is replete with targets. Thus, in general, ministries responsible for vocational training (of which there are said to be 17) have to expand infrastructure and its utilization by a factor of five, bringing the annual total of trained people from its current 3 to 15 million. This would then more than cover the annual increment to the workforce of 12.8 million (Planning Commission, 2008: 92-93). It can be seen that such an addition to the trained workforce would bring the total trained to something like 230 million by 2022, though this calculation is not made in the 11th Plan.

The Plan does however have another iconic notion to conjure with in the concept of 'demographic dividend'. This is the notion that India claims to have a unique 25-year window of opportunity, when it will have the world's youngest workforce, much younger than China or the OECD countries. If India gets its skill development strategy right, then it calculates it will be able not only to meet its own manpower needs but would have a manpower surplus of some 47 million workers to meet the estimated global manpower shortage of approximately 56 million.[9] The Plan notes optimistically: 'it is not inconceivable that within a decade we can become a global reservoir of skilled person power' (Planning Commission, 2008: 91). The demographic dividend idea gets picked up by many later commentators and is often presented along with the 500 million target; but what is not particularly clear is whether this expected surplus is somehow part of the 500 million. However, the Planning Commission is honest enough to admit that the demographic dividend could become a 'demographic nightmare' if India does not get its skill development strategy involved in a 'paradigm change' (Planning Commission, 2008). We shall turn to the elements of this paradigm shift shortly.

A third set of iconic target numbers relate to what may loosely be called the privatization of the hitherto public skill development system. The two Action Plans, within the 11th Plan, are called 'Government initiative in PPP mode' and 'Action Plan for component II – private sector initiatives'. In other words, they are both private-sector oriented. The first component was to take all parts of the government's institutional skills apparatus, in all its 20 or so relevant ministries, and link them directly to the private sector. This covers ITI/ITC, polytechnics, community polytechnics, secondary schools with vocational education streams, and all the parallel institutions in ministries such as Rural Development, Health, Tourism, etc. 'All these need to be restructured and repositioned in collaboration with private enterprises' (Planning Commission, 2008: 93). All new capacities are to be in the PPP mode. The

---

[9] The figure of 47 million labour surplus for India is drawn from a US Census Bureau BCG source for 2002-2003, but the source gives no surplus figures for Bangladesh or Sri Lanka (See Planning Commission, 2008: 126, annexure 5.2). The figure given for India is not concerned with skill level, just labour surplus according to population and age.

second component – private sector initiatives – is essentially to take 20 of the growth sectors in industry and services, and encourage them to set up corporations/trusts in the PPP mode to meet what are seen as the skills needs of the private arm of the Skills Development Mission.

What can be said about the achievements of this extraordinary ambition to change the character of the skill development system in India? If what was said above about the private sector preferring low-level systems of training on the job, including from casual labour, has there in fact been a sea-change? This is not of course just to do with getting private sector representation on to the management committee, but changing the entire structure into the PPP mode, and developing a whole set of private sector skills training initiatives.

Before leaving the skills initiatives of the 11th Plan we should recall that some 93% of the workforce is said to be in the unorganized sector, and yet very few of the ambitious targets just mentioned are directly related to the informal sector. This provides something of a conundrum for the key target of 500 million skilled people by 2022, since the very great majority of this promising pool of skilled people will have to have been in the informal sector. Yet in the 11th Plan's key chapter on skills, the unorganized sector is only mentioned once! Perhaps the situation would be very different once the ideas of the 11th Plan were turned into a National Skills Development Policy. To this we now turn.

3. National Skills Development Policy (NSDP)

Following hot on the heels of the 11th Plan came the NSDP. This document came from the Ministry of Labour and Employment (MOLE) and went to the Union Cabinet for approval in the autumn of 2008 and was passed by February 2009 (MOLE, 2009). It is intriguing to see how this much more policy-oriented document has taken the huge number of proposals and initiatives in the 11th Plan, and sought to make them part of policy. As might be anticipated, it only takes three sentences for the NSDP to announce that India has set a target for skilling 500 million people by 2022 (NSDP, 2). And only four sentences before the readers hear about India's advantage of a 'demographic dividend'. What is also claimed in these very first few sentences is that of the workforce (in 2004-2005) 'the target group for skill development comprises all those in the labour force; which is made up of no less than 433 million in the unorganised sector, and 26 million in the organised sector'. This makes absolutely clear that it is the unorganised sector that will need to provide the bulk of skill development initiatives if the 500 million target it to be reached. Not surprisingly there is, unlike the 11th Plan, a whole section of three pages of NSDP dedicated to Skill Development for the Unorganised Sector. Interestingly, there are lots of intentions and aspirations here but not a single quantitative target (MOLE, 2009).

In particular, the NDSP argues that the mode of informal apprenticeship and learning will be recognised by a National Vocational Qualifications Framework (NVQF). This mechanism had been mentioned once in the 11th Plan but there it was only said to be particularly useful for mobility between different formal vocational and technical qualifi-cations. Here in the NDSP, the NVQF is expected to integrate the testing and certification of skills acquired in non-formal and informal arrangements. Although there is a whole complex architecture set up to implement the National Skills Mission for the formal sector, there is no mention of which body will be responsible for upgrading the skills of the great bulk of the Indian labour force. The section on the unorganised sector ends with the following instead: 'Various successful models have been tried in India and around the world. In designing skill development strategies and programmes for the unorganised sector, successful models will be studied and adopted to suit local conditions' (MOLE, 2009). This does not sound like a strategy for rapid implementation. And the same might be said of the training providers for the unorganised sector. These turn out to be 'Various avenues/institutions including schools and public/private training institutions/civil society organizations/NGOs' (Ibid. 28). Particular mention is made of the role of skill development centres (SDCs) in relation to the unorganised sector. Interestingly, however, these SDCs were referred to in the 11th Plan in terms of becoming a 'Virtual skill development resource network' for web-based learning. Which sounds a little far from the ordinary realities of working in the informal sector.

One of the key chapters of the NSDP is certainly chapter 6: 'Benchmarking of skill deficit and plan to achieve target by 2022'. As can be seen from the title, this again takes the time-line of 2022, as in the phrase '500 million persons by 2022' (Ibid. 44), and presents an outline of which ministries and other institutions have responsibility for reaching how many millions of trained people. As we have said, the National Skill Development Corporation (NSDC), which is the private arm of the Skills Development Mission, has the largest number, 150 million; the Ministry of Labour and Employment (MOLE) has 100 million, and the MOHRD 50 million. The total across some 24 bodies actually comes to 530 million by 2022.

The only body out of all these that is mentioned as having the 'unorganised sector' as a target is the MOLE, in respect of its programme of Modular Employable Skills (MES). There is no indication, however, of the scale of this programme. All that we are told is that the MOLE has a current training capacity of just 12 million as against their suggested target of 100 million by 2022. We are told that it has no less than 33,000 institutions under its purview. It would seem that this figure, which is vastly higher than any other ministry, is made up of the 6,834 ITI/ITCs, and 23,800 'establishments' in which there are formal sector apprentices to be found. These employers, whether large or small-scale, can scarcely be counted as MOLE institutes.

The NDSP, therefore, claims that the MOLE has 23,800 'establishments' related to formal sector apprenticeship. But it is much less clear what is its strategy in relation to the upgrading of the hundreds of millions of workers in the informal sector. Even though the term 'unorganised sector' is only used explicitly of the MES programme, there is mention of many other vulnerable and marginal groups in connection with other ministry programmes: 'poorer sections of society'; 'unemployed rural youth'; 'disadvantaged and marginalised sections'; 'scheduled tribes'; 'scheduled castes'; 'child labour', etc. These many different categories of disadvantaged young and old people are certainly itemised as the targets of several programmes of various ministries. But of course when the NDSP allocates a single target figure to each ministry or institution, there is no way of telling what is its internal composition. We shall return to this question later as it is certainly of importance to be clear which constituencies in India are going to benefit from the extraordinary ambitions of the Skills Mission. Nevertheless the whole of NDSP's chapter three is on the Expansion of Outreach, Equity and Access, and within that all the main disadvantaged communities are mentioned. It is also mentioned that the intention is to 'better integrate skill development into broader poverty reduction programmes'. It will be remembered that this integration of skill development into poverty programmes was precisely what the NCEUS had recommended to government, in proposing linking the National Rural Employment Guarantee Act (NREGA) to skill development. This was also what was recommended by the Report of the Sub-Committee on Vision for Vocational Education, commissioned by the Planning Commission (2010:

6). It is precisely these kinds of linkages which would embed skills training more within income-generating programmes for the poor.

We end this comment on the NDSP by underlining the possibility that the NDSP, despite its name, may be seen less as a national strategy than as a strategy proposed by the Ministry of Labour and Employment. We note, for instance, that MOLE developed a proposal for a National Vocational Qualification Framework (NVQF) in August 2010, and organised a couple of review meetings on it along with the World Bank and the ILO in February and in May 2011, but by the end of May 2011, the MOHRD had also developed a full version of an NVQ, though it was now called a National Vocational Education Qualification Framework (NVEQF).[10]

4. A National Vocational Qualification (NVQ) for India – going the second mile?

It may seem surprising that in the midst of implementing the world's largest skill development initiative, two of the Government of India's Central Ministries should propose a National Vocational Qualification (NVQ). We have already mentioned that the idea of an NVQ had been touched upon by the Planning Commission but implementing a full-blown NVQ in a country of the size and complexity of India tells of very great ambition.

It may also appear strange that India, a country too proud to accept aid for the tsunami damage, should welcome with open arms several items in what McGrath and Lugg (2012) have termed the international travelling toolkit of TVET reform. But just as pride in economic self-reliance can be combined with demonstration that India too, like China, can play the role of aid donor in Africa, so its embrace of a national qualification framework is perhaps more of an assertion that India's skills are already internationally accepted – see the later discussion of India as the 'skills capital of the world'.

An alternative explanation is that there has been little indigenous thought on vocational education and training and even less coherent planning. The external toolkit offers some legitimation of policy action at a time when politically speed is of the essence. Krishna Kumar expands

---

[10] This divided interest in developing an NVQ goes right back to 2005, since the World Bank's January 2006 *Skill development in India* already referred to both ministries having developed separate proposals for an NVQ, 'although only covering their individual responsibilities' (World Bank, 2006: 41).

on this:

> A sense of hurry now prevails in this newly recognized 'skill' sector. Its recognition itself is a product of external pressure; hence it is not too surprising that India is using and moving along the current parlance which has developed elsewhere. This parlance conveys a feeling that something substantial is being done now, and that it might work differently from the schemes that have been chronically failing. (Kumar to KK, 1 February 2012).

The case for India pursuing a full NVQ seems to have been first made by the Ministry of Labour and Employment, though both ministries had had outline proposals by 2005. Although NVQs have certainly been promoted by some countries which already had these, it has not traditionally been easy to sell innovations to India which it had not itself considered important. However, advice on the international experience and on lessons to be learnt relating to NVQs was certainly sought from the ILO and World Bank offices in New Delhi, and a leading expert on the role of NVQs, Professor Michael Young, was brought out through them to lead two stake-holder meetings in New Delhi. These took place in February and May 2011.[11] But the sponsoring ministry was Labour; and there was little evidence of MOHRD in these events.

Meanwhile, and in parallel, the idea of the MOHRD being involved in an NVQ had developed from as early as 2005, as we have mentioned. But a briefing paper for the Minister was only finally prepared in August 2010. It sought to present a very positive case for India developing an NVQ. It will be worth reviewing this case very briefly, because it may cast light on India's readiness to take on board an additional really massive paradigm shift in the thinking about its TVET system, at the very time it was engaged in an already hugely complex sea change in TVET.

Amongst the apparent attractions of an NVQ or an NVQF as presented to the Minister of MOHRD in August 2010 are said to be the following, in a briefing note arguing why India needed an NVQF:

- It would lead to a user-driven and demand-driven training

---

[11] For the May meeting Young was accompanied by Stephanie Allais of the University of Witwatersrand. She powerfully drew the attention of the audience to the massive problems which South Africa had experienced in implementing its version of an NVQ. See also Allais, 2012.

system instead of a supply-driven one;

- It would involve employers as a key part of the training, assessment and certification;
- It would encourage progression, and linkage between work-based and academic qualifications (MOHRD, 2010: 1)

It can be seen how these claims would fit in with India's desire to shake up the TVET system and ensure it was employer-responsive.

Arguably, however, the briefing note over-sold the potential of an NVQF directly to affect the quality of India's training system. Thus it suggested to the Minister that one of the 'benefits to Government' would be the 'development of a highly skilled, high-quality, and competitive workforce' (Ministry, 2010). It was also suggested that the NVQF would 'support the creation of high performance organisations to improve living standards of the people'. In respect of its benefits to industry, it claimed that the NVQF would 'improve quality, productivity and competitiveness'. There were many other claims made for what the NVQF could do for India's government, employers, TVET providers and students. But it is doubtful if NVQF analysts would accept that a qualifications framework could have a direct effect on such outcomes. At the very most, an NVQF might contribute to such things, provided a whole set of other complementary changes were underway in TVET reform. Indeed, Young and Allais have made precisely this point in their commentary about lessons from international research for India:[12]

> Any realistic starting point has to recognize that international experience demonstrates that introducing an NVQF by itself will not improve the quality of TVET, increase the availability of TVET programs, or address skill gaps (Young and Allais, 2011: 5).

By the time that Young and Allais were leading a workshop in May 2011 on what could be learnt from international experience, and making a series of recommendations for Indian policy makers in respect of an NVQF, the MOHRD had already committed itself to the process, and a full-blown description of an Indian National Vocational Education Qualifications Framework (NVEQF) was being finalised for presentation and agreement to central and state-level ministries of education at the end of May and early June 2011.

---

[12] Master (2011) has made a similar point in her piece: 'India's NVEQF – sound policy or sheer madness', drawing on South Africa's experience of an NQF.

The sheer scale of what is now involved is hard to exaggerate, with the creation of Sector Skills Councils through the private sector, and their development of National Occupational Standards. These, in turn, have to be translated into a competency-based curriculum, again by the private sector, but in liaison with government at central and state levels. All this is happening not long after the entire school curriculum had been rethought through a national curriculum framework, including some very innovative analysis in rethinking the role of work and education (NCERT, 2005, 2007). Already, in 2011 the NVEQF was in the process of being piloted in one of the states, Haryana (Mehrotra, 2011), and by July 2012, it will begin to be rolled out to the rest of India, with the full support of the Central Advisory Board on Education.[13] Coordination between the now leading agency, MOHRD, and the MOLE was still very far from being evident.

5. Funding for skills development with the private sector

The massive aspirations completely to change the skills system and discourse in India involve a great deal of new funding, as all the relevant ministries have new targets for skilled workers, and many have obligations to create and or upgrade their existing institutional infra-structure. There is very little external financial assistance involved in this exercise, apart from the World Bank which had been financing the upgrading of 100 industrial training institutes from before the national skills mission took off. There is also a small EU programme of Support to Skills Development in India (€6.5 million) linked to capacity develop-ment, especially in relation to the Directorate General of Employment and Training of MOLE (EU, 2010). But the great bulk of all funding for the Skills Mission is from government and from the private sector in India.

It is in relation to the private sector that there would appear to be the greatest change in the last three years since the National Skills Development Policy and the National Skills Development Corporation came on stream. From being a country which we had characterised earlier in this paper as being very little interested in formal sector skills training, it would seem that there has been something of a revolution. Thanks to the dynamism of the NSDC and the promotion of opportunities in public private partnership with the Industrial Training

---

[13] Mehrotra to KK, 26th January 2012.

Institutes, there is suddenly a rush by many of the well-known corporate names to become involved in training deals brokered by the NSDC.

These deals are written up in the business press and corporate websites, and they have a number of features in common. First, and almost without exception, the particular deal is described as being part of the GOI's plan to produce 500 million skilled people by 2022. Here typically is a comment by the CEO of NSDC in relation to the training deal with the Indian Institute of Job Training (IIJT): "We are pleased to partner with IIJT to achieve our target of training 150 million youth by 2022". A second feature is that the deal is large-scale. Thus, Future Group and NIIT both agreed to partner with the NSDC to produce seven million trained people each over a 10 year period. Bharti Group's Centum Workskills is to train 12 million people in 11 years. Everonn's International Skills School will train 15 million people over 10 years, covering no less than 10% of the 150 million training target given to NSDC.[14] Third, the deals involve the use of very large numbers of training centres spread out across the country. Thus, the IIJT agreement mentioned above is for setting up of 1349 multi-skill development centres across the country. And lastly, quite a lot of financial incentive is present. For example the IIJT deal involved a soft loan of Indian Rupees 62 crores (or US$ 13 million). The upgrading of ITIs through the PPP linkage with major corporates would bring in from government over half a million dollars to each ITI in the PPP mode. There would be 300 upgraded each year with a cost of some US$ 400 million each year. The total number of ITIs to be upgraded would come to 1396.

But the intriguing issue is not just that the private sector appears to have 'entered the foray to run the ITIs' (in the words of the Con-federation of Indian Industry (CII)'s Skills Development Initiative) in a way that is very different from earlier years; but the discourse is distinct. Skilling India has been branded in a way that was unimaginable a few years earlier. Thus, the CII is proud to represent India as the 48th member of WorldSkills International, joining an organization that only has a handful of members from the developing world. From being a country with some of the most dismal skills rankings in the world, India is celebrated by CII in the following iconic way: 'Making India the Skills Capital of the World'. In Gujarat's social sector, one of the largest of the

---

[14] The Everonn project is said to have an investment of Rs. 153 crores (US$ 32 million) and a revenue generating potential of Rs. 14,250 crores (US$ 3 billion).

corporate-government partnerships, of some US$2 billion, aiming at generating over a million jobs through self-employment, no less than 30 of India's largest corporates are present, and NSDC is responsible for the training component of all the projects. The triumph of the venture is well captured in the following observation: "It will be a win-win situation for both the corporates as well as the grassroots entrepreneurs since it will follow the model of eradicating poverty through profits," exults an industry observer (*Financial Express*, January 12 2011).

6. Drivers and meanings

This short safari through some of the skills literature and developments of the last 6-7 years in India has raised more questions than provided answers. This is principally because many of the initiatives are just a year or two old. The five-year plan which launched many of these new approaches does not run its course till 2012. Even the mid-term appraisal (MTA) of the 11th Plan (Planning Commission, 2011) found that several of key initiatives were 'still in an early stage of implementation'. Not surprisingly, the NVQF was not even mentioned in the mid-term appraisal.

But there has been a shift in language. For instance, the term 'public private partnership' occurs more than 170 times in the MTA, suggesting that the term, and more importantly the ideology behind it, have come in from the cold, since the 11th Plan promoted the concept so strongly.

Connected directly to this, the role of corporate India appears to have become much more evident in the skills development architecture. The NSDC within a very short period has brokered a large number of links and partnerships.[15] Many of the nation's flagship companies, as well as the industry and commerce associations, have been drawn into activities in support of the 500 million target. As these very large-scale schemes fan out across India, it would be valuable to know more about who exactly are the beneficiaries of these five, 10 and 15 million person schemes.

Recalling that of the target of 500 million, a very large number would eventually need to come from the unorganised sector, high proportions of which still have only minimum schooling and literacy, we

---

[15] For a list of 23 NSDC partners as of April 2011, with numbers of dedicated centres and target numbers, see 'Making 500 million employable', *Business Today*, 3 April 2011. (http://businesstoday.intoday.in/story/indias-skill-revolution-training-people-to-make-them-employable/1/13909.html).

would anticipate that the earliest cohorts recruited to these corporate partnership schemes could well be from those who already have completed their basic or even secondary education. The millions of poorly or uneducated workers in the informal or unorganised sector will not be easily able to take part in these highly visible, and branded skills opportunities that are all captured on the web. As the MTA honestly admits in its just two paragraphs on skill development for the unorganised sector, 'the implementation of the policy for this sector remains a formidable challenge' (Planning Commission, 2011: 213).

The skills development mission has also brought new money into NGO activities in India, and here again it will be important to analyse who is now being reached as opposed to who was being reached before. The question to be raised however would be what is the additionality of these new funds going into the NGO sector (Sharma, 2011). Are government funds now substituting for some of the NGO funding rather than adding to them? Is there a possibility that the higher funding rates by the new government funding are actually resulting in two different levels of funding within the same NGO project activities?

But the new skills discourse is not just about changes in the public and private spheres of TVET; we have argued that it is also a discourse that is very manpower-based. It is about expansion, targets, and skills gaps. Even though the new paradigm is said to be demand-driven, the iconic target of 500 million has no rational base in employer demand at all. The same is true of the calculations around the famous demographic dividend; they are mostly about the mere supply of youthful labour in India, with the claimed surplus of 47 million by 2020. Admittedly, there is also the claim that the ageing economies of the world will have a skilled manpower shortage of some 56 million by 2020. But such a global calculation must be regarded as rather different from the usual sense of demand-driven.

In other words, the skills language is very narrowly focused on technical and vocational manpower, in quantitative terms, in what we referred to as the 'productivist' paradigm at the beginning of this paper. But what is missing in this manpower planning approach? Despite the extraordinary diversity and quality of artisanal crafts in India, there is very little discussion of this important dimension of skill. It is virtually invisible in the skills discussions, as are terms such as design and creativity. This may change when a sector skills council is set up in 2011 on handloom and handicrafts, but it may well continue to emphasise skills gap analysis like the series of 20 reports on the website of NSDC which examine skill requirements up to the inevitable date of 2022. This includes a report on the Gems and Jewellery Sector which is not at all about the nature of the skills in this sector, but only about the mapping of skills requirements, as in the sub-title: Study of mapping of human resource skills gaps in India till 2022 (NSDC, n.d.).

A concern with the need to develop a broader account of vocational education and training is evident in the Report of the Sub-committee on Vision for Vocational Education (Planning Commission, 2010). This was particularly the case in respect of relations between upper secondary schools with vocational courses and the industrial training institutes. Such linkages would allow both institutions to 'benefit from their own strengths in curriculum and pedagogy' and would help to develop 'a holistic vision of vocational education and training for young people'. This same emphasis on the need to rethink the character and 'epistemology of vocational education' runs through the work of the Sub-committee. Avoidance of a narrow curriculum focus is important because currently there is little concern with communication skills, knowledge related to health, safety and civic issues or an awareness of gender issues. The advance of the NVQF influence on narrower, modular approaches to competence could be another reason that the Sub-committee argued so strongly for a holistic, and more integrated vision of vocational education and training (Kumar, 2011).

7. Concluding reflections

We have touched upon most of the questions raised at the beginning of this paper. But running through our exploration has been an awareness of the paucity of long-term research on the TVET/skills development sector. With the massive growth of interest in the sector, this is sure to be remedied. But it would seem that the many different dimensions of skills development are up for major, even dramatic, change before there are coherent accounts of how the existing system works. Thus we lack detailed analysis of training in the informal, unorganised sector which is still the largest system for skills development in India. Often this would be better termed skill acquisition in the informal sector, as there may well be no explicit commitment to train, but just a process of learning on the job. We also lack critical accounts of vocational education in schools, or of the character of the industrial training institutes, at the point that they are suddenly being partnered by the private sector through the PPP schemes.

It may be important to have some insight into this current institutional architecture, as India, as a so-called emerging donor, is itself beginning to provide vocational training centres to Africa and to other countries in South Asia. What models of TVET, if any, is it drawing upon from its own experience to offer Africa?

But as a whole series of ambitious initiatives begin to be put in place, from NVEQF, to PPP, to competency-based curricula, and centres of excellence in upgraded ITIs, it will be important for research to be covering these many new explorations of very rapid policy learning and policy adaptation. Documenting the impact of the Skills Development Mission will need to cover many different dimensions, from TVET and lifelong learning (Singh, 2012), NGOs, new private sector skills companies and schools, and the very architecture of the Skills Mission itself.

Delivering change in the mission mode in India's tradition is to do with dramatically kick-starting something that needs massive political focus to be implemented. But the mission mode also tends, in Indian politics, to be time-bound. So one of the key questions must be the long-term sustainability of what has been started with such determination in the last few years. This particular Mission, almost by definition, cannot possibly be accomplished in a five-year cycle.

The year 2022 has already become an iconic date for India's skills ambitions. But with the benefit of hindsight it will prove important to have acknowledged that India cannot be made the world's skills capital overnight or even in a decade.

References

Allais, S., 2012. Will skills save us? Rethinking the relationships between vocational education, skills development policies, and social policy in South Africa, *International Journal of Educational* Development, 32, 5, 632-642.

Breman, J., 1996. *Footloose labour*. Cambridge University Press, Cambridge.

European Union (EU), 2010. *Support to skills development in India*. European Union, New Delhi.

Gandhi, M., 2008. *The collected works of Mahatma Gandhi* (May-August 1924). Obscure Press.

Institute of Applied Manpower Research (IAMR), 2010. *The challenges facing skills development in India: An issues paper*. IAMR, Planning Commission, New Delhi.

Jansen, J., 2005. Targeting education: the politics of performance and the prospects of education for all. *International Journal of Educational Development* 25, 368-380.

King, K., Palmer, R., 2011. New trends in international cooperation. Background paper for the *World Report on technical and vocational education and training*, UNESCO, Paris.

Khilnani, S., 1997. *The idea of India*. Penguin, London.

Kumar, K., 2011. Vocational education: tangled visions. *NORRAG News* No. 46, downloadable at www.norrag.org.

McGrath, S., 2012. Vocational education and training for development: A policy in need of a theory? *International Journal of Educational Development* 32 (5), 623-631.

McGrath, S., Lugg, R., 2012. Knowing and doing vocational education and training reform: Evidence, learning and the policy process. *International Journal of Educational Development* 32 (5), 696-708.

Master, L. 2011. India's NVEQF – sound policy or sheer madness? *NORRAG News* No.46, downloadable at www.norrag.org.

Mehrotra, S. 2011. Skill development initiatives: private-public partnership and private initiatives in India. *NORRAG News* No. 46, downloadable from www.norrag.org.

Ministry of Human Resource Development (MOHRD), 2010. Write-up on National Vocational Qualification Framework (NVQF) for the meeting of 12.8.2010 with Minister.

Ministry of Labour and Employment (MOLE), (2009). National Policy on Skills Development. Ministry of Labour and Employment, Delhi, Government of India. http://labour.nic.in/policy/NationalSkillDevelopment-PolicyMar09.pdf. Accessed on 07.09.11.

National Council of Educational Research and Training (NCERT), 2005. *National Curriculum Framework*, NCERT, New Delhi.

National Council of Educational Research and Training (NCERT), 2007. Position Paper. National Focus Group on Work and Education, Paper No. 3.7, NCERT, New Delhi.

National Commission for Enterprises in the Unorganised Sector (NCEUS), 2006. *Social security for unorganised workers*. Report NCEUS, New Delhi.

National Commission for Enterprises in the Unorganised Sector (NCEUS), 2009. *Skill formation and employment assurance in the unorganised sector.* NCEUS, New Delhi.

National Skills Development Corporation (NSDC), n.d. Human resource and skills requirements in the gems and jewellery sector (2022). A report. Study of mapping of human resource skills gaps in India till 2022. NSDC, New Delhi.

National Sample Survey Organisation (NSSO), 2006. *Employment and unemployment among social groups in India, 2004-2005,* NSS 61st round. NSSO, Ministry of Statistics & Programme Implementation, New Delhi.

Planning Commission, 2006. *Report of the Working Group on Skill Development and Vocational Training,* Planning Commission, New Delhi.

Planning Commission, 2007. *Report of the task force on skill development,* Planning Commission, Government of India, New Delhi.

Planning Commission, 2008. *Eleventh Five Year Plan, 2007-2012. vol. I. Towards inclusive growth.* Oxford University Press, New Delhi.

Planning Commission, 2010. Report of the Sub-Committee on Vision for Vocational Education, Planning Commission New Delhi.

Planning Commission, 2011. Mid-term appraisal of the eleventh five year plan, 2007-2012. Planning Commission, OUP, New Delhi.

Sharma, A. 2011. Expanding opportunities for marginalised groups. Paper to the UKFIET Oxford International Conference on Educational Development, 13-15 September, New College, Oxford.

Singh, M., 2012. India's national skills development policy and implications for TVET and lifelong learning. In: Matthias, P. (Ed.), *The future of vocational education and training in a changing world.* Springer, Dordrecht.

Ul-Haq, M., Ul-Haq, K. (Eds.), 1998. *Human Development Report in South Asia 1998,* Human Development Centre. Islamabad/Oxford University Press, Karachi.

Unni, J., 2011. Skilling the workforce in India. *NORRAG News* 46, September. Downloadable at www.norrag.org.

World Bank, 2006. *Skill development in India. The vocational education and training system.* Human Development Unit, South Asia, World Bank, New Delhi.

Young, M., Allais. S., 2011. Options for designing an NVQF for India. Discussion paper for stakeholder workshop, May 3rd 2011. Habitat Centre, New Delhi.

Chapter 13

Conclusions around Education, Skills, Knowledge and Work – and the Role of Aid

The year 2018 marked 50 years since completing my doctoral work on *Pan-Africanism and education* (King, 1968). That analysis put together the role of aid in policy transfer and priority setting for Sub-Saharan Africa along with the promotion of 'industrial' education over a particular time period – 1880 to 1930. [1] The focus was particularly derived from a detailed, critical investigation of just two major reports by the Phelps-Stokes Fund on education in Africa.

The value of using particularly significant reports, policy papers or commissions as an entry to wider issues of international importance to education has stayed with me. Thus, in the last conference before leaving a formal position in the Centre of African Studies in the University of Edinburgh in September 2005, my focus was woven round three influential policy papers of 2005: *Report of the Commission for Africa*, the World Bank's *Education sector strategy update*, and the report of the UN's Millennium Project, *Investing in development* (King, 2005). Equally when the 50th anniversary of the Centre of African Studies in Edinburgh came up in 2012, Simon McGrath and I used the occasion of *CAS@50* to look back at 'The lessons of the past 50 years for beyond 2015'. One dimension of our analysis of key shifts was the interrogation of central texts – such as the 1961 *Conference of African states on the development of education in Africa* (King and McGrath, 2012).

Another example, already referred to earlier, of reviewing a core issue over time would be the analysis of the international and national

---

Kenneth King (2019): *Education, Skills and International Cooperation: Comparative and Historical Perspectives*. Hong Kong: Comparative Education Research Centre (CERC), The University of Hong Kong, and Dordrecht: Springer. © CERC

[1] In 1881 Booker T. Washington was called to set up an institute in Tuskegee, Alabama. In the same year Edward Blyden, a West Indian scholar, gave his inaugural address as president of Liberia College in Monrovia.

© Springer Nature Switzerland AG 2019
K. King, *Education, Skills and International Cooperation*, CERC Studies in Comparative Education 36, https://doi.org/10.1007/978-3-030-29790-9_13

fascination with target-setting in education over a 100-year span – from the World Missionary Conference in Edinburgh in 1910 up to the final agreement about the world's educational goal and targets, set in the *2030 agenda for sustainable development* (King, 2015).

A mechanism that regularly institutionalised the critical analysis of potentially major international trends, milestones and reports came through my 30 years of editing *NORRAG News* every six months (1986-2017). This approach was first fully illustrated in *NORRAG News (NN)* 7 and *8* which focused entirely on the process of creating the *Declaration* and *Framework for Action* for Jomtien in 1990, but also in elaborating what actually happened in Jomtien. This same method could still be seen in the last issue of NN which I edited in January 2017: *Education, training and Agenda 2030: What progress one year on?* (NN 54). This took the Sustainable Development Goal 4 and its 10 targets, and teased out, through a diversity of 50 voices, the impact at international and country levels.

There were three special characteristics of this NORRAG approach. First, these analyses of large and complex bodies of work were not all written by the editor; rather my role was both commentator and catalyst. The unique side of NN was that a range of some 40-50 people – roughly half from the North, half from the South – brought their diverse perspectives and lenses to bear on the same topic. Second, they had to do so in some 500-750 words – the same length as a blog. Third, precisely because of the length, it was possible to have key policy-makers also contribute, which would have been impossible in a regular academic journal.

Another NORRAG approach consisted of interrogating a key term or phrase that had become commonplace, but whose multiple meanings were unclear or confusing. These would include terms like 'capacity-building', 'best practice', 'partnership', 'emerging donors', 'knowledge for development', 'sector-wide approaches' or 'value for money', and then unpeeling all the possible layers of policy analysis through many different lenses. *NORRAG News* also encouraged the tackling of a topic precisely because it had suddenly become hugely critical internationally – like *Refugees, displaced persons and education* (NN 53) in May 2016.[2]

This openness to burning new topics was different from the consultancy culture which had afflicted many university settings, particularly in Sub-Saharan Africa, where regular salaries were

---

[2] For all 54 issues of *NORRAG News* up to 2017, see http://resources. norrag.org/#search

insufficient for living. I was fortunate to be able to weave my longstanding threads of aid, education, skills and work into many of these special issues of NN and into my own research. This characteristic of being able to focus on a small series of interconnected themes over a period of two to five decades is one of the academic luxuries of work in the relatively well-resourced universities of OECD countries as well as in many institutions in so-called emerging economies such as India and China. The possibility to keep turning to one or more core themes, as the surrounding context and culture shift with global trends over time, is a feature of academia that is too easily taken for granted. It is of course made possible in these countries by the availability of multiple sources of research funding. It is hugely more demanding to create and deepen individual research capacity around a chosen subject when the only sources of funding are a series of one-off consultancies which may focus on many entirely different policy issues.

The other privilege of adequately resourced academia is that genuine research partnerships are possible. Several funding agencies encourage North-South academic partnerships, and these can work well and be greatly rewarding. It will be recalled that what was unique about the IDRC in its early years was that it did not require an academic link with the North as a precondition of its research funding in the South. All too often now, partnership is a condition of research for many of the agencies supporting research in the developing world. I have revisited this topic of the politics of higher education research partnership many times since IDRC days (e.g. King, 2009).

Working on a common project with colleagues, even when thousands of miles away, can be hugely rewarding and productive, as the very long-term research partnership of Ernesto Schiefelbein in Chile and Noel McGinn in the USA amply confirms (Schiefelbein and McGinn, 2017; also Schiefelbein and McGinn in *NORRAG News 41*).[3] But distance is not the only challenge; there are also issues of time-lines, communication, finance and, most crucially, shared commitment to a common project and outcome.

Joint research projects across thousands of miles require time together, not just intensive, brief project development meetings, but ideally weeks in each other's institutional settings and research cultures. They are very different from consultancies where rapid agreements and

---

[3] See also Farrell (2008) 'Reflections on 40 years of partnership'.

'deliverables' are of the essence. This is one reason why I have tried to avoid consultancies, except where it was necessary to bring additional funding into the Centre of African Studies.[4]

The British Council's higher education link schemes have encouraged many valuable long-term partnerships, as illustrated by the partnership which was put together by me, from 1993, between the Department of Educational Studies in the University of Edinburgh and the Faculty of Education in the University of Western Cape in South Africa. This exposed many members of staff on both sides to periods of two to three weeks in each others' institutions. But while the edited book which resulted from this was valuable and even influential, it was not based on a deep and extended period of shared research (Morrow and King (eds.), 1999).

Time is of the essence in partnership research. If one partner is trying to combine the shared project with a range of many other research, administration and teaching commitments, and the second partner is focusing primarily on the project, the unevenness will often mean that there cannot be a shared product. It is then better for each partner to recognise this, and produce their own publications from the project in their own time.

Even in the more symmetrical partnerships, where each partner has a similar commitment to investing time, it may be sensible to acknowledge that both the research and writing tasks are better divided than shared. In other words, productive partnerships are not about all partners doing the same thing, or doing everything together. A realistic division of labour is crucial. Early recognition about who is doing what writing by what deadline is necessary. When one partner is attached full-time to the research and the other is part-time, that will be reflected in the writing commitments.

The Centre of African Studies was fortunate in having Simon McGrath spend his first six years full-time with us after his masters and doctorate in the Centre. This made it possible for three different research projects and many conference publications to be jointly planned and undertaken with me. In some of these, Simon did the major writing,[5] while in others, responsibilities for writing were divided. Thus, in

---

[4] I once did a consultancy on the Danish tool-rooms to India where there were only five days of field visits allowed for the analysis of something that had been in India for 30 years. Never again.

[5] For instance, in King and McGrath. 2002. *Globalisation, enterprise and knowledge: Education, training and development in Africa*, Symposium Books, Oxford.

Knowledge for development (2004), the case studies of agencies were divided, with Simon covering Sida and DFID, and myself the World Bank and JICA. Simon and I drew many younger doctoral students into the experience of editing and reviewing through the annual conference publications of the Centre of African Studies.

Another example of a symmetrical partnership would be my work with Robert Palmer. Like Simon, he had done a masters and doctorate in Edinburgh. Thereafter, he joined the office of Queen Rania of Jordan, and later her Foundation. Over the last decade we have collaborated on a series of TVET-related publications. Most notably, these included a long report for the British Council and the UK National Commission for UNESCO entitled *Skills for work, growth and poverty reduction: challenges and opportunities in the global analysis and monitoring of skills* (King and Palmer, 2008). Then two years later, we jointly completed one of the series of IIEP's Fundamentals in Educational Planning, on *Technical and vocational skills development* (King and Palmer, 2010). Robert and I also collaborated on the skills side of the Research Consortium on Educational Outcomes and Policies. Robert initiated the NORRAG blog in May 2012, and to the extent possible I reviewed all of these until 2017. In parallel, Robert reviewed most of the articles in *NORRAG News* over the last many years.

NORRAG also provided the opportunity for the publication of books and regular reports. Thus, Simon McGrath was responsible for the conference reports of the Working Group for International Cooperation in Skills Development for some ten years.[6] Lene Buchert (of UNESCO and later the University of Oslo) and Kenneth collaborated to publish volumes on aid to higher education, consultancy and research, and shifts in international aid to education (Buchert and King, 1996; King and Buchert, 1995; 1999).

Partnerships for research and publication are not the only modality available for collaboration. Another career-long mechanism which has proved a vital source of ideas, insights and evidence is the informal network or invisible college.[7] This linkage mechanism has been crucial to my networking and exchange over the last 40 years, and it may be recommended to younger scholars almost as a method of work. Like symmetrical partnerships it is based on trust, commitment and

---

[6] See http://resources.norrag.org/#search for all the Working Group reports.
[7] Patricio Cariola of CIDE and Bob Myers of FORD and RRAG first used this phrase with me to apply to the personal commitments involved in academic networking.

friendship. It may not result in any single publication, but these email (or earlier fax) exchanges of about half a page or less are a way of engaging with emerging ideas, testing sources, histories, hunches or intriguing perspectives. It is a discursive approach, ensuring up to the moment interaction, and drawing them into the shared process. The masters and mistresses of this crucial form of lifelong learning and critical interrogation would include the following colleagues and friends, along with those just mentioned above. This is much more than acknowledging them; it is recognising a shared engagement to knowledge generation that has survived all the changes in technology since the manual typewriter and blue air-letters of my doctoral days:

Birger Fredriksen (formerly of UNESCO and the World Bank); Arvil Van Adams (formerly of the World Bank); Sheldon Shaeffer (formerly IDRC, UNICEF, and UNESCO); Alan Ogot (formerly University of Nairobi); Trevor Coombe (formerly Department of Education, South Africa); Mark Bray (University of Hong Kong); Kayashima Nobuko (JICA); Mark Mason (Education University of Hong Kong); Santosh Mehrotra (Jawaharlal Nehru University); Li Jun (University of Western Ontario); Ernesto Schiefelbein (Alberto Hurtado University, Santiago, Chile); Peter Williams (formerly Commonwealth Secretariat); Patricio Cariola (formerly Centre for Research on the Development of Education (CIDE), Santiago, Chile); Suzuki Shin'ichi (formerly Waseda University, Tokyo); Ingemar Gustafsson (formerly Sida); David Court (formerly Rockefeller Foundation, Nairobi); Yokozeki Yumiko (IICBA, Addis Ababa); Robert Myers (formerly Consultative Group on Early Childhood Care and Development and RRAG); Wolfgang Gmelin (formerly DSE, Bonn); Wolfgang Kuper (formerly GTZ, Eschborn); Barry Sautman (Hong Kong University of Science and Technology); Beatrice Avalos (University of Chile); William Ozanne (formerly *International Journal of Educational Development*); Keith Watson (formerly University of Reading); Sawamura Nobuhide (Osaka University); Beverly Young (formerly British Council); David Levesque (formerly DFID); Barbara Trudell (Summer Institute for Linguistics, Cape Town); Wim Biervliet (formerly CESO, the Hague); Mogens Jensen (formerly DANIDA); Wang Xiulan (Zhejiang Normal University); Barbara Bompani (University of Edinburgh); Matsunaga Masaei (JICA); Zhang Yuting (Zhejiang Normal University); Stephanie Allais (University of Witwatersrand);

Jacques Charmes (formerly Institute of Research for Development, Paris); Jandhyala Tilak (formerly, National University of Educational Planning and Administration, New Delhi); Alison Girdwood (British Council); Jamil Salmi (formerly World Bank); Manzoor Ahmed (BRAC University, Dhaka); Michael Crossley (University of Bristol); James Currey (formerly James Currey Publishers); James Foster (Nairobi); Noel McGinn (formerly Harvard); Caroline Dyer (University of Leeds); Elsbeth Court (School of Oriental and African Studies, London); Gordon Mwangi (Shikoku Gakuin University, Japan); Eric Krystall (formerly Family Programmes Promotion Services, Nairobi); Claudio da Moura Castro (formerly ILO and InterAmerican Development Bank); Colin Leys (formerly University of Nairobi); Tony Tillett (formerly IDRC); Camilla Toulmin (International Institute for Environment and Development, London); Liu Jing (Tokyo University, formerly Nagoya University); Natasha Gray (Monaco); Paul Nugent (University of Edinburgh). – There are many others who have been hugely helpful at particular moments.

I cannot end this account of 'partnerships for development' without acknowledging that Mark Bray has played a central partnership role in my academic life. Apart from being my first doctoral student in the University of Edinburgh, and having creatively stepped into my job in the Centre of African Studies while I was in IDRC, he invited me to apply for a position in the University of Hong Kong as distinguished visiting professor. This duly led to my researching China's aid and soft power in Africa. He also suggested in 2006 that I should prepare a book on what his colleague, Mark Mason, too generously called KK's Greatest Hits. It took me more than a decade to find the time to start this. But his help in bringing this volume to birth cannot be exaggerated.

The last partnership has been the most critical. I married Pravina the month I finished my PhD in June 1968. Because of our deciding early on in our married life to travel together whenever possible to seminars, conferences and presentations, she knows personally every one of those mentioned above in our invisible college. Perhaps this is also a research approach that can be suggested to others. She made it possible for me to produce my early book on *Pan-Africanism from within* (Makonnen, 1973), and was critical in the production of most of the first 30 issues of *NORRAG News*, until it went from hard copy to virtual. She also sat in on the informal management committee meetings of NORRAG up till 2016.

From 1992 till 2005, she was the administrator of the Centre of African Studies, and played a central role in organising and publishing our annual international conferences in that period. When we both retired from the Centre in September 2005, and went to the University of Hong Kong for a year in March 2006, she was able for the first time to participate in all the hundreds of interviews we conducted in China and in Africa for *China's aid and soft power in Africa* (2013). Though she was happy for me to write up the insights from our work together between 2006 and 2010, her critical eye was invaluable in the creation of the final product.

Now in 2018, we are engaged together in studying India's cooperation with Africa in human resource development. Although we have visited India many times since 1968, 2018 is the first time we have spent more than three months in India exploring India's human resource collaboration with Africa, and, along with that, some of the key themes that have run right through this book. This will inevitably involve histories and comparisons with the two other Asian giants engaged with Africa, China and Japan, and through these with China's Belt and Road Initiative and India and Japan's Asia-Africa Growth Corridor.[8]

It will engage with India's version of South-South Cooperation, its claims about its soft power and institution building in Africa, as well as the multiple faces of the slippery terms, capacity-building and people-to-people engagement. It will explore the symmetries and asymmetries of this complex relationship, as well as what India's agenda-setting and research priorities look like almost a hundred years after the Phelps-Stokes promoted its ideas about a differentiated education 'adapted' to Africa. There will be in-depth interviews with African students in India and Indian students in Africa, as well as with Indian NGOs and Indian firms working in Africa. There will need to be a critical examination of the texts on both sides claiming for the partnership 'equality, friendship, mutual benefit and solidarity' (IAFS, 2015:2). We won't obviously factor in serendipity, but will hope that Fortuna and Tyche will play a part along with Ganesh and Lakshmi.

---

[8] For the AAGC vision for Asia-Africa cooperation, and the role of African agency see King 2018.

References

Asia-Africa Growth Corridor (AAGC) 2017. *Asia-Africa Growth Corridor: Partnership for sustainable and innovative development: A vision document*, African Development Bank meeting, Ahmedabad, India, 22-26 May 2017.

Buchert, L. and King, K. (eds.) 1996. *Consultancy and research in international education: the new dynamics*, German Foundation for International Development (DSE)/NORRAG, Bonn.

Farrell, J. 2008. 'Reflections on 40 years of partnership', *NORRAG News 41*, Graduate Institute, Geneva, 49-50. Accessed at norrag.org

IAFS (India-Africa Forum Summit), 2015. *India-Africa framework for strategic cooperation*, Ministry of External Affairs, New Delhi.

King, K. 1968. *Pan-Africanism and education: A study of race, philanthropy and education in the Southern States of the USA and East Africa*, PhD. thesis, University of Edinburgh.

King, K. 1995. 'North-South academic links in a climate of audit, productivity and cost-effectiveness' in *Linkages revisited: The significance of linkages in higher education*, NUFFIC, The Hague.

King, K. 2005. 'Education, skills, knowledge and work on the world's development agenda', in Beveridge, M., King. K., Palmer, R. and Wedgwood, R. (eds.) *Re-integrating education, skills and work in Africa: Towards informal or knowledge economies? Towards autonomy or dependency in development?* Centre of African Studies, University of Edinburgh.

King, K. 2009. 'Higher education and international cooperation: The role of academic collaboration in the developing world' in Stephens, D. (Ed.) *Higher education and international capacity building: Twenty-five years of higher education links*, Symposium Books, Oxford.

King, K. 2013. *China's aid and soft power in Africa: The case of education and training*, James Currey, Woodbridge.

King, K. 2015. 'The global targeting of education and skill: Policy history and comparative perspectives', BAICE presidential lecture at UKFIET's Oxford Conference on Education and Development, 16th September 2015. Accessible at http://www.norrag.org/fileadmin/ Working Papers/Working_Paper_9_King.pdf. A shorter version is available in *Compare: A Journal of Comparative and International Education*, 46, 6.952-975.

King, K. 2018. 'Japan, India and China on Africa: Global Ambitions and Human Resource Development' in Panda, J. and Basu, T. (eds.)

China-India-Japan in the Indo-Pacific: Ideas, interests and infrastructure', Pentagon Press, New Delhi.

King, K. and Buchert, L. (eds.) 1995. *Learning from experience: Policy and practice in aid to higher education,* Centre for the Study of Education in Developing Societies (CESO) paperback no 24, The Hague.

King, K. and Buchert, L. (eds.) 1999. *Changing international aid to education: Global patterns and national contexts.* NORRAG, and UNESCO, Paris.

King, K. and McGrath, S. 2002 *Globalisation, enterprise and knowledge: Education, training and development in Africa,* Symposium Books, Oxford.

King, K. and McGrath, S. 2012. 'Education and development in Africa: Lessons of the past 50 years for Beyond 2015', paper to Conference on Centre of African Studies @ 50, Centre of African Studies, University of Edinburgh. Accessible at: http://eprints.nottingham.ac.uk/1640/1/Kenneth.King%26Simon.McGrath.CAS@50.pdf

King. K. and Palmer, R. 2008. Skills for work, growth and poverty reduction: challenges and opportunities in the global analysis and monitoring of skills. British Council, and UK National Commission for UNESCO, London.

King, K. and Palmer, R. 2010. *Planning of technical and vocational skills development,* Fundamentals in Educational Planning Series, International Institute for Educational Planning (IIEP), UNESCO, Paris.

Makonnen, T.R. (recorded and edited by King, K.) 1973. *Pan-Africanism from within,* Oxford University Press, Nairobi.

McGinn, N. 2008. 'North-South research partnerships: A personal viewpoint' *NORRAG News 41,* Graduate Institute, Geneva, 22-24. Accessed at norrag.org

Morrow, W. and King, K. (Eds.). 1999. *Changing education and training in South Africa,* University of Cape Town, Cape Town.

NORRAG News, NORRAG, Graduate Institute, Geneva, accessible at http://resources.norrag.org/#search

Schiefelbein, E. 2008. 'Good friends in several successful partnerships' *NORRAG News 41,* Graduate Institute, Geneva, 47-49. Accessed at norrag.org

Schiefelbein, E. and McGinn, N. 2017. *Learning to educate: Proposals for the reconstruction of education in developing countries,* International Bureau of Education (IBE), Geneva.

CERC Studies in Comparative Education (ctd)

15. Alan Rogers (2004): *Non-formal Education: Flexible Schooling or Participatory Education?*. ISBN 978-962-8093-30-4. 306pp. HK$200/US$32.
14. W.O. Lee, David L. Grossman, Kerry J. Kennedy & Gregory P. Fairbrother (eds.) (2004): *Citizenship Education in Asia and the Pacific: Concepts and Issues*. ISBN 978-962-8093-59-5. 313pp. HK$200/US$32.
13. Mok Ka-Ho (ed.) (2003): *Centralization and Decentralization: Educational Reforms and Changing Governance in Chinese Societies*. ISBN 978-962-8093-58-8. 230pp. HK$200/US$32.
12. Robert A. LeVine (2003, reprinted 2010): *Childhood Socialization: Comparative Studies of Parenting, Learning and Educational Change*. ISBN 978-962-8093-61-8. 299pp. HK$200/US$32.
11. Ruth Hayhoe & Julia Pan (eds.) (2001): *Knowledge Across Cultures: A Contribution to Dialogue Among Civilizations*. ISBN 978-962-8093-73-1. 391pp. HK$250/US$38. [Out of print]
10. William K. Cummings, Maria Teresa Tatto & John Hawkins (eds.) (2001): *Values Education for Dynamic Societies: Individualism or Collectivism*. ISBN 978-962-8093-71-7. 312pp. HK$200/US$32.
9. Gu Mingyuan (2001): *Education in China and Abroad: Perspectives from a Lifetime in Comparative Education*. ISBN 978-962-8093-70-0. 260pp. HK$200/US$32.
8. Thomas Clayton (2000): *Education and the Politics of Language: Hegemony and Pragmatism in Cambodia, 1979-1989*. ISBN 978-962-8093-83-0. 243pp. HK$200/US$32.
7. Mark Bray & Ramsey Koo (eds.) (2004): *Education and Society in Hong Kong and Macao: Comparative Perspectives on Continuity and Change*. Second edition. ISBN 978-962-8093-34-2. 323pp. HK$200/US$32.
6. T. Neville Postlethwaite (1999): *International Studies of Educational Achievement: Methodological Issues*. ISBN 978-962-8093-86-1. 86pp. HK$100/US$20.
5. Harold Noah & Max A. Eckstein (1998): *Doing Comparative Education: Three Decades of Collaboration*. ISBN 978-962-8093-87-8. 356pp. HK$250/US$38.
4. Zhang Weiyuan (1998): *Young People and Careers: A Comparative Study of Careers Guidance in Hong Kong, Shanghai and Edinburgh*. ISBN 978-962-8093-89-2. 160pp. HK$180/US$30.
3. Philip G. Altbach (1998): *Comparative Higher Education: Knowledge, the University, and Development*. ISBN 978-962-8093-88-5. 312pp. HK$180/US$30.
2. Mark Bray & W.O. Lee (eds.) (1997): *Education and Political Transition: Implications of Hong Kong's Change of Sovereignty*. ISBN 978-962-8093-90-8. 169pp. [Out of print]
1. Mark Bray & W.O. Lee (eds.) (2001): *Education and Political Transition: Themes and Experiences in East Asia*. Second edition. ISBN 978-962-8093-84-7. 228pp. HK$200/US$32.

CERC Monograph Series in Comparative and International Education and Development

12. Raymond E. Wanner (2015): *UNESCO's Origins, Achievements, Problems and Promise: An Inside/ Outside Perspective from the US*. ISBN 978-988-14241-2-9. 84pp. HK$100/US$16.
11. Maria Manzon (ed.) (2015): *Changing Times, Changing Territories: Reflections on CERC and the Field of Comparative Education*. ISBN 978-988-17852-0-6. 105pp. HK$100/US$16.
10. Mark Bray & Ora Kwo (2014): *Regulating Private Tutoring for Public Good: Policy Options for Supplementary Education in Asia*. ISBN 978-988-17852-9-9. 93pp. HK$100/US$16. [Also available in Chinese and Korean]
9. Mark Bray & Chad Lykins (2012): *Shadow Education: Private Supplementary Tutoring and Its Implications for Policy Makers in Asia*. ISBN 978-92-9092-658-0. (Print). ISBN 978-92-9092-659-7. (PDF). 100pp. HK$100/US$16.. [Also available in Chinese, Russian and Vietnamese]
8. Nirmala Rao & Jin Sun (2010): *Early Childhood Care and Education in the Asia Pacific Region: Moving Towards Goal 1*. ISBN 978-988-17852-5-1. 97pp. HK$100/US$16.

7.   Nina Ye. Borevskaya, V.P. Borisenkov & Xiaoman Zhu (eds.) (2010): *Educational Reforms in Russia and China at the Turn of the 21st Century: A Comparative Analysis*. ISBN 978-988-17852-4-4. 115pp. HK$100/US$16.

6.   Eduardo Andere (2008): *The Lending Power of PISA: League Tables and Best Practice in International Education*. ISBN 978-988-17852-1-3. 138pp. HK$100/US$16.

5.   Linda Chisholm, Graeme Bloch & Brahm Fleisch (eds.) (2008): *Education, Growth, Aid and Development: Towards Education for All*. ISBN 978-962-8093-99-1. 116pp. HK$100/US$16.

4.   Mark Bray & Seng Bunly (2005): *Balancing the Books: Household Financing of Basic Education in Cambodia*. ISBN 978-962-8093-39-7. 113pp. HK$100/US$16.

3.   Maria Manzon (2004): *Building Alliances: Schools, Parents and Communities in Hong Kong and Singapore*. ISBN 978-962-8093-36-6. 117pp. HK$100/US$16.

2.   Mark Bray, Ding Xiaohao & Huang Ping (2004): *Reducing the Burden on the Poor: Household Costs of Basic Education in Gansu, China*. ISBN 978-962-8093-32-8. 67pp. HK$50/US$10. [Also available in Chinese]

1.   Yoko Yamato (2003): *Education in the Market Place: Hong Kong's International Schools and their Mode of Operation*. ISBN 978-962-8093-57-1. 117pp. HK$100/US$16.

Order through bookstores or from:

Comparative Education Research Centre
Faculty of Education, The University of Hong Kong
Pokfulam, Hong Kong, China.

Fax:(852) 3917 4737
E-mail: cerc@hku.hk
Website: http://cerc.edu.hku.hk

The list prices above are applicable for order from CERC, and include sea mail postage. For air mail postage, please add US$10 for 1 copy, US$18 for 2-3 copies, US$40 for 4-8 copies. For more than 8 copies, please contact us direct. For CERC/Springer Series No.24 and 30, air mail postage is US$15 per copy.

CERC Studies in Comparative Education 19

Comparative Education Research
Approaches and Methods

second edition

Edited by
Mark Bray, Bob Adamson and
Mark Mason

Publishers:
Comparative Education Research Centre and
Springer
ISBN 978-988-17852-8-2
2014; 453 pages
HKD250/USD38

Approaches and methods in comparative education are of obvious importance, but do not always receive adequate attention. This second edition of a well-received book, containing thoroughly updated and additional material, contributes new insights within the long-standing traditions of the field.

A particular feature is the focus on different units of analysis. Individual chapters compare places, systems, times, cultures, values, policies, curricula and other units. These chapters are contextualised within broader analytical frameworks which identify the purposes and strengths of the field. The book includes a focus on intra-national as well as cross-national comparisons, and highlights the value of approaching themes from different angles. As already demonstrated by the first edition of the book, the work will be of great value not only to producers of comparative education re-search but also to users who wish to understand more thoroughly the parameters and value of the field.

The editors: Mark Bray is UNESCO Chair Professor of Comparative Education at the University of Hong Kong. Bob Adamson is Professor and Head of the Department of International Education and Lifelong Learning at the Hong Kong Institute of Education; and Mark Mason is Professor at the Hong Kong Institute of Education and a Senior Programme Specialist at the UNESCO International Bureau of Education (IBE) in Geneva.

This book is also available in Chinese, Farsi, French, Italian,
Japanese, Portuguese, Russian and Spanish.
Website: http://cerc.edu.hku.hk

Printed by Printforce, the Netherlands